PARADISE

DANTE

PARADISE

*Translated, Edited, and with an
Introduction by Anthony Esolen*

Illustrations by Gustave Doré

THE MODERN LIBRARY

NEW YORK

2004 Modern Library Edition

Translation, introduction, and notes copyright © 2004 by Random House, Inc.
Biographical note copyright © 1996 by Random House, Inc.

LIBRARY OF CONGRESS CATALOGING-IN-PUBLICATION DATA
Dante Alighieri, 1265–1321.
[Paradiso. English & Italian]
Paradise/Dante Alighieri; translated, edited, and with an introduction by Anthony Esolen;
illustrations by Gustave Doré.
p. cm.
Text of Dante's Paradise in English and Italian.
ISBN 0-679-64269-2
I. Esolen, Anthony M. II. Title.

PQ4315.4.E7613 2004
851'.1—dc22   2004049940

Modern Library website address: www.modernlibrary.com

2 4 6 8 9 7 5 3

Dante Alighieri

Dante Alighieri, the Italian poet whose great allegory *The Divine Comedy* has exerted a profound effect on Western literature and thought, was born in Florence in May 1265. He came from a noble though impoverished family, descendants of the city's Roman founders. Relatively little is known with certainty about Dante's early life, but it is noteworthy that he grew up during the restless period that followed decades of blood rivalry between two Florentine political groups, the Guelphs and the Ghibellines. His childhood was doubtless colored by stories of this partisan strife from which, as Machiavelli later wrote, "there resulted more murders, banishments, and destruction of families than ever in any city known to history."

Dante probably received his early schooling from the Franciscans and the Dominicans; later, he studied rhetoric with the Guelph statesman and scholar Brunetto Latini. Another significant mentor was the aristocratic poet Guido Cavalcanti, who strongly influenced his early work. For the young Dante, writing poetry became an important expression of his passion for art and learning, and of his abiding concern with the nature of love and spiritual fulfillment. A Florentine woman of exceptional beauty, Beatrice Portinari, provided a powerful stimulus to the poet's artistic development. Dante idealized her as the "bringer of blessings," a beatific guide capable of pointing him toward the inner perfection sought by every noble mind. Following her untimely death in 1290, Dante, overcome with grief, celebrated her grace and virtue in *La vita nuova* (1292–94), a small "book of memory" written in verse and prose. He then sought renewal in an extensive study of theology and philosophy.

In 1295 Dante entered public life and within a few years emerged as a prominent figure in Florentine politics. By then he had entered into an arranged marriage with Gemma Donati, a gentlewoman with whom he had several children. In the summer of 1300 Dante was named one of the six governing magistrates of Florence. During this time he was involved in the clash between two hostile factions of the Guelph party, the Whites and the Blacks. Aligning himself with the White Guelphs, Dante campaigned to preserve the independence of Florence and repeatedly opposed the machinations of Pope Boniface VIII, who was attempting to place all of Tuscany under papal control. In 1301, however, the Black Guelphs seized power, and Dante was banished at once on trumped-up charges of graft, embezzlement, and other transgressions. Later sentenced to death by fire if he returned to Florence, Dante never entered his native city again.

Dante's remaining years were spent with a series of patrons in various courts of Italy. Two uncompleted works date from his early period of exile. *De vulgari eloquentia* (1303–4), a scholarly tract in Latin on the eloquence of the Italian vernacular, is generally acknowledged to be the key to Dante's artistic inquiries. *Il convivio* (1304–7), a glorification of moral philosophy, is viewed as the cornerstone of his investigations into knowledge and wisdom. Perhaps as early as 1306, Dante began to compose *The Divine Comedy,* the greatest poem of the Middle Ages and the first masterpiece of world literature written in a modern European language. The Latin treatise *De monarchia* (1312–13), a practical guide calling for the restoration of peace in Europe under a secular ruler in Rome, is a statement of the poet's political theories. In his final years Dante was given asylum in Ravenna, where he completed *The Divine Comedy* shortly before his death in September 1321.

CONTENTS

LIST OF ILLUSTRATIONS

INTRODUCTION

Anthony Esolen

In a dark and superstitious age, with even the memory of learning fading like a dream, when the cultural conditions of life prevent most people from deriving real pleasure from the simple duties of home and family and village, men's vain imaginations invent for themselves another world. They project into that world what little they know of this one, imagining a God like a great and kindly old man, who forgives their failings unconditionally and allows them to continue in their present pastimes: to fish, to hunt, to gossip with friends, to lounge in the sun at the side of a lake. Such a God is a wonderfully convenient balm to their bruised hearts and egos; for in this world of ours, man is terribly small, born in pain, living through trouble and heartache, and dying in doubt or despair. Men cry not so much to be made whole and good as to be let off the hook, to get away without dying, and so they attribute magical powers, even on this side of the grave, to cards, stones, powders, herbs, and ointments, reducing the almighty Creator of the universe to an easily manipulable force, to a tool, like a stock or a stone.

Thankfully, it has not always been so.

It is commonly said that the *Paradise* is the most medieval of the three canticles of Dante's masterpiece. I am not sure what the epithet means. If it means that it is the most firmly grounded in Dante's culture, in the embroilments of Dante's time and place, I must wonder what has happened to all the Guelphs and Ghibellines in Hell, and all the poets and patriots making their slow way up the Mountain of Purgatory. With the exception of the Cacciaguida cantos, what the annotator of *Paradise* notices is that there are far fewer names to give references for and far fewer historical events to explain than in the other two canticles.

If "medieval" means that the *Paradise* is the least accessible of the three to the modern reader, I concur. It surely is; but it was also the least accessible to the medieval reader. If it means that in *Paradise* we do not find those time-transcending moments of tragedy or human grief that the *Inferno* and *Purgatory* are so justly famous for, again I concur. There is no moment in *Paradise* like the finality of Farinata's revelation of the future all-encompassing ignorance of the damned; no concentrated bursts of accusation and despair, as when Jacopo Rusticucci blames his damnation on his shrewish wife; not even the womanly regret of Pia, recalling her murder at the hands of the man who once put his ring upon her finger. This is all true; but then nothing in *Inferno* can compare with the stunning ending of Canto Ten, with its delicate evocations of simple village life, the gears of the church clock ringing the bells and lifting the hearts of those who hear them from afar; nor is there anything in *Purgatory* quite like the human and heroic joy of Francis of Assisi. If "medieval" means "preoccupied with abstruse trivialities," the charge is beneath contempt, since they who make it know less about the Middle Ages than they do about the *Paradise*.

I would like to understand it, then, in this sense: the *Paradise* is indeed the most medieval of the three canticles, in that it most fully embodies the striving of the medieval mind to understand all of reality—material and intellectual, legal and moral and religious, earthly and heavenly, logical and supralogical—as one grand and harmonious whole. And more, if there be more to assert: the *Paradise* strives to show forth that whole in a work of art that is itself, like the playful and soaring cathedrals of France, a work of ineffable beauty and complexity. For it is *Paradise* that resumes and perfects the themes and motifs of the other two canticles. It is the work by which the unity of the whole *Comedy* must be judged.

But even in itself *Paradise* exhibits more of this unity in complexity than do the other canticles. By reason of the walls separating the categories of the damned, *Inferno* is necessarily somewhat episodic; discussion, like travel, is freer in *Purgatory,* and we often find someone's words or thoughts repeated later on, from a different perspective, with the possibility of delving deeper into the matter in question. In *Paradise*—where all souls are present before the face of God yet at the same time are presented "elsewhere" in Heaven, moving with the speed of thought—the intellectual probing is ever returning, ever spiraling, because we are dealing with mysteries that the human mind can apprehend but not comprehend, can glimpse but not fathom. The apparently minor question of the shadows on the moon is actually a reprise of the subtle distinctions in the *Inferno* between sinners of the same class, and of the particular graces granted to such sinners in the *Purgatory* as the negligent kings and, most strikingly, Provenzan Salvani; and it is visited again and again, in different forms, even unto Bernard's showing Dante that the baptized infants are endowed with various degrees of grace. It is the mystery of God's immanence in a universe composed of diverse things, a mystery that Dante, struggling to find an analogy fit for its harmony and power, beholds directly only near the last few lines of the poem—the last few lines of the *Comedy.*

The question of man's nature, the natural propensity of man to rise unto the heights in intellect and love, is a reprise of the many motifs of heaviness, weariness, and immobility in the *Inferno,* and of the growing lightness in the step as one climbs the Mountain of Purgatory. It is broached with a calm whimsy in the first canto, when Beatrice explains to the astounded poet that what is really unnatural in man is to fall. That question too, after many probings, meets its resolution at the end of the poem, when Dante tells us, looking into the end of all human desire, into the unsurpassable light of God, that had he turned anywhere else, he would have gone blind—yet he had not the power to turn. And of course, any discussion of man's nature must lead to a discussion of sin. In the *Inferno* Dante beheld the consequences of wickedness and indeed beheld wickedness in action, and had to be instructed by Virgil on what justified certain categorizations of evil; in the *Purgatory* he probes more deeply, asking whether our wills are wholly determined from without and whether, in that case, the term "evil" makes any sense; in the *Paradise* he is given a full lesson on what human freedom is, and he speaks to the very source of sin, Adam himself, who defines the original sin as a violation of man's created nature.

Discussion of sin and its just punishment leads to discussion of the hope for mercy and redemption. Thus when Beatrice surprises us by answering for Dante, telling the apostle James that the Church Militant has no son of greater hope than is the poet, we should recall the very beginning of the poem, when, lost in the dark wood, Dante "lost all hope to reach the mountaintop" (*Inferno* 1.54); the terrible finality of the inscription over Hell's gates, "Abandon all hope, you who enter here" (3.9); and the poignant striving of the souls in Purgatory, for whom hope is the well-spring of their joy in suffering. Those souls long for the peace denied the souls in *Inferno*—denied the banner-racing hollow men, the tempest-flung lechers, the rain-battered gluttons, the itching counterfeits, the weary traitor-chawing Satan; they long for peace, and in *Paradise* we find a peace defined by Piccarda as to dwell within the will of God. It is a peace magnificently expressed not by rest, exactly, but by the glee of motion—of ringing bells, of country dances, of high-hearted pilgrims, of lovers in love.

And that leads, inevitably for the Christian, to Christ, who is unquestionably at the center of the entire scheme of the *Comedy*, its structure, its arguments, its aspirations, its harmony. His name is not uttered in *Inferno*, though he with the other Persons of the Trinity created it, and we hear that his harrowing of Hell has left its walls and cliffs in dilapidation. His name is uttered but not rhymed upon in *Purgatory*, where we see him mystically symbolized by the Griffin leading his Church, and where his mother, Mary, is given as the model of virtue to counter each of the capital vices. His name resounds through *Paradise*. A lesser poet would give us theology lessons about Christ. Dante strives for more: to give us Christ himself, the Second Person of the Trinity, begotten by the Father from all eternity in the Love that is the Spirit, embodied in the saints and their lives, visible mysteriously in the heavens and the earth that were made through him, and, absolutely centrally, manifest as the God-Man in whose very being is expressed the mystery of the union of God and redeemed creation.

No doubt the medieval mind dwelt lovingly upon the humanity of Jesus. It is to the Middle Ages that we owe our first and sweetest Christmas carols, and it is from the popular medieval devotion to the meekness and humility of Jesus, expressed so vividly by the women mystics of the age, that the modern Christian derives the convenient and comfortable vision of Jesus as a saintly older brother who enjoys being around children and would therefore naturally enjoy being around us. Nor is Jesus far from Dante's poetry—the beatitudes are one of the organizing principles of *Purgatory*, and the words of Jesus are cited there and in *Paradise* well over a hundred times. Still, the medieval mystic Richard of Saint Victor claimed that the universe was created as it was through Christ because it was to be redeemed as it was to be redeemed through Christ; its redemption was provided for and was implicit in its very creation. In Christ, then, according to this line of thought, reside the answers to all man's questions about himself and the universe. As it happens, the most pressing question for Dante is the same as it was for Job and for Gilgamesh, for Aeschylus and Sophocles and Plato, for Milton and Dostoyevsky: the question of justice. If, as a work of art, the *Paradise* is to be the just and fitting completion of *Inferno* and *Purgatory*, it must bring to its fitting conclusion the probing of justice begun in *Inferno* and deepened— by the consideration of the wondrous action of mercy—in *Purgatory*.

A poem about the universe provides a universe of possibilities for its introducer. I hope the reader will pardon me if here I choose this one. For Dante, the problem of justice is Christological: it is the problem of reconciling love and mercy with truth and righteousness—of reconciling the Christ who forgave his enemies from the Cross with that same Christ by whom Hell itself was made and who will return to judge all mankind and give to each according to his deserts. And of all the corollary problems of justice—the difficulty in finding harmony among creatures of such astonishing diversity; the apparent success of wickedness in the world; the government of so party-riven a city as Florence—the one that stirs Dante's heart most deeply involves the just worship of God and the fate of pagans who, though virtuous, through no fault of their own could not pay that just worship. And so I would like to examine that matter, not only for its own sake, but because such an examination may illustrate what I have been struggling to say about the *Paradise*. For the resolution of the issue will, we will see, involve the resolution of the following, too:

The worth of the human body, first asserted by Virgil in *Inferno* 6, when he says that the body is a part of man's perfection
The body as vehicle of eternal reward
The problem of the union of human body and human soul, discussed so painstakingly in the embryology of *Purgatory* 25
The relation of physical space to Paradise and of time to eternity
The efficacy of prayer, inasmuch as prayer seems to alter events in time yet is part of God's unalterable providence
How the natural is impregnated with the supernatural, or, more specifically, how human virtues embodied by finite beings dwelling in space and time can reflect or be analogous to divine virtues

How the human—body and soul united and made in the image and
likeness of God—reflects, in microcosm, the origin, the form, the
matter, and the goal of the cosmos

How grace works from beyond man, within man, by means of man, to
redeem man and make man like God

In the *Paradise* these and many other themes of the *Comedy* either find
their fulfillment or are directed toward it, and this fulfillment is found
nowhere other than in the person of Christ.

Diligite Iustitiam Qui Iudicatis Terram

"Delight in justice, ye who rule the earth." That seems an obvious
thing for the constellation of blessed souls to spell out in the circle of the
just rulers in Canto Eighteen. Nothing odd about it: if one is to rule—lit-
erally, if one is to "judge"—then one should love justice.

But what does "justice" mean? For Dante, justice implied no a priori
system or procedure or social contract ensuring a fair chance for all; nor
did it imply an a posteriori, ideal result whose attainment would justify
the means. Such Platonic or Enlightenment ideations divorce justice
from the created, time-bound beings we are. They mistake the nature of
man. They violate our boundaries—or better, they pretend that we have
none. But that was the very sin of Adam:

> "My son, it wasn't tasting from the tree
>   that led me into exile; but alone
>   but trespassing the mark set down for me."
>   (26.115–17)

Justice is not what hypothetical man has established in the beginning, nor
what a hypothetical state will provide at the end, but a winnowing of
good from evil in the here and now, in the stories of our lives, within our
bounded and mortal bodies, by the One who is eternally just, who actu-
ally works in the world, to whose justice we must conform our own, and
whom we are called to worship in righteousness.

And so, if Dante is to discuss justice, he must needs refer to that Being,
because he dwells in a universe of beings and their stories, and those sto-
ries are meaningful stories, not bare chronicles. That helps explain an odd
thing about Dante's circle of the just rulers. Nowhere does he describe
practically how these rulers were just. What methods of rule did they use?

What did their ideal society look like? Did they establish circuit courts, enlarge the franchise, require writs of habeas corpus, enrich the public dole? We do not know. But we need not know, if "justice" is defined as a relationship to a just God rather than as a philosophical formula or a political program.

For the rulers of this earth are adjured to "love" justice. Let us not take the word lightly. It is exactly the same word Augustine uses for the love we are commanded to have for God and for neighbor. We are to delight in, rejoice in, justice—not hate it, as do the damned, nor wish it were otherwise, as the poet seems to do several times early in the *Inferno*. Now, since it is justice we are talking about, it must be explicable and accessible to reason; a Virgil must be able to apprehend it. But since it is a divine justice, we will not be able to understand all, or even to understand wholly the smallest part. Our love for justice can be requited only by something—or someone—beyond ourselves, by the One whom, as it happened, Virgil did not know. Also, just as time is both passing away and eternally present before God, so justice too must partake of both the timely and the eternal. It cannot, as I have suggested, exist in a metaphysical world of ideal sexless beings making constitutional choices *ab ovo*; since it is justice for created, embodied beings, it will be particular. It will embrace what would be fair for this person, at this time, in this situation; recall the rule-breaking that frees Provenzan Salvani from waiting at the base of the Mountain of Purgatory (*Purgatory* 11); recall that the entire journey of the poet has been enabled by Mary, who in mercy for Dante "broke the rigid sentence from above" (*Inferno* 2.96). Yet there must, too, be general laws, for reason itself can discover them: for example, the notion of oneself as a being teaches us the incommensurable worth of beings and objects, and thus teaches us that we should not do to others what we would not like done to ourselves. Because we created beings are also ensouled, the working out of justice on earth must transcend the particulars and find itself in accord with divine law. In other words, justice is both what is justly done here and now within the story and what informs the story as a whole from above. Since we ourselves are in the story, and can thus know little of it, our love of justice must always be accompanied by a painful awareness of our ignorance, and by awe before the providence of God. To love justice, then, is to go on an ardent quest, as did Plato and Aristotle, for wisdom both human and divine. It is to long in wonder for what abides beyond us yet is with us still. Dante and Aquinas would say that it is to long for Christ.

And that explains why Dante has chosen this line, the first verse of the Old Testament book of Wisdom. For here in Paradise justice transcends this or that juridical system, just as reasoning in Paradise transcends this or that language. On earth, justice is the result of wisdom in the ruler, and the beginning of wisdom is the fear of the Lord. A just ruler will be wise, and a wise ruler will fear the Lord. Why? Because the Lord's judgments are unsearchable. A trap closes upon us: a wise and just ruler will look to the Lord, whose wisdom is inaccessible and whose judgments cannot be explained. But the trap opens as it could not have for Aeschylus and Sophocles: the Wisdom of God is a Person who made himself accessible—as accessible indeed as a child or an unjustly condemned man: "But we preach Christ crucified, unto the Jews a stumbling block, and unto the Greeks foolishness; but unto them which are called, both Jews and Greeks, Christ the power of God, and the wisdom of God. Because the foolishness of God is wiser than men" (1 Cor. 1:23–25).

For a materialist this is all absurd. How can the unexampled stand as an example? How can a principle be a person? But faith sees warm and vital truths here, no less true for being paradoxical. The first qualification of justice in a ruler is that he be wise, that he understand how he himself is but a small motif in a story written by someone else, appointed to enact measures in accord with principles that, in a shadowy way, the Author has revealed directly and through natural reason; yet he must enact these measures without losing sight of the individual beings to whom he is to show this justice. He is the agent of Wisdom, of whose design he can never be more than dimly or fitfully aware. Yet in faith he grasps that all on earth will earn their just rewards, even when he and other just rulers cannot perceive all that is happening; and that is exactly as he would have it. In Dante's vision, just as no proud man could ever retain his pride and really give his soul to Beatrice, so only the humble man can love justice.

And so it is in *Paradise* that the cantos on justice are devoted to supralogical, law-exploding examples of divine grace enforcing law and enacting a justice beyond the expectations of, yet fulfilling the longings of, the just. And Dante prepares us for this celebration of justice by first celebrating and defining the wisdom of Solomon.

In Canto Ten, Dante hears Thomas Aquinas say that "no second ever rose" to match the wisdom of the Hebrew king. The praise confuses the poet, who considers Adam and Jesus. Surely whatever wisdom man can possess was granted to those two? If so, says Thomas later, characteristically taking the objection from his disputer's mouth, "How can this man have been without a peer?" (13.89). Lest we blaspheme, we must resolve the crux. The key is an equivocation. By the word "rose," Thomas explains, he meant "rose to power." Solomon is not the wisest man but the wisest king who ever lived, and his request of the gift of wisdom is best seen in the context of his dedication to the wise ruling of his people. It had nothing to do with being the sharpest logician, mathematician, or philosophical strategist. Dante the poet has allowed Dante the character to commit a blunder in order to teach the reader humility in judging of the divine. Under the guidance of Beatrice, Dante has been soaring at instantaneous speeds, to realms past human thought, "soaring beyond man" (1.70). Such intellectual expansion is humbling in one way, as Thomas's admonition is humbling in another:

> "And should you rush to what you don't perceive,
> let my words drag like lead weights on your feet
> and make you slow to answer yes or no..."
>
> (13.112–14)

The problem is not simply rational capacity. Our lives are journeys—the very poem begins *nel mezzo del cammin di nostra vita,* "midway upon the journey of our life." We are creatures of time. And we have bodies, too; it is not possible to imagine embodied beings assenting to the most abstract intellectual untruth without being changed, psychically and physically, by that untruth. The result is a literal, not merely metaphorical, straying from the path, that dangerous straying which found Dante in the midst of a deep wilderness at the beginning of the *Comedy,* his salvation all but lost. Thus Thomas warns us to keep our feet to the sure road:

> "For scurrying thought will often enough deflect
> a man's opinions into false terrain,
> and then his self-love binds his intellect."
>
> (118–20)

The quick forming of an erroneous opinion may be caused by heedlessness, but it is pride that keeps the man from retracing his steps. The man in error is not simply wrong. He has gone wrong; he has erred, in the Latin sense of *error.* He has wandered, and in his obstinacy he refuses to seek the way back. The link between wisdom and justice is again shown to be humility—ironic but Christlike virtue, for the ruler exalted so! Conversely, the link between folly and injustice is pride, which renders a man truly low, regardless of how high he may be stationed:

> "For of all fools that man's the most complete
> who'll affirm or deny but not reflect,
> impetuous in his haste down either street..."
>
> (115–17)

Again, Christianity is not a philosophy, if by a philosophy we mean a rationally analyzable set of timeless propositions. It is (Dante would say, and I agree) rational, and it does present analyzable propositions. But it is more. Christianity is a faith that makes particular claims on particular people. It is for beings, not for abstractions. To err is to mistake the story cleanly. In Aquinas's words—and Aquinas is for Dante simply the greatest Christian philosopher—it is to run before one's time. A simple misapprehension of one word, "wisest," becomes a sin against providential order:

> "People besides should never be too sure
> of what they judge, like farmers in the corn
> who count their crop before the ears mature.
> For I've seen all the winter a bare thorn
> looking like nothing but a stiff rough stick,
> whose top would blossom when the rose was born,
> And I have seen a vessel sleek and quick,
> racing through all its course along the main,
> founder as it was putting into port."
>
> (130–38)

Here Thomas illustrates the disjunction between human and divine wisdom by two parables that involve our misapprehension of time. We cannot always see the "season," the right time for a thing to happen. Our sins against justice are sins against wisdom. Thinking we know more than we do, we think we can tell what must happen by what we suppose has happened. We see, or think we see, a dead rosebush, reduced to a thorny stick by the winter, and we judge that the thing is ready to be thrown into the fire. We see a brave ship, sailing stalwartly for months, hoving confidently into port. We judge that it will soon be harbored. Yet the bare branch puts forth a rose, and the ship goes down. Our hastiness is a metaphor for our incomplete reading of the human heart; and as long as we are not God, and as long as our fellows are beings rather than sets of genetic code, that reading must be incomplete. Not the greatest of intellects, not Thomas himself, can comprehend the mystery of another being. Thus not Thomas himself can say who will or who will not be saved. So much the more laughable it is in the ordinary man or woman to presume to do so:

> "So let not Master Dick or Lady Jane,
> seeing one rob, another give his all,
> think they can see with providence divine,
> Because the one can rise, the other fall."
>
> (139–42)

So it was in fact at Jesus' passion, when the almsgiving Pharisees mocked him to their condemnation, but the humble and repentant thief, admitting that he was but suffering the just penalty for his actions, heard these consoling words: "Today you will be with me in Paradise" (Luke 23:43).

Now, what does this humility imply for the purveyor of justice? It keeps the ruler within his proper, limited sphere (and Dante's political career springs from his conviction that Church and secular leaders had transgressed their proper spheres, with bitter consequences). If the man loves divine justice, he will feel his human limitations the more keenly, and will confine himself to keeping good order in the state by judging cautiously of what he can see, and refraining from judging what he cannot see. Only so will his time-bound decisions be informed by the eternal wisdom of God.

The rewards of such humility surpass anything that a sensible man would expect; any but those moved by ardent charity toward God and one another would be ashamed to claim them. These rewards are just in this sense: it is the just God who grants them. But they are to our notions of justice as is the ocean to a puddle. Let us examine what it is given the humble—the wise—to see.

Dante asks Solomon whether the blessed will be more jubilant after they have been reunited with their bodies. Now it seems I have strayed far from the question of justice: what does that have to do with the resurrection of the body? And why, after Thomas has just told Dante that

Solomon's wisdom consisted in rulership rather than in abstractions, does Dante ask Solomon what looks like a purely theological question? We dare not suppose that Dante forgot what he was doing. Nor dare we suppose that Dante has clumsily proceeded to another, separate matter. Consider that for Solomon justice involved the just treatment of particular, embodied human beings; to love justice is to search, with heart and mind and soul, for the just One in accord with whose decrees one is ardent to act. It is an exalted virtue whose matter may be quite humble—as was the case with the two women who both claimed to be the mother of the same infant, and whose maternal feelings Solomon depended upon to solve the problem (1 Kings 3:16–28). The just ruler will thus be the most earthy of lovers of wisdom, like Saint Louis the king deciding small disputes between peasants under an oak tree outside of Paris, or like Sancho Panza, refusing to be called Don, using all his shrewdness and powers of observation to untangle riddles that stump the aristocrats who watch him in amazement. He knows who and what he is, and how small he is, and that his glory rests in that smallness. To deny the resurrection of the body is, in a small but significant way, to assert that we are too proud to be what we are: unions of body and soul. It is to deny, subtly, our connection to time and the worms of time.

The question is a counterpart to the question Dante has asked of Farinata, the political agitator (no ruler) and heretic (no wise man), in *Inferno* 10: why can the souls in hell see the future but not the present? Both questions have to do with the transcending of human limitations, specifically our relationship to time and space. It has been chillingly put that in Heaven there is eternity, while in Hell there is time—endless time, wearying time, with only such petty and inconsequential change as to mark time, yet within an essential sameness, now and forever, cut off from its origin and goal in eternity. It is to suffer the burden of, without dwelling in, time. And of all the souls in Hell, the Epicurean heretics must feel this time the most wearying, intellectually. Wise in their own minds, they denied the immortality of the soul—for why should we have been created for such absurd heights? Yet it occurs to Dante to ask Farinata, the worldly patriot—a failed patriot, we might add—about the strange knowledge and ignorance of the souls in Hell. And what will happen when the world has ceased to be, and there is no more future to know? Farinata's reply tolls a death knell to the mind. Through the same divine light they denied, the souls are granted sight of coming events, but when those events draw near, they lose sight of them completely. They lose the very memory of the sight, for what else is it to foresee an event, if not to see it in the imagination, or to remember an event, if not to be able to recall an image of it? The souls are thus punished by an inversion of the typical action of the human mind. For us the future is dim and the present is clear; for them the future is clear and the present invisible. The natural, time-related, threefold ability of the mind—memory, perception, and imagination, linked by Augustine to the Trinity—is thwarted. What should have been evidence, while these proud men lived, of their participation in a mind not bound by time now mocks them with their folly and, with the slabs above their fiery tombs, imprisons them in their false humility, their presumptuous self-limitation.

For Dante, as for Plato and Aristotle, evidence of the soul's immortality is inherent in the soul's activity. To deny this immortality is to deny one's proper humanity, a grievous affront to the Creator; it is also to deny the telos of one's humanity, the enjoyment of the eternally true. That is why the Epicureans are punished so severely, while the other pagan philosophers are but relegated to Limbo. But the question of the resurrection of the body—of our transcending time and space *in corpore*, while remaining creatures of time and space still—is another matter. This curious exaltation of the lowly body was such an obstacle to the Greeks that even Paul's enthusiastic converts at Corinth wanted to be sensible by refusing to believe it. I say they were right, by their lights, to reject the offensive doctrine, for it makes too much and too little of us. Too little, indeed, for why should we be reminded of this shell we wear, let alone reassume it for eternity? Too much, for why should our bodies enjoy so unlooked-for a gift? But then, life of any sort, to the believer, is a gift. Even to exist as a creature, to the believer, is a source of wonder. Then to reject this high gift is to take from God only such things as accord with our view of ourselves. It is pride or aloofness in the guise of modesty, diffidence and distance in place of faith and burning love. We (so we should like to think) do not require quite so much resurrection: that of the noble soul will suffice, thank you. But God is a fool and will have us all. Christ assumed a body to save souls, and not souls alone.

And so it falls to the wise ruler Solomon to answer Dante's question about the resurrection of the body. The question implies the logic of faithlessness, and its answer implies the paradox of the union of human and divine in Christ. Granted that the souls in Heaven already enjoy the perfection of bliss, how can their union with the body add any more to that? How can what is already all be added to? And if the body is reunited with the soul, will not the soul's radiance have to be reduced if the body is to endure it? Note that the questions erase God from the picture; the problem is presented as abstract, mathematical. What can increase what is already all? Any notion of what one is created for, or of perfection as a state that implies a Perfecter and a being who has been perfected—in other words, any implication of justice as love—is absent. It is, strange to say, a carnal imagination that denies the beauty and dignity of the flesh.

Solomon's response is preceded by motifs of self-transcending sublimity. First, in a humble, refreshingly fleshly image (also, and fittingly, an image that foreshadows the utter transcendence at the conclusion of the poem), the souls who hear Dante's question and who anticipate the answer show immediately that especially in Paradise, perfect bliss can be increased:

> As dancers dancing in a merry reel
>   will raise their voices in a rush of glee,
>   all of their gestures lighter in the heel,
> So, to that most devout and ready plea,
>   the holy circlings showed me a new joy
>   in their revolving and their wondrous song.
>   (14.19–24)

Then the poet reminds us of the wonder already accepted by any Christian doubtful of bodily resurrection, and that is that there should be a resurrection at all:

> Whoever on earth laments that we must die
>   to live above in Heaven, does not see
>   the sweet refreshment of the eternal rain.
>   (25–27)

He reminds us that God himself is the Lord over number, picking up Thomas's refusal to define wisdom as the ability to tell whether one can inscribe in a semicircle a scalene triangle whose base is the diameter (an impossibility) and looking forward to the final canto and Dante's incapacity to understand the how of the Incarnation, where he is like a geometer trying to square the circle (also an impossibility):

That ever-living One and Two and Three
    that ever reigns in Three and Two and One,
    uncircumscribed and circumscribing all,
Three times was hymned in praise by every one
    of those souls in so sweet a melody
    as would reward all merit.

(28–33)

The praise itself is a trinity, a duality, and a unity—three songs, two rings, one harmony—to the Trinity and to Christ and to the one God, and both music and object are beyond the poet's power to describe. Then when Solomon actually begins to speak, it is with "a gentle voice" that "might have been the angel's when he spoke to Mary" (35–37). The angel is the gallant Gabriel, whispering to Mary those words of incomprehensible love that announced the Incarnation of Christ, for whom it was no loss of glory to be clothed in human flesh.

So too with the souls who, though robed in bliss, will become even more blessed at the resurrection of the body:

"When, blessed and glorified,
    the flesh is robed about us once again,
    we shall be lovelier for being whole;
Whence the gift of illuminating grace
    granted us by the highest Good shall grow—
    light that disposes us to see His face,
And in that light then must our vision grow,
    grow then the ardent love it sets aflame,
    wherein the radiance of the flesh shall grow."

(43–51)

What is fascinating about this passage is the unabashed argument *per consequens*. Granted the revealed and logically inaccessible premise of the resurrection of the body, it follows logically that human beings, made up of soul and body, should then be more perfectly blessed, because more perfectly human, more perfectly what their inner design and their outer Designer intend them to be. There is, in other words, no measure of blessedness outside the relationship of God, who blesses with the human being who is blessed. Yet that conclusion involves us in an overleaping of logic. If a thing is already perfectly blessed, how can its blessedness increase? Such a question implies the faithless pseudoquestion, answered by Dante twice, "If God was self-sufficient, why did he bother to create at all?" As flawless as Solomon's reasoning is, the answer lies not in demonstrable logic but in the matter, the body, that which Solomon is actually reasoning about: love. And once love and beatitude are admitted, the Christian vision is seen to follow as neatly as a geometric proof.

But how can a mere body be reunited with a soul without hampering the soul? As always, the question hides another faithless one, rejecting Christ: "How can God, who is spirit, not degrade himself by creating material things or going so far as to become a material thing?" Dante's answer is a defiant reversal of our expectations. He uses the image of a glowing coal to show not merely that the body will be no clog in heaven, but that, as the last shall be first, the body will actually outshine the soul in glory:

> "But as a fiery coal that gives off flame
>   conquers it with its incandescent white,
>   preserving its appearance all the same,
> So this surrounding gleam of heavenly light
>   will be defeated by the luminous flesh
>   that now lies tombed in earth. Nor will the might
> Of its new radiance trouble us with pain,
>   for strong enough will be its organs then
>   to bear all things that bring us more delight."
>
> (52–60)

For we are embodied beings. As Joseph Pieper says, referring to Aquinas, it is no contradiction that God is more perfect for being pure spirit, but we are more perfect in the union of body and soul, for then we will be more perfectly ourselves. The doctrine, we see, is incomprehensible without a Designer, an Author, a Creator who made us to be the particular sort of beings we are. In Heaven, the body, which in our fallen state we feel as a husk or as a chain upon the soul, will be the soul's principle of individuation. It will be the coal both giving off the light of the soul and, as it were, defining that soul, making it something particular, the blessed life of this human being, and not an indistinguishable instance of general blessedness.

Beyond our enjoying our own perfection, of what use will a body be in eternity? Here we tap again the wellspring of Christian paradox. What the rationalist finds really offensive is not the bald possibility of a Creator, so long as that Creator remains a nameless, faceless, and even timeless force. In such a case, it hardly matters whether one is a theist or an atheist; it is rather like preferring one sort of mildly socialist party to another. Such a God never says, "My ways are not your ways," because those ways would be eminently discoverable and comprehensible by us; nor would they even be "ways," for that implies a personality, a preference for certain ways rather than others. There would be no *mysterium tremendum* about such a God. There would be none of the surprises, the apparent rebuffs, the reversals of a love affair. But Dante's is precisely a God who commits the offense to our dignity of loving us, and better than we love ourselves. As Kierkegaard says, no true lover enumerates for himself three reasons why it is a good thing for him to be in love. There can be no rational answer to the question "Why should God love us?"—first, because God is God and needs nothing from us; second, because we are we and can give nothing to God; and finally, because love is love and quite reasonably rules the question out. Well then, it is not we who attain perfection for ourselves by stripping ourselves of those features, like the body, which we deduce are hindrances to our becoming like angels or gods; rather it is God in love who bestows perfection upon us by giving us those features which he created and which he loves, and giving them to us perfectly, so that we become perfectly what he made us, in love, to be. That is exactly what the souls in bliss desire too, and their love for their bodies (to be contrasted with the weepy solicitude the suicides show for the bodies they had heedlessly tossed away [*Inferno* 13] is not a love for themselves as perfect, but a love for the God who made them, and a love for the other embodied beings about them. And since we are embodied beings, as Pieper happily puts it, we cannot live with the stars all the time. We must have roofs over our heads. To love a human being is also to love the body. To love the body is to love the small, the local, the particular. It is to love those things enjoyed by that body—even to love Florence, or to use Burke's phrase, the small platoon into which one was born. It is to love Bag End and the beer from a particularly good harvest. For Dante, the small and the local are delicately expressed in terms of human intimacy:

> So prompt and ready was the loud "Amen!"
>   both choirs responded, it was clear to me
>   how much they yearned to see their flesh again,

> Maybe less for themselves than for their mamas,
> their fathers, and the others they held dear
> before they had become eternal flames.
>
> (61–66)

Mamme, "mamas": the word evokes the beauty not only of a relationship but of an entire state of innocent life, characterized by the gentle and particular care of a *mamma*. It is a touch of earth, exalted in heaven. And Dante will develop the motif—for as the scene now shifts from the sun to Mars, the first person he meets among the holy warriors will be his own great-great-grandfather, Cacciaguida, a Florentine patriot with choice things to say about Florence now, and wistfully nostalgic memories of its humbler past, when virtuous mamas soothed their children with lullabies. And beyond that there is one Mama into whose eyes a child once looked, and whose face Dante will behold in Heaven; if Christ redeemed the world by becoming flesh of the Virgin, then the eyes he looked upon at his birth are blessed—and though they are but human, they plumb the divine more deeply than any created vision can.

Let us go over our territory. We have seen that, for Dante, justice must always be oriented toward the Creator. We have also considered that this Creator has made us as embodied, time-bound beings, who can know some things but who cannot know them all. Thus the just man will be aware of his limitations, and will be humble. His wisdom will echo the Wisdom of God, who is Christ. In particular, he will accept the gifts of soul and body; his awareness of his own ignorance is the counterpart to his knowledge, by faith, of what God promised that man might be. And the motive force behind his just rule will not be intellect, as it is not intellect that makes the dancers dance more swiftly when they consider the resurrection of the body. It will be love. He sees what he sees because he has fallen in love, and what he sees makes him love all the more.

Now let us return to the circle of just rulers.

The first thing to notice is that the souls sing individually and speak corporately. Their constellation is a kind of starry body politic or body of Christ. Also, the constellation is that of an Eagle, first because the eagle is a symbol of keen sight, and also because it is the imperial symbol, as the bird of Jupiter. Why should Dante now exalt the bird of imperial Rome, and what does that decision have to do with the preceding discussion?

Much, if we consider one of the premises of Christian (then Catholic) history, affirmed by G. K. Chesterton in *The Everlasting Man*. According to Chesterton, it was fitting that Christ was born when he was, for the Roman world was the best that paganism had to offer. At its finest, Rome embodied patriotism, self-restraint, a decent regard for the dignity of labor (even menial labor), a love for marriage, and a clearheaded concern for the practical as against the theoretical. Under Augustus Caesar, Rome reduced a warring world to peace and provided it with some real prosperity. Whether or not Chesterton exaggerates the merits of Rome, the Christians of Dante's day certainly saw a divine hand in the triumph of Augustus Caesar, who brought about the fitting earthly peace into which the true Prince of Peace might be born—and who did so quite unwittingly. This view of history was commonplace, and is what raised Virgil to the status of prophet. For in his Fourth Eclogue, a tribute to a patron and politician whose wife had recently borne a son, Virgil predicts a time of perfect peace to come, a Golden Age ushered in by this great birth. In the providence of God, Augustus prepares the way of the Lord, though he does not know it. So too, as Dante would have it, Virgil's song becomes the means for the conversion of Roman pagans after him—for instance, of the poet Statius. Virgil, says Dante's Statius, is like a man with a lantern, who lights the way for those behind him, though he himself cannot see.

In a way, Virgil sums up in himself all of Roman history leading up to the birth of Christ and the triumph of the Catholic Church. Thus when, at the beginning of the *Comedy*, the poet doubts whether it would be a good idea to journey with Virgil to the hereafter, he notes the example of two who have done so, one to bring comfort to the Christian Church, the other to discover the way to found the city of Rome:

> "You tell of Silvius' father, who descended
>   to the immortal world, still in the flesh,
>   and with his flesh's senses all aware.
> Yet if the Adversary of all evil
>   showed him this grace, it does not seem unfit
>   to intellects that see the great result,
> Both who and what was meant to spring from him;
>   for he was chosen in the heaven of heavens
>   father of sacred Rome and her command,
> And these, if we would speak the truth, were set
>   firmly in place to be the holy throne
>   where the successor to great Peter sits.

> Upon this journey which you celebrate
>> he learned of things which were the cause of both
>> his triumph, and the mantle of the pope.
> Later, the Chosen Vessel also went
>> to bring back comfort, strengthening the faith
>> which is the first step on salvation's way."
>
> *(Inferno* 2.13–30)

Aside from Dante's preoccupation with the relationship between Church and state—which, though it too forms a large part of his treatment of justice, I shall not delve into here—we should note that both Paul and Aeneas were providentially ordained to see what they saw beyond this world, so that there would be a Rome and a papacy. In this context Paul is most aptly called the *vas d'elezione,* the Chosen Vessel, for in his letters and in his own life he illustrates the unsearchable choices of God. No one would see any reason beforehand why either Aeneas or Paul should be granted such a privilege—Paul, the erstwhile persecutor of the Church, and Aeneas, the fugitive from a leveled city! Furthermore, Aeneas is to be the preparer for a Church whose existence he can never have foreseen. Faith in providence grants the vision, which includes two turns of history that reveal an unexpectedly complex order behind the appearances.

If we ask, "Why did God choose Rome?" we ask a question, then, that refers *after* the choice to the fitness of the choice, though the choice came unexpectedly to men of the time. If we ask it in any other sense, we presume upon the rights of providence. There was no more reason to choose Rome to be the ruler of the world than there was reason to choose Israel to introduce that world to the worship of the one true God. Ultimately, God chose Rome because God chose Rome. Again we must remind ourselves that Christianity is not a philosophy. God is more than the author of a set of principles; he is the author of a story, wherein Rome—not Peking, not Moscow, not Memphis, not Carthage—was to play one most important role. The particular is so significant that even in heaven the Roman symbol—a pre-Christian, indeed pagan, symbol—is exalted. To accept the fitness of the Roman eagle as a symbol for just rulers is, then, to accept in humility the workings of divine providence, those very workings which the eagle discusses and which, keen-sighted though it may be, it can never fathom utterly.

The prominent souls in this circle of just rulers, those to whom the eagle points Dante's attention, form the constellation's pupil and brow. It would be natural for us to conclude that these were either the most righteous rulers ever or the rulers who saw most deeply into justice. Neither, absolutely, seems to be the case; and that lack of neat fitness is most fit, lest we set ourselves up as judges above our Judge. Instead, each of the six souls is shown as one who *did not see* something on earth, but who, enjoying the pleasure of irony, does see it now. In each case, the something not seen verges upon the supralogical. We expect the appropriate, and receive the unexpected, which turns out to be more appropriate still. As the discussion in Canto Twenty takes the form of a song or liturgy—a rhapsody of wonder, a drama of redemption—each soul is presented in a tercet, followed by a tercet illuminating the irony of the soul's career, the disjunction between his knowledge then and his knowledge now. The effect is not that of irresistible proof, but of thunder building to a climax.

The first soul is David:

> "He in the center, as the pupil, gleams
> > who was the singer of the Holy Spirit,
> > the king who moved the Ark from house to house;
> Now does he understand his songs have merit
> > insofar as they spring from his own will,
> > by the concordant blessings they inherit."

(20.37–42)

Notice that no aspect of David's rule is mentioned—rather, the prerequisite for just rule, which is humility. Dante introduces David by calling him the king who took the Ark of God from town to town—because he felt unworthy to house it in his own city, and had to be advised by God to do so. He is not, here, the builder of a great temple, and indeed God was to rebuke him later for his human assumption that a great God deserves a great house built by a great man, David! The occasion to which Dante alludes is David's triumphant bringing of the Ark into Jerusalem, while he, "more and less than king," as Dante has deftly put it, the "humble psalmist" (*Purgatory* 10.65–66), danced so breathlessly and joyously that his robes rose up over his shame, all while his sour-eyed queen, Michal, looked on contemptuously at the display of her husband's flesh before mere townswomen (2 Sam. 6). The Ark too is a paragon of particularity and humility. Why should the Ark be more sacred than any other chest dedicated to the Lord? How can the God of the universe take up special residence here? Why here, and not elsewhere, or everywhere? To ask such questions, again, is to presume upon the providence of God, to turn away from his wondrous being toward some abstract and comprehensible force of one's own supposition. Why, God should do what we would have a god do! And that Ark, as Dante or any of his fellow worshipers would tell us, was a foreshadowing of the womb of Mary, who housed within her humble womb the New Covenant for all men. David, in other words, danced before a particular manifestation of God's purposeful activity in the world, as providentially preparing the way for the womb of a woman particularly graced—for the Incarnation and for the Church on earth.

Does David know this? He did not, when he sang those songs. Yet prompted by love he became, in those Psalms, a prophet of things he could not see. For his humility God grants him a blissful reward, out of all proportion to the humble service David rendered, yet a fit reward for that service, too.

If one had to choose a second just king from among the Israelites, the fit choice might seem to be the zealous destroyer of idols, Josiah. But Dante chooses a great but somewhat lesser king, Hezekiah, because, I think, of a moment of humbling and mercy in that king's life. In particular, Dante shows the ironic disjunction between our reasoning, based upon temporal causes, and the wisdom of the Creator and Ruler of time:

> "The following soul in this circumference,
>   where the arch rises, gained a long delay,
>   and stayed his death by genuine penitence;
> Now does he understand, when just men pray,
>   eternal judgment does not change, deferring
>   until tomorrow what's decreed today."
>
> (49–54)

Hezekiah had received word by the prophet that he would die that day, whereupon he earnestly besought the Lord, who granted him fifteen more years of life, asking him to look upon the miraculously reversing shadow upon a sundial (2 Kings 20). Does not the efficacy of prayer, more than any other result brought about by our willed actions, call into doubt the whole notion of divine providence? If a thing is decreed by God, how can prayer deflect it? If prayer can alter God's will, how can we then speak of an eternally ordained plan? The answer, given by Boethius, rests in a rich difference: that between how we time dwellers know and how God knows. Our prayer is just one of those freely chosen causes, spurred by love, which God foresees and has from the beginning folded into the divine plan. For Hezekiah, the result here is longer life; at another time, it is the obliteration of the seemingly insurmountable Assyrian army.

Things turn out not as they should, but as they should. That is the paradoxical lesson two more souls learn. First is Constantine, who with goodwill gave (so Dante and everyone of his day thought) a measure of temporal power to the pope, thus (so Dante thought) muddling the spiritual and temporal authorities and bringing about the bloody controversies between pope and emperor in the Middle Ages:

> "The next soul bore me off with all the laws
>   and made us Greek, to grant the Shepherd Rome,
>   a good intent that sprouted up bad fruit;
> Now does he understand the plagues that come
>   from his good deed will never harm his soul,
>   even should they destroy all Christendom."
>
> (55–60)

It is a stunning exculpation. "Ye shall know them by their fruits," says Jesus (Matt. 7:16), and Dante uses the same image to argue that Constantine was just, despite the fact that his action bore bad fruit. How can this be? Here we must not be carnal judges. The "fruit" Jesus was talking about included acts of malice, fraud, violence, lewdness. We are not the masters of time. No one can then judge a man's actions and thus his soul according to the results of time. To do so would be to subject good and evil to our own judgment and comprehension, when we are warned that only God knows the heart. Just as no action evil in itself can be justified beforehand by our foolish "certainty" that good will result, so no action good in itself can be condemned after the fact by our perception that evil has resulted. Time is the Lord's, and all its chances and changes.

Therefore we cannot infallibly interpret the events in the story we ourselves inhabit. Sometimes, as in the case of Constantine, apparent (but only apparent) evil is rewarded, while in the case of William the Good, justice goes apparently unrewarded:

> "The spirit at the semicircle's fall
>   was William, whom they weep for in that land
>   that weeps for Charles and Frederick living still;

> Now does he understand how deeply Heaven
> loves a just king, and in his lightning blaze
> he shows it still, for all to understand."
>
> (61–66)

William of Sicily was followed by the worthless Charles and Frederick, for no fault of William's. For being that exception in Dante's Italy, a just king, William is rewarded by the love of Heaven—the heart of Heaven inclines to him, as it had once granted the unexpected grace to the prayerful Hezekiah.

I have, as the reader may have noticed, omitted until now the discussion of the two souls whose presence here or anywhere in Paradise is the most surprising: the Roman emperor Trajan and the Trojan Ripheus. These men were unbaptized pagans, apparently, yet they enjoy eternal bliss. How is this possible? If this is possible, why are not all the souls of the just pagans in Paradise? In particular, why is Dante's beloved Virgil not in Paradise?

Let us take the more general question first, and let us allow Dante, in the words of the eagle, to present it for us:

> " 'Upon the Indus' banks a man is born,
>   and in that country no one's there to preach
>   on Christ, no one to read of Him, or write;
> And all his actions and desires are good,
>   as far as human reason can perceive,
>   without a sin in either deed or speech.
> He dies unbaptized and without the faith.
>   Where is the justice that condemns the man?
>   Where is his fault, if he does not believe?' "
>
> (19.70–78)

It is the question of the virtuous pagans. Why should what looks like an accident of life determine one's eternal destiny? Or, seeing that there are no true accidents, how can God hold a man responsible for neglecting a faith that was never offered to him? For Dante, no question is more erosive of faith than this. He has been troubled with it from the beginning. In the *Inferno*, when, for Dante's salvation (and for nothing that Virgil himself can gain!), Virgil proposes the journey to the underworld, the Roman poignantly contrasts Dante's good fortune, or, we should say, the grace

Dante has received, with his own. For Dante was born in a Christian land and had the chance to know Christ, for which he had better be grateful. Thus Virgil tells Dante that he cannot guide him into Paradise itself to meet the blessed:

> "If you then wish to rise and go to them,
>   another soul, worthier than I, will come;
>   I will leave you with her when I depart.
> For that great Emperor who reigns above,
>   because I was a rebel to his law,
>   allows no man to enter there by me.
> Everywhere he commands, from there he rules,
>   there stand his city and his lofty throne.
> Happy the man he chooses for his house!"
>
>   (*Inferno* 1.121–29)

Now, there is a way out of this problem that Dante does not take. I have always found the way to be tainted. It asserts, with Calvin, that the virtue of the pagans was only nominal. It did not really exist. If the Roman general Regulus advised his country against a truce and, once the senate had taken his advice, kept his vow to return to his captors in Carthage though he knew it would mean his death, how do we know that his bravery was not motivated by a desire for glory? How do we know that what looks like an act of love was not really an act of pride? The problem of the virtuous pagans is ruled out from the beginning: there are no virtuous pagans.

It may be possible to persuade someone of this, theologically; but I would wager that even Calvin saw it as special pleading. A variation on this answer is to argue that, since the human race has been so depraved by original sin that all deserve damnation, if a certain person by "accident" hears no word of God, that person's damnation was but just anyway. Salvation, after all, is a free gift; no one can merit it. But Dante does not take this way out, either, which also solves the problem by theological fiat. In the case of damnation, such justice bears not the slightest resemblance to what human beings might see as just: the pagan who murders and the pagan who gives his life to save another are damned alike. Here it is not that the justice of God is incomprehensible; it is rather that God's actions are what they are, and the name "justice" is applied to them a posteriori. The disjunction between the human and the divine is so radical that nothing, or everything, God does can be made to seem fit or unfit.

The problem with both these solutions is the same. They turn Christian faith into a faith in a theology, rather than a faith in a Being. Theologies do not intervene in the course of events; a Being may. If God is just, and if he is a Being whose relationship to us we can in part understand, because it has been revealed to us, and because it has come down and dwelt among us, then we must also be able to understand, in part, God's justice. It is not our justice; it is infinitely high above our justice; but somehow it must be, as Aquinas would put it, *like* our justice, analogous to our justice. It is both like and vastly different, and therein lies the possibility for the poetically appropriate. If such is the case, we can never dispense with the details of a pagan's life. They are part of his story, and Christian justice dwells in the realm of story: because you have done this, you will suffer that.

Thus Dante does not really give us an abstraction for a virtuous pagan. He is the very human Virgil, who, as Dante portrays him, was so predisposed toward Christianity that he helped to bring his admirer Statius to the faith. He is, as I read Canto Nineteen, the unnamed man who lives on the banks of the Indus, who follows his natural reason as best he can. How should the story turn out for these people, so as to preserve both the fitness of the ending and the transcendent wisdom of the One who has written the ending?

First let us note that the question does hinge upon the nature of Christ—on the possibility of really meaningful action on the part of God and man. If God must save anyone who tries hard enough to be good, then we have no need for Christ. Our own concept of justice would rule, and if we like we can tack the name "God" to it. If God takes no consideration whatsoever of human attempts, however flawed, to worship him in truth, then his arbitrary will rules, and if we like we can tack the name "justice" to it, or "mercy." But in that case Christ is perfectly unapproachable.

We should also notice that to require mathematical equality as a precondition for justice is incompatible with a created, material universe in which interesting things happen. Dante understood this point quite clearly. A universe of theoretical baseball players, all of whom possess the same prior abilities subject to the same probabilistic laws, who will all face the same sequence of pitches, and who will all be granted three outs and nine innings, is no universe of stories. It may turn out one way or it may turn out another, but in its very probability it is as determined as stone, nor would anyone be so sentimental as to attach the name of "being" to an individual batter. These nominal individuals, all depressingly the same, could not be objects of love. It makes no sense to say that one loves another because there is absolutely nothing distinguishable about that other, not even a face. No, if we are to have a universe dwelt in by true beings capable of love, of heroism, of suffering, and of triumph, we must have a various universe, and variety implies inequality in at least one respect, the one that varies. All of this is another way of saying that, by the very nature of God, of human beings, and of this physical universe, no philosophical justification of God's ways is possible, if by justification we mean an analytical exposition of the equal chances every nominal "individual" possesses for equal bliss. God in his dangerous love has created something infinitely more lovely: a world peopled by beings free to love or to hate. A man's free choice to walk smugly by the beggar on the bridge may have no consequence to speak of, or eternal consequences. It is a world into which, to save a race gone awry, the Author himself has entered in a particular way at a particular place, to atone for men's sins and to reveal particular things about the world and its Father, ultimately to return to that world and restore its lost innocence. God did not create a philosophy. He created, as Dante saw, a comedy.

So it makes sense that if Trajan and Ripheus are saved, it is not by some predetermining law, some calculable threshold of virtue beyond which if any pagan should pass, even if by a hair's breadth, the Lord would be bound by the rules of fair play to save him. Rather, Trajan and Ripheus are saved by surprising things that happen to them in their lives (and in Trajan's case, the words "in life" take on a shocking meaning). These things, surprising though they may be, happen with fitness, though they need not have happened at all. To tell the truth, not one of us need be saved; and in the story of the salvation of any man there are bound to be many fit but surprising turns of providence.

Trajan's is the more obviously miraculous, exceptional case, and thus it is the easier to deal with. Skeptical of legends (he sets the record straight regarding the death of Saint John, 25.122–29), Dante repeats, apparently without a trace of skepticism, the tale of Pope Gregory the Great, who was devoted to the memory of the good emperor. Gregory prayed that somehow Trajan might be saved. The Lord worked out the means: Trajan was resurrected briefly from the grave, and Gregory preached to him, and he, naturally enough when one has been resurrected from the grave, believed. God did not simply translate Trajan from

Hell to Heaven, but from death to life, and Trajan, momentarily in life again, and thus momentarily in possession of a newly free will, could hear the word of God and respond to it:

> "To flesh and bone
>   the one returned from never-repenting Hell,
>   and that was the reward of living hope,
> Of living hope, with power to impel
>   prayers to God that he might rise once more,
>   and live, and so be moved to willing well.
> Returned unto his flesh the briefest hour,
>   the glorious spirit I've been speaking of
>   believed in Him and sought His help and power,
> And in believing, kindled into love
>   so true, the second time he fell asleep
>   he merited his coming to this joy."
>
> (20.106–17)

Note that this resuscitation is the reward of "living hope." It does not follow necessarily. Hope is the métier of our lives. It is the condition of man who sees as through a glass, darkly. Thus the hopeful man understands that God admits of possibilities for our lives that are far beyond, yet somehow corresponding to, what we might imagine. The whole event—and it is an event, not a deduction—evinces all the surprise and the warmth of a love story, which, in fact, it is.

The best way to think of the difference between a sublime event and a bald rational deduction is to consider the wonder of the event as an event; that is, to ask whether the event could have turned out otherwise. What would have happened to Cinderella had she not lost one of her slippers? Only if such a question is possible does the tale mean anything. What would have happened to Trajan had Gregory not prayed for him, or had he prayed for someone else instead? The answer is simple. A child will accept it; a rationalist will rebel. Trajan would not now enjoy eternal bliss. Prayer, as I have said, is but one of our actions that are really consequential. God provides for those actions, without, however, robbing those actions of their fit consequences. It is a part of his power that he gives men power, even the power of prayer. It does not follow of necessity that an omnipotent God should do this; but then, God is not a proposition but a Being. He gives men power because that is the sort of self-humbling God he is. The God who created the material universe, and who assumed human flesh to save a world from woe, deigns to allow human beings a real part in the working out of his story. They are, as Tolkien puts it, "sub-creators," not puppets. That is a logical consequence of the scandalous fact, undiscoverable by logic, that he loves us. Had Trajan not humbled himself (and he was on the verge of not humbling himself) and inconvenienced his army to hear out the widow (cf. *Purgatory* 10.73–93), Gregory would not have fallen in love with his memory. Lacking that devotion, he would not have prayed; had he not prayed, he would not have moved God to the miracle; Trajan would remain with the other virtuous pagans at the rim of Hell. I have said "miracle," referring to the resuscitation, but the real miracle, the one the rationalist must fear more than scorn, is that God should have created a Gregory and a Trajan at all and, having created them, should in his love have endowed them too with the ability to create, and thus to love.

What fitting irony can we see in retrospect! Trajan had no idea, when the widow was pleading with him, that his eternal destiny hung in the balance. A drama was being enacted, of whose full cast of characters the particular characters onstage at the time—the emperor, the widow, the impatient lieutenants, the bored soldiers—were quite unaware. Of course, now we see Trajan in Heaven looking back in wonder at the Trajan who came before him, ever enjoying the contrast between what he knows now and what he knew then:

> "Now does he understand what debt you owe
> not following Christ, by the experience
> of this sweet life, and the opposite below."
> (20.46–48)

I have suggested the stark particularities of Trajan's case—a resurrection the like of which, according to the biography of Gregory whence its legend derives, there was to be no other. But I think we can also argue that Trajan stands as an example of a multitude of possible particular cases. For the really mysterious thing about the event was not that Gregory's prayer for Trajan should be answered, but that any prayer should be answered—any prayer by any Gregory for any Trajan. That prayer should be answered is itself a fact that points to the ultimate link between God and man, namely a being who is himself both God and man. The God who makes creatures to be like him, and who humbled himself to put their errant ways to rights, wishes to be overcome by prayer; if it is not blasphemous to say so, he in his power grants to dust the power to move Omnipotence:

> "The kingdom of Heaven suffers violence
>   from living hope and burning charity
>   that overcome the will of the divine,
> Not as a man will overcome a man—
>   the divine wins because it would be won,
>   and won, it wins with its benignity."
>
> (20.94–99)

In Trajan we may see all those whose presence in the flock is unsuspected but whose salvation has depended upon the prayers of those made righteous in Christ; not that they might be saved without Christ, but that Christ might save them in ways beyond human comprehension.

The case of Ripheus is more difficult, because the event that changes his life is an inward prompting of the soul, moved by God's grace. For movements of the soul are also events; they happen to us, in the same way that we might turn a corner and see something frightful or terribly lovely, or stumble upon a stone. None of them are wholly in the control of our wills, and some of them come to us quite from outside. The latter sort of event occurred for Ripheus. Again, there is absolutely no sense here that God's grace was consequent upon Ripheus's actions, as if what Ripheus did necessitated God's response. Otherwise it would not be grace but debt, not story but law. Yet, having been given, the grace is fitting:

> "By grace that showers from a spring so deep
>   no creature's sight can penetrate into
>   its first upwelling wave, the other soul
> Placed all his love in righteousness below;
>   for which, grace upon grace, God raised his eye
>   and showed him our redemption yet to come,
> And he believed in it, and from that day
>   he could not bear the stink of paganism,
>   and he reproached the people gone awry.
> Those Ladies then endewed him with baptism,
>   the three at the right wheel of the chariot,
>   a thousand years before the Baptist came."
>
> (118–29)

Before baptism was ever heard of, Ripheus was really baptized, by the three great sponsors, Faith, Hope, and Charity—three ladies, not three equations. What Dante has done here is astonishing. He has taken a character from Virgil's *Aeneid,* a character mentioned in passing, whose epithet was that he was the Trojan who loved justice the most and ever strove to do the right. It was ironic, in the *Aeneid,* that he should be so, for he was about to die, inasmuch as Jupiter, in his own surprising design, had destined that Troy should fall so that Rome would be built. Beyond being just and dying with the nameless multitude, Ripheus plays no part in the story of the *Aeneid.* But not as the world sees does God see. What happened to Ripheus is exceptional, yet it is the kind of exceptional thing that could be happening to any pagan anywhere, with his neighbors, even his Christian neighbors if he has any, being none the wiser. There is the story we think we see, a story in which even for his own people Ripheus plays a very small part, and then there is the story as it really is, disjunct from but not wholly unlike the first. It is a richer, deeper story, wherein justice is fulfilled beyond calculations:

> "Who would believe, down in the world that errs,
>> that Ripheus the Trojan in this round
>> would be the fifth among the holy flares?
> Far more he understands of grace divine
>> than all the world can see, although his eye
>> can still not plumb the depth of the profound."
>
> (67–72)

Who would believe it? asks the eagle, changing the formula for its introduction of the souls and striking thereby a note of wonder. The just are rapt in a charity transcending justice, as is right. In a sense, it is as reasonable to believe in the salvation of Ripheus as it is to believe in the ever-self-humbling, godlike-creature-making God, who, omnipotence himself, wishes to be overcome by prayer, and so conquers in a complex and personal way. Ripheus then may stand, not as symbol but as an instance of those to whom, of his own free choice and without regard to prayer, God has graced with vision, a vision of a Redeemer. Beyond this speculative point it is perilous for the wayfaring Christian to go. But as one can have love only by giving it away, so one can possess one's will wholly only by submitting it wholly in love. If God's love conquers by allowing itself to be conquered, it is because his love is conquered by a will not to know any more than God wills that we know:

"Mortals, withhold your judgment: even we
who see the face of God do not yet know
the number chosen from eternity—
And it is sweet, this lack in what we know,
because in this good is our good made fine,
and what the Lord may will, we too will so."

(133–38)

And why not? For who in love ever wished that his beloved were any the less glorious?

The answer, then, to the question of the virtuous pagans is also no proposition, but a Being. God himself is the answer. He will, we trust, give what is just, and will give it beyond our ability to add or to detract. We do not know who will be saved; we cannot know unless he reveals it. If we could know, of our own, he would not be God. But we have plenty of circumstantial evidence, as it were, to suggest that whatever God does will not only be fitting and proper but will strike us as most surprising. The believer would not have it any other way. Thus in love with Love, Trajan and Ripheus delight in what they know, and what they do not know, for it is all a delight in him:

And as an expert hand on the guitar
follows the singer with a trembling chord,
lending a greater pleasure to the air,
So while the eagle spoke I can recall
those two blest gleams of light, that I could see
flashing their happy flames at every word,
Like eyes that blink in perfect harmony.

(142–48)

Stupendous, that in such a homely image—the natural, effortless blinking of two eyes—we should have an emblem of seeing and not seeing, bound up with now natural, effortless, ardent love.

And that leads us to the most striking case of the salvation of a pagan soul, that of Cato. Dante meets Cato at the base of the Mountain of Purgatory, where Virgil names him as one who died "for liberty in Utica" (1.74), and then, as I read it, he foretells Cato's inclusion among the blessed, robed again with the "garment that will shine / So bright on the great day" (75–76). We must not think that Cato merits salvation by his apparently suicidal death. As Dante conceived it, Cato was a witness to—literally a martyr to—liberty, and thus, in dying only to show how inestimably valuable liberty is, he testified to the Truth that sets men free. Yet the martyrdom (for Dante sees it as such) of Cato points to Christ in the same way as the life of Francis points to Christ, and that is through the power of the indwelling Spirit working in their minds and hearts. We must consider the possibility that as Christ dwelled in Francis, so conforming him to himself that Francis was graced with the terrible wounds of the stigmata, so Christ—the Truth that Cato could name only indirectly—dwelled in Cato, so conforming him to himself that Cato was graced with that sacrificial death.

In the three cases of Trajan, Ripheus, and Cato, then, we see nothing that is not consonant with justice, since mercy is itself an action of justice and presupposes justice. None are saved in contradiction to a damnation they merit; each is saved by Christ: Trajan, through the instrumentality of prayer (so central to the themes of liberation and friendship in *Purgatory*), a prayer spoken on his behalf that he might see the truth; Ripheus, by God's direct revelation, a gift consonant with Ripheus's ardent love for the light he was given; Cato, by the grace of God conforming him in his last great action to Christ himself. One is prayed for, two are not; two see the truth, and one in action becomes like unto the Truth. Their salvation is just—but grace and mercy have seen to it that it be so.

In different ways the souls in Hell, proud, mendacious, and treacherous, are distortions of Christ; in different ways the souls in Purgatory are fired with longing for Christ; in different ways the souls in Paradise manifest Christ. In that One who is both God and man—and God as one of three Persons in one God—is hidden the key to that unity in diversity. In that One dwells the ground of the possibility of godlike action on the part of man—action that is enabled by grace and that explains the mercy of Purgatory and, by contrast, the justice of Hell. In that One are the local, the specific, and the bodily exalted forever; even Florence cannot be forgotten, then. In that One are the good and the true united, since the loving humility that led Christ to the Cross is the love wherein God first created all the universe; to understand the one is to understand the other. Dante will not rhyme on the name of Christ, since he considers no word worthy of it. But more: it is *the* word, the name, the key to all knowledge and all love. It is for that reason that Dante ends the *Paradise,* and thus the *Comedy,* neither with the Trinity nor with man in beatitude but with both in the Incarnate Christ. That mystery, bursting the bounds of logic while violating none, is what the poet most struggles to understand. Not by his own merits does he finally understand, but through the grace of Christ; and when he understands this, he understands everything, and he himself becomes one with the heavens, one with the vast design of the Word through whom all things were made:

> That circle which appeared—in my poor style—
>   like a reflected radiance in Thee,
>   after my eyes had studied it awhile,
> Within, and in its own hue, seemed to be
>   tinted with the figure of a Man,
>   and so I gazed on it absorbedly.
> As a geometer struggles all he can
>   to measure out the circle by the square,
>   but all his cogitation cannot gain
> The principle he lacks: so did I stare
>   at this strange sight, to make the image fit
>   the aureole, and see it enter there:
> But mine were not the feathers for that flight,
>   Save that the truth I longed for came to me,
>   smiting my mind like lightning flashing bright.
> Here ceased the powers of my high fantasy.
>   Already were all my will and my desires
>   turned—as a wheel in equal balance—by
> The Love that moves the sun and the other stars.
>
> (33.127–45)

The poet rests in silence. Those to whom it has been granted, let them believe.

TRANSLATOR'S NOTE

Dante's *Paradise* is a musical and intellectual feast, full of delicacies of sound and touched everywhere with images derived from what innocence remains in the life of man. For such a poem a strictly literal translation will not do. Music must be rendered into music, and so I have found it appealing, even necessary, to rhyme. But since English is a language notoriously poor in rhymes (unless one is willing to invert syntax, employ archaisms, or crack the meter), I have committed myself to no particular rhyme. The result, I hope, will provide a shadow of the music of Dante's terza rima without, however, calling undue attention to itself. My translation of *Paradise* rhymes more frequently than does my translation of *Purgatory,* while my *Inferno* rhymed hardly at all; I considered sweetness of music one of the rewards of the ascent, completed by the last canto of *Paradise,* which, allowing for slant rhymes, is rendered in full terza rima.

I wish to express my gratitude to the editors of the Modern Library, particularly Will Murphy, who encouraged this project and guided it to its happy port. As ever, wishing but to be numbered in their company, I am indebted to the valiant translators who have come before me, and to the editors of Dante's poem, most notably Umberto Bosco and Giovanni Reggio, who have assisted me immeasurably in understanding and in translating this, the most astounding poem ever written. Finally, to my comrades, my colleagues in the Program in Western Civilization at Providence College, many thanks for unfailing support, suggestions, and good cheer; and to my wife, Debra, whose love for me and our children is my own proof of a love and a providence that will not fail.

PARADISE

La gloria di colui che tutto move
    per l'universo penetra, e risplende
    in una parte più e meno altrove.
Nel ciel che più de la sua luce prende   4
    fu' io, e vidi cose che ridire
    né sa né può chi di là sù discende;
perché appressando sé al suo disire,   7
    nostro intelletto si profonda tanto,
    che dietro la memoria non può ire.
Veramente quant' io del regno santo   10
    ne la mia mente potei far tesoro,
    sarà ora materia del mio canto.
O buono Appollo, a l'ultimo lavoro   13
    fammi del tuo valor sì fatto vaso,
    come dimandi a dar l'amato alloro.
Infino a qui l'un giogo di Parnaso   16
    assai mi fu; ma or con amendue
    m'è uopo intrar ne l'aringo rimaso.
Entra nel petto mio, e spira tue   19
    sì come quando Marsïa traesti
    de la vagina de le membra sue.

Canto One

*Dante and Beatrice are at the threshold of Heaven. She explains to him that it is **the nature of the human soul** to rise.*

The glory of the One who moves all things
    penetrates the universe with light,
    more radiant in one part and elsewhere less:
I have been in that heaven He makes most bright,°   4
    and seen things neither mind can hold nor tongue
    utter, when one descends from such great height,
For as we near the One for whom we long,   7
    our intellects so plunge into the deep,
    memory cannot follow where we go.
Nevertheless what small part I can keep   10
    of that holy kingdom treasured in my heart
    will now become the matter of my song.
O good Apollo, for this last work of art,   13
    make me as fit a vessel of your power
    as you demand when you bestow the crown
Of the beloved laurel. Till this hour   16
    one peak of twin Parnassus° has sufficed,
    but if I am to enter the lists now
I shall need both. Then surge into my breast   19
    and breathe your song, as when you drew the vain
    Marsyas° from the sheath of his own limbs.

°*that heaven He makes most bright:* literally, the tenth sphere, the Empyrean. But Dante is referring to his sight of the beatific vision in Canto 33.

°*Parnassus:* Thessalian mountain sacred to the god of music, Apollo, and to the nine Muses.

°*Marsyas:* the vain satyr who challenged Apollo to a duel on the lutes. Apollo won and, avenging the blasphemy, flayed Marsyas alive—or as Dante puts it, devaginated him from his members (Ovid, *Metamorphoses* 6.382–400).

O divina virtù, se mi ti presti   22
    tanto che l'ombra del beato regno
    segnata nel mio capo io manifesti,
vedra'mi al piè del tuo diletto legno   25
    venire, e coronarmi de le foglie
    che la materia e tu mi farai degno.
Sì rade volte, padre, se ne coglie   28
    per trïunfare o cesare o poeta,
    colpa e vergogna de l'umane voglie,
che parturir letizia in su la lieta   31
    delfica deïtà dovria la fronda
    peneia, quando alcun di sé asseta.
Poca favilla gran fiamma seconda: 34
    forse di retro a me con miglior voci
    si pregherà perché Cirra risponda.
Surge ai mortali per diverse foci   37
    la lucerna del mondo; ma da quella
    che quattro cerchi giugne con tre croci,
con miglior corso e con migliore stella   40
    esce congiunta, e la mondana cera
    più a suo modo tempera e suggella.
Fatto avea di là mane e di qua sera   43
    tal foce, e quasi tutto era là bianco
    quello emisperio, e l'altra parte nera,
quando Beatrice in sul sinistro fianco   46
    vidi rivolta e riguardar nel sole:
    aguglia sì non li s'affisse unquanco.
E sì come secondo raggio suole   49
    uscir del primo e risalire in suso,
    pur come pelegrin che tornar vuole,

Father, virtue divine, should you but deign 22
    that I make manifest a shadow of
    the blessed kingdom sealed upon my brain,

At the foot of that tree whose wood you love 25
    you'll see me stand and crown my brows with green,
    made worthy by the subject, and by you.

Poets and Caesars now so rarely glean 28
    those leaves to celebrate a victory
    (man's fault and shame, for our desires are mean),

the Peneian branches must give birth to joy 31
    when any man should thirst for their high fame,
    in the glad heart of the Delphic deity.°

A little spark gives birth to a great flame. 34
    Better voices perhaps will follow mine,
    praying to hear what Cyrrha° shall proclaim!

By various spills of light the sun will shine 37
    dawning upon the world of men that die,
    but at the three-cross intersection of

Four rings° it rises in the company 40
    of a more favorable time of year,
    happier stars, to stamp this worldly clay

With its most perfect seal. One hemisphere 43
    lay brightening in that stream and one grew dim,
    as it made morning there and evening here,°

When I saw Beatrice turn upon her left 46
    and look to Heaven to gaze into the sun:
    no eagle ever held a gaze so firm.°

As a reflecting ray will follow upon 49
    the first and in a glance, an instant, rise
    just like a pilgrim longing to turn home,

°*Delphic deity:* Apollo, the god whose prophesies were uttered by the oracle of Delphi. Dante alludes to the myth of Apollo and the daughter of Peneus, Daphne, whose virginity was preserved from the god's advances by her being transformed into a laurel tree. Apollo then dedicated the laurel to the honoring of poets and, as Ovid would have it, such emperors as Augustus Caesar (cf. Metamorphoses 1.452–567).

°*Cyrrha:* One of the twin peaks of Parnassus, the mountain sacred to Apollo.

°*Four rings:* It is the spring equinox. For the astronomy and allegory, see notes.

°*morning there and evening here:* evening atop the Mountain of Purgatory, morning in Jerusalem. That befits the moment of Dante's ascent to Heaven and the New Jerusalem.

°*a gaze so firm:* Eagles were thought to be able to stare into the sun; cf. 20.31–33.

così de l'atto suo, per li occhi infuso   52
   ne l'imagine mia, il mio si fece,
   e fissi li occhi al sole oltre nostr' uso.
Molto è licito là, che qui non lece   55
   a le nostre virtù, mercé del loco
   fatto per proprio de l'umana spece.
Io nol soffersi molto, né sì poco,   58
   ch'io nol vedessi sfavillar dintorno,
   com' ferro che bogliente esce del foco;
e di sùbito parve giorno a giorno   61
   essere aggiunto, come quei che puote
   avesse il ciel d'un altro sole addorno.
Beatrice tutta ne l'etterne rote   64
   fissa con li occhi stava; e io in lei
   le luci fissi, di là sù rimote.
Nel suo aspetto tal dentro mi fei,   67
   qual si fé Glauco nel gustar de l'erba
   che 'l fé consorto in mar de li altri dèi.
Trasumanar significar *per verba*   70
   non si poria; però l'essemplo basti
   a cui esperïenza grazia serba.
S'i' era sol di me quel che creasti   73
   novellamente, amor che 'l ciel governi,
   tu 'l sai, che col tuo lume mi levasti.
Quando la rota che tu sempiterni   76
   desiderato, a sé mi fece atteso
   con l'armonia che temperi e discerni,
parvemi tanto allor del cielo acceso   79
   de la fiamma del sol, che pioggia o fiume
   lago non fece alcun tanto disteso.
La novità del suono e 'l grande lume   82
   di lor cagion m'accesero un disio
   mai non sentito di cotanto acume.

So she instilled her gazing—through my eyes—   52
    into my powers of fancy, and I too
    stared at the sun more than our sight can bear.
With our weak powers on earth one may not do   55
    what there one may—thanks to the special place°
    created as the proper home for man.
Not long could I sustain the brilliant rays   58
    before they seemed to flash like sparks that play
    round steel still white-hot from the forge's blaze,
And suddenly it seemed that day and day   61
    were fused, as if the One who wields the might
    adorned the heavens with a second sun.
Into the everlasting wheels of light   64
    Beatrice gazed with silent constancy;
    on her I gazed, far from that central sight.
Her countenance had the same effect in me   67
    as did the plant that Glaucus° tasted when
    it made him share the godhood of the sea.
To signify man's soaring beyond man   70
    words will not do: let my comparison
    suffice for them for whom the grace of God
Reserves the experience. If I bore alone   73
    that part of me which you created last,°
    O Love that steers the heavens, you surely know,
For your light lifted me. And when the vast   76
    wheel you have made eternal by desire
    held me intent to hear the harmony
You tune in all its parts, the sunlight-fire   79
    lit so much of the sky, no flooding stream
    or rain could ever fill so broad a lake.
The newness of the sound, the swelling gleam   82
    lighted desire in me to learn their cause—
    keener than any appetite I'd known.

°*special place:* Earthly Paradise.

°*Glaucus:* a fisherman who ate a sea plant and found himself transformed into a sea god (Ovid, *Met.* 13.898–968).

°*created last:* the soul. Dante neither asserts nor denies that he was brought into Heaven bodily. Cf. Paul's ascent to the third heaven, 2 Cor. 12:1–4.

Ond' ella, che vedea me sì com' io,   85
    a quïetarmi l'animo commosso,
    pria ch'io a dimandar, la bocca aprio
e cominciò: "Tu stesso ti fai grosso   88
    col falso imaginar, sì che non vedi
    ciò che vedresti se l'avessi scosso.
Tu non se' in terra, sì come tu credi;   91
    ma folgore, fuggendo il proprio sito,
    non corse come tu ch'ad esso riedi".
S'io fui del primo dubbio disvestito   94
    per le sorrise parolette brevi,
    dentro ad un nuovo più fu' inretito
e dissi: "Già contento *requïevi*   97
    di grande ammirazion; ma ora ammiro
    com' io trascenda questi corpi levi".
Ond' ella, appresso d'un pïo sospiro,   100
    li occhi drizzò ver' me con quel sembiante
    che madre fa sovra figlio deliro,
e cominciò: "Le cose tutte quante   103
    hanno ordine tra loro, e questo è forma
    che l'universo a Dio fa simigliante.
Qui veggion l'alte creature l'orma   106
    de l'etterno valore, il qual è fine
    al quale è fatta la toccata norma.
Ne l'ordine ch'io dico sono accline   109
    tutte nature, per diverse sorti,
    più al principio loro e men vicine;
onde si muovono a diversi porti   112
    per lo gran mar de l'essere, e ciascuna
    con istinto a lei dato che la porti.
Questi ne porta il foco inver' la luna;   115
    questi ne' cor mortali è permotore;
    questi la terra in sé stringe e aduna;
né pur le creature che son fore   118
    d'intelligenza quest' arco saetta,
    ma quelle c'hanno intelletto e amore.

And she, who saw within me what I was,   85
    to still the troubled waters of my soul,
    opened her lips before I could inquire,
And thus began: "You're making your mind dull   88
    with false imagining—you don't perceive
    what you would see, if you could shake it off.
You are not on the earth, as you believe.   91
    Lightning that flees its proper realm is not
    so swift as your returning to your own."
I admit I was shorn of my first doubt   94
    by the brief words she flashed me with a smile,
    but in another net my feet were caught:
"My first amazement is at peace—but still   97
    I am amazed that I should rise so high,
    beyond the lightness of the air and fire."
She turned her eyes to me then with a sigh   100
    of pity, as a mother in distress
    whose child is ill and talks deliriously,
So she made matters plain: "All things possess   103
    order amongst themselves: this order is
    the form that makes the world resemble God.
Thence the high beings° read the signs, the trace   106
    of that eternal Power who is the end
    for which the form is set in time and place.
All natures in this order lean and tend   109
    each in distinctive manner to its Source,
    some to approach more near and others less—
Whence from their various ports all creatures move   112
    on the great sea of being, with each one
    ferried by instinct given from above.
This is what makes the fire rise toward the moon;   115
    this, the prime mover of the mortal heart;
    this makes the heavy earth condense in one;
Nor does this bow with target-cleaving art   118
    strike only things that lack intelligence,
    but beings made with intellect and love.

°*high beings:* angels and men.

La provedenza, che cotanto assetta,   121
    del suo lume fa 'l ciel sempre quïeto
    nel qual si volge quel c'ha maggior fretta;
e ora lì, come a sito decreto,   124
    cen porta la virtù di quella corda
    che ciò che scocca drizza in segno lieto.
Vero è che, come forma non s'accorda   127
    molte fïate a l'intenzion de l'arte,
    perch' a risponder la materia è sorda,
così da questo corso si diparte   130
    talor la creatura, c'ha podere
    di piegar, così pinta, in altra parte;
e sì come veder si può cadere   133
    foco di nube, sì l'impeto primo
    l'atterra torto da falso piacere.
No dei più ammirar, se bene stimo,   136
    lo tuo salir, se non come d'un rivo
    se d'alto monte scende giuso ad imo.
Maraviglia sarebbe in te, se, privo   139
    d'impedimento, giù ti fossi assiso,
    com'a terra quïete in foco vivo".
Quinci rivolse inver'lo cielo il viso.   142

The glorious world-ordaining providence   121
   forever stills the highest heaven with light,
   beyond the spinning of the swiftest sphere,°
And to that place as to our destined site   124
   we're speeded by the power of that cord
   shooting each arrow in its happy flight.
Often it's true a form may not accord   127
   with the intent of him who works the art
   because the matter's deaf and won't respond:
So, from this course, a creature may depart   130
   if it should have the power, despite the push,
   to swerve away and veer off from its start,
And as you'll see a fall of lightning flash   133
   from the high clouds, so cheating pleasures skew
   that first urge, and they plunge it to the earth.
No more amazement should it bring to you   136
   that you ascend, than if a mountain stream
   should tumble rushing to the plains below.
But it would be a cause of just surprise   139
   if, free of every bar, you should remain
   like a still flame on earth, and not arise."
Then to the heavens she turned her gaze again.   142

°*the swiftest sphere:* the ninth, or Primum Mobile (cf. 27.99).

O voi che siete in piccioletta barca,
    desiderosi d'ascoltar, seguiti
    dietro al mio legno che cantando varca,
tornate a riveder li vostri liti: 4
    non vi mettete in pelago, ché forse,
    perdendo me, rimarreste smarriti.
L'acqua ch'io prendo già mai non si corse;   7
    Minerva spira, e conducemi Appollo,
    e nove Muse mi dimostran l'Orse.
Voialtri pochi che drizzaste il collo   10
    per tempo al pan de li angeli, del quale
    vivesi qui ma non sen vien satollo,
metter potete ben per l'alto sale   13
    vostro navigio, servando mio solco
    dinanzi a l'acqua che ritorna equale.
Que' glorïosi che passaro al Colco   16
    non s'ammiraron come voi farete,
    quando Iasón vider fatto bifolco.

CANTO TWO

*Rising to **the first sphere, the moon,** Dante asks Beatrice about the markings, and learns that they are due to the diversity of gifts with which God has endowed all creatures.*

O all you in your shallops following
   my furrows as I sail across the sea,
   you who desire to listen as I sing,
Don't try the open ocean—turn and see   4
   your own familiar shores, for you'd remain
   forever lost, should you lose sight of me.
I venture waters never sailed by man!   7
   Apollo steers me, Pallas° breathes the winds,
   nine Muses point me to the Bears on high.
You other few who long have raised your minds   10
   unto the bread of angels,° such a food
   as brings men life and never fills them full,
Well may you set your ships of sturdy wood   13
   upon the deep salt, keeping in my wake
   before the splashes settle evenly.
Never such wonder they who sailed to take   16
   the golden fleece once felt as you shall feel,
   not when they saw how Jason bore the yoke!°

  °*Apollo, Pallas:* Apollo is the god of music and prophecy, Pallas (Latin Minerva) the goddess of wisdom.

  °*bread of angels:* theology.

  °*Jason ... yoke:* In his quest for the golden fleece, one of the tests Jason had to pass was to plow a field with two fire-breathing oxen (Ovid, *Met.* 7.100–121); he had been made proof against the fire by a potion given him by the sorceress Medea.

La concreata e perpetüa sete   19
  del deïforme regno cen portava
  veloci quasi come 'l ciel vedete.
Beatrice in suso, e io in lei guardava;   22
  e forse in tanto in quanto un quadrel posa
  e vola e da la noce si dischiava,
giunto mi vidi ove mirabil cosa   25
  mi torse il viso a sé; e però quella
  cui non potea mia cura essere ascosa,
volta ver' me, sì lieta come bella,   28
  "Drizza la mente in Dio grata", mi disse,
  "che n'ha congiunti con la prima stella".
Parev' a me che nube ne coprisse   31
  lucida, spessa, solida e pulita,
  quasi adamante che lo sol ferisse.
Per entro sé l'etterna margarita   34
  ne ricevette, com' acqua recepe
  raggio di luce permanendo unita.
S'io era corpo, e qui non si concepe   37
  com' una dimensione altra patio,
  ch'esser convien se corpo in corpo repe,
accender ne dovria più il disio   40
  di veder quella essenza in che si vede
  come nostra natura e Dio s'unio.
Lì si vedrà ciò che tenem per fede,   43
  non dimostrato, ma fia per sé noto
  a guisa del ver primo che l'uom crede.
Io rispuosi: "Madonna, sì devoto   46
  com' esser posso più, ringrazio lui
  lo qual dal mortal mondo m'ha remoto.
Ma ditemi: che son li segni bui   49
  di questo corpo, che là giuso in terra
  fan di Cain favoleggiare altrui?".

The lasting thirst, created with the soul,   19
    for that deiform kingdom swept us far,
    swift as the mind-seen wheeling of the skies.
Beatrice gazed upward, and I gazed at her,   22
    and in the instant of an arrow's flight—
    sunk in the target, whistling off the nock—
I saw I'd reached a place that turned my sight   25
    toward something to behold in awe; so she,
    from whom no care of mine could be concealed,
As glad as she is lovely, said to me,   28
    "Direct your thought to God in gratitude,
    for He has led us to the lowest star."
It seemed to me all swaddled in a cloud,   31
    dense, solid, soaked with light and polished clean,
    as if the sunshine struck a diamond stone.
The pearl of everlasting took us in,   34
    receiving us as water will receive
    a ray of light, remaining whole and one.
If I was body (and here we can't conceive   37
    how one bulk can permit a second bulk
    to slip into its place, as body in body),
The more should our desire be touched aflame   40
    to see that Being in whom it shall appear
    how Godhead and our nature were made one.
What now we hold by faith will then be clear,   43
    seen without proof, self-evident and known,
    like the first principles of human thought.
"My Lady, as devoutly as I can   46
    I thank the One whose grace has raised me far
    out of the world of dying," I began,
"But say, what are these shadowy signs that mar   49
    this body, making some on earth below
    tell tales of Cain condemned to walk the moon?"°

°*condemned to walk the moon:* Popular lore had it that Cain was the man in the moon; exiled for his murder of Abel, he became the perpetual wanderer.

Ella sorrise alquanto, e poi "S'elli erra   52
  l'oppinïon", mi disse, "d'i mortali
  dove chiave di senso non diserra,

certo non ti dovrien punger li strali   55
  d'ammirazione omai, poi dietro ai sensi
  vedi che la ragione ha corte l'ali.

Ma dimmi quel che tu da te ne pensi".   58
  E io: "Ciò che n'appar qua sù diverso
  credo che fanno i corpi rari e densi".

Ed ella: "Certo assai vedrai sommerso   61
  nel falso il creder tuo, se bene ascolti
  l'argomentar ch'io li farò avverso.

La spera ottava vi dimostra molti   64
  lumi, li quali e nel quale e nel quanto
  notar si posson di diversi volti.

Se raro e denso ciò facesser tanto,   67
  una sola virtù sarebbe in tutti,
  più e men distribuita e altrettanto.

Virtù diverse esser convegnon frutti   70
  di princìpi formali, e quei, for ch'uno,
  seguiterieno a tua ragion distrutti.

Ancor, se raro fosse di quel bruno   73
  cagion che tu dimandi, o d'oltre in parte
  fora di sua materia sì digiuno

esto pianeto, o, sì come comparte   76
  lo grasso e 'l magro un corpo, così questo
  nel suo volume cangerebbe carte.

Se 'l primo fosse, fora manifesto   79
  ne l'eclissi del sol, per trasparere
  lo lume come in altro raro ingesto.

Questo non è: però è da vedere   82
  de l'altro; e s'elli avvien ch'io l'altro cassi,
  falsificato fia lo tuo parere.

She smiled a little. "If opinions go   52
    roving on earth when senses cannot spring
    the lock of truth for mortal man, by now

You should no longer feel surprise's sting.   55
    No cause for wonder, for you see that wit,
    though led by sense, flaps with too short a wing.

But come, you tell me what you think of it."   58
    "What look down there like different spots," I said,
    "are caused by thin or denser matter here."

"You'll see for certain how your theory's plunged   61
    deep into falsehood, if," said she, "you heed
    the refutation I will offer you.

The eighth sphere shows you many stars of light,   64
    and in their quantities and qualities
    you can note different faces, dim and bright.

If that were caused by various densities,   67
    a single starry power would dwell in all,
    portioned in every place, some more, some less.

Since power springs from a formal principle,   70
    all individual virtues° of the stars,
    following your line of thought, would come to null,

Save that alone. Grant, thinness is the cause   73
    of the gray spots: then either it would be lean
    of stellar matter everywhere across

This planet or, as strips of fat and lean   76
    under the skin, press pages rare and dense
    in layers beneath its binding. Of the first,

The sun's eclipse should bring clear evidence: 79
    the moon in front should shine with a fair glow,
    like a slight object steeped in radiance.

So we examine—since that is not so—   82
    the second case. Canceling that one too,
    I'll have proved your opinion false. Suppose

°*individual virtues:* particular powers shed by the influence of each star. Beatrice argues that differences in the quality and the magnitude of light from the stars must bespeak different virtues—*formal* differences—rather than merely a difference of degree in the possession of a single virtue.

S'elli è che questo raro non trapassi,   85
  esser conviene un termine da onde
  lo suo contrario più passar non lassi;
e indi l'altrui raggio si rifonde   88
  così come color torna per vetro
  lo qual di retro a sé piombo nasconde.
Or dirai tu ch'el si dimostra tetro   91
  ivi lo raggio più che in altre parti,
  per esser lì refratto più a retro.
Da questa instanza può deliberarti   94
  esperïenza, se già mai la provi,
  ch'esser suol fonte ai rivi di vostr' arti.
Tre specchi prenderai; e i due rimovi   97
  da te d'un modo, e l'altro, più rimosso,
  tr'ambo li primi li occhi tuoi ritrovi.
Rivolto ad essi, fa che dopo il dosso   100
  ti stea un lume che i tre specchi accenda
  e torni a te da tutti ripercosso.
Ben che nel quanto tanto non si stenda   103
  la vista più lontana, lì vedrai
  come convien ch'igualmente risplenda.
Or, come ai colpi de li caldi rai   106
  de la neve riman nudo il suggetto
  e dal colore e dal freddo primai,
così rimaso te ne l'intelletto   109
  voglio informar di luce sì vivace,
  che ti tremolerà nel suo aspetto.
Dentro dal ciel de la divina pace   112
  si gira un corpo ne la cui virtute
  l'esser di tutto suo contento giace.
Lo ciel seguente, c'ha tante vedute,   115
  quell' esser parte per diverse essenze,
  da lui distratte e da lui contenute.

This thinness doesn't pass all the way through: 85
    then it must not allow its opposite,
    the dense, to pass a certain boundary,
And at that very depth the rills of light 88
    will be reflected, as the rays that splash
    from glass made leaden on the hidden side.
Now you might say the rays look rather bleak 91
    just in those spots the moon is rarefied—
    reflections are more distant there, and weak.
Experience, if you let it be your guide, 94
    the fount for every stream of human art,
    can set you free from this objection too.
You take three mirrors. Two you set apart 97
    at the same distance, with the other one
    exactly in the center of your sight
Yet farther back. Now, from behind, you shine 100
    a light that kindles all three in a blaze
    and ricochets the radiance back to you.
You'll see, although the sight of the far glass 103
    will fall short of the other two in size,
    equal intensity in all the rays.
As, struck by the warming sun, what underlies 106
    snow° is denuded of the cold and white,
    so now—yourself remaining what you are—
I wish to fill your intellect with light, 109
    light so aflame with life that cannot cease,
    in your eyes it will tremble like a star.
Within that heaven of divinest peace° 112
    revolves a body in whose influence lies
    the being of all things in its embrace.
The following heaven of the spangled eyes 115
    portions that being out in essences,
    distinguishing the powers of Paradise.

°*what underlies snow:* water, stripped of the accidental features of whiteness and cold.

°*heaven of divinest peace:* the Empyrean (see 30.39 and note). The next is the Primum Mobile, imparting motion to the *following heaven of the spangled eyes,* the sphere of the fixed stars.

Li altri giron per varie differenze   118
  le distinzion che dentro da sé hanno
  dispongono a lor fini e lor semenze.

Questi organi del mondo così vanno,   121
  come tu vedi omai, di grado in grado,
  che di sù prendono e di sotto fanno.

Riguarda bene omai sì com' io vado   124
  per questo loco al vero che disiri,
  sì che poi sappi sol tener lo guado.

Lo moto e la virtù d'i santi giri,   127
  come dal fabbro l'arte del martello,
  da' beati motor convien che spiri;

e 'l ciel cui tanti lumi fanno bello,   130
  de la mente profonda che lui volve
  prende l'image e fassene suggello.

E come l'alma dentro a vostra polve   133
  per differenti membra e conformate
  a diverse potenze si risolve,

così l'intelligenza sua bontate   136
  multiplicata per le stelle spiega,
  girando sé sovra sua unitate.

Virtù diversa fa diversa lega   139
  col prezïoso corpo ch'ella avviva,
  nel qual, sì come vita in voi, si lega.

Per la natura lieta onde deriva,   142
  la virtù mista per lo corpo luce
  come letizia per pupilla viva.

Da essa vien ciò che da luce a luce   145
  par differente, non da denso e raro;
  essa è formal principio che produce,

conforme a sua bontà, lo turbo e 'l chiaro".   148

The lower wheels with all their differences 118
    dispose those individual powers, and sow
    the seeds and bring the cause to meet its end.
These organs of the universe thus go 121
    from one step to the next, as you can see:
    take from above, and set in act below.
Follow my reasoning attentively 124
    as I pass to the truth that you desire,
    so you may ford the river on your own.
As from the blacksmith springs the hammer's art, 127
    so power and motion in each holy wheel
    breathe from the blessed beings° that move the sphere;
So too that heaven so many lights adorn. 130
    From the deep Mind that turns it, it receives
    its image, and it makes itself the seal.
As soul within your human dust resolves 133
    its animate self into the various powers
    of various members fit and formed for them,
So the intelligence of the eighth sphere pours 136
    its bounty multiplied by all the stars,
    turning upon itself in unity.
The diverse virtues make the bonds diverse 139
    that bind the spheres, their power enlivening
    the precious body of the universe,
As soul in you. And so the matter shines, 142
    as gladness lights the apple of the eye,
    by power deriving from that joyful spring.
This is the principle—not 'dense' and 'rare'— 145
    endowing light in all variety,
    gleaming its power in all things dim and clear,
Conforming to their own nobility." 148

°*blessed beings:* angelic intelligences, thought to be the motive force in each sphere.

Quel sol che pria d'amor mi scaldò 'l petto,
   di bella verità m'avea scoverto,
   provando e riprovando, il dolce aspetto;
e io, per confessar corretto e certo   4
   me stesso, tanto quanto si convenne
   leva' il capo a proferer più erto;
ma visïone apparve che ritenne   7
   a sé me tanto stretto, per vedersi,
   che di mia confession non mi sovvenne.
Quali per vetri trasparenti e tersi,   10
   o ver per acque nitide e tranquille,
   non sì profonde che i fondi sien persi,
tornan d'i nostri visi le postille   13
   debili sì, che perla in bianca fronte
   non vien men forte a le nostre pupille;
tali vid' io più facce a parlar pronte;   16
   per ch'io dentro a l'error contrario corsi
   a quel ch'accese amor tra l'omo e 'l fonte.
Sùbito sì com' io di lor m'accorsi,   19
   quelle stimando specchiati sembianti,
   per veder di cui fosser, li occhi torsi;

CANTO THREE

*Dante and Beatrice enter **the first circle** of Heaven, the circle of **the moon.**
Here, among the souls of those who neglected their vows, Dante encounters **Pic-
carda,** who explains to him the diversity of blessedness among the saints.*

The sun who first had warmed my breast with love
    in proving and reproving showed to me
    the sweet and lovely visage of the truth,
For which I raised my head just so, to say   4
    that she had made me certain, and confess
    myself corrected from my errant way,
But a new vision rose before my eyes,   7
    so seizing me to fathom what it was
    that my confession vanished from my mind.
As in a polished and transparent glass,   10
    or on the sunlit water clear and still
    but not too deep to see the bed beneath,
The glosses of our lineaments will show,   13
    but the eye finds their traces faint and weak,
    as the trace of a pearl on a fair brow,
Such faces did I see, ready to speak—   16
    and I ran counter to the wandering
    that kindled love between the boy and pool.°
Supposing each was but a mirroring,   19
    when I became aware of them I turned
    to find out whose reflections they might be,

°*the boy and pool:* Narcissus, the handsome lad who fell in love with his own reflection (Ovid,
Met. 3.407–510).

THE MOON

e nulla vidi, e ritorsili avanti   22
   dritti nel lume de la dolce guida,
   che, sorridendo, ardea ne li occhi santi.
"Non ti maravigliar perch' io sorrida",   25
   mi disse, "appresso il tuo püeril coto,
   poi sopra 'l vero ancor lo piè non fida,
ma te rivolve, come suole, a vòto: 28
   vere sustanze son ciò che tu vedi,
   qui rilegate per manco di voto.
Però parla con esse e odi e credi;   31
   ché la verace luce che le appaga
   da sé non lascia lor torcer li piedi".
E io a l'ombra che parea più vaga   34
   di ragionar, drizza'mi, e cominciai,
   quasi com' uom cui troppa voglia smaga:
"O ben creato spirito, che a' rai   37
   di vita etterna la dolcezza senti
   che, non gustata, non s'intende mai,
grazïoso mi fia se mi contenti   40
   del nome tuo e de la vostra sorte".
   Ond'ella, pronta e con occhi ridenti:
"La nostra carità non serra porte   43
   a giusta voglia, se non come quella
   che vuol simile a sé tutta sua corte.
I' fui nel mondo vergine sorella;   46
   e se la mente tua ben sé riguarda,
   non mi ti celerà l'esser più bella,
ma riconoscerai ch'i' son Piccarda,   49
   che, posta qui con questi altri beati,
   beata sono in la spera più tarda.
Li nostri affetti, che solo infiammati   52
   son nel piacer de lo Spirito Santo,
   letizian del suo ordine formati.
E questa sorte che par giù cotanto,   55
   però n'è data, perché fuor negletti
   li nostri voti, e vòti in alcun canto".

Saw nothing—so I turned again, to gaze   22
    upon the soft light of my guide, who smiled,
    and in her holy eyes the glowing rays
Shone like a fire. "You're thinking like a child,"   25
    said she. "No need to wonder why I smile.
    For you don't dare to trust your steps to truth,
But still go toddling back to empty thought.   28
    These are true substances you now perceive,
    bound here for failing to fulfill their vows.
So speak with them and hear them and believe: 31
    for the true Luminary, their delight,
    will never let their footsteps go astray."
I turned to face the shadow that, by sight,   34
    seemed eagerest to speak, and I began
    as one almost disabled by desire:
"O well created spirit, you who know   37
    and feel the sweetness of eternal life,
    which no one understands unless he tastes,
Content me now, do me the courtesy,   40
    tell me your name, tell of your blessed fate."
    With laughing eyes she answered readily:
"Our charity will never bolt the gate   43
    against a just desire: as His love, who
    would have His whole court like Himself. I was
A virgin sister in the world below,   46
    and if you peer into your memory,
    I will not hide in being lovelier now—
That won't prevent your recognizing me.   49
    I am Piccarda, blest with all the blest
    who dwell within the slowest of the spheres.
The Holy Spirit kindles in our breast   52
    all we desire, for His delight is ours,
    and in His order we rejoice and rest.
Because we were neglectful in our vows   55
    and left them empty then in some respect,
    this place which seems so low is given us."

Ond' io a lei: "Ne' mirabili aspetti   58
    vostri risplende non so che divino
    che vi trasmuta da' primi concetti:
però non fui a rimembrar festino;   61
    ma or m'aiuta ciò che tu mi dici,
    sì che raffigurar m'è più latino.
Ma dimmi: voi che siete qui felici,   64
    disiderate voi più alto loco
    per più vedere e per più farvi amici?".
Con quelle altr' ombre pria sorrise un poco;   67
    da indi mi rispuose tanto lieta,
    ch'arder parea d'amor nel primo foco:
"Frate, la nostra volontà quïeta   70
    virtù di carità, che fa volerne
    sol quel ch'avemo, e d'altro non ci asseta.
Se disïassimo esser più superne,   73
    foran discordi li nostri disiri
    dal voler di colui che qui ne cerne;
che vedrai non capere in questi giri,   76
    s'essere in carità è qui *necesse,*
    e se la sua natura ben rimiri.
Anzi è formale ad esto beato *esse*   79
    tenersi dentro a la divina voglia,
    per ch'una fansi nostre voglie stesse;
sì che, come noi sem di soglia in soglia   82
    per questo regno, a tutto il regno piace
    com' a lo re che 'n suo voler ne 'nvoglia.
E 'n la sua volontade è nostra pace;   85
    ell' è quel mare al qual tutto si move
    ciò ch'ella crïa o che natura face".
Chiaro mi fu allor come ogne dove   88
    in cielo è paradiso, *etsi* la grazia
    del sommo ben d'un modo non vi piove.
Ma sì com' elli avvien, s'un cibo sazia   91
    e d'un altro rimane ancor la gola,
    che quel si chere e di quel si ringrazia,

And I: "I wasn't quick to recollect,   58
    because your wondrous countenances shine
    with something that transforms their images,
Something, I cannot fathom it, divine.   61
    But what you say helps make the vision clear,
    and I can nearly trace your form again.
But tell me, you who are so happy here,   64
    do you desire a place of greater height
    to see more, know more, and be held more dear?"
With the rest of those shades she smiled a bit,   67
    then with such gladness she replied to me,
    as a girl in the gleaming of first love:
"Brother, the virtue of our charity   70
    brings quiet to our wills, so we desire
    but what we have, and thirst for nothing else.
If we should feel a yearning to be higher,   73
    such a desire would strike disharmony
    against His will who knows, and wills us here.
That cannot catch these wheels, as you shall see: 76
    recall love's nature, recall that Heaven is
    to live in loving, necessarily.
For it is of the essence of this bliss   79
    to hold one's dwelling in the divine Will,
    who makes our single wills the same, and His,
So that, although we dwell from sill to sill   82
    throughout this kingdom, that is as we please,
    as it delights the King in whose desire
We find our own. In His will is our peace: 85
    that is the sea whereto all creatures fare,
    fashioned by Nature or the hand of God."
Then it was clear to me that everywhere   88
    in Heaven is Paradise, though the high Good
    does not rain down His grace on all souls there
Equally. But as it happens that one food   91
    satisfies, and you give thanks, while you yearn
    for yet another and you beg for it,

così fec' io con atto e con parola,   94
  per apprender da lei qual fu la tela
  onde non trasse infino a co la spuola.

"Perfetta vita e alto merto inciela   97
  donna più sù", mi disse, "a la cui norma
  nel vostro mondo giù si veste e vela,

perché fino al morir si vegghi e dorma   100
  con quello sposo ch'ogne voto accetta
  che caritate a suo piacer conforma.

Dal mondo, per seguirla, giovinetta   103
  fuggi'mi, e nel suo abito mi chiusi
  e promisi la via de la sua setta.

Uomini poi, a mal più ch'a bene usi,   106
  fuor mi rapiron de la dolce chiostra:
  Iddio si sa qual poi mia vita fusi.

E quest' altro splendor che ti si mostra   109
  da la mia destra parte e che s'accende
  di tutto il lume de la spera nostra,

ciò ch'io dico di me, di sé intende;   112
  sorella fu, e così le fu tolta
  di capo l'ombra de le sacre bende.

Ma poi che pur al mondo fu rivolta   115
  contra suo grado e contra buona usanza,
  non fu dal vel del cor già mai disciolta.

Quest' è la luce de la gran Costanza   118
  che del secondo vento di Soave
  generò 'l terzo e l'ultima possanza".

Così parlommi, e poi cominciò *Ave,*   121
  Maria' cantando, e cantando vanio
  come per acqua cupa cosa grave.

So by my words and look I begged to learn   94
   about the thread she didn't all unspool.
   "A Lady° is emparadised above
By perfect life and merit, in whose rule   97
   they take the habit in your world," said she,
   "and set upon their heads the bridal veil,°
That they may wake and sleep, until they die,   100
   with that Spouse who will take each vow to heart
   which love has made conform to His delight.
Following her, when young I fled the world   103
   and donned the habit of her sisterhood,
   housing myself within her way of life.
Then men more given to evil than to good   106
   from the sweet cloistered garden ravished me°—
   God knows what, after that, my life became.
This other spirit gleaming splendidly   109
   with all the kindling light that lights our sphere,
   showing herself now to the right of me,
Knows what I say I also say of her.   112
   She was a sister, and the holy bands
   that veiled her brow in shade, they snatched away,
Casting her to the world by violent hands,   115
   against her wish, against all decency.
   And yet she never unbound the veil that robed
Her heart. From the great Constance° shines this light,   118
   who by the second gale of Swabia
   bore the third, and the final, heir of might."
So did she speak, then she began to sing,   121
   "Hail, Mary," and so singing she was gone,
   like a smooth heavy object vanishing

°*Lady:* Saint Clare, to whose order Piccarda belonged. Clare of Assisi (1194–1253) was a friend of Saint Francis, whose order of Little Brothers inspired her to found an order of nuns similarly devoted to poverty.

°*bridal veil:* the veil of the nun, dedicating her life to her Spouse, Christ.

°*ravished me:* Piccarda was taken from the cloister and compelled to marry.

°*Constance:* Empress Constance (1154–98), wife of Holy Roman Emperor Henry VI of Swabia, *the second gale,* as Henry was the son of the emperor Frederick I Barbarossa and the father of *the third, and the final, heir,* Frederick II. For a fuller discussion of the politics, see notes.

La vista mia, che tanto lei seguio 124
    quanto possibil fu, poi che la perse,
    volsesi al segno di maggior disio,
e a Beatrice tutta si converse; 127
    ma quella folgorò nel mïo sguardo
    sì che da prima il viso non sofferse;
e ciò mi fece a dimandar più tardo. 130

Into a shadowy pool. Still I looked on,   124
    following her as far as possible,
    then, wondering, I turned to Beatrice,
My vision's greater yearning and true goal,   127
    but in my glance she blazed like lightning fire,
    so bright I found it unendurable.
That made me hesitate to ask her more.   130

Intra due cibi, distanti e moventi
  d'un modo, prima si morria di fame,
  che liber' omo l'un recasse ai denti;
sì si starebbe un agno intra due brame   4
  di fieri lupi, igualmente temendo;
  sì si starebbe un cane intra due dame:
per che, s'i' mi tacea, me non riprendo,   7
  da li miei dubbi d'un modo sospinto,
  poi ch'era necessario, né commendo.
Io mi tacea, ma 'l mio disir dipinto   10
  m'era nel viso, e 'l dimandar con ello,
  più caldo assai che per parlar distinto.
Fé sì Beatrice qual fé Danïello,   13
  Nabuccodonosor levando d'ira,
  che l'avea fatto ingiustamente fello;
e disse: "Io veggio ben come ti tira   16
  uno e altro disio, sì che tua cura
  sé stessa lega sì che fuor non spira.
Tu argomenti: 'Se 'l buon voler dura,   19
  la vïolenza altrui per qual ragione
  di meritar mi scema la misura?'.

Canto Four

*Beatrice explains to Dante **the true location of the blessed**, and then, distinguishing absolute from conditional will, asserts **the sanctity and inviolability of holy vows.***

Between two morsels for the appetite,
    just as appealing, just as far away,
    before a free man ever took one bite
He'd die of hunger; so a lamb will stay   4
    frozen in fear between two ravenous wolves;
    so will a hound stop short between two deer.
So I don't blame myself for holding still,   7
    since my two doubts gave me an equal push—
    nor praise it—it was unavoidable.
I held my peace, but in my cheek a flush   10
    painted the wish and asked the questions too,
    with greater warmth than if I'd spoken them.
Beatrice did what Daniel had to do   13
    soothing the angry king of Babylon,°
    easing the wrath that fired his felonies.
"I see how you're so pulled by either one   16
    of two desires," said she, "this care of yours
    straps itself in confusion and can't breathe.
You argue, 'If my good intent endures,   19
    why should another person's violence
    cause any waning in what I deserve?'

°*king of Babylon:* Nebuchadnezzar. Troubled by a dream, he executed his advisers when they could not divine its contents. But Daniel, inspired by God, told the king his dream and interpreted it (Dan. 2:1–46).

Ancor di dubitar ti dà cagione 22
    parer tornarsi l'anime a le stelle,
    secondo la sentenza di Platone.
Queste son le question che nel tuo *velle* 25
    pontano igualmente; e però pria
    tratterò quella che più ha di felle.
D'i Serafin colui che più s'india, 28
    Moïsè, Samuel, e quel Giovanni
    che prender vuoli, io dico, non Maria,
non hanno in altro cielo i loro scanni 31
    che questi spirti che mo t'appariro,
    né hanno a l'esser lor più o meno anni;
ma tutti fanno bello il primo giro, 34
    e differentemente han dolce vita
    per sentir più e men l'etterno spiro.
Qui si mostraro, non perché sortita 37
    sia questa spera lor, ma per far segno
    de la celestïal c'ha men salita.
Così parlar conviensi al vostro ingegno, 40
    però che solo da sensato apprende
    ciò che fa poscia d'intelletto degno.
Per questo la Scrittura condescende 43
    a vostra facultate, e piedi e mano
    attribuisce a Dio e altro intende;
e Santa Chiesa con aspetto umano 46
    Gabrïel e Michel vi rappresenta,
    e l'altro che Tobia rifece sano.
Quel che Timeo de l'anime argomenta 49
    non è simile a ciò che qui si vede,
    però che, come dice, par che senta.
Dice che l'alma a la sua stella riede, 52
    credendo quella quindi esser decisa
    quando natura per forma la diede;

Another reason for your hesitance 22
    is that returning souls appear to dwell,
    as Plato speculated, in the stars.
These are the questions pushing at your will 25
    with equal force: so I will first disprove
    the more poisonous error. Not the most
Endeitied of Seraphim above, 28
    not Moses, Samuel, not whichever John°
    you wish to take, I say not even Mary
In any other heaven holds his throne 31
    or enjoys more or fewer years in being
    than do those spirits that appeared to you,
But all lend beauty to the inmost ring 34
    and live sweet life, as each one, more or less,
    enjoys the breath of the eternal spring.
They showed themselves to you here to express 37
    (not that they've been assigned this sphere below)
    the lowest stair of heavenly blessedness.
One has to greet your native powers so: 40
    for from the senses man's mind apprehends
    all it makes fit for intellect to know.
That is why Holy Scripture condescends 43
    to your minds and attributes to the Lord
    a hand or foot, intending something more,
And with a human face the Church's word 46
    portrays for you Michael and Gabriel
    and him who had Tobias' sight restored.°
What the *Timaeus* posits of the soul 49
    and what you see here are not similar,
    because he seems to mean just what he says.
He says the soul goes to its proper star, 52
    believing that it thence was cut away
    when nature lent it as the body's form.

°*whichever John:* the herald Baptist or the visionary evangelist.
°*who had Tobias' sight restored:* the angel Raphael, who restored the wealth and the eyesight of the old Tobias (Tob. 11:7–15).

e forse sua sentenza è d'altra guisa   55
   che la voce non suona, ed esser puote
   con intenzion da non esser derisa.

S'elli intende tornare a queste ruote   58
   l'onor de la influenza e 'l biasmo, forse
   in alcun vero suo arco percuote.

Questo principio, male inteso, torse   61
   già tutto il mondo quasi, sì che Giove,
   Mercurio e Marte a nominar trascorse.

L'altra dubitazion che ti commove   64
   ha men velen, però che sua malizia
   non ti poria menar da me altrove.

Parere ingiusta la nostra giustizia   67
   ne li occhi d'i mortali, è argomento
   di fede e non d'eretica nequizia.

Ma perché puote vostro accorgimento   70
   ben penetrare a questa veritate,
   come disiri, ti farò contento.

Se vïolenza è quando quel che pate   73
   nïente conferisce a quel che sforza,
   non fuor quest' alme per essa scusate:

ché volontà, se non vuol, non s'ammorza,   76
   ma fa come natura face in foco,
   se mille volte vïolenza il torza.

Per che, s'ella si piega assai o poco,   79
   segue la forza; e così queste fero
   possendo rifuggir nel santo loco.

Se fosse stato lor volere intero,   82
   come tenne Lorenzo in su la grada,
   e fece Muzio a la sua man severo,

così l'avria ripinte per la strada   85
   ond' eran tratte, come fuoro sciolte;
   ma così salda voglia è troppo rada.

E per queste parole, se ricolte   88
   l'hai come dei, è l'argomento casso
   che t'avria fatto noia ancor più volte.

Perhaps he can be read another way,   55
    with an intention not to raise a laugh,
    if his words aren't taken literally.
If he means that the blame or honor due   58
    the influence of these stars returns on high,
    his arrow clips a portion of the true.
Once almost the whole world was twisted by   61
    this principle, misunderstood, and men
    named the stars Jove and Mars and Mercury
And ran astray. There is less venom in   64
    the other doubt that troubles you, because
    its malice cannot lead you far from me.
That in mortal eyes the justice of our laws   67
    appears unjust is yet a proof of faith
    and not the crookedness of heresies.
Because you have the power to see this truth   70
    and penetrate it by intelligence,
    I will content you, as you wish, with proof.
If violence means that he who suffers lends   73
    no contribution to the violent,
    then these souls can lay claim to no excuse:
For when the will's unwilling, it's not spent,   76
    but acts as nature in a leaping flame,
    though violence buffet it a thousand times.
If will bends much or little, all the same   79
    it does assist the force: such were these souls
    who could have fled back to their holy place.
But had their wills been steadfast and entire,   82
    such as held holy Lawrence on the grate
    and made Mucius sentence his hand to fire,
They would have willed to hasten to that street   85
    whence they were seized, when they were freed once more—
    but wills so resolute you rarely meet.
Gather my words in, glean their truth like grain, 88
    and you will see that argument destroyed
    which would have hurt you often and again.

Ma or ti s'attraversa un altro passo   91
   dinanzi a li occhi, tal che per te stesso
   non usciresti: pria saresti lasso.
Io t'ho per certo ne la mente messo   94
   ch'alma beata non poria mentire,
   però ch'è sempre al primo vero appresso;
e poi potesti da Piccarda udire   97
   che l'affezion del vel Costanza tenne;
   sì ch'ella par qui meco contradire.
Molte fïate già, frate, addivenne   100
   che, per fuggir periglio, contra grato
   si fé di quel che far non si convenne;
come Almeone, che, di ciò pregato   103
   dal padre suo, la propria madre spense,
   per non perder pietà si fé spietato.
A questo punto voglio che tu pense   106
   che la forza al voler si mischia, e fanno
   sì che scusar non si posson l'offense.
Voglia assoluta non consente al danno;   109
   ma consentevi in tanto in quanto teme,
   se si ritrae, cadere in più affanno.
Però, quando Piccarda quello spreme,   112
   de la voglia assoluta intende, e io
   de l'altra; sì che ver diciamo insieme".
Cotal fu l'ondeggiar del santo rio   115
   ch'uscì del fonte ond' ogne ver deriva;
   tal puose in pace uno e altro disio.
"O amanza del primo amante, o diva",   118
   diss' io appresso, "il cui parlar m'inonda
   e scalda sì, che più e più m'avviva,
non è l'affezion mia tanto profonda,   121
   che basti a render voi grazia per grazia;
   ma quei che vede e puote a ciò risponda.
Io veggio ben che già mai non si sazia   124
   nostro intelletto, se 'l ver non lo illustra
   di fuor dal qual nessun vero si spazia.

But now before your eyes another road   91
   rises, a pass so difficult, you'd find
   no strength to overcome it on your own.
I've set it down for certain, in your mind,   94
   that blessed souls can never speak a lie,
   for they are standing near the fount of truth.
Nevertheless you heard Piccarda say   97
   what appears to have contradicted me,
   that Constance kept her true love for the veil.
Brother, it often happens that to flee   100
   peril, we do what never should be done,
   against what we would wish, and grudgingly—
As at his father's pleading, Alcmaeon   103
   put out the life of his own mother and
   pitilessly preserved his piety.
In such a case I'd have you understand   106
   that will and force commingle and prevent
   excuse for the offense. Unto the evil,
Absolute will refuses its consent,   109
   but when contingent will yields to the fear
   of falling to worse harm should it withstand,
Will does consent. We've spoken truly here: 112
   Piccarda's words referred to the first will,
   the absolute; and to the other, mine."
Such was the rippling of the holy rill   115
   whose fountain was the spring of every truth.
   It brought both yearnings peace, and made them still.
"O soul divine, beloved of the first Lover,"   118
   said I, "whose words wash over me and steep
   me in such warmth, I grow in life and youth,
The ocean of my love is not so deep   121
   as to suffice to give you grace for grace;
   let Him who sees, and can, give you your due.
I see our intellects cannot be filled   124
   unless the one Truth floods them with its light,
   beyond which nothing true can find a place.

Posasi in esso, come fera in lustra,   127
    tosto che giunto l'ha; e giugner puollo:
    se non, ciascun disio sarebbe *frustra*.
Nasce per quello, a guisa di rampollo,   130
    a piè del vero il dubbio; ed è natura
    ch'al sommo pinge noi di collo in collo.
Questo m'invita, questo m'assicura   133
    con reverenza, donna, a dimandarvi
    d'un'altra verità che m'è oscura.
Io vo' saper se l'uom può sodisfarvi   136
    ai voti manchi sì con altri beni,
    ch'a la vostra statera non sien parvi".
Beatrice mi guardò con li occhi pieni   139
    di faville d'amor così divini,
    che, vinta, mia virtute diè le reni,
e quasi mi perdei con li occhi chini.   142

Like a beast in its den, we rest in it   127
   when we have reached it, as we can indeed—
   if not, our longings would be all in vain.
Those high desires sprout forth, as from a seed,   130
   doubt, at the foot of truth—and doubt, by nature,
   urges us, hill to hill, up to the peak.
This is what welcomes me, what makes me sure,   133
   Lady, that I may ask with reverence
   about another truth I find obscure.
I'd like to know if man can recompense   136
   the failing in his vow with works well done,
   so one side of your scales won't be too light."
Beatrice looked at me with eyes that shone   139
   so full of scintillating love divine
   they put to flight the powers of my own,
And down I cast them, nearly overcome.   142

"S'io ti fiammeggio nel caldo d'amore
di là dal modo che 'n terra si vede,
sì che del viso tuo vinco il valore,
non ti maravigliar, ché ciò procede   4
da perfetto veder, che, come apprende,
così nel bene appreso move il piede.
Io veggio ben sì come già resplende   7
ne l'intelletto tuo l'etterna luce,
che, vista, sola e sempre amore accende;
e s'altra cosa vostro amor seduce,   10
non è se non di quella alcun vestigio,
mal conosciuto, che quivi traluce.
Tu vuo' saper se con altro servigio,   13
per manco voto, si può render tanto
che l'anima sicuri di letigio".
Sì cominciò Beatrice questo canto;   16
e sì com' uom che suo parlar non spezza,
continüò così 'l processo santo:
"Lo maggior don che Dio per sua larghezza   19
fesse creando, e a la sua bontate
più conformato, e quel ch'e' più apprezza,
fu de la volontà la libertate;   22
di che le creature intelligenti,
e tutte e sole, fuoro e son dotate.

CANTO FIVE

*Beatrice explains to Dante **the irrevocability of sacred vows.** They enter **the second sphere** and meet spirits, represented by **Mercury,** who paid too much attention to worldly honor when on earth.*

"If I am kindled in such warmth of love
    it overwhelms the power of your sight
    with far more force than earth has vision of,
You need not wonder, for it comes from light   4
    of perfect vision which, the more it sees,
    the deeper does it journey into good.
I see the splendor of the eternal rays   7
    pouring their light into your intellect,
    which ever and alone enkindles love
Once beheld; and should something else deflect   10
    your love, it is no more than a faint glow,
    a trace of that first light you don't suspect.
You'd like to know if for a broken vow   13
    the soul can offer service for the wrong,
    enough to clear it from the claims of law."
So then did Beatrice begin this song,   16
    continuing her holy reasoning thus
    as one who does not break his speech in two:
"The greatest gift God made for any creature   19
    by His own bounty, gift most perfectly
    like His own excellence, gift He holds most dear,
Was from the first the will at liberty: 22
    all creatures made to be intelligent
    were and are so endowed, and only they.

Or ti parrà, se tu quinci argomenti,   25
    l'alto valor del voto, s'è sì fatto
    che Dio consenta quando tu consenti;
ché, nel fermar tra Dio e l'omo il patto,   28
    vittima fassi di questo tesoro,
    tal quale io dico; e fassi col suo atto.
Dunque che render puossi per ristoro?   31
    Se credi bene usar quel c'hai offerto,
    di maltolletto vuo' far buon lavoro.
Tu se' omai del maggior punto certo;   34
    ma perché Santa Chiesa in ciò dispensa,
    che par contra lo ver ch'i' t'ho scoverto,
convienti ancor sedere un poco a mensa,   37
    però che 'l cibo rigido c'hai preso,
    richiede ancora aiuto a tua dispensa.
Apri la mente a quel ch'io ti paleso   40
    e fermalvi entro; ché non fa scïenza,
    sanza lo ritenere, avere inteso.
Due cose si convegnono a l'essenza   43
    di questo sacrificio: l'una è quella
    di che si fa; l'altr' è la convenenza.
Quest' ultima già mai non si cancella   46
    se non servata; e intorno di lei
    sì preciso di sopra si favella:
però necessitato fu a li Ebrei   49
    pur l'offerere, ancor ch'alcuna offerta
    si permutasse, come saver dei.
L'altra, che per materia t'è aperta,   52
    puote ben esser tal, che non si falla
    se con altra materia si converta.
Ma non trasmuti carco a la sua spalla   55
    per suo arbitrio alcun, sanza la volta
    e de la chiave bianca e de la gialla;

You'll see, then, from this line of argument,   25
   the high value of vows if they're so made
   that God consents as soon as you consent.
For when both God and man have sealed the pact   28
   they slay this treasure in a sacrifice,
   and do so, as I say, by a free act.
What could restore the loss, what could suffice?   31
   To turn your gift to holy works would be
   to put what you have pilfered out to use.
The major premise° now you surely see: 34
   but because Holy Church grants dispensation,
   and appears to deny what I have shown,
You need a bit more help for your digestion   37
   because you've sunk your teeth into tough food,
   and have to sit at table yet a while.
Open your mind to what I now make plain,   40
   hold it within, for there's no knowledge when
   you understand a thing you don't retain.
The essence of this sacrifice lies in   43
   two necessary things: the first is what
   you sacrifice, the second is the pact.
This second's never canceled if it's not   46
   fulfilled, as we've declared—precisely so,
   and therefore in Leviticus we're taught
The ancient Hebrews were required by law,   49
   even when they could change the offering,
   to offer something still, as you must know.
The first (what I have called the offered thing)   52
   has to be what will cause no sinful lack
   if it should be exchanged for something else.
No one should change the burden on his back   55
   by his own judgment, though, without the turn
   of both the silver and the yellow keys;°

°*major premise:* that man can sacrifice to God nothing more precious than the freedom of the will.
   °*the silver and the yellow keys:* the authority of the Church; see notes.

e ogne permutanza credi stolta,   58
  se la cosa dimessa in la sorpresa
  come 'l quattro nel sei non è raccolta.

Però qualunque cosa tanto pesa   61
  per suo valor che tragga ogne bilancia,
  sodisfar non si può con altra spesa.

Non prendan li mortali il voto a ciancia;   64
  siate fedeli, e a ciò far non bieci,
  come Ieptè a la sua prima mancia;

cui più si convenia dicer 'Mal feci',   67
  che, servando, far peggio; e così stolto
  ritrovar puoi il gran duca de' Greci,

onde pianse Efigènia il suo bel volto,   70
  e fé pianger di sé i folli e i savi
  ch'udir parlar di così fatto cólto.

Siate, Cristiani, a muovervi più gravi: 73
  non siate come penna ad ogne vento,
  e non crediate ch'ogne acqua vi lavi.

Avete il novo e 'l vecchio Testamento,   76
  e 'l pastor de la Chiesa che vi guida;
  questo vi basti a vostro salvamento.

Se mala cupidigia altro vi grida,   79
  uomini siate, e non pecore matte,
  sì che 'l Giudeo di voi tra voi non rida!

Non fate com' agnel che lascia il latte   82
  de la sua madre, e semplice e lascivo
  seco medesmo a suo piacer combatte!".

Così Beatrice a me com' ïo scrivo;   85
  poi si rivolse tutta disïante
  a quella parte ove 'l mondo è più vivo.

Lo suo tacere e 'l trasmutar sembiante   88
  puoser silenzio al mio cupido ingegno,
  che già nuove questioni avea davante;

And let him trust he juggles things in vain   58
    if what he takes for what he gives away
    is not worth more than half as much again.
Sometimes a thing's so valuable it may   61
    never be bought with other coin, but drags
    the scale of every balance. Mortal men
Should not think vows a deal of scraps and rags!   64
    Be faithful, and not addled in the eye,
    as Jephthah° was in offering his first sight,
Who'd better said, "I have done wrong," than by   67
    keeping his vow, done worse; the same's the case
    with the Greek chief° and his stupidity,
Whence Iphigenia wept for her fair face   70
    and made both fool and wise man mourn her fate
    when they heard of such piety. Be grave
In moving, Christians, be deliberate: 73
    not like a feather tossed by every puff;
    and don't think any splash will cleanse a fault!
You have the Testaments, the Old and New;   76
    you have the Church's shepherd as your guide.
    For your salvation these should be enough.
If avarice calls you to the other side,   79
    be men, not silly sheep who cannot think!
    Don't give your Jews good reason to deride.
Don't be the lamb who leaves his mother's milk   82
    and, scampering in ignorant delight,
    scraps with himself and butts at empty air."
Beatrice spoke exactly what I write,   85
    then she turned with an all-desiring glance
    to where the world enjoys its fullest life.
Her quiet and transfigured countenance   88
    imposed a silence on my eager wit,
    before whose sight new questions had already

°*Jephthah:* The Israelite judge, after victory in battle, vowed to slay to the Lord the first thing he saw on his return. That turned out to be his only child, his daughter rushing forth to greet him (Judg. 11.30–39).

°*Greek chief:* Agamemnon, who sacrificed his daughter *Iphigenia* to placate the goddess Artemis and win favorable winds for sailing to Troy.

e sì come saetta che nel segno 91
    percuote pria che sia la corda queta,
    così corremmo nel secondo regno.
Quivi la donna mia vid' io sì lieta, 94
    come nel lume di quel ciel si mise,
    che più lucente se ne fé 'l pianeta.
E se la stella si cambiò e rise, 97
    qual mi fec' io che pur da mia natura
    trasmutabile son per tutte guise!
Come 'n peschiera ch'è tranquilla e pura 100
    traggonsi i pesci a ciò che vien di fori
    per modo che lo stimin lor pastura,
sì vid' io ben più di mille splendori 103
    trarsi ver' noi, e in ciascun s'udia:
    "Ecco chi crescerà li nostri amori".
E sì come ciascuno a noi venìa, 106
    vedeasi l'ombra piena di letizia
    nel folgór chiaro che di lei uscia.
Pensa, lettor, se quel che qui s'inizia 109
    non procedesse, come tu avresti
    di più savere angosciosa carizia;
e per te vederai come da questi 112
    m'era in disio d'udir lor condizioni,
    sì come a li occhi mi fur manifesti.
"O bene nato a cui veder li troni 115
    del trïunfo etternal concede grazia
    prima che la milizia s'abbandoni,
del lume che per tutto il ciel si spazia 118
    noi semo accesi; e però, se disii
    di noi chiarirti, a tuo piacer ti sazia".
Così da un di quelli spirti pii 121
    detto mi fu; e da Beatrice: "Dì, dì
    sicuramente, e credi come a dii".
"Io veggio ben sì come tu t'annidi 124
    nel proprio lume, e che de li occhi il traggi,
    perch' e' corusca sì come tu ridi;

Risen—and as an arrowhead will hit
 the mark before the cord has ceased to hum,
 so did we speed into the second realm.

Such joy my Lady beamed when she had come
 into the radiance pouring from that sphere,
 she lent the planet brightness of her own.

If she brought flashing laughter to a star,
 what then to me, who am so changeable
 by nature, for whatever may appear?

As in a fishing pool pristine and still,
 the fishes swim to something dropped below
 should they believe it's good to feed upon,

More than a thousand splendors all aglow
 I saw approach us, and I heard them say,
 "Look, here is one to make our friendships grow!"

And just as every radiance came our way
 a shadow filled with gladness could be spied
 within the gleaming of their purity.

Think, reader, if the supper I provide
 were cut short at the start of its career,
 how pitiably you'd hunger to know more,

And you'll see clearly how I longed to hear
 the names and graces of these blessed ones,
 soon as they showed themselves before my eyes.

"O born in happy hour, to see the thrones
 of the eternal triumph, led by grace
 before your discharge from the earth's platoons,

We burn with heavenly light that fills all space,
 so satisfy your hunger as you please,
 if you desire to hear the truth of us."

Such were the words addressed by one of these
 devoted souls. "Speak, speak!" said Beatrice.
 "Trust in them, as if they were deities."

"I see the gladness shining in your eyes,
 how when you laugh it splashes in a blaze,
 how you dwell in the nest of your own light,

91

94

97

100

103

106

109

112

115

118

121

124

ma non so chi tu se', né perché aggi,   127
     anima degna, il grado de la spera
     che si vela a' mortai con altrui raggi".
Questo diss' io diritto a la lumera   130
     che pria m'avea parlato; ond' ella fessi
     lucente più assai di quel ch'ell' era.
Sì come il sol che si cela elli stessi   133
     per troppa luce, come 'l caldo ha róse
     le temperanze d'i vapori spessi,
per più letizia sì mi si nascose   136
     dentro al suo raggio la figura santa;
     e così chiusa chiusa mi rispuose
nel modo che 'l seguente canto canta.   139

But don't know who you are, O worthy soul,   127
    nor why yours is the level of that ring°
    hidden behind another's radiant veil."
So I, directly to the shimmering   130
    that spoke, and when it heard it grew more bright,
    such the delight it gleaned in listening.
As the sun hides in its exceeding light   133
    when morning warmth has eaten up the haze
    that softened it enough for human sight,
The holy figure in a happy blaze   136
    concealed himself by his bright reveling
    and from within those secret secret rays
Responded as the following song will sing.   139

°*that ring:* Mercury, often invisible in the glare of the nearby sun.

"Poscia che Costantin l'aquila volse
    contr' al corso del ciel, ch'ella seguio
    dietro a l'antico che Lavina tolse,
cento e cent' anni e più l'uccel di Dio   4
    ne lo stremo d'Europa si ritenne,
    vicino a' monti de' quai prima uscìo;
e sotto l'ombra de le sacre penne   7
    governò 'l mondo lì di mano in mano,
    e, sì cangiando, in su la mia pervenne.
Cesare fui e son Iustinïano,   10
    che, per voler del primo amor ch'i' sento,
    d'entro le leggi trassi il troppo e 'l vano.
E prima ch'io a l'ovra fossi attento,   13
    una natura in Cristo esser, non piùe,
    credea, e di tal fede era contento;
ma 'l benedetto Agapito, che fue   16
    sommo pastore, a la fede sincera
    mi dirizzò con le parole sue.
Io li credetti; e ciò che 'n sua fede era,   19
    vegg' io or chiaro sì, come tu vedi
    ogne contradizione e falsa e vera.

Canto Six

*Justinian describes the history of **the eagle of Rome**, its most glorious victory the avengement of the death of Christ. After decrying **the corruption of both Guelphs and Ghibellines**, he points out the soul of the honorable courtier **Romeo**.*

"When Constantine had turned the eagle's wing°
    against the course of Heaven, which it had flown
    following him who made Lavinia queen,°
Two centuries and more the bird of God   4
    nested on Europe's farthest coast, and held
    near to the mountains whence it came of old,
And passed from hand to hand and steered the world   7
    under the shadow of its sacred wings,
    till finally it passed into my own.
Caesar I was and am Justinian,   10
    who by the prompting of the primal Love°
    pruned the law of all rank and useless things.
I held there was in Christ, before I strove   13
    to do this work, one nature and not two,
    and was contented in my misbelief,
Until I was directed to the true   16
    and perfect faith by blest Agapetus,
    the highest Shepherd, who persuaded me.
I put my trust in what he preached, and thus   19
    I see the points of faith as you now see
    that contradictories are true and false.

°*the eagle's wing:* symbol of Rome and her empire. For the eagle's career, see notes.
°*him who made Lavinia queen:* Aeneas, legendary father of the Roman race. His betrothal to Lavinia embroiled him in war against the natives of central Italy.
°*the primal Love:* the Holy Spirit (cf. *Inferno* 3.6).

Tosto che con la Chiesa mossi i piedi,   22
    a Dio per grazia piacque di spirarmi
    l'alto lavoro, e tutto 'n lui mi diedi;
e al mio Belisar commendai l'armi,   25
    cui la destra del ciel fu sì congiunta,
    che segno fu ch'i' dovessi posarmi.
Or qui a la question prima s'appunta   28
    la mia risposta; ma sua condizione
    mi stringe a seguitare alcuna giunta,
perché tu veggi con quanta ragione   31
    si move contr' al sacrosanto segno
    e chi 'l s'appropria e chi a lui s'oppone.
Vedi quanta virtù l'ha fatto degno   34
    di reverenza; e cominciò da l'ora
    che Pallante morì per darli regno.
Tu sai ch'el fece in Alba sua dimora   37
    per trecento anni e oltre, infino al fine
    che i tre a' tre pugnar per lui ancora.
E sai ch'el fé dal mal de le Sabine   40
    al dolor di Lucrezia in sette regi,
    vincendo intorno le genti vicine.
Sai quel ch'el fé portato da li egregi   43
    Romani incontro a Brenno, incontro a Pirro,
    incontro a li altri principi e collegi;
onde Torquato e Quinzio, che dal cirro   46
    negletto fu nomato, i Deci e ' Fabi
    ebber la fama che volontier mirro.

God in His grace was pleased to breathe in me   22
    the lofty work to which I gave my all,
    when with the Church I walked in harmony.
To Belisarius my general   25
    did I entrust my troops, and Heaven's right hand
    lent his such strength, it was my sign to rest
From action in the field. So I reply   28
    to your first question, but what I've had to say
    presses me to append an explanation,
That you may see with how much justice they   31
    move against the most holy Roman sign,
    they who suborn this symbol as their own
And who oppose it.° See what power divine   34
    has made it worthy of reverence, from the hour
    when Pallas° died to set it in its reign.
You know it harbored on the Alban shore   37
    over three centuries, till the three at last
    battled the three° and brought it to Rome once more.
You know that from the Sabine rape° it passed   40
    through seven kings until Lucretia's woe,°
    conquering all the peoples roundabout.
You know the glorious Romans raised it high   43
    when they met Brennus in the field of war,
    met Pyrrhus, met the other kings and councils,
Where Quinctius of the careless shock of hair,   46
    Torquatus, the Decii, and the Fabii
    won glory I keep forever fresh with myrrh.

°*they who suborn ... who oppose it:* Ghibellines and Guelphs, the pro- and anti-imperial parties of Dante's day. See notes to lines 103–8 below.

°*Pallas:* noble Arcadian youth who died fighting in the cause of Aeneas and the Trojans (Virgil, *Aeneid* 10.439–89).

°*the three:* the famous combat between the three Roman Horatii and the three Alban Curiatii, to decide which people would rule Rome (Livy, *History* 1.23–26).

°*Sabine rape:* Suffering a shortage of women, Romulus and his men lured the neighboring Sabines to a religious feast and then kidnapped their daughters (Livy, *Hist.* 1.9).

°*Lucretia's woe:* Sextus Tarquinius, son of King Tarquin the Proud, raped Lucretia, wife of a Roman senator. Avenging this evil, Lucius Junius Brutus (*Inf.* 4.127) and his allies expelled Tarquin and established the Roman Republic (Livy, *Hist.* 1.56–60).

Esso atterrò l'orgoglio de li Aràbi 49
   che di retro ad Anibale passaro
   l'alpestre rocce, Po, di che tu labi.
Sott' esso giovanetti trïunfaro 52
   Scipïone e Pompeo; e a quel colle
   sotto 'l qual tu nascesti parve amaro.
Poi, presso al tempo che tutto 'l ciel volle 55
   redur lo mondo a suo modo sereno,
   Cesare per voler di Roma il tolle.
E quel che fé da Varo infino a Reno, 58
   Isara vide ed Era e vide Senna
   e ogne valle onde Rodano è pieno.
Quel che fé poi ch'elli uscì di Ravenna 61
   e saltò Rubicon, fu di tal volo,
   che nol seguiteria lingua né penna.
Inver' la Spagna rivolse lo stuolo, 64
   poi ver' Durazzo, e Farsalia percosse
   sì ch'al Nil caldo si sentì del duolo.
Antandro e Simeonta, onde si mosse, 67
   rivide e là dov' Ettore si cuba;
   e mal per Tolomeo poscia si scosse.
Da indi scese folgorando a Iuba; 70
   onde si volse nel vostro occidente,
   ove sentia la pompeana tuba.
Di quel che fé col baiulo seguente, 73
   Bruto con Cassio ne l'inferno latra,
   e Modena e Perugia fu dolente.
Piangene ancor la trista Cleopatra, 76
   che, fuggendoli innanzi, dal colubro
   la morte prese subitana e atra.

This standard cast the Arabs' pride to earth 49
   who crossed your rugged wellsprings, River Po,
   following Hannibal over the rough north.
Beneath this standard the lads Scipio 52
   and Pompey rode in triumph, and it proved
   harsh to that mountain you were born below.°
And near the hour when the whole heaven strove 55
   to lead the world to its serenity,
   Caesar, at Rome's desire, took up the flag.
What it did then in Gaul and Germany, 58
   from the Var to the Rhine, each stream that fills the Rhône,
   the Loire, the Yser, and the Saône may see.
Leaving Ravenna for the Rubicon 61
   it leapt over that river with a flight
   no quill can follow, and no tongue describe:
It swept its squadrons into Spain to fight, 64
   then made the hot Nile feel the lash of pain
   when it had soared over the Adriatic
To crush Pharsalia.° Then it saw again 67
   Simoïs and Antandros° and the tomb
   where Hector lies; and shook its wings to bring
Ptolemy down. Like lightning hammering doom 70
   it swooped on Juba, then swerved west of you,
   where trumpets roused the last of Pompey's hosts.
For its deeds in the second steward's keeping° 73
   Brutus and Cassius yelp like dogs in Hell,
   and Modena and Perugia went weeping.
The dismal Cleopatra mourns it still, 76
   who feared its flight and tried to flee before—
   and from the asp took swift and bitter death.

  °*that mountain you were born below:* Fiesole, overlooking Florence. Dante alludes to the legend that traitors to the Roman Republic, following the notorious Catiline, fled to Fiesole, where they were overtaken and slain by Pompey.
  °*Pharsalia:* The climactic battle won by Julius Caesar over the troops of Pompey; Dante read of it in Lucan's epic of the same name.
  °*Simoïs and Antandros:* rivers of Troy, in Asia Minor.
  °*the second steward's keeping:* that of Augustus Caesar, emperor at the time of the birth of Christ.

Con costui corse infino al lito rubro;   79
    con costui puose il mondo in tanta pace,
    che fu serrato a Giano il suo delubro.
Ma ciò che 'l segno che parlar mi face   82
    fatto avea prima e poi era fatturo
    per lo regno mortal ch'a lui soggiace,
diventa in apparenza poco e scuro,   85
    se in mano al terzo Cesare si mira
    con occhio chiaro e con affetto puro;
ché la viva giustizia che mi spira,   88
    li concedette, in mano a quel ch'i' dico,
    gloria di far vendetta a la sua ira.
Or qui t'ammira in ciò ch'io ti replìco: 91
    poscia con Tito a far vendetta corse
    de la vendetta del peccato antico.
E quando il dente longobardo morse   94
    la Santa Chiesa, sotto le sue ali
    Carlo Magno, vincendo, la soccorse.
Omai puoi giudicar di quei cotali   97
    ch'io accusai di sopra e di lor falli,
    che son cagion di tutti vostri mali.
L'uno al pubblico segno i gigli gialli   100
    oppone, e l'altro appropria quello a parte,
    sì ch'è forte a veder chi più si falli.
Faccian li Ghibellin, faccian lor arte   103
    sott' altro segno, ché mal segue quello
    sempre chi la giustizia e lui diparte;
e non l'abbatta esto Carlo novello   106
    coi Guelfi suoi, ma tema de li artigli
    ch'a più alto leon trasser lo vello.

With him it sped unto the Red Sea's shore,   79
    with him it brought such peace to every land,
    in Rome they bolted Janus' temple door.°
But what the standard that inspires this speech   82
    had ever done or was to do, through all
    the mortal realms that lay in its command,
Appears of dim significance and small   85
    if you regard it—with clear vision, with
    pure love—in the third Caesar's hand:° because
The living justice that instills my breath   88
    granted to that third hand a glorious boon,
    the glory of the vengeance of His wrath.
Be stunned by what I now reveal, for soon   91
    with Titus° did the eagle fly to take
    vengeance for vengeance for the ancient sin!
And later, when the fangs of the Lombard snake   94
    had bitten Holy Church, victorious Charles
    the Great° assisted her beneath its wings.
Now you can judge the men I have accused,   97
    their falsehood and the evil that are cause
    of all your trials. For this one has opposed
The yellow lilies° to the people's sign,   100
    while that one claims it as his party's own:
    hard to see who has gone the farther wrong.
Ghibellines, go, go on and ply your art   103
    under another standard, for no man
    can follow the sign well who severs it
From right; nor let this lad Charles° think he can   106
    batter it with his Guelphs, but let him fear
    talons so sharp they've stripped the very mane

°*Janus' temple door:* Janus was the Roman god of doors, and thus of beginnings. His temple was shut whenever (which was almost never) Rome was at peace with all her neighbors.

°*the third Caesar's hand:* that of Tiberius, emperor when Christ was crucified.

°*Titus:* destroyer of Jerusalem in 70 A.D., son and successor of the emperor Vespasian.

°*Charles the Great:* Charlemagne defeated the Lombards at the entreaty of the pope, and was then crowned emperor in Rome on Christmas Day in 800.

°*the yellow lilies:* symbol of France. The French consistently opposed imperial designs in Italy.

°*this lad Charles:* scornful reference to Charles II, duke of Anjou and king of Naples; see notes.

Molte fïate già pianser li figli   109
   per la colpa del padre, e non si creda
   che Dio trasmuti l'armi per suoi gigli!
Questa picciola stella si correda   112
   d'i buoni spirti che son stati attivi
   perché onore e fama li succeda:
e quando li disiri poggian quivi,   115
   sì disvïando, pur convien che i raggi
   del vero amore in sù poggin men vivi.
Ma nel commensurar d'i nostri gaggi   118
   col merto è parte di nostra letizia,
   perché non li vedem minor né maggi.
Quindi addolcisce la viva giustizia   121
   in noi l'affetto sì, che non si puote
   torcer già mai ad alcuna nequizia.
Diverse voci fanno dolci note;   124
   così diversi scanni in nostra vita
   rendon dolce armonia tra queste rote.
E dentro a la presente margarita   127
   luce la luce di Romeo, di cui
   fu l'ovra grande e bella mal gradita.
Ma i Provenzai che fecer contra lui   130
   non hanno riso; e però mal cammina
   qual si fa danno del ben fare altrui.
Quattro figlie ebbe, e ciascuna reina,   133
   Ramondo Beringhiere, e ciò li fece
   Romeo, persona umìle e peregrina.
E poi il mosser le parole biece   136
   a dimandar ragione a questo giusto,
   che li assegnò sette e cinque per diece.
Indi partissi povero e vetusto;   139
   e se 'l mondo sapesse il cor ch'elli ebbe
   mendicando sua vita a frusto a frusto,
assai lo loda, e più lo loderebbe".   142

From greater lions than he! If sons must bear   109
    grief for the father's sins, let *him* not think
    God will exchange his eagle for French *fleurs!*
This little star is ornamented by   112
    all the brave souls who live their lives that fame
    and honor might succeed them when they die—
But when desire is set on things below,   115
    it wanders from the road, and so the rays
    of true love mount with less life in the flame.
That our rewards are measured as our days   118
    have merited, for us is happiness—
    that we may see them neither less nor more.
The living justice has so sweetened us   121
    that we can never twist our hearts toward wrong,
    for our desires are rendered pure and just.
Various voices make the sweeter song: 124
    here in our life the various thrones endow
    the wheels of Heaven with sweet harmony.
Shining within the pearl before you now   127
    is one whose work was beautiful and grand
    but ill repaid: the gleam of Romeo.
But they're not laughing now, those Provençals   130
    who slandered him: an evil road, to glean
    one's losses from the good of someone else.
He had four daughters and each one a queen,   133
    had Raymond Berenguer; that was the work
    of humble Romeo, the foreigner.
But cross-eyed gossip goaded the old duke   136
    to demand a full reckoning from that just
    counselor who had rendered twelve for ten.
He left that country, poor and full of years;   139
    and if the world knew with what heart he bore
    his life of beggary, from crust to crust,
For all their praise, they'd praise him all the more."   142

"Osanna, sanctus Deus sabaòth,
  superillustrans claritate tua
  felices ignes horum malacòth!".
Così, volgendosi a la nota sua,   4
  fu viso a me cantare essa sustanza,
  sopra la qual doppio lume s'addua;
ed essa e l'altre mossero a sua danza,   7
  e quasi velocissime faville
  mi si velar di sùbita distanza.
Io dubitava e dicea 'Dille, dille!'   10
  fra me, 'dille' dicea, 'a la mia donna
  che mi diseta con le dolci stille'.
Ma quella reverenza che s'indonna   13
  di tutto me, pur per *Be* e per *ice,*
  mi richinava come l'uom ch'assonna.
Poco sofferse me cotal Beatrice   16
  e cominciò, raggiandomi d'un riso
  tal, che nel foco faria l'uom felice:
"Secondo mio infallibile avviso,   19
  come giusta vendetta giustamente
  punita fosse, t'ha in pensier miso;
ma io ti solverò tosto la mente;   22
  e tu ascolta, ché le mie parole
  di gran sentenza ti faran presente.

CANTO SEVEN

*Beatrice explains the necessity of **Christ's atoning sacrifice** and the justice of
God's **vengeance against the Jews** who put Christ to death.*

"Hosanna, holy God of power and might,
    illuminating with your clarity
    these armies and their joyful flames of light!"
I heard, in rhythm with the harmony   4
    of hosts, the singing of that radiance°
    bright with the twinning of a double ray;
Then all the souls commingled in a dance,   7
    and with the slashing swiftness of a flame
    in sudden distance veiled themselves from sight.
"Speak, speak to your Lady," I began to exclaim   10
    within myself, but wavering. "Speak to her!
    She slakes your thirst with her sweet drops of truth."
But reverence played the mistress over me   13
    and like an old man nodding off I bowed
    when in my mind I heard the name of "Bee."
Beatrice for a little while allowed   16
    my speechlessness, then flashed me such a smile
    as would bring gladness to a man in fire.
"By what I see, a view that cannot fail,   19
    the punished vengeance plunges you in thought—
    how it is just to punish what was just,"°
Said she, "but I'll soon free your mind of doubt.   22
    Then heed my words, for they will help you gain
    a gift of precious truth. Since he could not

°*that radiance:* Justinian.
°*just to punish what was just:* If it was just that Christ died on the cross for men's sins, why was
it also just to punish those who put him to death? Beatrice recalls Justinian's words, 6.91–93.

Per non soffrire a la virtù che vole   25
    freno a suo prode, quell' uom che non nacque,
    dannando sé, dannò tutta sua prole;
onde l'umana specie inferma giacque   28
    giù per secoli molti in grande errore,
    fin ch'al Verbo di Dio discender piacque
u' la natura, che dal suo fattore   31
    s'era allungata, unì a sé in persona
    con l'atto sol del suo etterno amore.
Or drizza il viso a quel ch'or si ragiona: 34
    questa natura al suo fattore unita,
    qual fu creata, fu sincera e buona;
ma per sé stessa pur fu ella sbandita   37
    di paradiso, però che si torse
    da via di verità e da sua vita.
La pena dunque che la croce porse   40
    s'a la natura assunta si misura,
    nulla già mai sì giustamente morse;
e così nulla fu di tanta ingiura,   43
    guardando a la persona che sofferse,
    in che era contratta tal natura.
Però d'un atto uscir cose diverse: 46
    ch'a Dio e a' Giudei piacque una morte;
    per lei tremò la terra e 'l ciel s'aperse.
Non ti dee oramai parer più forte,   49
    quando si dice che giusta vendetta
    poscia vengiata fu da giusta corte.
Ma io veggi' or la tua mente ristretta   52
    di pensiero in pensier dentro ad un nodo,
    del qual con gran disio solver s'aspetta.
Tu dici: 'Ben discerno ciò ch'i' odo;   55
    ma perché Dio volesse, m'è occulto,
    a nostra redenzion pur questo modo'.
Questo decreto, frate, sta sepulto   58
    a li occhi di ciascuno il cui ingegno
    ne la fiamma d'amor non è adulto.

Suffer, not for his benefit, a rein   25
 upon his will, the man who was not born,°
 damning himself, damned all his children too,
Whence the whole human race was weak, forlorn,   28
 and through the many centuries they roved,
 all lost, until the Word of God came down
Uniting human nature long removed   31
 from its Creator with Himself, one Person,
 by the sole act of His eternal Love.
Now turn your eyes to this result of reason.   34
 The human nature He adopted, one
 with its Creator, was as pure and good
As it was made to be, but of its own,   37
 it too was banned from Paradise, because
 it had strayed from the way of truth and life.
The punishment delivered by the Cross   40
 never with more precise a justice bit,
 when measured by the nature He assumed,
Yet never a lawless wrong was more unfit,   43
 considering where that nature was compact:
 the Person they compelled to suffer it.
Different effects resulted from one act,   46
 for the same death pleased both the Jews and God:
 for it all the earth trembled, the skies cracked,
The heavens opened. No more think it hard   49
 when it is said a just tribunal brought
 vengeance for a just vengeance. But I see
Your mind is tangled in a trap of thought,   52
 longing most eagerly that someone lay
 your doubts to rest, and free you of the knot.
'I can make out all I have heard,' you say,   55
 'yet still can't see the reason why God chose
 that man should be redeemed in just this way.'
More secret than a tomb is this decree,   58
 brother, from anyone whose native wit
 hasn't been fostered in the fire of love.

°*man who was not born:* Adam.

Veramente, però ch'a questo segno   61
  molto si mira e poco si discerne,
  dirò perché tal modo fu più degno.
La divina bontà, che da sé sperne   64
  ogne livore, ardendo in sé, sfavilla
  sì che dispiega le bellezze etterne.
Ciò che da lei sanza mezzo distilla   67
  non ha poi fine, perché non si move
  la sua imprenta quand' ella sigilla.
Ciò che da essa sanza mezzo piove   70
  libero è tutto, perché non soggiace
  a la virtute de le cose nove.
Più l'è conforme, e però più le piace;   73
  ché l'ardor santo ch'ogne cosa raggia,
  ne la più somigliante è più vivace.
Di tutte queste dote s'avvantaggia   76
  l'umana creatura, e s'una manca,
  di sua nobilità convien che caggia.
Solo il peccato è quel che la disfranca   79
  e falla dissimìle al sommo bene,
  per che del lume suo poco s'imbianca;
e in sua dignità mai non rivene,   82
  se non rïempie, dove colpa vòta,
  contra mal dilettar con giuste pene.
Vostra natura, quando peccò *tota*   85
  nel seme suo, da queste dignitadi,
  come di paradiso, fu remota;
né ricovrar potiensi, se tu badi   88
  ben sottilmente, per alcuna via,
  sanza passar per un di questi guadi:
o che Dio solo per sua cortesia   91
  dimesso avesse, o che l'uom per sé isso
  avesse sodisfatto a sua follia.

It's a mark he may study hard to hit;   61
    he stares—but precious little he discerns.
    I'll tell you, then, why this way was most fit.
Bounty divine, which in its goodness burns,   64
    spurns every envy and flashes forth in love
    to unfold the beauties of eternity.
All it distills without a medium   67
    is infinite: for when it stamps its seal,
    the imprint cannot alter or remove;
All it rains down without a medium   70
    is wholly free: not subject to the might
    of any new-made thing or starry wheel.°
More like to Him, the more is His delight,   73
    for then that sacred love whose radiance
    shines the world forth burns with more living light,
And man was formed to benefit from all   76
    three gifts; but should he fail in any one,
    it follows, his nobility will fall.
What steals his liberty is sin alone,   79
    makes him dissimilar to that Good most high
    and dims in him the brightness of Its glow,
Never returning to his dignity   82
    unless where sin has emptied he suffice
    for wrong delight with righteous penalty.
When in its seed your human nature sinned   85
    utterly, it was exiled far away
    from both its dignity and Paradise,
Which to regain, there is no other way—   88
    if you attend to this with subtlety—
    if not by crossing one of these two fords:
Either the Lord alone for courtesy   91
    pardon the sin, or for his foolishness
    mankind make satisfaction on his own.

°*not subject . . . wheel:* created directly by God, without the intermediaries of planetary influence or angelic intelligence.

Ficca mo l'occhio per entro l'abisso   94
    de l'etterno consiglio, quanto puoi
    al mio parlar distrettamente fisso.
Non potea l'uomo ne' termini suoi   97
    mai sodisfar, per non potere ir giuso
    con umiltate obedïendo poi,
quanto disobediendo intese ir suso;   100
    e questa è la cagion per che l'uom fue
    da poter sodisfar per sé dischiuso.
Dunque a Dio convenia con le vie sue   103
    riparar l'omo a sua intera vita,
    dico con l'una, o ver con amendue.
Ma perché l'ovra tanto è più gradita   106
    da l'operante, quanto più appresenta
    de la bontà del core ond' ell' è uscita,
la divina bontà che 'l mondo imprenta,   109
    di proceder per tutte le sue vie,
    a rilevarvi suso, fu contenta.
Né tra l'ultima notte e 'l primo die   112
    sì alto o sì magnifico processo,
    o per l'una o per l'altra, fu o fie:
ché più largo fu Dio a dar sé stesso   115
    per far l'uom sufficiente a rilevarsi,
    che s'elli avesse sol da sé dimesso;
e tutti li altri modi erano scarsi   118
    a la giustizia, se 'l Figliuol di Dio
    non fosse umilïato ad incarnarsi.
Or per empierti bene ogne disio,   121
    ritorno a dichiararti in alcun loco,
    perché tu veggi lì così com' io.
Tu dici: 'Io veggio l'acqua, io veggio il foco,   124
    l'aere e la terra e tutte lor misture
    venire a corruzione, e durar poco;
e queste cose pur furon creature;   127
    per che, se ciò ch'è detto è stato vero,
    esser dovrien da corruzion sicure'.

Now fix your eyes, peer into the abyss   94
    of the eternal plans of providence,
    holding yourself as closely as you can

To what I say. Man, set within his bounds,   97
    could never bow so low to satisfy
    by humbly following in obedience,

As he tried, disobeying, to mount high,   100
    and so he is shut out, for just this cause,
    from making satisfaction for himself.

It had to be by God's own ways, God's laws,   103
    that to his true life man might be restored:
    I mean by both God's pardon and the Cross.

For since the more a work stands in accord   106
    with the outpouring of his generous heart,
    the more it's cherished by its architect,

The divine bounty that has sealed its art   109
    upon the world was pleased to use each way
    to raise you to the glory you had lost.

Unto earth's final night from earth's first day   112
    no deed so grand or lofty has been done
    by justice or by pardon, nor shall be,

For when God gave Himself, enabling man   115
    to rise again, His gift was all the more
    mighty than had He pardoned him, alone;

And all other means would have left justice poor,   118
    had not the Son of God in charity
    humbled Himself to take on human flesh.

And now, that you may see the truth I see   121
    and fill your yearnings, I'll go back and clear
    another difficulty. For you say,

'I see the fire, the water, and the air,   124
    I see the earth, and all their combinations
    decaying, and enduring but a while,

And these things were the Lord's direct creations.   127
    But if what you have said just now is right,
    the elements should never fear decay.'

Li angeli, frate, e 'l paese sincero 130
    nel qual tu se', dir si posson creati,
    sì come sono, in loro essere intero;
ma li alimenti che tu hai nomati 133
    e quelle cose che di lor si fanno
    da creata virtù sono informati.
Creata fu la materia ch'elli hanno; 136
    creata fu la virtù informante
    in queste stelle che 'ntorno a lor vanno.
L'anima d'ogne bruto e de le piante 139
    di complession potenzïata tira
    lo raggio e 'l moto de le luci sante;
ma vostra vita sanza mezzo spira 142
    la somma beninanza, e la innamora
    di sé sì che poi sempre la disira.
E quinci puoi argomentare ancora 145
    vostra resurrezion, se tu ripensi
    come l'umana carne fessi allora
che li primi parenti intrambo fensi". 148

The angels, brother, and this realm of light   130
    where you now stand, by God's own hand were formed,
    created in their fullness, as they are.
But the elements you name were all informed   133
    by a created power, a second cause,
    they and all other things they constitute.
Created was the matter they possess,   136
    created was the forming influence
    raining upon them from these circling stars.
The souls of the brute animals and plants   139
    are drawn by the revolving of these fires
    out of the potencies of elements,
But the peak of Beneficence inspires   142
    your life without a means—your living soul,
    and so enamoring it that it desires
Its Maker ever. And if you recall   145
    how God first formed man's flesh in Paradise°
    when he made both our parents, you shall see
That after death your bodies shall arise."   148

° *how God first formed man's flesh in Paradise:* directly, that is.

Solea creder lo mondo in suo periclo
  che la bella Ciprigna il folle amore
  raggiasse, volta nel terzo epiciclo;
per che non pur a lei faceano onore   4
  di sacrificio e di votivo grido
  le genti antiche ne l'antico errore;
ma Dïone onoravano e Cupido,   7
  quella per madre sua, questo per figlio,
  e dicean ch'el sedette in grembo a Dido;
e da costei ond' io principio piglio   10
  pigliavano il vocabol de la stella
  che 'l sol vagheggia or da coppa or da ciglio.
Io non m'accorsi del salire in ella;   13
  ma d'esservi entro mi fé assai fede
  la donna mia ch'i' vidi far più bella.
E come in fiamma favilla si vede,   16
  e come in voce voce si discerne,
  quand' una è ferma e altra va e riede,

CANTO EIGHT

*Dante and Beatrice rise to **the third sphere, Venus,** where they meet souls who were too ardent in their attachment to fleshly love. Here Dante speaks with **Charles Martel of Anjou,** who discusses the cause of **degeneracy among noble families** and the evils wrought by **confusion of vocations.***

Back in its perilous time the world believed
    the lovely Cyprian queen° beamed maddening love
    from the revolving wheel of the third sphere,
And they gave, not only to her, the honor of   4
    the cries of prayer and flames of sacrifice,
    those men of old in their old wandering ways,
Honoring all her line of deities,   7
    the mother Dione, Cupid the son,
    saying the child once sat in Dido's lap;°
And by that goddess with whom I begin   10
    they named the evening and the morning star
    the sunlight flirts with, at her brow, her chin.
I hadn't sensed the climb, but when I saw   13
    how much more lovely Beatrice became,
    easily I believed we were within.
And as you'll find the flickerings in a flame   16
    or song in song when one voice holds the note
    while the other comes and goes in melody,

°*Cyprian queen:* Venus, goddess of love, daughter of Jupiter and *Dione,* and mother of *Cupid.* One of Venus's traditional haunts was the island of Cyprus.

°*in Dido's lap:* to cause her to fall in love with Aeneas, to her destruction, as it turned out. Dante's line is taken nearly verbatim from Virgil (*Aen.* 1.718).

vid' io in essa luce altre lucerne   19
   muoversi in giro più e men correnti,
   al modo, credo, di lor viste interne.
Di fredda nube non disceser venti,   22
   o visibili o no, tanto festini,
   che non paressero impediti e lenti
a chi avesse quei lumi divini   25
   veduti a noi venir, lasciando il giro
   pria cominciato in li alti Serafini;
e dentro a quei che più innanzi appariro   28
   sonava 'Osanna' sì, che unque poi
   di rïudir non fui sanza disiro.
Indi si fece l'un più presso a noi   31
   e solo incominciò: "Tutti sem presti
   al tuo piacer, perché di noi ti gioi.
Noi ci volgiam coi principi celesti   34
   d'un giro e d'un girare e d'una sete,
   ai quali tu del mondo già dicesti:
'Voi che 'ntendendo il terzo ciel movete';   37
   e sem sì pien d'amor, che, per piacerti,
   non fia men dolce un poco di quïete".
Poscia che li occhi miei si fuoro offerti   40
   a la mia donna reverenti, ed essa
   fatti li avea di sé contenti e certi,
rivolsersi a la luce che promessa   43
   tanto s'avea, e "Deh, chi siete?" fue
   la voce mia di grande affetto impressa.
E quanta e quale vid' io lei far piùe   46
   per allegrezza nova che s'accrebbe
   quando parlai, a l'allegrezze sue!
Così fatta, mi disse: "Il mondo m'ebbe   49
   giù poco tempo; e se più fosse stato,
   molto sarà di mal, che non sarebbe.

I saw a host of lamp glows in that light 19
    more or less swiftly moving all a-dance
    according to their grace of inner sight.
From a cold cloud never shot lightning's lance 22
    or cyclone's whirl with such velocity
    that it would not seem reined, in a dead trance,
To anyone who'd seen those spirits fly 25
    our way, leaving the radiant turning train
    the Seraphim first turn.° And from the heart
Of those approaching nearest swelled the strain 28
    of a Hosanna sung with such a voice
    as all my yearning is to hear again.
Whence one of them, alone, came close to us, 31
    beginning, "We're all ready, as you please!
    We wish to speak and make your heart rejoice.
We turn with those high Principalities, 34
    one in our thirst, one wheeling, and one dance,
    whom you entreated in the world: 'O you
Who move third heaven by intelligence,' 37
    and are so filled with love, for your delight
    even a little quiet will be sweet."
After my lady had assured my sight, 40
    for I had offered her my reverent eyes,
    I turned again to look upon the light
That promised me so much, so graciously, 43
    and with a voice that bore for him the seal
    of great affection, asked, "Ah, who are you?"
How great I saw that spirit swell, how bright 46
    in his rejoicing luminosity,
    my words but multiplying his delight!
So grown, "The world below," he said to me, 49
    "held me a little while; had it been more,
    much evil would not have been, that came to be.

°*leaving...turn:* The souls leave the Empyrean and are turned by the Primum Mobile, itself moved by the love of the Seraphim.

La mia letizia mi ti tien celato 52
    che mi raggia dintorno e mi nasconde
    quasi animal di sua seta fasciato.
Assai m'amasti, e avesti ben onde; 55
    che s'io fossi giù stato, io ti mostrava
    di mio amor più oltre che le fronde.
Quella sinistra riva che si lava 58
    di Rodano poi ch'è misto con Sorga,
    per suo segnore a tempo m'aspettava,
e quel corno d'Ausonia che s'imborga 61
    di Bari e di Gaeta e di Catona,
    da ove Tronto e Verde in mare sgorga.
Fulgeami già in fronte la corona 64
    di quella terra che 'l Danubio riga
    poi che le ripe tedesche abbandona.
E la bella Trinacria, che caliga 67
    tra Pachino e Peloro, sopra 'l golfo
    che riceve da Euro maggior briga,
non per Tifeo ma per nascente solfo, 70
    attesi avrebbe li suoi regi ancora,
    nati per me di Carlo e di Ridolfo,
se mala segnoria, che sempre accora 73
    li popoli suggetti, non avesse
    mosso Palermo a gridar: 'Mora, mora!'
E se mio frate questo antivedesse, 76
    l'avara povertà di Catalogna
    già fuggeria, perché non li offendesse;

The arrowing rays of gladness round me here   52
   are hiding me and hold me veiled from you,
   like the live silkworm in his silken bands.
You loved me much, and had good reason to,   55
   for had I lived there longer, I'd have shown
   not fronds of friendship, but the ripe fruit too.
The land washed on the left banks of the Rhône,°   58
   after its waves have mingled with the Sorgue,
   waited the time when I would be its lord,
With that horn of Ausonia° towned and towered   61
   at Bari, Gaeta, and Catona, down
   from where the Verde and Tronto touch the sea.
Already upon my brow there flashed the crown   64
   of the Danube-watered land of Hungary,
   after the river leaves its German shores.
And that fair triple-cornered Sicily   67
   upon the gulf the hot scirocco lashes,
   smoking not from Typhoeus' forge° but by
Its self-born sulfur belching fire and ashes,   70
   to this day would have looked to crown its kings—
   born in my line—from Rudolph and from Charles,
If evil government, which ever wrings   73
   the hearts of poor souls prone beneath its load,
   hadn't compelled Palermo to cry out,
'Die, die!'°—and had my brother paid good heed,   76
   before he paid the price he would have fled
   the miser-hearted Catalonian greed.

°*land . . . Rhône:* Provence. Charles Martel was crowned king of Hungary in 1292, and was heir to Provence, Puglia, and Sicily.

°*Ausonia:* Italy. The *horn* is the southern end of the peninsula; the *Verde* and *Tronto* empty into the Tyrrhenian and Adriatic Seas, respectively, roughly dividing Charles's kingdom of Naples from the rest of Italy.

°*Typhoeus' forge:* In mythology, the Titan Typhoeus rebelled against Jove and was thrust beneath Mount Aetna, where he and other Titans were compelled to labor at the foundry of the blacksmith god, Vulcan (cf. *Inf.* 31.124).

°*Die, die:* Charles refers to the bloody uprising in *Palermo* known as the Sicilian Vespers (1282), when the people revolted against his father, Charles II of Anjou, crying, "Death to all the French!" Charles's *brother* Robert succeeded his father.

Venus—Charles Martel

ché veramente proveder bisogna 79
   per lui, o per altrui, sì ch'a sua barca
   carcata più d'incarco non si pogna.

La sua natura, che di larga parca 82
   discese, avria mestier di tal milizia
   che non curasse di mettere in arca".

"Però ch'i' credo che l'alta letizia 85
   che 'l tuo parlar m'infonde, segnor mio,
   là 've ogne ben si termina e s'inizia,

per te si veggia come la vegg' io, 88
   grata m'è più; e anco quest' ho caro
   perché 'l discerni rimirando in Dio.

Fatto m'hai lieto, e così mi fa chiaro, 91
   poi che, parlando, a dubitar m'hai mosso
   com' esser può, di dolce seme, amaro".

Questo io a lui; ed elli a me: "S'io posso 94
   mostrarti un vero, a quel che tu dimandi
   terrai lo viso come tien lo dosso.

Lo ben che tutto il regno che tu scandi 97
   volge e contenta, fa esser virtute
   sua provedenza in questi corpi grandi.

E non pur le nature provedute 100
   sono in la mente ch'è da sé perfetta,
   ma esse insieme con la lor salute:

per che quantunque quest' arco saetta 103
   disposto cade a proveduto fine,
   sì come cosa in suo segno diretta.

Se ciò non fosse, il ciel che tu cammine 106
   producerebbe sì li suoi effetti,
   che non sarebbero arti, ma ruine;

e ciò esser non può, se li 'ntelletti 109
   che muovon queste stelle non son manchi,
   e manco il primo, che non li ha perfetti.

Vuo' tu che questo ver più ti s'imbianchi?". 112
    E io: "Non già; ché impossibil veggio
   che la natura, in quel ch'è uopo, stanchi".

Now he or someone else should look ahead   79
    and make sure his emburdened ship of state
    doesn't take on a cargo heavier yet.
He, a degenerate from a rich estate,   82
    would then need soldiers whose sole drill does not
    consist in sticking money in their chests."
"Since I believe that you see as I see   85
    (for you behold the end and source of good)
    the jubilance your words instill in me,
It brings me all the more delight, my lord!   88
    And this too is a truth that makes it dear:
    you read it by your gazing into God.
You've gladdened me, but now make one thing clear—   91
    because your speech has put me in some doubt.
    How, from sweet seed, can bitter fruit appear?"
"If I can show you but one truth about   94
    what you have asked," so did the soul respond,
    "you'll face—and see—what's now behind your back.
The Good that turns and soothes with fullest peace   97
    all of the realm you're climbing, lends these grand
    bodies° the power to form what It foresees,
Providing for the natures of mankind,   100
    with all that's fit to make them blest and whole—
    for that is also in that perfect Mind.
So all the powers this heavenly bow may shoot   103
    must fall well aimed to strike the end foreseen,
    just as a thing directed to its goal.
Were that not so, these heavens you walk would rain   106
    their influence down, producing such effects
    as would be ruin, not the work of art—
Which cannot be, unless those intellects   109
    that move the stars were lacking in some way—
    the First too, that had not perfected them.
Now shall I make this truth as bright as day?"   112
    Said I, "No need. I see that nature can-
    not flag, when fashioning what has to be."

° *these grand bodies:* the spheres.

Ond' elli ancora: "Or dì: sarebbe il peggio   115
   per l'omo in terra, se non fosse cive?".
"Sì", rispuos' io; "e qui ragion non cheggio".

"E puot' elli esser, se giù non si vive   118
   diversamente per diversi offici?
   Non, se 'l maestro vostro ben vi scrive".

Sì venne deducendo infino a quici;   121
   poscia conchiuse: "Dunque esser diverse
   convien di vostri effetti le radici:

per ch'un nasce Solone e altro Serse,   124
   altro Melchisedèch e altro quello
   che, volando per l'aere, il figlio perse.

La circular natura, ch'è suggello   127
   a la cera mortal, fa ben sua arte,
   ma non distingue l'un da l'altro ostello.

Quinci addivien ch'Esaù si diparte   130
   per seme da Iacòb; e vien Quirino
   da sì vil padre, che si rende a Marte.

Natura generata il suo cammino   133
   simil farebbe sempre a' generanti,
   se non vincesse il proveder divino.

Or quel che t'era dietro t'è davanti: 136
   ma perché sappi che di te mi giova,
   un corollario voglio che t'ammanti.

Sempre natura, se fortuna trova   139
   discorde a sé, com' ogne altra semente
   fuor di sua regïon, fa mala prova.

And he pressed on, "Would it be worse for man 115
   if he were not a citizen? Come, tell."
   "Surely it would—I need no proof of that."
"Can there be citizens unless men dwell 118
   in various ways, with various offices?
   Not if your Teacher° has advised you well."
He came by his deductions down to this, 121
   concluding, "Then they too must be diverse,
   the roots of all the leanings men possess,
So this man's born a Solon and that man 124
   a Xerxes and another the high priest
   Melchizedek, or he who lost his son°
While soaring through the air. The good seal's pressed 127
   on mortal wax, these wheels fulfill their art—
   but draw no lines dividing house and house.
That's how it is that Esau could depart 130
   from Jacob's seed, or how Quirinus° came
   from so lowborn a father they conferred
His siring on the war god. Quite the same 133
   as the begetting sire would be the son—
   but providence enjoys the victory.
What lay behind you, now you look upon, 136
   but so you'll know how you delight me, here,
   this corollary is a robe to don!
Like any seed far from its just terrain, 139
   if fortune clashes with its inborn power,
   one's nature yields a paltry crop of grain.

°*your Teacher:* Aristotle (*Politics* 1.1.2: "Man is by nature a political animal").

°*he who lost his son:* The inventor Daedalus fashioned waxen wings for himself and his son, Icarus, to escape from Crete. Icarus flew too close to the sun and drowned in the sea when his wings melted (Ovid, *Met.* 8.159–235; see also *Inf.* 17.109–11).

°*Quirinus:* Romulus, legendary founder of the city of Rome. Livy suggests that Romulus's mother, a Vestal Virgin, told her tale of being ravished by Mars in order to hide a likelier story (*Hist.* 1.3); Dante attributes the embarrassment to the citizens, inventing a legend to shore up the glory of their deceased founder.

E se 'l mondo là giù ponesse mente   142
   al fondamento che natura pone,
   seguendo lui, avria buona la gente.
Ma voi torcete a la religïone   145
   tal che fia nato a cignersi la spada,
   e fate re di tal ch'è da sermone;
onde la traccia vostra è fuor di strada".   148

If all the world down there would set their minds   142
    to follow the foundation nature brings,
    they'd have a populace that's good and strong.
But you wrench someone to religious things   145
    who has been born to strap the sheath and sword,
    and of the sermon givers you make kings.
And that is why your strides go off the road."   148

Da poi che Carlo tuo, bella Clemenza,
      m'ebbe chiarito, mi narrò li 'nganni
      che ricever dovea la sua semenza;
ma disse: "Taci e lascia muover li anni";   4
      sì ch'io non posso dir se non che pianto
      giusto verrà di retro ai vostri danni.
E già la vita di quel lume santo   7
      rivolta s'era al Sol che la rïempie
      come quel ben ch'a ogne cosa è tanto.
Ahi anime ingannate e fatture empie,   10
      che da sì fatto ben torcete i cuori,
      drizzando in vanità le vostre tempie!
Ed ecco un altro di quelli splendori   13
      ver' me si fece, e 'l suo voler piacermi
      significava nel chiarir di fori.
Li occhi di Bëatrice, ch'eran fermi   16
      sovra me, come pria, di caro assenso
      al mio disio certificato fermi.
"Deh, metti al mio voler tosto compenso,   19
      beato spirto", dissi, "e fammi prova
      ch'i' possa in te refletter quel ch'io penso!".
Onde la luce che m'era ancor nova,   22
      del suo profondo, ond' ella pria cantava,
      seguette come a cui di ben far giova:

Canto Nine

*Still in **the third sphere**, Dante speaks with **Cunizza da Romano**, who proph-esies woe for her homeland, and with the bishop and troubadour **Folquet**; he shows to Dante the brightest soul in the sphere of Venus, that of **Rahab**.*

Beautiful Clemence,° once your Charles had done
    enlightening me, he told me of your seed,
    of the deceits your children would endure,
But said, "Be silent, let the years proceed,"   4
    so I say nothing, save that they who bring
    ruin to them will justly weep indeed.
By now, the life of that illumining   7
    had faced the Sun, the source that fills it full,
    the all-sufficing Good of everything.
Impious creatures, souls so gullible   10
    you turn your temples unto vanity,
    twisting your hearts from good that cannot fail!
Then look! another splendor came to me,   13
    and that she wished to bring me pleasure was
    manifest in her welling brilliancy.
Steady above me as before, the eyes   16
    of Beatrice gave my wish their dear consent,
    once more assuring me of my desire.
"Ah, blessed spirit, make it evident—   19
    place the truth in the balance with my will—
    that you can mirror all my thought's intent."
That radiance still unknown and new to me,   22
    out of the depths from whence she sang, replied
    as one rejoicing in her charity,

°*Clemence:* Either Charles Martel's wife or his daughter.

"In quella parte de la terra prava   25
  italica che siede tra Rïalto
  e le fontane di Brenta e di Piava,
si leva un colle, e non surge molt' alto,   28
  là onde scese già una facella
  che fece a la contrada un grande assalto.
D'una radice nacqui e io ed ella: 31
  Cunizza fui chiamata, e qui refulgo
  perché mi vinse il lume d'esta stella;
ma lietamente a me medesma indulgo   34
  la cagion di mia sorte, e non mi noia;
  che parria forse forte al vostro vulgo.
Di questa luculenta e cara gioia   37
  del nostro cielo che più m'è propinqua,
  grande fama rimase; e pria che moia,
questo centesimo anno ancor s'incinqua: 40
  vedi se far si dee l'omo eccellente,
  sì ch'altra vita la prima relinqua.
E ciò non pensa la turba presente   43
  che Tagliamento e Adice richiude,
  né per esser battuta ancor si pente;
ma tosto fia che Padova al palude   46
  cangerà l'acqua che Vincenza bagna,
  per essere al dover le genti crude;
e dove Sile e Cagnan s'accompagna,   49
  tal signoreggia e va con la testa alta,
  che già per lui carpir si fa la ragna.
Piangerà Feltro ancora la difalta   52
  de l'empio suo pastor, che sarà sconcia
  sì, che per simil non s'entrò in malta.

"Sitting between Rialto° by the tide   25
　　and where the Brenta and the Piave spring,
　　in just that part of crooked Italy,
A hill arises to no special height,   28
　　but from its top a burning brand° swept down
　　and wrought destruction on the countryside.
From the same root this torch and I were born.   31
　　Cunizza was my name, and here I glow
　　because on earth this starlight conquered me;
But I am glad my fate has placed me so.   34
　　I pardon my old sin; though that might well
　　seem hard to fathom for your herd below.
Nearest me gleams a jewel steeped in light,   37
　　a precious gem to glitter in our sky,
　　who left great fame that will not die before
They multiply the century by five.   40
　　See how a man should strive for excellence,
　　that life may leave a legacy alive!
But they don't think of that, that rabble penned   43
　　between the Adige and the Tagliament.
　　Not though the hand of Heaven has battered them
Will duty-shrugging Padua repent,   46
　　but soon they'll turn Vicenza's marshes red
　　with their own blood for being insolent,
And where the Sile and Cagnan share one bed°   49
　　somebody lords it now with head cocked high,
　　a rat for whom they're stitching nets to spread.
Feltro° will weep yet for the treachery   52
　　its ruthless shepherd stooped to: sin so great,
　　no cleric's in the clink for such a crime.

°*Rialto:* largest island of Venice. Cunizza is mapping out the March of Treviso, bounded by
the Alps to the north and by the republic of Venice to the south and east.

°*a burning brand:* Cunizza's brother Ezzelino III, whose fortress stood on the top of Mount
Romano; see notes.

°*where the Sile and Cagnan share one bed:* at Treviso, where the rivers remain distinguishable
after their confluence. Cunizza alludes to Rizzardo da Camino, tyrant of Treviso, hated by no-
bility and commons, and assassinated.

°*Feltro:* The bishop of Feltro treacherously handed over three exiled *Ferrarese* to the custody
of the papal (and Angevin) legate in Ferrara, where the men were decapitated.

Troppo sarebbe larga la bigoncia   55
    che ricevesse il sangue ferrarese,
    e stanco chi 'l pesasse a oncia a oncia,
che donerà questo prete cortese   58
    per mostrarsi di parte; e cotai doni
    conformi fieno al viver del paese.
Sù sono specchi, voi dicete Troni,   61
    onde refulge a noi Dio giudicante;
    sì che questi parlar ne paion buoni".
Qui si tacette; e fecemi sembiante   64
    che fosse ad altro volta, per la rota
    in che si mise com' era davante.
L'altra letizia, che m'era già nota   67
    per cara cosa, mi si fece in vista
    qual fin balasso in che lo sol percuota.
Per letiziar là sù fulgor s'acquista,   70
    sì come riso qui; ma giù s'abbuia
    l'ombra di fuor, come la mente è trista.
"Dio vede tutto, e tuo veder s'inluia",   73
    diss' io, "beato spirto, sì che nulla
    voglia di sé a te puot' esser fuia.
Dunque la voce tua, che 'l ciel trastulla   76
    sempre col canto di quei fuochi pii
    che di sei ali facen la coculla,
perché non satisface a' miei disii?   79
    Già non attendere' io tua dimanda,
    s'io m'intuassi, come tu t'inmii".
"La maggior valle in che l'acqua si spanda",   82
    incominciaro allor le sue parole,
    "fuor di quel mar che la terra inghirlanda,
tra ' discordanti liti contra 'l sole   85
    tanto sen va, che fa meridïano
    là dove l'orizzonte pria far suole.

You'd have to cart quite a large vineyard crate   55
    to catch the blood of the three Ferrarese—
    a weary job, to weigh it ounce by ounce!
Which this priest donates to their enemies,   58
    showing his party by his generous love—
    that land's fine customs make for gifts like these.
Mirrors there are, what you call Thrones,° above—   61
    flashing upon us the reflected light
    of God the Judge; and that is why to speak
Of such affairs, and in such words, seems right."   64
    Here she fell silent, showing she had turned
    elsewhere, reentering the dancing wheel.
That other gladness she'd made known to me   67
    as rare and dear approached us, like the sight
    of a fine ruby glimmering in the sun.
By gladness there the spirits glean more light—   70
    like laughter here—but all the countenance dims
    in shades below, when gloom has touched the mind.
"God sees all, and your vision so in-Hims,   73
    O blessed soul," said I, "no will of man
    can fly or be concealed from what you see.
Then why do you by whom this heaven rings   76
    in merry concord with those pious flames
    who weave their silken cowls with their six wings,
Not raise your voice and satisfy my wish?   79
    I wouldn't wait for you to speak your will,
    if I could so in-you as you in-me."
"The broadest valley° that your rivers fill,"   82
    for in this fashion had his words begun,
    "besides the Ocean garlanding the world,
Eastward extends so far against the sun,   85
    washing its way between discordant shores,
    it's dawn at one end, at the other, noon.

° *Thrones:* third of the nine angelic orders. The Thrones execute the just decrees of God.
° *broadest valley:* the basin of the Mediterranean, the largest known body of water except the Atlantic, the *Ocean* that was thought to circle the world.

Di quella valle fu' io litorano   88
    tra Ebro e Macra, che per cammin corto
    parte lo Genovese dal Toscano.
Ad un occaso quasi e ad un orto   91
    Buggea siede e la terra ond' io fui,
    che fé del sangue suo già caldo il porto.
Folco mi disse quella gente a cui   94
    fu noto il nome mio; e questo cielo
    di me s'imprenta, com' io fe' di lui;
ché più non arse la figlia di Belo,   97
    noiando e a Sicheo e a Creusa,
    di me, infin che si convenne al pelo;
né quella Rodopëa che delusa   100
    fu da Demofoonte, né Alcide
    quando Iole nel core ebbe rinchiusa.
Non però qui si pente, ma si ride,   103
    non de la colpa, ch'a mente non torna,
    ma del valor ch'ordinò e provide.
Qui si rimira ne l'arte ch'addorna   106
    cotanto affetto, e discernesi 'l bene
    per che 'l mondo di sù quel di giù torna.
Ma perché tutte le tue voglie piene   109
    ten porti che son nate in questa spera,
    procedere ancor oltre mi convene.
Tu vuo' saper chi è in questa lumera   112
    che qui appresso me così scintilla
    come raggio di sole in acqua mera.
Or sappi che là entro si tranquilla   115
    Raab; e a nostr' ordine congiunta,
    di lei nel sommo grado si sigilla.

Between the Ebro and Magra,° whose short course   88
    divides the Tuscan from the Genovese,
      I was a dweller on that valley's coast.
Near to one line of sunset and sunrise   91
    sit Bougiah and the city whence I came,
      whose harbor once steamed hot with its own blood.
The people in that land who knew my name   94
    called me Folquet, and now upon this sphere
      I stamp my seal, as once it did the same
On me: for Dido never burned so hot,   97
    paining Sychaeus and Creusa both
      by her offense, as I burned till my pate
Peeked through the strands, nor she of Rhodope   100
    gulled by Demophoön, nor Hercules
      when he first clasped Iole to his heart.
Yet we don't feel remorse, we smile at ease—   103
    not for the sin we have no memory of,
      but for the power that orders and foresees.
We gaze on the adorning art of love,   106
    the good that makes creation beautiful,
      that turns the world below by world above.
But that you'll leave fulfilled in every will   109
    risen in you to know about this sphere,
      I must go on a little longer still.
You'd like to know who shines beside me here   112
    as scintillating in her lamping fire
      as rays of sunlight when the lake is clear.
Know that within it Rahab finds her peace.   115
    The highest of our saints, she seals her light
      on every rank of spirits in our choir.

°*between the Ebro and Magra:* The Ebro empties into the sea on the northeastern coast of Spain; the Magra (the boundary between Tuscany and Liguria, the region surrounding Genoa), on the northwestern coast of Italy. Between lies Marseilles, on roughly the same line of longitude as *Bougiah,* a port in Algeria.

Da questo cielo, in cui l'ombra s'appunta 118
    che 'l vostro mondo face, pria ch'altr' alma
    del trïunfo di Cristo fu assunta.
Ben si convenne lei lasciar per palma 121
    in alcun cielo de l'alta vittoria
    che s'acquistò con l'una e l'altra palma,
perch' ella favorò la prima gloria 124
    di Iosüè in su la Terra Santa,
    che poco tocca al papa la memoria.
La tua città, che di colui è pianta 127
    che pria volse le spalle al suo fattore
    e di cui è la 'nvidia tanto pianta,
produce e spande il maladetto fiore 130
    c'ha disvïate le pecore e li agni,
    però che fatto ha lupo del pastore.
Per questo l'Evangelio e i dottor magni 133
    son derelitti, e solo ai Decretali
    si studia, sì che pare a' lor vivagni.
A questo intende il papa e ' cardinali; 136
    non vanno i lor pensieri a Nazarette,
    là dove Gabrïello aperse l'ali.
Ma Vaticano e l'altre parti elette 139
    di Roma che son state cimitero
    a la milizia che Pietro seguette,
tosto libere fien de l'avoltero". 142

To here, where earth's shade funnels to a point,°   118
    she was assumed in Christ's triumphal ride,
    the first of all the souls. It was but right
To grant to her in one of Heaven's rings   121
    the palm of the exalted victory
    gained by the palms when He was crucified,
Since she gave gracious aid to the first glory   124
    achieved by Joshua in the Holy Land—
    that hardly stirs the pontiff's memory.
Your city, planted by the prideful hand   127
    of him° who snubbed his Maker with his shoulder,
    whose envy in the beginning wrought such tears,
Begot and sowed broadside the cursed flower,°   130
    leading the sheep and lambs to go astray
    after it turned their shepherd into a wolf.
To gain those flowers the gospel's flung away,   133
    the Doctors too. Canon law fires their zeal,
    they gloss well-thumbed *Decretals* all the day.
Those grip the minds of pope and cardinal;   136
    their thoughts don't journey forth where Nazareth
    beheld the opened wings of Gabriel.
But Vatican and all the hills of Rome,   139
    where Peter's soldiers were ordained to die,
    the graveyard for their holy martyrdom,
Will soon be free of the adultery."   142

°*earth's shade funnels to a point:* It was thought that the conical shadow of the earth terminated at the sphere of Venus.

°*him:* Satan.

°*the cursed Flower:* the florin, the coin of Florence.

Guardando nel suo Figlio con l'Amore
   che l'uno e l'altro etternalmente spira,
   lo primo e ineffabile Valore
quanto per mente e per loco si gira   4
   con tant' ordine fé, ch'esser non puote
   sanza gustar di lui chi ciò rimira.
Leva dunque, lettore, a l'alte rote   7
   meco la vista, dritto a quella parte
   dove l'un moto e l'altro si percuote;
e lì comincia a vagheggiar ne l'arte   10
   di quel maestro che dentro a sé l'ama,
   tanto che mai da lei l'occhio non parte.
Vedi come da indi si dirama   13
   l'oblico cerchio che i pianeti porta,
   per sodisfare al mondo che li chiama.
Che se la strada lor non fosse torta,   16
   molta virtù nel ciel sarebbe in vano,
   e quasi ogne potenza qua giù morta;
e se dal dritto più o men lontano   19
   fosse 'l partire, assai sarebbe manco
   e giù e sù de l'ordine mondano.

CANTO TEN

*Dante and Beatrice have risen to **the fourth circle, the sun,** the dwelling of **the wise.** Dante is addressed by **Thomas Aquinas,** who names for him the eleven other spirits in the heavenly garland.*

That inexpressible and primal Power,
    looking on his begotten Son with Love
    they breathe eternally, created all
That turns through mind or place in Heaven above   4
    with an order so sweet, no one can gaze
    upon the world without a taste of Him.
Unto those lofty wheels, then, Reader, raise   7
    your eyes with me, direct them to that part
    where two celestial circles° cross and pass,
And fall enamored of that Master's art   10
    whose gaze will never part from what He's made,
    so deeply does He love it in His heart.
See how the ring that sweeps the planets round   13
    tilts as it shoots from there, to satisfy
    the world that calls upon their influence:
For had their highway not been pitched awry   16
    it would have quelled the power of many a star
    and rendered almost every potency
Dead here below; but to come just too near   19
    or veer a little further from the level
    would rob the order of each hemisphere.

°*two celestial circles:* the path of the sun and the other planets (the ecliptic) and the celestial equator, at 23.5 degrees declination. Dante asserts below that the angle is pitched perfectly for the actualization of various starry influences and for the habitability of both earth's hemispheres.

Or ti riman, lettor, sovra 'l tuo banco,   22
    dietro pensando a ciò che si preliba,
    s'esser vuoi lieto assai prima che stanco.
Messo t'ho innanzi: omai per te ti ciba;   25
    ché a sé torce tutta la mia cura
    quella materia ond' io son fatto scriba.
Lo ministro maggior de la natura,   28
    che del valor del ciel lo mondo imprenta
    e col suo lume il tempo ne misura,
con quella parte che sù si rammenta   31
    congiunto, si girava per le spire
    in che più tosto ognora s'appresenta;
e io era con lui; ma del salire   34
    non m'accors' io, se non com' uom s'accorge,
    anzi 'l primo pensier, del suo venire.
È Bëatrice quella che sì scorge   37
    di bene in meglio, sì subitamente
    che l'atto suo per tempo non si sporge.
Quant' esser convenia da sé lucente   40
    quel ch'era dentro al sol dov' io entra'mi,
    non per color, ma per lume parvente!
Perch' io lo 'ngegno e l'arte e l'uso chiami,   43
    sì nol direi che mai s'imaginasse;
    ma creder puossi e di veder si brami.
E se le fantasie nostre son basse   46
    a tanta altezza, non è maraviglia;
    ché sopra 'l sol non fu occhio ch'andasse.
Tal era quivi la quarta famiglia   49
    de l'alto Padre, che sempre la sazia,
    mostrando come spira e come figlia.
E Bëatrice cominciò: "Ringrazia,   52
    ringrazia il Sol de li angeli, ch'a questo
    sensibil t'ha levato per sua grazia".

Stay at your bench now, Reader, stay and dwell   22
    on these small hints that whet the appetite,
    and taste elation long before you tire!
I've set the table; take you now and eat;   25
    for now the matter calls on all my care,
    turning my mind to the command, to write
What I have seen. The noblest minister   28
    of Nature,° he whose light divides the day,
    who most imprints the world with heavenly power,
Touching those crossing circles in the sky,   31
    turned in the spirals of his summertime
    of ever earlier rising; there was I
Turning with him, but did not feel the climb,   34
    unless I noticed it as someone feels
    thought on the instant, when the thought has come.
For it is Beatrice who so reveals   37
    the good and better, with such sudden flight,
    her act has no extent in time. The souls
Within that sun I entered, ah how bright!   40
    For not by color were they visible,
    but by their own intensity of light.
On wit and use and art I'll call and still   43
    never find words for you to picture it.
    Believe, and thirst to see it for yourselves.
And if our fancy cannot touch such height,   46
    no wonder: for the eye has never known
    splendor on earth surpassing the sun's light.
So the fourth family of the Father shone,   49
    who fills their hunger ever, revealing how
    He breathes His Spirit and begets His Son.
And Beatrice began, "Give thanks, give thanks   52
    to the Sun of the angels, Him whose grace
    has raised you to this sun that men can see."

°*noblest minister / of Nature:* the sun, now past the spring equinox.

Cor di mortal non fu mai sì digesto   55
    a divozione e a rendersi a Dio
    con tutto 'l suo gradir cotanto presto,
come a quelle parole mi fec' io;   58
    e sì tutto 'l mio amore in lui si mise,
    che Bëatrice eclissò ne l'oblio.
Non le dispiacque, ma sì se ne rise,   61
    che lo splendor de li occhi suoi ridenti
    mia mente unita in più cose divise.
Io vidi più folgór vivi e vincenti   64
    far di noi centro e di sé far corona,
    più dolci in voce che in vista lucenti:
così cinger la figlia di Latona   67
    vedem talvolta, quando l'aere è pregno,
    sì che ritenga il fil che fa la zona.
Ne la corte del cielo, ond' io rivegno,   70
    si trovan molte gioie care e belle
    tanto che non si posson trar del regno;
e 'l canto di quei lumi era di quelle;   73
    chi non s'impenna sì che là sù voli,
    dal muto aspetti quindi le novelle.
Poi, sì cantando, quelli ardenti soli   76
    si fuor girati intorno a noi tre volte,
    come stelle vicine a' fermi poli,
donne mi parver, non da ballo sciolte,   79
    ma che s'arrestin tacite, ascoltando
    fin che le nove note hanno ricolte.
E dentro a l'un senti' cominciar: "Quando   82
    lo raggio de la grazia, onde s'accende
    verace amore e che poi cresce amando,
multiplicato in te tanto resplende,   85
    che ti conduce su per quella scala
    u' sanza risalir nessun discende;

Mortal heart never fed on any food   55
    that made it readier to sing the Lord's
    praises, and give itself in gratitude,
Than I was when I heard my Lady's words: 58
    I gave my love to Him so utterly,
    Beatrice was forgotten in eclipse.
She wasn't displeased—rather so smiled at me   61
    that the resplendence of her laughing eyes
    clove my mind, drawing it from unity.°
For I saw flames of overwhelming life   64
    wreathing us round to form a flashing crown,
    sweeter in song than radiant to the sight:
As when the evening air is filled with mist,   67
    we sometimes see Latona's daughter° weave
    her moonlight for a sash about her waist.
In Heaven's court, whence I have come again,   70
    shine many gems so beautiful and rare,
    laden with them the memory cannot leave:
Such was the hymning of the brilliant there.   73
    To fly to them, fashion yourself a wing—
    or wait for tidings from the deaf and dumb!
Those ardent suns that had not ceased to sing,   76
    as stars revolving round the pole nearby,
    revolved about us three times in a ring,
Then stopped: as ladies pausing in their glee   79
    hold the reel's places and resume the dance
    when they catch the returning melody.
Began one dancer: "When the radiance   82
    of the Lord's grace, which lights the flames of true
    love and by love still grows in eminence,
With such multiplication shines in you   85
    it leads you up these stairs no man may take
    descending, without climbing up anew,

°*drawing it from unity:* Dante now notices a plurality of beings in and through whom the unitary wisdom of God works.

°*Latona's daughter:* Diana, goddess of the moon.

qual ti negasse il vin de la sua fiala   88
    per la tua sete, in libertà non fora
    se non com' acqua ch'al mar non si cala.
Tu vuo' saper di quai piante s'infiora   91
    questa ghirlanda che 'ntorno vagheggia
    la bella donna ch'al ciel t'avvalora.
Io fui de li agni de la santa greggia   94
    che Domenico mena per cammino
    u' ben s'impingua se non si vaneggia.
Questi che m'è a destra più vicino,   97
    frate e maestro fummi, ed esso Alberto
    è di Cologna, e io Thomas d'Aquino.
Se sì di tutti li altri esser vuo' certo,   100
    di retro al mio parlar ten vien col viso
    girando su per lo beato serto.
Quell' altro fiammeggiare esce del riso   103
    di Grazïan, che l'uno e l'altro foro
    aiutò sì che piace in paradiso.
L'altro ch'appresso addorna il nostro coro,   106
    quel Pietro fu che con la poverella
    offerse a Santa Chiesa suo tesoro.
La quinta luce, ch'è tra noi più bella,   109
    spira di tale amor, che tutto 'l mondo
    là giù ne gola di saper novella:
entro v'è l'alta mente u' sì profondo   112
    saver fu messo, che, se 'l vero è vero,
    a veder tanto non surse il secondo.
Appresso vedi il lume di quel cero   115
    che giù in carne più a dentro vide
    l'angelica natura e 'l ministero.

He who'd deny his flask of wine to slake   88
    your thirst would not be free, would have such power
    as rivers not returning to the sea!

You long to know who are the plants that flower,   91
    engarlanding your lady with our love,
    the lovely one who strengthens you for Heaven.

I was a lamb among the holy flock   94
    Dominic leads to pasture by his rule,
    where you can fatten well, if you don't rove.

My brother and my master was the soul   97
    nearest my right, great Albert of Cologne,
    and Thomas of Aquino was my name.

If you wish to be sure of everyone,   100
    follow my words, follow them with your eyes,
    turning them round about this blessed crown.

This the third flaming rises from the smile   103
    of Gratian, he who lent both realms of law°
    assistance that delighted Paradise.

The other near him who adorns our choir   106
    was Peter,° he who gave his widow's mite,
    his simple treasure, to the Holy Church.

Most beautiful among us, the fifth light°   109
    breathes with such love that all the world below
    is gluttonous to hear of him: within

That radiance is the high mind blessed to know   112
    to such great depths, no second ever rose
    who saw so much, if what is true is true.

See where the candle there beyond him glows: 115
    he° in the flesh most deeply peered into
    angelic being and its ministries.

   °*both realms of law:* probably the civil and the ecclesiastical.

   °*Peter:* Peter Lombard (1090?–1160), Victorine monk, author of the *Sentences,* a collection of
and commentary upon opinions of the Church Fathers on points of theology.

   °*the fifth light:* Solomon, who prayed to God for wisdom (1 Kings 3:9).

   °*he:* Dionysius, named the Areopagite (converted by Saint Paul in Athens, when he preached
on the Areopagus; cf. Acts 17:34). Dante refers to the *Celestial Hierarchy,* a work of angelology in-
correctly attributed to Dionysius; cf. 28.130–39 and note.

Ne l'altra piccioletta luce ride   118
    quello avvocato de' tempi cristiani
    del cui latino Augustin si provide.
Or se tu l'occhio de la mente trani   121
    di luce in luce dietro a le mie lode,
    già de l'ottava con sete rimani.
Per vedere ogne ben dentro vi gode   124
    l'anima santa che 'l mondo fallace
    fa manifesto a chi di lei ben ode.
Lo corpo ond' ella fu cacciata giace   127
    giuso in Cieldauro; ed essa da martiro
    e da essilio venne a questa pace.
Vedi oltre fiammeggiar l'ardente spiro   130
    d'Isidoro, di Beda e di Riccardo,
    che a considerar fu più che viro.
Questi onde a me ritorna il tuo riguardo,   133
    è 'l lume d'uno spirto che 'n pensieri
    gravi a morir li parve venir tardo:
essa è la luce etterna di Sigieri,   136
    che, leggendo nel Vico de li Strami,
    silogizzò invidïosi veri".
Indi, come orologio che ne chiami   139
    ne l'ora che la sposa di Dio surge
    a mattinar lo sposo perché l'ami,

The following lantern glimmers with the joy 118
  of that defender° of the Christian days
  who helped Augustine by his history.

Now if your mind will follow upon my praise, 121
  your eyes proceeding on from light to light,
  you'll thirst to know about the eighth.° Because

He saw all that was good, now in delight 124
  shimmers that spirit who made manifest
  how the world cheats—to all who hear him right.

The flesh whence he was driven lies at rest 127
  in the crypts of Ciel d'Oro; but he came
  from martyrdom and exile to this peace.

Beyond him see the ardent souls, the flame 130
  of Isidore, of Bede, of Richard,° he
  who was, in contemplation, more than man.

This one, at whom your sight comes round to me, 133
  is the gleam of a soul who came to bear
  thoughts that so burdened him, death seemed too slow:

He is the light eternal of Siger, 136
  who when he lectured in the Street of Straw,
  syllogized truths that made him hated there."°

Then like a tower clock that tolls the hour 139
  when the bride of the Lord rises to sing
  morningsong to her Spouse, to win His love,

°*that defender:* Paulus Orosius, who wrote a history of the world at the request of Saint Augustine, to show forth Augustine's thesis of the everlasting strife between the City of God and the city of man.

°*the eighth:* Boethius (480–526). Framed by his political enemies, imprisoned and awaiting execution for a crime he did not commit, Boethius wrote *Consolation of Philosophy.* His bones rest in Pavia, in the Church of San Pietro in *Ciel d'Oro.*

°*Isidore . . . Bede . . . Richard:* Isidore of Seville, the Venerable Bede, and Richard of Saint Victor; see notes.

°*syllogized . . . there:* Siger's orthodoxy was questioned when he lectured at the University of Paris; see notes.

che l'una parte e l'altra tira e urge,   142
   tin tin sonando con sì dolce nota,
   che 'l ben disposto spirto d'amor turge;
così vid' ïo la gloriosa rota   145
   muoversi e render voce a voce in tempra
   e in dolcezza ch'esser non pò nota
se non colà dove gioir s'insempra.   148

Sounding so sweet a knelling of ting ting 142
    as all the gears within it push and pull,
    a soul that's well disposed must hear the ring
And swell with love: so now I saw that wheel 145
    rendering voice to voice in harmony,
    and in sweet temper that no man can feel
If not where joy is for eternity. 148

O insensata cura de' mortali,
    quanto son difettivi silogismi
    quei che ti fanno in basso batter l'ali!
Chi dietro a *iura* e chi ad amforismi   4
    sen giva, e chi seguendo sacerdozio,
    e chi regnar per forza o per sofismi,
e chi rubare e chi civil negozio,   7
    chi nel diletto de la carne involto
    s'affaticava e chi si dava a l'ozio,
quando, da tutte queste cose sciolto,   10
    con Bëatrice m'era suso in cielo
    cotanto glorïosamente accolto.
Poi che ciascuno fu tornato ne lo   13
    punto del cerchio in che avanti s'era,
    fermossi, come a candellier candelo.
E io senti' dentro a quella lumera   16
    che pria m'avea parlato, sorridendo
    incominciar, faccendosi più mera:
"Così com' io del suo raggio resplendo,   19
    sì, riguardando ne la luce etterna,
    li tuoi pensieri onde cagioni apprendo.
Tu dubbi, e hai voler che si ricerna   22
    in sì aperta e 'n sì distesa lingua
    lo dicer mio, ch'al tuo sentir si sterna,

CANTO ELEVEN

Thomas Aquinas recounts for Dante the life of Francis of Assisi, and concludes by decrying the corruption of the Dominicans of the present day.

O senseless strife of mortals! How unsound
    are all the syllogisms that make you flap
    your wings against the earth! One runs his round
For lawyering and one for medicine,   4
    one chases down a priestly benefice,
    and one, to reign by force or quibbling trap;
That man's a robber, and a councillor this;   7
    one struggles in the tangled luxury
    of flesh, one gives himself to lazy ease,
While I from all these things at last set free   10
    was there with Beatrice in Heaven above,
    welcomed and gathered in so gloriously.
And when the souls had rounded all the ring,   13
    like candles set within a chandelier
    they halted in their first positioning,
And from within his lamplight I could hear   16
    the soul who spoke to me before° now say,
    with smiles that made his voice more pure and clear,
"As I reflect the splendor of His ray,   19
    gazing into the everlasting light,
    I recognize your thoughts, and whence they rise.
You waver—you would have me set things right, 22
    in words so plain and understandable
    they will submit with ease before your sight—

°*the soul who spoke to me before:* Saint Thomas Aquinas.

ove dinanzi dissi: 'U' ben s'impingua',   25
    e là u' dissi: 'Non nacque il secondo';
    e qui è uopo che ben si distingua.
La provedenza, che governa il mondo   28
    con quel consiglio nel quale ogne aspetto
    creato è vinto pria che vada al fondo,
però che andasse ver' lo suo diletto   31
    la sposa di colui ch'ad alte grida
    disposò lei col sangue benedetto,
in sé sicura e anche a lui più fida,   34
    due principi ordinò in suo favore,
    che quinci e quindi le fosser per guida.
L'un fu tutto serafico in ardore;   37
    l'altro per sapïenza in terra fue
    di cherubica luce uno splendore.
De l'un dirò, però che d'amendue   40
    si dice l'un pregiando, qual ch'om prende,
    perch' ad un fine fur l'opere sue.
Intra Tupino e l'acqua che discende   43
    del colle eletto dal beato Ubaldo,
    fertile costa d'alto monte pende,
onde Perugia sente freddo e caldo   46
    da Porta Sole; e di rietro le piange
    per grave giogo Nocera con Gualdo.
Di questa costa, là dov' ella frange   49
    più sua rattezza, nacque al mondo un sole,
    come fa questo talvolta di Gange.
Però chi d'esso loco fa parole,   52
    non dica Ascesi, ché direbbe corto,
    ma Orïente, se proprio dir vuole.

About my saying, 'Where you fatten well,'°   25
    and where I said, 'No second ever rose,'
    and here we need to make distinctions tell.

That providence which steers the universe   28
    with such a plan that all created sight
    is overcome before it plumbs the depths,

To lead unto her Love and her delight   31
    the Spouse° of Him who took her as His Bride
    when with a cry He shed His blessed blood,

Raised up two princes° in His grace, to guide   34
    her confidence and make her true to Him,
    firming her faithfulness on either side.

One felt the fire love of the seraphim;   37
    the other, for his wisdom on the earth,
    was one in splendor with the cherubim.

Of one I'll speak, and yet he speaks of both—   40
    because their works were aimed at the same ends—
    who showers either man with praise. Between

Tupino° and the river that descends   43
    from the hill chosen by the blest Ubaldo,
    a rich slope eases from the peak, and lends

Perugia warmth and shade by the Sun Gate,   46
    but to the west the looming summit makes
    for harsh distress in Nocera and Gualdo.

On the side where the slope more gently breaks,   49
    into the world was born another sun,
    as at times this sun's born in the Ganges;

So, speaking of his birthplace, let no one   52
    call it *Ascesi*—far too short a name—
    but *Oriente*, Rising in the Dawn.

° *Where you fatten well:* See 10.96 above; for *No second ever rose,* see 10.113.
° *Spouse:* the Church, Bride of Christ (cf. Eph. 5:22–23).
° *two princes:* Saint Francis (who *felt the fire love of the seraphim*) and Saint Dominic, founders of the two great orders of mendicant friars.
° *Tupino:* Thomas describes the location of Assisi, between the valleys of the Tupino and the Chiascio, the river that falls from the mountain where Saint *Ubaldo,* later bishop of nearby Gubbio, built his hermitage. The *rich slope* is Mount Subasio, overshadowing *Perugia.* Since the winds carrying moisture blow from west to east, the towns of *Nocera* Umbra and *Gualdo* Tadino, lying on the wrong side, suffer for it.

Non era ancor molto lontan da l'orto,   55
  ch'el cominciò a far sentir la terra
  de la sua gran virtute alcun conforto;
ché per tal donna, giovinetto, in guerra   58
  del padre corse, a cui, come a la morte,
  la porta del piacer nessun diserra;
e dinanzi a la sua spirital corte   61
  et coram patre le si fece unito;
  poscia di dì in dì l'amò più forte.
Questa, privata del primo marito,   64
  millecent' anni e più dispetta e scura
  fino a costui si stette sanza invito;
né valse udir che la trovò sicura   67
  con Amiclate, al suon de la sua voce,
  colui ch'a tutto 'l mondo fé paura;
né valse esser costante né feroce,   70
  sì che, dove Maria rimase giuso,
  ella con Cristo pianse in su la croce.
Ma perch' io non proceda troppo chiuso,   73
  Francesco e Povertà per questi amanti
  prendi oramai nel mio parlar diffuso.
La lor concordia e i lor lieti sembianti,   76
  amore e maraviglia e dolce sguardo
  facieno esser cagion di pensier santi;
tanto che 'l venerabile Bernardo   79
  si scalzò prima, e dietro a tanta pace
  corse e, correndo, li parve esser tardo.
Oh ignota ricchezza! oh ben ferace!   82
  Scalzasi Egidio, scalzasi Silvestro
  dietro a lo sposo, sì la sposa piace.
Indi sen va quel padre e quel maestro   85
  con la sua donna e con quella famiglia
  che già legava l'umile capestro.

Not long after his dawning then he came   55
    to let the earth begin to feel his power,
    the comfort of his manhood. Still a lad,

Against his father he swept off to war   58
    to win his lady love: and such was she,
    no one for her unfastens pleasure's door,

As not for death. He made her one with him   61
    before his father and the spiritual court,
    and with each passing day he loved her more.

Widowed of the first Spouse who took her hand,   64
    until he came, a thousand years and more
    she stood uncalled, ignored, despised, and banned—

Of no worth, that men found her faith secure   67
    in Amyclas' poor dwelling, at the voice°
    that set the whole world trembling in its fear;

Of none, that she was constant and so fierce   70
    that when his mother Mary stood below,
    she alone wept with Christ upon the Cross.

My words have walked at length, and darkly so: 73
    Francis it was and Lady Poverty,
    they are the lovers I have drawn for you.

Their happy countenances, their harmony,   76
    the love, the wonder, and each tender look
    instilled, in others, thoughts of sanctity,

So that the venerable Bernard° took   79
    his shoes off—he the first, and for such peace
    ran, and in running seemed to come too slow.

O unknown riches! Field of such increase!   82
    Egidio and Silvestro doff their shoes
    behind the bridegroom, so the bride did please!

And from that place the lord and father goes   85
    beside his lady and that family
    harnessed already by the humble cord.°

°*the voice:* that of Julius Caesar. Being so poor, the fisherman *Amyclas* had nothing to fear from Caesar or his soldiers (Lucan, *Pharsalia* 5.519ff.).

    °*Bernard:* first disciple of Saint Francis, followed soon by *Egidio* and *Silvestro;* see notes.

    °*the humble cord:* the rope belt the Franciscans used to bind their simple tunics. Dante, a third order (lay) Franciscan, may have worn one (cf. *Inf.* 16.106).

Né li gravò viltà di cuor le ciglia   88
   per esser fi' di Pietro Bernardone,
   né per parer dispetto a maraviglia;
ma regalmente sua dura intenzione   91
   ad Innocenzio aperse, e da lui ebbe
   primo sigillo a sua religïone.
Poi che la gente poverella crebbe   94
   dietro a costui, la cui mirabil vita
   meglio in gloria del ciel si canterebbe,
di seconda corona redimita   97
   fu per Onorio da l'Etterno Spiro
   la santa voglia d'esto archimandrita.
E poi che, per la sete del martiro,   100
   ne la presenza del Soldan superba
   predicò Cristo e li altri che 'l seguiro,
e per trovare a conversione acerba   103
   troppo la gente e per non stare indarno,
   redissi al frutto de l'italica erba,
nel crudo sasso intra Tevero e Arno   106
   da Cristo prese l'ultimo sigillo,
   che le sue membra due anni portarno.
Quando a colui ch'a tanto ben sortillo   109
   piacque di trarlo suso a la mercede
   ch'el meritò nel suo farsi pusillo,
a' frati suoi, sì com' a giuste rede,   112
   raccomandò la donna sua piu cara,
   e comandò che l'amassero a fede;
e del suo grembo l'anima preclara   115
   mover si volle, tornando al suo regno,
   e al suo corpo non volle altra bara.
Pensa oramai qual fu colui che degno   118
   collega fu a mantener la barca
   di Pietro in alto mar per dritto segno;

No cowardice bowed his eye for being born 88
    the merchant son of Pietro Bernardone,
      nor his appearance rousing wondrous scorn,
But like a princely champion he spoke 91
    his stern intentions to Pope Innocent,
      and from him took his rule's initial seal.
And when his band of little poor men grew, 94
    following him whose life of miracle
      were better sung of to the glory of Heaven,
A second laurel crowned the holy will 97
    of this chief shepherd, for the Eternal Breath°
      inspired Honorius to confirm his rule.
And later, thirsting for a martyr's death, 100
    in presence of the Sultan high and proud,
      he preached of Christ and of His followers,
But when he'd found that nation was too crude 103
    for true conversion, not to stay in vain
      he turned to tend the Italian garden's fruit,
And on the naked rock that looms between 106
    Tiber and Arno took his final seal°
      from Christ, and two years bore it on his flesh.
When it pleased Him who chose him for such good 109
    to draw him heavenward for the legacy
      he merited in making himself small,
Unto his brothers as his lawful heirs 112
    he gave the lady whom he held most dear,
      that they might love her in fidelity.
Then from that lady's lap this soul so clear 115
    wished to depart, returning to its realm,
      and for its bones would have no other bier.
Think what a worthy man he must have been 118
    to be his comrade, and maintain the Bark
      of Peter° on the deep, with a true helm—

°*the Eternal Breath:* the Holy Spirit.
°*his final seal:* the stigmata, which he received on Mount La Verna, when he had retreated there to his tiny cell; see notes.
°*the Bark / of Peter:* the Church.

e questo fu il nostro patrïarca;   121
    per che qual segue lui, com' el comanda,
    discerner puoi che buone merce carca.
Ma 'l suo peculio di nova vivanda   124
    è fatto ghiotto, sì ch'esser non puote
    che per diversi salti non si spanda;
e quanto le sue pecore remote   127
    e vagabunde più da esso vanno,
    più tornano a l'ovil di latte vòte.
Ben son di quelle che temono 'l danno   130
    e stringonsi al pastor; ma son sì poche,
    che le cappe fornisce poco panno.
Or, se le mie parole non son fioche,   133
    se la tua audïenza è stata attenta,
    se ciò ch'è detto a la mente revoche,
in parte fia la tua voglia contenta,   136
    perché vedrai la pianta onde si scheggia,
    e vedra' il corrègger che argomenta
'U' ben s'impingua, se non si vaneggia' ".   139

That man was Dominic, our patriarch.
  Whoever follows him as he commands
  will put in with good cargo in his ark.   121

But his fold have gone off to distant lands,
  gluttoning for food finer than the old,
  alien food to crop from alien sands.   124

And as his sheep stray farther from his hold
  and love to wander by the way, the worse
  do they return, empty of milk, to the fold.   127

True, there are some who fear eternal loss
  and press close to the shepherd; but so few,
  a scrap of cloth would serve to cut their cowls.   130

Now if my words haven't seemed hoarse to you,
  and if your listening has been intent,
  recalling what I said a while ago,   133

In one part will your wishes rest content:
  you'll see the stump whose rot I've spoken of
  and how I qualified my argument: 136

'Where you can fatten well, *if you don't rove.*' "   139

THE SUN—GLORIFIED SOULS

Sì tosto come l'ultima parola
   la benedetta fiamma per dir tolse,
   a rotar cominciò la santa mola;
e nel suo giro tutta non si volse   4
   prima ch'un'altra di cerchio la chiuse,
   e moto a moto e canto a canto colse;
canto che tanto vince nostre muse,   7
   nostre serene in quelle dolci tube,
   quanto primo splendor quel ch'e' refuse.
Come si volgon per tenera nube   10
   due archi paralelli e concolori,
   quando Iunone a sua ancella iube,
nascendo di quel d'entro quel di fori,   13
   a guisa del parlar di quella vaga
   ch'amor consunse come sol vapori,
e fanno qui la gente esser presaga,   16
   per lo patto che Dio con Noè puose,
   del mondo che già mai più non s'allaga:

CANTO TWELVE

*Out of a second garland of spirits another soul speaks: it is the soul of **Bonaventure**, who describes the life of **Dominic** and concludes by decrying the corruption of the Franciscans of the present day.*

And when the blessed flame of joy was still,
    soon as his final word had taken wing,
    the wheel went turning in the sacred mill
And hadn't spun a full turn round the ring   4
    when, look! a second, garlanding about,
    moving as they move, singing as they sing,
Such song as puts our poetry to rout—   7
    our siren muses—with their flutes so sweet,
    as direct rays of sunlight overcome
A vague reflection. When the clouds are fine   10
    and Juno sends her herald° to the earth,
    two arches equal in their color shine
In parallel, the outer taking birth   13
    from the inner, echoing like her fading cries°
    whom love consumed as sun dissolves the dew;
Rainbows that make us mortals early wise   16
    by the pact God made Noah, with his vow
    that he would never flood the world again.°

°*her herald:* Iris, goddess of the rainbow.

°*her fading cries:* those of Echo, the nymph who fell in love with Narcissus and who wasted away in pining for him, until at last she was only a stone and a voice (Ovid, *Met.* 3.339–510).

°*never flood the world again:* God set the rainbow in the sky as a sign of that promise (Gen. 9:8–17).

così di quelle sempiterne rose   19
   volgiensi circa noi le due ghirlande,
   e sì l'estrema a l'intima rispuose.
Poi che 'l tripudio e l'altra festa grande,   22
   sì del cantare e sì del fiammeggiarsi
   luce con luce gaudïose e blande,
insieme a punto e a voler quetarsi,   25
   pur come li occhi ch'al piacer che i move
   conviene insieme chiudere e levarsi;
del cor de l'una de le luci nove   28
   si mosse voce, che l'ago a la stella
   parer mi fece in volgermi al suo dove;
e cominciò: "L'amor che mi fa bella   31
   mi tragge a ragionar de l'altro duca
   per cui del mio sì ben ci si favella.
Degno è che, dov' è l'un, l'altro s'induca: 34
   sì che, com' elli ad una militaro,
   così la gloria loro insieme luca.
L'essercito di Cristo, che sì caro   37
   costò a rïarmar, dietro a la 'nsegna
   si movea tardo, sospeccioso e raro,
quando lo 'mperador che sempre regna   40
   provide a la milizia, ch'era in forse,
   per sola grazia, non per esser degna;
e, come è detto, a sua sposa soccorse   43
   con due campioni, al cui fare, al cui dire
   lo popol disvïato si raccorse.
In quella parte ove surge ad aprire   46
   Zefiro dolce le novelle fronde
   di che si vede Europa rivestire,
non molto lungi al percuoter de l'onde   49
   dietro a le quali, per la lunga foga,
   lo sol talvolta ad ogne uom si nasconde,

So the two garlands circled round us now,　　　　　19
　　wreathed of the roses of eternity,
　　the outer answering the inner bow.
When the dance and the second jubilee,　　　　　22
　　responding in their flames and hymning feast
　　with light to light in gentle love and joy,
Instantly with one will had come to rest,　　　　　25
　　as twin eyelashes twinkling in delight
　　will shut and open with a single flash,
So from the heart of a new gleam of light　　　　　28
　　came a voice—and I turned as by the pull
　　that points the compass needle to the star.
Then he: "The love that makes me beautiful　　　　31
　　draws me to speak about the other guide,
　　who made the first souls praise my own so well.
Where one abides, the other should abide.　　　　34
　　So let their brilliant fame be blazoned out
　　together, who were soldiers side by side!
Christ's army, that had claimed so dear a price　　37
　　to arm again, was following the banner
　　hesitantly, but few, and filled with doubt,
When the high Emperor who reigns forever,　　　40
　　through grace alone, and for no merits they
　　had earned, provided for his wavering troops,
And, as we've said, He gave His Spouse the stay　　43
　　of those two champions, whose deeds and speech
　　mustered again the people gone astray.
In that land° where the soft wind rises each　　　46
　　April to open up the light new leaves
　　wherein we see our Europe newly clad,
Near to the crashing of the ocean waves　　　　　49
　　where in its weary travel, seeking rest,
　　the sun at times will hide from sight of man,

°*that land:* Saint Bonaventure describes the birthplace of Saint Dominic, in Castile, close to the Atlantic and the western coasts of Europe.

siede la fortunata Calaroga   52
  sotto la protezion del grande scudo
  in che soggiace il leone e soggioga:
dentro vi nacque l'amoroso drudo   55
  de la fede cristiana, il santo atleta
  benigno a' suoi e a' nemici crudo;
e come fu creata, fu repleta   58
  sì la sua mente di viva vertute
  che, ne la madre, lei fece profeta.
Poi che le sponsalizie fuor compiute   61
  al sacro fonte intra lui e la Fede,
  u' si dotar di mutüa salute,
la donna che per lui l'assenso diede,   64
  vide nel sonno il mirabile frutto
  ch'uscir dovea di lui e de le rede;
e perché fosse qual era in costrutto,   67
  quinci si mosse spirito a nomarlo
  del possessivo di cui era tutto.
Domenico fu detto; e io ne parlo   70
  sì come de l'agricola che Cristo
  elesse a l'orto suo per aiutarlo.
Ben parve messo e famigliar di Cristo: 73
  ché 'l primo amor che 'n lui fu manifesto,
  fu al primo consiglio che diè Cristo.
Spesse fïate fu tacito e desto   76
  trovato in terra da la sua nutrice,
  come dicesse: 'Io son venuto a questo'.

Sits Calaruega fortunate and blest   52
   under protection of the mighty shield
   whose lion both subdues and is suppressed.°
In that town was the amorous servant born,   55
   mild to his own but bitter to the foe,
   the holy athlete dueling on the field
For Christian faith. When it was fashioned, so   58
   filled was his soul with living manliness,
   he made his mother a prophet while he lay
Yet in her womb. And when he and Lady Faith   61
   were fully wedded at the holy font,
   and each endowing each with gifts of health,
The woman° who had answered for him there   64
   saw, in a dream, the fruit so marvelous
   that he and his inheritors would bear;
And, that the word might correspond to truth,   67
   a heavenly spirit inspired her with the name
   of His possessive, whose he wholly was.
Dominic he was called: I speak of him   70
   as of a tender of the fields whom Christ
   chose to increase his crop. Well might he seem
A steward and a courier of Christ,   73
   for when he showed the world his first young love,
   it was for the first counsel given by Christ.°
Many a time his nurse would find the lad   76
   awake at night and kneeling silently,
   as if he'd said, 'It is for this I've come.'

°*lion…suppressed:* The arms of Castile bore a lion above a tower on one side and a tower above a lion on the other.

° *The woman:* his godmother, who answered the questions posed to the child in the baptismal rite. When asked the child's name, she responded, "Dominic," a name that means "belonging to the Lord."

°*first counsel given by Christ:* humble poverty, in the first beatitude: "Blessed are the poor in spirit, for theirs is the kingdom of heaven" (Matt. 5:3).

Oh padre suo veramente Felice!   79
    oh madre sua veramente Giovanna,
    se, interpretata, val come si dice!
Non per lo mondo, per cui mo s'affanna   82
    di retro ad Ostïense e a Taddeo,
    ma per amor de la verace manna
in picciol tempo gran dottor si feo;   85
    tal che si mise a circüir la vigna
    che tosto imbianca, se 'l vignaio è reo.
E a la sedia che fu già benigna   88
    più a' poveri giusti, non per lei,
    ma per colui che siede, che traligna,
non dispensare o due o tre per sei,   91
    non la fortuna di prima vacante,
    non *decimas, quae sunt pauperum Dei,*
addimandò, ma contro al mondo errante   94
    licenza di combatter per lo seme
    del qual ti fascian ventiquattro piante.
Poi, con dottrina e con volere insieme,   97
    con l'officio appostolico si mosse
    quasi torrente ch'alta vena preme;
e ne li sterpi eretici percosse   100
    l'impeto suo, più vivamente quivi
    dove le resistenze eran più grosse.
Di lui si fecer poi diversi rivi   103
    onde l'orto catolico si riga,
    sì che i suoi arbuscelli stan più vivi.
Se tal fu l'una rota de la biga   106
    in che la Santa Chiesa si difese
    e vinse in campo la sua civil briga,

O Felix,° father truly blessed by fate!   79
  O Joan his mother truly full of grace,
  if things are as their names denominate!
Not for the world, for whose sake men may chase   82
  after Thaddaeus or the Ostian,°
  but for the love of the true manna's taste°
He soon became so deeply taught a man   85
  he took his doctrine round about the vine°
  whose leaves will curl white, if the dresser's bad.
And from the chair° that once was more benign   88
  to poor and righteous men—the chair is just,
  though he who sits there strays across the line—
He did not beg to dole a half or third,°   91
  or the wealth of the earliest vacancy,
  or tithes due to the paupers of the Lord,
But against the world in error to be free   94
  to fight for the seed of faith that bore good grain
  in this surrounding sheaf of twenty-four.
Then armed with zeal and doctrine and the charge   97
  of apostolic duty, he fell quick
  as torrents bursting from a mountain vein
And slammed the thickets of the heretic,   100
  pummeling onward with his surging drive
  where the resistance was most harsh and thick;
And from his torrent other streams derive   103
  that water all the Catholic garden plot
  and leave its little bushes more alive.
If that was one wheel of the chariot   106
  wherein the Holy Church fought off the foe
  and won her civil conflict on the field,

°*Felix:* Dante here translates the meanings of Latin *Felix* ("blessed") and of *Joan* (Hebrew: "grace of God").

° *Thaddaeus or the Ostian:* Thaddaeus is probably Taddeo d'Alderotto, founder of the medical faculty at the University of Bologna. The Ostian is Henry of Susa, thirteenth-century professor of canon law. Dante's point is that Dominic sought no means of garnering fame and wealth.

°*the true manna's taste:* that of wisdom.

°*the vine:* the Church (cf. Mark 12:1–11, John 15:1–8).

°*the chair:* the papacy.

°*a half or third:* of alms given for distribution to the poor, while keeping the rest.

ben ti dovrebbe assai esser palese 109
  l'eccellenza de l'altra, di cui Tomma
  dinanzi al mio venir fu sì cortese.
Ma l'orbita che fé la parte somma 112
  di sua circunferenza, è derelitta,
  sì ch'è la muffa dov' era la gromma.
La sua famiglia, che si mosse dritta 115
  coi piedi a le sue orme, è tanto volta,
  che quel dinanzi a quel di retro gitta;
e tosto si vedrà de la ricolta 118
  de la mala coltura, quando il loglio
  si lagnerà che l'arca li sia tolta.
Ben dico, chi cercasse a foglio a foglio 121
  nostro volume, ancor troveria carta
  u' leggerebbe 'I' mi son quel ch'i' soglio';
ma non fia da Casal né d'Acquasparta, 124
  là onde vegnon tali a la scrittura,
  ch'uno la fugge e altro la coarta.
Io son la vita di Bonaventura 127
  da Bagnoregio, che ne' grandi offici
  sempre pospuosi la sinistra cura.
Illuminato e Augustin son quici, 130
  che fuor de' primi scalzi poverelli
  che nel capestro a Dio si fero amici.
Ugo da San Vittore è qui con elli, 133
  e Pietro Mangiadore e Pietro Spano,
  lo qual giù luce in dodici libelli;
Natàn profeta e 'l metropolitano 136
  Crisostomo e Anselmo e quel Donato
  ch'a la prim' arte degnò porre mano.

It should be manifestly clear to you 109
   how excellent is the other one, whom Tom
   so courteously praised before I came.
But now the furrow of his turning wheel 112
   has been abandoned by his family;
   the crust of good wine now is mold and scum.
They used to follow his traces faithfully, 115
   but now they've veered so far wrong, they begin
   to put the toe down where the heel should be,
Yet they'll see when the grain is gathered in 118
   from all that evil sowing, how the weed
   will wail at being cast outside the bin.
Search our book over leaf by leaf, and read— 121
   I'll grant you'll find some page among them all
   that says, 'I'm still what I have always been,'
But not from Acquasparta or Casal, 124
   for when such friars come to read our rule,
   one cramps it while the other shirks and runs.
I am the life of Bonaventure, born 127
   in Bagnoregio: in my greater care
   I spurned the left-hand bounty of the world.
First of the brothers,° of the poor unshod, 130
   here are Augustine and Illuminato,
   who wore the rope to be the friends of God;
Hugh of Saint Victor is beside them too, 133
   both Peters,° the Book Eater and he of Spain,
   who still shines in his twelve small books below,
The prophet Nathan, Metropolitan 136
   Chrysostom, Anselm, and Donatus, he
   who humbly set his hand to the first art.°

°*the brothers:* Franciscans. *Augustine and Illuminato* were among the first of Francis's disciples.

°*both Peters:* Pietro Mangiadore ("the Book Eater") was chancellor of the University of Paris in the mid–twelfth century. Peter *of Spain,* later Pope John XXI (r. 1276–77), wrote works on medicine and philosophy, including *twelve small* textbooks on logic, the *Summulae logicales.*

°*the first art:* grammar, first in the studies of the medieval schoolboy. *Donatus* was a fourth-century grammarian.

Rabano è qui, e lucemi dallato   139
    il calavrese abate Giovacchino
    di spirito profetico dotato.
Ad inveggiar cotanto paladino   142
    mi mosse l'infiammata cortesia
    di fra Tommaso e 'l discreto latino;
e mosse meco questa compagnia".   145

Here's Rabanus, and gleaming next to me   139
   is the Calabrian abbot Joachim,
     endowed with the Spirit's gift of prophecy.
To emulate so great a paladin,   142
   I was moved by the kindled courtesy
     of brother Thomas and his crisp discourse—
And all this band of souls were moved with me."   145

Imagini, chi bene intender cupe
　　quel ch'i' or vidi—e ritegna l'image,
　　mentre ch'io dico, come ferma rupe—,
quindici stelle che 'n diverse plage　　　　　　　　　　4
　　lo cielo avvivan di tanto sereno
　　che soperchia de l'aere ogne compage;
imagini quel carro a cu' il seno　　　　　　　　　　　7
　　basta del nostro cielo e notte e giorno,
　　sì ch'al volger del temo non vien meno;
imagini la bocca di quel corno　　　　　　　　　　　10
　　che si comincia in punta de lo stelo
　　a cui la prima rota va dintorno,
aver fatto di sé due segni in cielo,　　　　　　　　　13
　　qual fece la figliuola di Minoi
　　allora che sentì di morte il gelo;
e l'un ne l'altro aver li raggi suoi,　　　　　　　　　16
　　e amendue girarsi per maniera
　　che l'uno andasse al primo e l'altro al poi;

CANTO THIRTEEN

Thomas Aquinas explains what Scripture means and what he meant in describing Solomon as the wisest man who ever lived. He concludes by condemning the rashness of human judgment.

Imagine, if you wish to fathom well
   what I now saw—and while I speak, retain
   the image like a rock-built citadel—
From all the starry shores the bright fifteen°   4
   livening Heaven with such peaceful rays
   they lift all haze and make the air serene;
Imagine then that northern Wain° that stays   7
   full in our view, however its helm may turn,
   finding our skies sufficient, nights and days;
Imagine the two pan stars of that horn°   10
   beginning with the axis pinned in place
   round which the first great wheel of Heaven revolves,
Forming themselves into two signs in space,   13
   like the bright crown of Minos' daughter° as
   she felt death coming with the touch of ice—
Flashing each other's radiance like glass,   16
   each turning but in opposite career,
   circling together as they cross and pass—

°*the bright fifteen:* stars of the first magnitude as denominated by Ptolemy.

°*northern Wain:* the Wain or Wagon, which we know as the Big Dipper; because of its nearness to the North Star, in most northern latitudes it never appears to rise or set.

°*that horn:* the Little Dipper, shaped like a horn opening out from the celestial axis at the North Star, its two brightest stars at the mouth of the horn.

°*crown of Minos' daughter:* the constellation Corona. When Ariadne was deserted by Theseus, whom she had helped slay the Minotaur, the god Bacchus took her in love and transformed her garland into a constellation; Dante's Italian suggests that the crown was rather Ariadne herself (cf. Ovid, *Met.* 8.172–82).

e avrà quasi l'ombra de la vera   19
   costellazione e de la doppia danza
   che circulava il punto dov' io era:
poi ch'è tanto di là da nostra usanza,   22
   quanto di là dal mover de la Chiana
   si move il ciel che tutti li altri avanza.
Lì si cantò non Bacco, non Peana,   25
   ma tre persone in divina natura,
   e in una persona essa e l'umana.
Compié 'l cantare e 'l volger sua misura;   28
   e attesersi a noi quei santi lumi,
   felicitando sé di cura in cura.
Ruppe il silenzio ne' concordi numi   31
   poscia la luce in che mirabil vita
   del poverel di Dio narrata fumi,
e disse: "Quando l'una paglia è trita,   34
   quando la sua semenza è già riposta,
   a batter l'altra dolce amor m'invita.
Tu credi che nel petto onde la costa   37
   si trasse per formar la bella guancia
   il cui palato a tutto 'l mondo costa,
e in quel che, forato da la lancia,   40
   e prima e poscia tanto sodisfece,
   che d'ogne colpa vince la bilancia,
quantunque a la natura umana lece   43
   aver di lume, tutto fosse infuso
   da quel valor che l'uno e l'altro fece;
e però miri a ciò ch'io dissi suso,   46
   quando narrai che non ebbe 'l secondo
   lo ben che ne la quinta luce è chiuso.
Or apri li occhi a quel ch'io ti rispondo,   49
   e vedräi il tuo credere e 'l mio dire
   nel vero farsi come centro in tondo.

And of this double dance you'll have a mere   19
    shadow, a ghost of that true constellation
    revolving round the point where I was standing:
As far above our usual conversation   22
    as Chiana's swamp's more sluggish than the ring°
    that sends the other heavens in rotation.
Not Bacchus there, not Paean° do they sing;   25
    three Persons in one nature, the divine,
    and in one Person the divine and man.
The dance had reached the end of its design,   28
    and then the holy lanterns turned our way,
    leaving their own care, gladdening with mine.
The silence of those powers in harmony   31
    was broken by the light that spoke about
    the wondrous life of God's poor man,° to say,
"When one row of the corn is trodden out,   34
    and when its fruit is safely in the crib,
    sweet love now lures me on to thresh the other.
You're thinking of the breast that gave its rib,   37
    drawn forth to form the woman of fair cheek
    whose palate made the whole world pay so dearly,
And of that breast pierced with a lance to make   40
    full recompense for future sins and past,
    causing the scales of human debt to break.
Whatever light our nature has possessed   43
    must have been, so you argue, wholly infused
    into the hearts of these two, by that first
Power that created them. So you're confused   46
    when I say that no second has been found
    to match the wisdom housed in the fifth light.
Open your eyes to what I shall expound: 49
    you'll see what you believe and what I say
    stand in truth's ring, two points upon one round.

°*Chiana's swamp's ... the ring:* The Val di Chiana was a malarial swamp near Orvieto (cf. *Inf.* 29.47); the ring is the Primum Mobile, swiftest of created things.

°*Paean:* Apollo, whose revelers would cry out, "Io Paean!"

°*God's poor man:* Saint Francis.

Ciò che non more e ciò che può morire   52
   non è se non splendor di quella idea
   che partorisce, amando, il nostro Sire;
ché quella viva luce che sì mea   55
   dal suo lucente, che non si disuna
   da lui né da l'amor ch'a lor s'intrea,
per sua bontate il suo raggiare aduna,   58
   quasi specchiato, in nove sussistenze,
   etternalmente rimanendosi una.
Quindi discende a l'ultime potenze   61
   giù d'atto in atto, tanto divenendo,
   che più non fa che brevi contingenze;
e queste contingenze essere intendo   64
   le cose generate, che produce
   con seme e sanza seme il ciel movendo.
La cera di costoro e chi la duce   67
   non sta d'un modo; e però sotto 'l segno
   idëale poi più e men traluce.
Ond' elli avvien ch'un medesimo legno,   70
   secondo specie, meglio e peggio frutta;
   e voi nascete con diverso ingegno.
Se fosse a punto la cera dedutta   73
   e fosse il cielo in sua virtù supprema,
   la luce del suggel parrebbe tutta;
ma la natura la dà sempre scema,   76
   similemente operando a l'artista
   ch'a l'abito de l'arte ha man che trema.
Però se 'l caldo amor la chiara vista   79
   de la prima virtù dispone e segna,
   tutta la perfezion quivi s'acquista.

What has to die and what can never die   52
    are nothing but the glimmerings of that Word
    our Father has begotten by His Love,

Because that living Radiance° which derives   55
    from its Light Giver, never to dis-one
    from Him nor from the threeing of their Love,

Through His great bounty makes His rays all one,   58
    mirroring them in nine subsistencies,°
    yet everlastingly remaining one.

Thence light descends to the last potencies   61
    from sphere to sphere, until from it proceed
    what are no more than brief contingencies,

I mean all generated things, that need   64
    not be, but change and die, and come to light
    by heaven in motion,° with or without seed.

Since their wax and the hand that shapes them vary,   67
    the heavenly impress, varying in degree,
    will shine in every object, dim or bright.

And that is how it happens that one tree   70
    bears better and worse fruit, and men are born
    with various gifts of ingenuity.

Clear the wax to perfection and return   73
    the heavens to where their powers are at the peak:
    then you will see the seal in fullest shine;

But nature always comes up lame and weak,   76
    works like an artist with a trembling hand
    who falters, though he knows his art's technique.

But when the ardent Love has brought to bear   79
    the Wisdom of the primal Power, and sealed,
    every perfection is embodied there.°

°*Radiance:* Christ, Second Person of the Trinity, the Wisdom through whom all things are made.

°*nine subsistencies:* the nine spheres, or angelic intelligences. These subsist because they depend upon no material cause for their continued existence. All other things are contingent.

°*heaven in motion:* stellar influences, that is. Rarely, Thomas says, are the stars aligned to create perfection in an object (come to being *without seed*) or human being (born *with seed*).

°*But…there:* God (in Power, Wisdom, and Love; cf. *Inf.* 3.4–6) created Adam and the human nature of Jesus directly.

Così fu fatta già la terra degna
di tutta l'animal perfezïone;
così fu fatta la Vergine pregna; 82

sì ch'io commendo tua oppinïone,
che l'umana natura mai non fue
né fia qual fu in quelle due persone. 85

Or s'i' non procedesse avanti piùe,
'Dunque, come costui fu sanza pare?'
comincerebber le parole tue. 88

Ma perché paia ben ciò che non pare,
pensa chi era, e la cagion che 'l mosse,
quando fu detto 'Chiedi', a dimandare. 91

Non ho parlato sì, che tu non posse
ben veder ch'el fu re, che chiese senno
acciò che re sufficïente fosse; 94

non per sapere il numero in che enno
li motor di qua sù, o se *necesse*
con contingente mai *necesse* fenno; 97

non *si est dare primum motum esse,*
o se del mezzo cerchio far si puote
trïangol sì ch'un retto non avesse. 100

Onde, se ciò ch'io dissi e questo note,
regal prudenza è quel vedere impari
in che lo stral di mia intenzion percuote; 103

e se al 'surse' drizzi li occhi chiari,
vedrai aver solamente respetto
ai regi, che son molti, e ' buon son rari. 106

Con questa distinzion prendi 'l mio detto;
e così puote star con quel che credi
del primo padre e del nostro Diletto. 109

E questo ti sia sempre piombo a' piedi,
per farti mover lento com' uom lasso
e al sì e al no che tu non vedi: 112

So once the earth was well prepared to yield   82
    every perfection of a living soul;
      so once the Virgin Mother was with child.

Thus do I say your reasoning is quite true,   85
    that human nature never has been nor
      shall again be as it was in those two.

But now your words might well begin, 'Therefore   88
    how could this man have been without a peer?'
      unless I walked with you a little more.

To clarify what isn't yet quite clear,   91
    you should recall the person and the cause,
      when God said, 'Ask,' that moved him to his prayer.°

From what I've spoken you can see he was   94
    a king, and asked for the capacity
      to fulfill a king's duties—not to muse

About the angels and the quantity   97
    of movers of the stars; or if a *must*
      and *might* together make necessity;°

Or whether an uncaused motion can exist,   100
    or if on a half circle you can fit
      a triangle unless one angle's right.

That's where the arrow of my intention hit: 103
    he had no peer in foresight for a king,
      if you note what I say, comparing it

With what I said before. By my word 'rose'   106
    you'll see that kings alone were those I meant—
      of whom are many, but the good are few.

With this distinction take my argument   109
    so you may stand upon what you believe
      of our first father and of our Delight.°

And should you rush to what you don't perceive,   112
    let my words drag like lead weights on your feet
      and make you slow to answer yes or no,

°*his prayer:* God offered Solomon any request, and the young king asked him for the wisdom to rule his people well (1 Kings 3:5–12).

°*must* and *might… necessity:* whether a necessary condition can combine with a nonnecessary condition and still yield a necessary conclusion.

°*our Delight:* Christ.

ché quelli è tra li stolti bene a basso,   115
    che sanza distinzione afferma e nega
    ne l'un così come ne l'altro passo;
perch' elli 'ncontra che più volte piega   118
    l'oppinïon corrente in falsa parte,
    e poi l'affetto l'intelletto lega.
Vie più che 'ndarno da riva si parte,   121
    perché non torna tal qual e' si move,
    chi pesca per lo vero e non ha l'arte.
E di ciò sono al mondo aperte prove   124
    Parmenide, Melisso e Brisso e molti,
    li quali andaro e non sapëan dove;
sì fé Sabellio e Arrio e quelli stolti   127
    che furon come spade a le Scritture
    in render torti li diritti volti.
Non sien le genti, ancor, troppo sicure   130
    a giudicar, sì come quei che stima
    le biade in campo pria che sien mature;
ch'i' ho veduto tutto 'l verno prima   133
    lo prun mostrarsi rigido e feroce,
    poscia portar la rosa in su la cima;
e legno vidi già dritto e veloce   136
    correr lo mar per tutto suo cammino,
    perire al fine a l'intrar de la foce.
Non creda donna Berta e ser Martino,   139
    per vedere un furare, altro offerere,
    vederli dentro al consiglio divino;
ché quel può surgere, e quel può cadere".   142

For of all fools that man's the lowest ass   115
   who'll affirm or deny but not reflect,
     impetuous in his haste down either pass,

For scurrying thought will often enough deflect   118
   a man's opinion into false terrain,
     and then his self-love binds his intellect.

From the banks they depart worse than in vain   121
   who fish for truth but haven't learned the art—
     as they've set out, they won't return again.

The world's been furnished open proofs of that: 124
   Melissus, Bryson, and Parmenides,
     who knew no destination from the start,

Nor did Sabellius, Arius, and those   127
   fools° who were swords to slash the Holy Scripture
     or glasses to distort its simple face.

People besides should never be too sure   130
   of what they judge, like farmers in the corn
     who count their crop before the ears mature.

For I've seen all the winter a bare thorn   133
   looking like nothing but a stiff rough stick,
     whose crown would blossom when the rose was born,

And I have seen a vessel sleek and quick,   136
   racing through all its course along the main,
     founder as it was putting into port.

So let not Master Dick and Lady Jane,   139
   seeing one rob, another give his all,
     think they can see with providence divine,

Because the one can rise, the other fall."   142

°*those fools:* other heretics.

Dal centro al cerchio, e sì dal cerchio al centro
    movesi l'acqua in un ritondo vaso,
    secondo ch'è percosso fuori o dentro:
ne la mia mente fé sùbito caso   4
    questo ch'io dico, sì come si tacque
    la glorïosa vita di Tommaso,
per la similitudine che nacque   7
    del suo parlare e di quel di Beatrice,
    a cui sì cominciar, dopo lui, piacque:
"A costui fa mestieri, e nol vi dice   10
    né con la voce né pensando ancora,
    d'un altro vero andare a la radice.
Diteli se la luce onde s'infiora   13
    vostra sustanza, rimarrà con voi
    etternalmente sì com' ell' è ora;
e se rimane, dite come, poi   16
    che sarete visibili rifatti,
    esser porà ch'al veder non vi nòi".
Come, da più letizia pinti e tratti,   19
    a la fïata quei che vanno a rota
    levan la voce e rallegrano li atti,
così, a l'orazion pronta e divota,   22
    li santi cerchi mostrar nova gioia
    nel torneare e ne la mira nota.

Canto Fourteen

King Solomon answers Dante's last question to the wise, a question about the resurrection of the body. Then Dante and Beatrice ascend to Mars, the fifth sphere, the place for the warriors for Christ.

Water in a round pail will swirl about
    from center to the ring, or the reverse,
    if the pail's jarred from inside, or without:
That image came to me with sudden force,   4
    sweeping into my mind as soon as he,
    the glorious life of Thomas, held his peace,
Due to the newborn similarity   7
    it showed to how he spoke with Beatrice,
    who, when he'd finished, said delightedly,
"He has a need he cannot yet express   10
    to follow another truth down to the root,
    a need he cannot utter with his voice
Or set forth in his mind. Tell if the light   13
    garlanding you like soul-adorning flowers
    remains, for all eternity, so bright;
And if the light retains its brilliant powers,   16
    say why the vision will not make you feel
    pain, when your forms are visible once more."
As dancers dancing in a merry reel,   19
    will raise their voices in a rush of glee,
    all of their gestures lighter in the heel,
So, to that most devout and ready plea,   22
    the holy circlings showed me a new joy
    in their revolving and their wondrous song.

Qual si lamenta perché qui si moia   25
   per viver colà sù, non vide quive
   lo refrigerio de l'etterna ploia.
Quell' uno e due e tre che sempre vive   28
   e regna sempre in tre e 'n due e 'n uno,
   non circunscritto, e tutto circunscrive,
tre volte era cantato da ciascuno   31
   di quelli spirti con tal melodia,
   ch'ad ogne merto saria giusto muno.
E io udi' ne la luce più dia   34
   del minor cerchio una voce modesta,
   forse qual fu da l'angelo a Maria,
risponder: "Quanto fia lunga la festa   37
   di paradiso, tanto il nostro amore
   si raggerà dintorno cotal vesta.
La sua chiarezza séguita l'ardore;   40
   l'ardor la visïone, e quella è tanta,
   quant' ha di grazia sovra suo valore.
Come la carne glorïosa e santa   43
   fia rivestita, la nostra persona
   più grata fia per esser tutta quanta;
per che s'accrescerà ciò che ne dona   46
   di gratüito lume il sommo bene,
   lume ch'a lui veder ne condiziona;
onde la visïon crescer convene,   49
   crescer l'ardor che di quella s'accende,
   crescer lo raggio che da esso vene.
Ma sì come carbon che fiamma rende,   52
   e per vivo candor quella soverchia,
   sì che la sua parvenza si difende;
così questo folgór che già ne cerchia   55
   fia vinto in apparenza da la carne
   che tutto dì la terra ricoperchia;
né potrà tanta luce affaticarne: 58
   ché li organi del corpo saran forti
   a tutto ciò che potrà dilettarne".

Whoever on earth laments that we must die 25
   to live above in Heaven, does not see
   the sweet refreshment of the eternal rain.
That ever-living One and Two and Three 28
   that ever reigns in Three and Two and One,
   uncircumscribed and circumscribing all,
Three times was hymned in praise by every one 31
   of those souls in so sweet a melody
   as would reward all merit. From the light°
Most fully radiant with divinity 34
   in the inner ring, I heard a gentle voice;
   it might have been the angel's when he spoke
To Mary. "In the feast of Paradise, 37
   for the length of eternity our love
   will fold us in the vestment of these rays.
They blaze according to the ardor of 40
   that love, ardor from vision, vision as wide
   and deep as grace abounding far above
Our worth allows. When, blessed and glorified, 43
   the flesh is robed about us once again,
   we shall be lovelier for being whole;
Whence the gift of illuminating grace 46
   granted us by the highest Good shall grow—
   light that disposes us to see His face,
And in that light then must our vision grow, 49
   grow then the ardent love it sets aflame,
   wherein the radiance of the flesh shall grow.
But as a fiery coal that gives off flame 52
   conquers it with its incandescent white,
   preserving its appearance all the same,
So this surrounding gleam of heavenly light 55
   will be defeated by the luminous flesh
   that now lies tombed in earth. Nor will the might
Of its new radiance trouble us with pain, 58
   for strong enough will be its organs then
   to bear all things that bring us more delight."

° *the light:* that of Solomon.

Tanto mi parver sùbiti e accorti   61
   e l'uno e l'altro coro a dicer "Amme!",
   che ben mostrar disio d'i corpi morti:
forse non pur per lor, ma per le mamme,   64
   per li padri e per li altri che fuor cari
   anzi che fosser sempiterne fiamme.
Ed ecco intorno, di chiarezza pari,   67
   nascere un lustro sopra quel che v'era,
   per guisa d'orizzonte che rischiari.
E sì come al salir di prima sera   70
   comincian per lo ciel nove parvenze,
   sì che la vista pare e non par vera,
parvemi lì novelle sussistenze   73
   cominciare a vedere, e fare un giro
   di fuor da l'altre due circunferenze.
Oh vero sfavillar del Santo Spiro!   76
   come si fece sùbito e candente
   a li occhi miei che, vinti, nol soffriro!
Ma Bëatrice sì bella e ridente   79
   mi si mostrò, che tra quelle vedute
   si vuol lasciar che non seguir la mente.
Quindi ripreser li occhi miei virtute   82
   a rilevarsi; e vidimi translato
   sol con mia donna in più alta salute.
Ben m'accors' io ch'io era più levato,   85
   per l'affocato riso de la stella,
   che mi parea più roggio che l'usato.
Con tutto 'l core e con quella favella   88
   ch'è una in tutti, a Dio feci olocausto,
   qual conveniesi a la grazia novella.
E non er' anco del mio petto essausto   91
   l'ardor del sacrificio, ch'io conobbi
   esso litare stato accetto e fausto;
ché con tanto lucore e tanto robbi   94
   m'apparvero splendor dentro a due raggi,
   ch'io dissi: "O Elïòs che sì li addobbi!".

So prompt and ready was the loud "Amen!"   61
  both choirs responded, it was clear to me
  how much they yearned to see their flesh again,
Maybe less for themselves than for their mamas,   64
  their fathers, and the others they held dear
  before they had become eternal flames.
And look—as when the glints of dawn appear—   67
  around them all and shining just as bright,
  more gleaming dawned beyond the gleaming there,
And as the early evening climbs the height,   70
  new lights begin to glimmer in the skies,
  seeming and yet not seeming true to sight,
New spiritual beings in that place   73
  began to shine on me and form a host
  ringing the other two circumferences.
O the true shimmering of the Holy Ghost!   76
  With what a flame of sudden radiancy
  they quelled my eyes, that all their might was lost!
But Beatrice turned her lovely glance to me,   79
  smiling in beauty I surrender with
  visions remembrance can't accompany.
From her the strength returned to raise my eyes,   82
  and I saw my lady and I had been assumed
  unto a loftier bliss of Paradise.
Easy to tell that I was lifted higher,   85
  by the enkindled laughter of that star,°
  which seemed to blush with even ruddier fire
Than usual. Then with wholehearted prayer,   88
  the language that is one for all mankind,
  I offered up a holocaust to God
For the new grace—and while the flames yet burned   91
  within my sacrificing breast, I knew
  my gift had been accepted by the Lord,
For then so rubylike a radiant glow   94
  appeared within two rays, it made me say,
  "O Helios,° who trim their tassels so!"

°*that star:* Mars.
°*Helios:* the sun, here a symbol for God Himself.

Come distinta da minori e maggi   97
  lumi biancheggia tra ' poli del mondo
  Galassia sì, che fa dubbiar ben saggi;
sì costellati facean nel profondo   100
  Marte quei raggi il venerabil segno
  che fan giunture di quadranti in tondo.
Qui vince la memoria mia lo 'ngegno;   103
  ché quella croce lampeggiava Cristo,
  sì ch'io non so trovare essempro degno;
ma chi prende sua croce e segue Cristo,   106
  ancor mi scuserà di quel ch'io lasso,
  vedendo in quell' albor balenar Cristo.
Di corno in corno e tra la cima e 'l basso   109
  si movien lumi, scintillando forte
  nel congiugnersi insieme e nel trapasso:
così si veggion qui diritte e torte,   112
  veloci e tarde, rinovando vista,
  le minuzie d'i corpi, lunghe e corte,
moversi per lo raggio onde si lista   115
  talvolta l'ombra che, per sua difesa,
  la gente con ingegno e arte acquista.
E come giga e arpa, in tempra tesa   118
  di molte corde, fa dolce tintinno
  a tal da cui la nota non è intesa,
così da' lumi che lì m'apparinno   121
  s'accogliea per la croce una melode
  che mi rapiva, sanza intender l'inno.
Ben m'accors' io ch'elli era d'alte lode,   124
  però ch'a me venìa "Resurgi" e "Vinci"
  come a colui che non intende e ode.
Ïo m'innamorava tanto quinci,   127
  che 'nfino a lì non fu alcuna cosa
  che mi legasse con sì dolci vinci.
Forse la mia parola par troppo osa,   130
  posponendo il piacer de li occhi belli,
  ne' quai mirando mio disio ha posa;

As wisest men must feel their musings sway,   97
    seeing adorned with great and little stars
    the pole-to-polar whitening Milky Way,
So now star-patterned in the deeps of Mars   100
    those rays had formed the venerable sign
    that intersects a circle with a cross.
Here memory conquers any wit of mine,   103
    for that cross lightninged forth the form of Christ—
    I find for it no metaphor so fine—
But who takes up his cross and follows Christ   106
    will pardon what I pass by in this place,
    seeing in that bright tree the light of Christ.
From horn to horn, from summit to the base,   109
    lovingly joining and then crossing by,
    moved lights that flashed in scintillating grace,
As here you'll see in straight lines or awry,   112
    swiftly or slowly and ever changing view,
    tiny or tinier motes of matter fly
Along a sunbeam that is crossed askew   115
    by the band of a shade to screen the light,
    when art and genius do what they can do—
And as a tempered harp of many a string   118
    or a guitar sounds sweetly, tinklingly,
    for him who—almost—hears the music ring,
So from the lights that there appeared to me   121
    a melody welled up throughout the cross
    which, though I couldn't understand the hymn,
Swept me away. Of lofty praise it was,   124
    for came to me the hardly fathomed sound
    of "You arise" and "Conquer." In that place
I was enchanted and fell so in love,   127
    nothing had ever fixed so firm a hold,
    no sweeter bands had ever held me bound.
Perhaps these words of mine may seem too bold,   130
    placing the pleasure of her lovely eyes—
    wherein I gaze that my desire may rest—

ma chi s'avvede che i vivi suggelli 133
    d'ogne bellezza più fanno più suso,
    e ch'io non m'era lì rivolto a quelli,
escusar puommi di quel ch'io m'accuso 136
    per escusarmi, e vedermi dir vero:
    ché 'l piacer santo non è qui dischiuso,
perché si fa, montando, più sincero. 139

Second; but if you see that as they rise
    these living seals of every beauty shine
    more mightily, nor had I turned to them,
You will excuse me for what I accuse
    myself of, to excuse myself and speak
    truth: for that holy bliss is not shut out
But grows the purer as it scales the peak.

133

136

139

THE CROSS

Benigna volontade in che si liqua
    sempre l'amor che drittamente spira,
    come cupidità fa ne la iniqua,
silenzio puose a quella dolce lira,   4
    e fece quïetar le sante corde
    che la destra del cielo allenta e tira.
Come saranno a' giusti preghi sorde   7
    quelle sustanze che, per darmi voglia
    ch'io le pregassi, a tacer fur concorde?
Bene è che sanza termine si doglia   10
    chi, per amor di cosa che non duri
    etternalmente, quello amor si spoglia.
Quale per li seren tranquilli e puri   13
    discorre ad ora ad or sùbito foco,
    movendo li occhi che stavan sicuri,
e pare stella che tramuti loco,   16
    se non che da la parte ond' e' s'accende
    nulla sen perde, ed esso dura poco:
tale dal corno che 'n destro si stende   19
    a piè di quella croce corse un astro
    de la costellazion che lì resplende;
né si partì la gemma dal suo nastro,   22
    ma per la lista radïal trascorse,
    che parve foco dietro ad alabastro.

CANTO FIFTEEN

Dante speaks with his ancestor **Cacciaguida,** *who describes the courtly virtues of* **the Florentines of old.**

The will for good wherein we ever see
   a righteous love like water shining clear,
   as twisted will reveals cupidity,
Had set a silence on that gentle lyre   4
   and let the trembling of the strings be still,
   those drawn or loosened by the hand of Heaven.
How can those spirits be insensible   7
   to righteous prayers, when in still harmony
   they cheered my heart to ask and have my will?
Well should he suffer without ending, he   10
   who strips himself of that love, for the love
   of things that do not last eternally.
As through the pure and starry peace above   13
   from time to time will flash a sudden flare,
   causing the eye that is at rest to move,
Appearing like a place-exchanging star   16
   (except no star is lost where it takes flight,
   and its fresh flame won't light it very far),
Such from the arm extending to the right   19
   to the foot of the cross a starlight came
   sweeping from the resplendent song of light,
Nor from its setting did the gemstone pass,   22
   but ran along the radius, and shone
   like flame behind an alabaster glass.

Sì pïa l'ombra d'Anchise si porse,   25
    se fede merta nostra maggior musa,
    quando in Eliso del figlio s'accorse.
"O sanguis meus, o superinfusa   28
    gratïa Deï, sicut tibi cui
    bis unquam celi ianüa reclusa?".
Così quel lume: ond' io m'attesi a lui;   31
    poscia rivolsi a la mia donna il viso,
    e quinci e quindi stupefatto fui;
ché dentro a li occhi suoi ardeva un riso   34
    tal, ch'io pensai co' miei toccar lo fondo
    de la mia gloria e del mio paradiso.
Indi, a udire e a veder giocondo,   37
    giunse lo spirto al suo principio cose,
    ch'io non lo 'ntesi, sì parlò profondo;
né per elezïon mi si nascose,   40
    ma per necessità, ché 'l suo concetto
    al segno d'i mortal si soprapuose.
E quando l'arco de l'ardente affetto   43
    fu sì sfogato, che 'l parlar discese
    inver' lo segno del nostro intelletto,
la prima cosa che per me s'intese,   46
    "Benedetto sia tu", fu, "trino e uno,
    che nel mio seme se' tanto cortese!".
E seguì: "Grato e lontano digiuno,   49
    tratto leggendo del magno volume
    du' non si muta mai bianco né bruno,
solvuto hai, figlio, dentro a questo lume   52
    in ch'io ti parlo, mercé di colei
    ch'a l'alto volo ti vestì le piume.
Tu credi che a me tuo pensier mei   55
    da quel ch'è primo, così come raia
    da l'un, se si conosce, il cinque e 'l sei;

With such a loving piety for his son,   25
   if we may trust our greater muse,° Anchises
   once hailed Aeneas in Elysium.
"O blood of mine, O overbrimming grace   28
   poured out by God! For whom has Heaven's door
   been opened twice, as it has been for you?"
So spoke that light—I waited to hear more,   31
   and then I turned again to Beatrice,
   and so was stunned with wonder on each hand,
For such a smile was burning in her eyes   34
   I thought my own had plumbed to touch the ground
   of all my glory and my Paradise.
Then showering gladness by his sight and sound,   37
   the spirit joined new words to his first speech,
   but all was in a language too profound—
Not that he chose to veil his thoughts from me.   40
   Such is necessity, when concepts move
   beyond the mark a mortal mind can reach.
And when the crossbow of his burning love   43
   slackened enough to slope the arrow down
   to strike the target of our intellect,
The first words I could fathom on my own,   46
   "You who have been so courteous to my seed,"
   I heard him say, "be blessed, Three and One!"
"My son," he followed, "you have filled, have freed   49
   my long sweet hunger, roused within the light
   wherein I speak, by reading in the tome°
Whose leaves never can turn to brown or white,   52
   and thanks to her whose magnanimity
   has robed you with the feathers for this flight.
You believe that your thoughts make way to me   55
   through Him that is the first, as in a ray
   shining forth five and six from unity.°

°*our greater muse:* Virgil; see notes.
°*the tome:* the book of eternal providence.
°*shining... unity:* The oneness of God's light shines forth the plurality of the world, just as the number one can be repeated to form *five and six.*

e però ch'io mi sia e perch' io paia   58
  più gaudïoso a te, non mi domandi,
  che alcun altro in questa turba gaia.
Tu credi 'l vero; ché i minori e ' grandi   61
  di questa vita miran ne lo speglio
  in che, prima che pensi, il pensier pandi;
ma perché 'l sacro amore in che io veglio   64
  con perpetüa vista e che m'asseta
  di dolce disïar, s'adempia meglio,
la voce tua sicura, balda e lieta   67
  suoni la volontà, suoni 'l disio,
  a che la mia risposta è già decreta!".
Io mi volsi a Beatrice, e quella udio   70
  pria ch'io parlassi, e arrisemi un cenno
  che fece crescer l'ali al voler mio.
Poi cominciai così: "L'affetto e 'l senno,   73
  come la prima equalità v'apparse,
  d'un peso per ciascun di voi si fenno,
però che 'l sol che v'allumò e arse,   76
  col caldo e con la luce è sì iguali,
  che tutte simiglianze sono scarse.
Ma voglia e argomento ne' mortali,   79
  per la cagion ch'a voi è manifesta,
  diversamente son pennuti in ali;
ond' io, che son mortal, mi sento in questa   82
  disagguaglianza, e però non ringrazio
  se non col core a la paterna festa.
Ben supplico io a te, vivo topazio   85
  che questa gioia prezïosa ingemmi,
  perché mi facci del tuo nome sazio".
"O fronda mia in che io compiacemmi   88
  pur aspettando, io fui la tua radice":
  cotal principio, rispondendo, femmi.
Poscia mi disse: "Quel da cui si dice   91
  tua cognazione e che cent' anni e piùe
  girato ha 'l monte in la prima cornice,

Therefore you do not ask who I may be 58
    nor why I feel more joy to see you here
    than any in this festive company.
What you believe is true, for in this life 61
    all souls gaze into the reflecting lake
    wherein, before you think, your thoughts appear.
But that the sacred love wherein I wake 64
    and keep perpetual watch, a love to feed
    sweet yearning, may be filled the fuller, make
Your voice resound now, sure and bold and glad, 67
    resound the great desire, resound your will—
    for my reply already is decreed!"
I turned to Beatrice, who heard my still 70
    unspoken wish, and smiled me her assent,
    lending me wings to seek my will in full.
So I began: "Love and the intellect 73
    were balanced in your souls with but one weight
    once you beheld the prime Equality
That burns with such an equal light and heat, 76
    the love-enkindling and enlightening Sun,
    that no analogy is adequate.
But love and intellect in mortal man, 79
    for reasons that are manifest to you,
    feather their wings unequally—so I,
A mortal, feel my own imbalance now, 82
    and from my heart alone have power to speak
    and thank you for so fatherly a greeting.
Then, jewel set within this precious gem, 85
    O living topaz, now I bend the knee.
    Fulfill my longing, let me know your name!"
"O frond of mine who brought delight to me 88
    even in expectation," he replied,
    "I was the root of all your family!
The man from whom you take your name, the man 91
    who has," said he, "a hundred years and more,
    rounded the first ring of the mountainside,°

°*the first ring of the mountainside:* that of pride, in Purgatory. Proneness to that sin evidently runs in the family.

mio figlio fu e tuo bisavol fue: 94
  ben si convien che la lunga fatica
  tu li raccorci con l'opere tue.
Fiorenza dentro da la cerchia antica,   97
  ond' ella toglie ancora e terza e nona,
  si stava in pace, sobria e pudica.
Non avea catenella, non corona,   100
  non gonne contigiate, non cintura
  che fosse a veder più che la persona.
Non faceva, nascendo, ancor paura   103
  la figlia al padre, ché 'l tempo e la dote
  non fuggien quinci e quindi la misura.
Non avea case di famiglia vòte;   106
  non v'era giunto ancor Sardanapalo
  a mostrar ciò che 'n camera si puote.
Non era vinto ancora Montemalo   109
  dal vostro Uccellatoio, che, com' è vinto
  nel montar sù, così sarà nel calo.
Bellincion Berti vid' io andar cinto   112
  di cuoio e d'osso, e venir da lo specchio
  la donna sua sanza 'l viso dipinto;
e vidi quel d'i Nerli e quel del Vecchio   115
  esser contenti a la pelle scoperta,
  e le sue donne al fuso e al pennecchio.
Oh fortunate! ciascuna era certa   118
  de la sua sepultura, e ancor nulla
  era per Francia nel letto diserta.
L'una vegghiava a studio de la culla,   121
  e, consolando, usava l'idïoma
  che prima i padri e le madri trastulla;
l'altra, traendo a la rocca la chioma,   124
  favoleggiava con la sua famiglia
  d'i Troiani, di Fiesole e di Roma.

Was my own son and your great-grandfather.   94
   You would do well to hasten his release,
   shortening his long labor by your prayer.
Florence, surrounded by the ancient wall   97
   whose tower still tolls the hours of tierce and none,°
   was sober, modest—and it stood in peace.
It had no gaudy necklaces, no crown,   100
   no sash that lures more lookers when it's worn
   than does the wearer, no brocaded gown;
No fear for fathers when a girl was born,   103
   for marrying age and dowries hadn't fled
   beyond all measure yet, in youth and cost;
No house was vacant of its family;   106
   no Sardanapalus° had come to town
   to shut the door and show them things in bed;
Mount Malus° hadn't yet been conquered by   109
   that Bird Tower you bricked up in a spurt—
   quicker in rising, quicker going down!
Bellincion Berti I have seen go, girt   112
   in leather and bone, his good wife coming from
   her mirror with no paint upon her face;
I have seen Nerli and Vecchietto come   115
   content to carry wallets of mere skin,
   their wives contented with the wool and loom.
Fortunate women! Sure of tombs within   118
   their own town walls—and no one left to lie
   alone by husbands moneying in France:
One at the cradle watches quietly   121
   and in her parents' own sweet lisping talk
   consoles her baby with a lullaby;
Another draws the wool skein off the shock   124
   and with her household spins the ancient lays
   of Trojans, of Fiesole, and Rome.

°*tierce and none:* midmorning (the third hour) and midafternoon (the ninth hour), two of the canonical times for daily prayer.

°*Sardanapalus:* king of Assyria (667–626 B.C.), notorious for his decadence and lechery.

°*Mount Malus:* a hill near Rome. Cacciaguida predicts as swift a fall in Florence's fortunes as her *Bird Tower* was swift going up.

Saria tenuta allor tal maraviglia 127
    una Cianghella, un Lapo Salterello,
    qual or saria Cincinnato e Corniglia.
A così riposato, a così bello 130
    viver di cittadini, a così fida
    cittadinanza, a così dolce ostello,
Maria mi diè, chiamata in alte grida; 133
    e ne l'antico vostro Batisteo
    insieme fui cristiano e Cacciaguida.
Moronto fu mio frate ed Eliseo; 136
    mia donna venne a me di val di Pado,
    e quindi il sopranome tuo si feo.
Poi seguitai lo 'mperador Currado; 139
    ed el mi cinse de la sua milizia,
    tanto per bene ovrar li venni in grado.
Dietro li andai incontro a la nequizia 142
    di quella legge il cui popolo usurpa,
    per colpa d'i pastor, vostra giustizia.
Quivi fu' io da quella gente turpa 145
    disviluppato dal mondo fallace,
    lo cui amor molt' anime deturpa;
e venni dal martiro a questa pace". 148

A Lapo or Cianghella° in those days   127
     would have as greatly stunned the minds of men
     as Cincinnatus or Cornelia now.
Unto so handsome and serene a life   130
     among my fellow townsmen, brave and true,
     unto so sweet a dwelling Mary gave me
When she was cried to in the pains of birth—   133
     and in your ancient Baptistery, I became
     at once a Christian man and Cacciaguida.
Moronto and Eliseo were my brothers;   136
     my wife came from the valley of the Po,
     and from her family you take your name.
I followed the emperor Conrad to the East   139
     and won such favor by my valorous deeds
     he raised me to the knighthood. In his host
I struck in war against that twisted creed   142
     whose people filch your just and proper place,
     shame to your shepherds, for they do not lead.
And in the East by that most filthy race   145
     I was unfettered from the world that lies,
     the love of which defiles so many souls.
From martyrdom I came unto this peace."   148

°*Lapo or Cianghella:* notorious Florentines of Dante's day, to be contrasted with the noble Roman hero *Cincinnatus* and the virtuous matron *Cornelia*. For a fuller discussion of these and the other persons Cacciaguida names, see notes.

O poca nostra nobiltà di sangue,
  se glorïar di te la gente fai
  qua giù dove l'affetto nostro langue,
mirabil cosa non mi sarà mai: 4
  ché là dove appetito non si torce,
  dico nel cielo, io me ne gloriai.
Ben se' tu manto che tosto raccorce: 7
  sì che, se non s'appon di dì in die,
  lo tempo va dintorno con le force.
Dal 'voi' che prima a Roma s'offerie,   10
  in che la sua famiglia men persevra,
  ricominciaron le parole mie;
onde Beatrice, ch'era un poco scevra,   13
  ridendo, parve quella che tossio
  al primo fallo scritto di Ginevra.
Io cominciai: "Voi siete il padre mio;   16
  voi mi date a parlar tutta baldezza;
  voi mi levate sì, ch'i' son più ch'io.
Per tanti rivi s'empie d'allegrezza   19
  la mente mia, che di sé fa letizia
  perché può sostener che non si spezza.
Ditemi dunque, cara mia primizia,   22
  quai fuor li vostri antichi e quai fuor li anni
  che si segnaro in vostra püerizia;

CANTO SIXTEEN

*Cacciaguida discourses on the rise and fall of noble **Florentine families.***

O our nobility of blood so small!
    If here men glory in their clannish pride,
    where human love is weak and apt to fall,
That will no longer leave me stupefied,   4
    for there where cravings do not turn awry—
    I say in Heaven—I felt glorified.
You are a mantle that soon shrinks away: 7
    time's scissors shear you all around the hem
    unless we patch in new cloth day by day.
With the *voi*° that was offered first at Rome   10
    (usage in which they do not persevere),
    my words to him resumed, and Beatrice,
Who stood a little separate from us there,   13
    smiling, seemed like the one° who gave a cough
    at the first fault they write of Guinevere.
"You are my father," I began in reply.   16
    "You fill my heart with confidence to speak,
    you raise me so, that I am more than I!
So many rivers of exhilaration   19
    now flood my heart that it's a joy for me
    even to bear the gladness and not break.
Tell me, beloved father of my tree,   22
    who were your elders and how many years
    they numbered to record your infancy;

°voi: polite pronoun for singular "you." For its connection with Rome, see notes.
    °*the one:* the lady of Malehaut. As Lancelot and Guinevere were revealing their love to each
other, she coughed to let them know she was in earshot.

ditemi de l'ovil di San Giovanni   25
   quanto era allora, e chi eran le genti
   tra esso degne di più alti scanni".
Come s'avviva a lo spirar d'i venti   28
   carbone in fiamma, così vid' io quella
   luce risplendere a' miei blandimenti;
e come a li occhi miei si fé più bella,   31
   così con voce più dolce e soave,
   ma non con questa moderna favella,
dissemi: "Da quel dì che fu detto *'Ave'*   34
   al parto in che mia madre, ch'è or santa,
   s'alleviò di me ond' era grave,
al suo Leon cinquecento cinquanta   37
   e trenta fiate venne questo foco
   a rinfiammarsi sotto la sua pianta.
Li antichi miei e io nacqui nel loco   40
   dove si truova pria l'ultimo sesto
   da quei che corre il vostro annüal gioco.
Basti d'i miei maggiori udirne questo: 43
   chi ei si fosser e onde venner quivi,
   più è tacer che ragionare onesto.
Tutti color ch'a quel tempo eran ivi   46
   da poter arme tra Marte e 'l Batista,
   erano il quinto di quei ch'or son vivi.
Ma la cittadinanza, ch'è or mista   49
   di Campi, di Certaldo e di Fegghine,
   pura vediesi ne l'ultimo artista.
Oh quanto fora meglio esser vicine   52
   quelle genti ch'io dico, e al Galluzzo
   e a Trespiano aver vostro confine,

Tell me about the sheepfold of Saint John,°   25
    how many it enclosed, and who they were
    worthy among them of the noblest chairs."

As coals in fire flame lively at a mere   28
    puff of the wind, so did I see that soul
    stirring in splendor at my courteous praise.

As his appearance grew more beautiful,   31
    so with a voice of sweet gentility,
    not with the dialect we use today,

"From the day of the angel's 'Hail,' " said he,   34
    "to when my mother, now among the blest,
    eased herself of the weight of bearing me,

Flaming again beneath his Lion's fist°   37
    this fiery star's been kindled in its trace
    five hundred eighty times across the sky.

My elders and I were born in the place   40
    where you would enter the sixth parish as
    you ran the last leg of your annual race.

Enough to hear about my forebears, this.   43
    Of who they were and whence they might derive,
    it's fitting not to speak, but to let pass.

In number, all the grown men then alive   46
    between Mars and the Baptist,° who bore arms,
    were to your living men as one to five.

That citizenry—which now is laced with swarms   49
    from Campi, from Certaldo, from Fegghine°—
    was pure down to the humblest artisan.

Far better had you drawn your borderline   52
    up to Trespiano and Galluzzo's° brink,
    and held the folks I've mentioned as your neighbors,

°*the sheepfold of Saint John:* Florence, whose patron saint was John the Baptist.

°*beneath his Lion's fist:* in the constellation Leo. Mars was thought to complete one revolution through the zodiac every 687 days. It would take 580 such periods to go from the annunciation to Cacciaguida's birth—in 1091, therefore.

°*between Mars and the Baptist:* between the remains, on the Ponte Vecchio, of a statue thought to be of Mars (cf. *Inf.* 13.146–47) and the Baptistery of Saint John. Cacciaguida's Florence was far smaller than the city of Dante's day.

°*Campi . . . Certaldo . . . Fegghine:* small locales in the countryside around Florence.

°*Trespiano and Galluzzo:* walled villages just outside of Florence.

che averle dentro e sostener lo puzzo   55
   del villan d'Aguglion, di quel da Signa,
   che già per barattare ha l'occhio aguzzo!
Se la gente ch'al mondo più traligna   58
   non fosse stata a Cesare noverca,
   ma come madre a suo figlio benigna,
tal fatto è fiorentino e cambia e merca,   61
   che si sarebbe vòlto a Simifonti,
   là dove andava l'avolo a la cerca;
sariesi Montemurlo ancor de' Conti;   64
   sarieno i Cerchi nel piovier d'Acone,
   e forse in Valdigrieve i Buondelmonti.
Sempre la confusion de le persone   67
   principio fu del mal de la cittade,
   come del vostro il cibo che s'appone;
e cieco toro più avaccio cade   70
   che cieco agnello; e molte volte taglia
   più e meglio una che le cinque spade.
Se tu riguardi Luni e Orbisaglia   73
   come sono ite, e come se ne vanno
   di retro ad esse Chiusi e Sinigaglia,
udir come le schiatte si disfanno   76
   non ti parrà nova cosa né forte,
   poscia che le cittadi termine hanno.
Le vostre cose tutte hanno lor morte,   79
   sì come voi; ma celasi in alcuna
   che dura molto, e le vite son corte.
E come 'l volger del ciel de la luna   82
   cuopre e discuopre i liti sanza posa,
   così fa di Fiorenza la Fortuna:
per che non dee parer mirabil cosa   85
   ciò ch'io dirò de li alti Fiorentini
   onde è la fama nel tempo nascosa.

Than bring them in and have to bear the stink   55
   of the plowboys of Signa and Aguglion,
   whose eyes are keen for graft, and they don't blink!
But had the world's most deviating men°   58
   not been stepmothers to the emperor,
   but loved him as a mother loves her son,
Some new-made Florentines who trade and deal   61
   would have turned back to hoe in Simifonti,
   where their grandfathers roved to scratch a meal;
Montemurlo would still wall up the Conti;   64
   the Cerchi would be living in Acone,
   and in the Valdigreve the Buondelmonti.
As when you bolt two different suppers down   67
   you rouse diseases, so a town grows sick
   from populations all confused in one:
And a blind lamb will fall, but not so quick   70
   as a blind bull; and oftentimes it's true
   a single sword can cut sharper than five.
Take Luni and Orbisaglia, look at how   73
   they've gone to ruin, and are followed by
   Chiusi and Sinigaglia falling now:
Then, that a branch should wither and turn dry   76
   won't seem a thing so difficult or strange,
   for entire cities too must someday die,
And as men die, men's works must suffer change   79
   and meet their death; but some things can endure
   so long, they hide the end from your short lives.
And as the tides reveal and hide the shore   82
   according to the moon's revolving ring,
   so Florence fares as Fortune's less or more;
Then you can have no cause for marveling   85
   at what I'll say of olden Florentines
   whose fame is hidden in the deeps of time.

°*world's most deviating men:* the leaders of the Church, locked in opposition against the emperor. Opposing imperial rule, Florence allied herself with her countryside, effectively drawing its people into her citizenry.

Io vidi li Ughi e vidi i Catellini, 88
    Filippi, Greci, Ormanni e Alberichi,
    già nel calare, illustri cittadini;
e vidi così grandi come antichi, 91
    con quel de la Sannella, quel de l'Arca,
    e Soldanieri e Ardinghi e Bostichi.
Sovra la porta ch'al presente è carca 94
    di nova fellonia di tanto peso
    che tosto fia iattura de la barca,
erano i Ravignani, ond' è disceso 97
    il conte Guido e qualunque del nome
    de l'alto Bellincione ha poscia preso.
Quel de la Pressa sapeva già come 100
    regger si vuole, e avea Galigaio
    dorata in casa sua già l'elsa e 'l pome.
Grand' era già la colonna del Vaio, 103
    Sacchetti, Giuochi, Fifanti e Barucci
    e Galli e quei ch'arrossan per lo staio.
Lo ceppo di che nacquero i Calfucci 106
    era già grande, e già eran tratti
    a le curule Sizii e Arrigucci.
Oh quali io vidi quei che son disfatti 109
    per lor superbia! e le palle de l'oro
    fiorian Fiorenza in tutt' i suoi gran fatti.
Così facieno i padri di coloro 112
    che, sempre che la vostra chiesa vaca,
    si fanno grassi stando a consistoro.
L'oltracotata schiatta che s'indraca 115
    dietro a chi fugge, e a chi mostra 'l dente
    o ver la borsa, com' agnel si placa,

I saw the Hughs and saw the Catellines,   88
   Filippi, Greci, Ormanni, and Alberichi,
   illustrious but already in decline,
And I saw families as great as old,   91
   with those of La Sannella and the Ark,
   and Soldanieri, Ardinghi, and Bostichi.
Above the portage gate that's laden now   94
   with strange new felony in such amount
   it will capsize and sink the little bark,
Once lived the Ravignani, from whom Count   97
   Guido descends, and all who take their names
   from noble Bellincione. Della Pressa
Already held the reins of government   100
   and ruled them well; and Galigaio's house
   was honored with the golden knob and hilt.°
The band of vair festooned the illustrious   103
   Pigli, Fifanti, Giuochi, and Barucci,
   the Galli and Sacchetti and those who blush
For the false bushel.° The stump of the Calfucci   106
   had borne fruit, and the loftiest cares of state
   had drawn the Sizii and the Arrigucci.
How I have seen them fall who once were great,   109
   destroyed by pride! That house of golden balls,°
   even they once flowered for Florence in grand deeds.
Such were the fathers of your ministers°   112
   who, while the seat is vacant, grow obese
   sitting at council in the bishop's halls.
That arrogant tribe,° dragons to those who flee,   115
   but who, if someone bares a tooth—or purse!—
   are lambs for meekness and humility,

° *the golden knob and hilt:* They had been knighted.

° *who blush for the false bushel:* the Chiaramontesi, one of whom used false scales at the customs office (cf. *Purgatory* 12.105).

° *house of golden balls:* the Lamberti. They and their allies the degli Uberti were banished from Florence; see notes.

° *your ministers:* The Visdomini and Tosinghi families enriched themselves by administering diocesan funds while the see was vacant.

° *arrogant tribe:* the Adimari, allied with the Argenti (cf. *Inf.* 8.32–61).

già venìa sù, ma di picciola gente;   118
     sì che non piacque ad Ubertin Donato
     che poï il suocero il fé lor parente.
Già era 'l Caponsacco nel mercato   121
     disceso giù da Fiesole, e già era
     buon cittadino Giuda e Infangato.
Io dirò cosa incredibile e vera: 124
     nel picciol cerchio s'entrava per porta
     che si nomava da quei de la Pera.
Ciascun che de la bella insegna porta   127
     del gran barone il cui nome e 'l cui pregio
     la festa di Tommaso riconforta,
da esso ebbe milizia e privilegio;   130
     avvegna che con popol si rauni
     oggi colui che la fascia col fregio.
Già eran Gualterotti e Importuni;   133
     e ancor saria Borgo più quïeto,
     se di novi vicin fosser digiuni.
La casa di che nacque il vostro fleto,   136
     per lo giusto disdegno che v'ha morti
     e puose fine al vostro viver lieto,
era onorata, essa e suoi consorti: 139
     o Buondelmonte, quanto mal fuggisti
     le nozze süe per li altrui conforti!
Molti sarebber lieti, che son tristi,   142
     se Dio t'avesse conceduto ad Ema
     la prima volta ch'a città venisti.
Ma conveniesi, a quella pietra scema   145
     che guarda 'l ponte, che Fiorenza fesse
     vittima ne la sua pace postrema.

Had come up, true, but such a paltry clan   118
    was theirs, it rankled Ubertin Donato
    when his wife's father made of them his kin.
The Caponsacchi had already come   121
    from Fiesole to market; Guida too
    was a full citizen, and Infangato.
I'll say what's unbelievable but true: 124
    you entered the town's little wall by gates
    named for the della Pera. All those who
Bore the fine flag of Hugh the Great, whose name   127
    and praise the reverent citizen recites
    on the feast of Saint Thomas, took from him
The titles and the heraldry of knights—   130
    though one who binds his flag with bands of gold
    has allied with the commons. Gualterotti
And Importuni were by then quite bold—   133
    and Borgo, had it kept its diet spare
    of all newcomers, and maintained the old,
Would still have peace. The house° that bore your tears,   136
    begotten by a righteous indignation,
    putting an end to all your happy life,
Was honored, with their kin. O Buondelmonte,   139
    what ruin did you bring us when you fled
    their wedding for the sweet kiss of another!
Many would still know joy who now are sad,   142
    if on that first day you approached the town
    God had been gracious to the Ema°—had
Granted that in its waters you should drown!   145
    Fitting that Florence, though, in her last peace,
    should slay a victim° at the broken stone

°*The house:* the Amidei. Florence's civil strife began with the feud between the Amidei and the Buondelmonti; see notes to line 110 above.

°*Ema:* a stream that the Buondelmonti would have crossed on their way from their old country estate to Florence.

°*a victim:* Buondelmonte dei Buondelmonti, slain on Easter morning in 1216 at the Ponte Vecchio.

Con queste genti, e con altre con esse,   148
   vid' io Fiorenza in sì fatto riposo,
   che non avea cagione onde piangesse.
Con queste genti vid' io glorïoso   152
   e giusto il popol suo, tanto che 'l giglio
   non era ad asta mai posto a ritroso,
né per divisïon fatto vermiglio".   154

Relic of Mars that guards the bridge. With these   148
    and others I saw Florence in repose,
    never a cause to shed a tear. With these
I saw them lead a just and glorious life,   151
    townsmen who never saw some victor drag
    their lily backward in the field, nor strife
Of party turn it red upon the flag."   154

Qual venne a Climenè, per accertarsi
   di ciò ch'avëa incontro a sé udito,
   quei ch'ancor fa li padri ai figli scarsi;
tal era io, e tal era sentito   4
   e da Beatrice e da la santa lampa
   che pria per me avea mutato sito.
Per che mia donna "Manda fuor la vampa   7
   del tuo disio", mi disse, "sì ch'ella esca
   segnata bene de la interna stampa:
non perché nostra conoscenza cresca   10
   per tuo parlare, ma perché t'ausi
   a dir la sete, sì che l'uom ti mesca".
"O cara piota mia che sì t'insusi,   13
   che, come veggion le terrene menti
   non capere in trïangol due ottusi,
così vedi le cose contingenti   16
   anzi che sieno in sé, mirando il punto
   a cui tutti li tempi son presenti;

CANTO SEVENTEEN

*Cacciaguida foretells **Dante's exile from Florence**, revealing the patronage he will enjoy from **Cangrande della Scala**. When Dante suggests that his poetry may give scandal to many on earth, Cacciaguida recommends absolute honesty, for **the poet's mission** depends upon it.*

As he who went to Clymene° to learn
   if what he'd heard to his own harm were true—
   who makes a father loath to give his son
All he might ask him for—so was I too;   4
   Beatrice felt it, and the holy lamp
   who had changed place upon the cross for me.
"Let forth the leaping ardor of desire,"   7
   my Lady said to me, "that it may go
   well sealed with your intention's inner stamp,
Not that your words will help our knowledge grow,   10
   but that you learn to let your thirst be known,
   so one may pour you wine." "Beloved root
Enheavened so high, that as our earthly minds   13
   see that two obtuse angles cannot lie
   within one triangle, you look upon
Contingent things before they come to be,   16
   gazing into the never-changing point
   where times are present to eternity.

°*he who went to Clymene:* When Phaëthon had heard he was not his father's son, his mother, Clymene, told him he was the son of Apollo. To prove it was so, Phaëthon asked Apollo for permission to drive the chariot of the sun. But the boy lost control of the horses, and was struck down by a lightning bolt from Jove, who feared that the wayward sun might burn the earth to a cinder (Ovid, *Met.* 1.750–2.324).

mentre ch'io era a Virgilio congiunto   19
   su per lo monte che l'anime cura
   e discendendo nel mondo defunto,
dette mi fuor di mia vita futura   22
   parole gravi, avvegna ch'io mi senta
   ben tetragono ai colpi di ventura;
per che la voglia mia saria contenta   25
   d'intender qual fortuna mi s'appressa:
   ché saetta previsa vien più lenta".
Così diss' io a quella luce stessa   28
   che pria m'avea parlato; e come volle
   Beatrice, fu la mia voglia confessa.
Né per ambage, in che la gente folle   31
   già s'inviscava pria che fosse anciso
   l'Agnel di Dio che le peccata tolle,
ma per chiare parole e con preciso   34
   latin rispuose quello amor paterno,
   chiuso e parvente del suo proprio riso:
"La contingenza, che fuor del quaderno   37
   de la vostra matera non si stende,
   tutta è dipinta nel cospetto etterno;
necessità però quindi non prende   40
   se non come dal viso in che si specchia
   nave che per torrente giù discende.
Da indi, sì come viene ad orecchia   43
   dolce armonia da organo, mi viene
   a vista il tempo che ti s'apparecchia.
Qual si partio Ipolito d'Atene   46
   per la spietata e perfida noverca,
   tal di Fiorenza partir ti convene.

While I and Virgil journeyed up the mount   19
 that heals the soul, and when we ventured down
 to the dead world, some things were said to me
That weighed upon me heavily, I own,   22
 about my future; though I'm confident
 and feel as solid as a tetragon°
Against the blows to come. Make me content,   25
 tell me the fortune that awaits me now!
 Arrows foreseen are slower in descent."
Such were my words to that most brilliant glow   28
 who had addressed me; my will had its say,
 as Beatrice wished. Never by roundabouts,°
Wherein the foolish lands that went astray   31
 had limed themselves, before mankind had slain
 the Lamb of God who takes our sins away,
But in crisp language chosen to explain—   34
 so that paternal love did now respond,
 both dark and radiant in his smile of joy.
"Contingency, which cannot reach beyond   37
 the pages of your foursquare elements,
 is fully painted in the eternal sight,
But derives nothing necessary thence   40
 save such as in the mirror of the eye
 will show a boat that's sweeping down the stream.°
From that Mind into mine, as to one's ear   43
 arrives the organ's gentle harmony,
 come visions of your future drawing near.
As Hippolytus of Athens had to flee   46
 the treachery of his father's ruthless wife,°
 so will your fleeing Florence also be.

°*a tetragon:* a cube, foursquare on all sides.

°*roundabouts:* Cacciaguida speaks directly, not in the devious enigmas used by pagan oracles.

°*save … stream:* One sees a boat moving downstream, and thus it is necessary that it be doing so; yet the sight of the boat does not necessitate its moving downstream (cf. Boethius, *Consolation of Philosophy* 5 pr. 6). God foresees events but does not compel them.

°*his father's ruthless wife:* Phaedra, wife of Theseus, fell in love with her stepson *Hippolytus.* When he resisted her she accused him of rape (Ovid, *Met.* 15.493–546); see notes.

Questo si vuole e questo già si cerca,
    e tosto verrà fatto a chi ciò pensa
    là dove Cristo tutto dì si merca.   49

La colpa seguirà la parte offensa
    in grido, come suol; ma la vendetta
    fia testimonio al ver che la dispensa.   52

Tu lascerai ogne cosa diletta
    più caramente; e questo è quello strale
    che l'arco de lo essilio pria saetta.   55

Tu proverai sì come sa di sale
    lo pane altrui, e come è duro calle
    lo scendere e 'l salir per l'altrui scale.   58

E quel che più ti graverà le spalle,
    sarà la compagnia malvagia e scempia
    con la qual tu cadrai in questa valle;   61

che tutta ingrata, tutta matta ed empia
    si farà contr' a te; ma, poco appresso,
    ella, non tu, n'avrà rossa la tempia.   64

Di sua bestialitate il suo processo
    farà la prova; sì ch'a te fia bello
    averti fatta parte per te stesso.   67

Lo primo tuo refugio e 'l primo ostello
    sarà la cortesia del gran Lombardo
    che 'n su la scala porta il santo uccello;   70

ch'in te avrà sì benigno riguardo,
    che del fare e del chieder, tra voi due,
    fia primo quel che tra li altri è più tardo.   73

Con lui vedrai colui che 'mpresso fue,
    nascendo, sì da questa stella forte,
    che notabili fier l'opere sue.   76

It's wished already and it's sought, but soon 49
    he'll seal it who has got it on his mind
    where Christ is hawked at market all day long.°
They'll rail against the beaten, as men do— 52
    but God's just vengeance shall give witness of
    the slander, vengeance dealt by what is true.
You'll leave behind you everything you love 55
    most dearly: this will be the arrow shot
    first from the bow of exile. You shall prove
How someone else's bread can taste of salt, 58
    and how it is a hard and bitter walk,
    climbing and coming down another's stairs.
But the most grievous weight to bend your back 61
    will be the company who share your fall,
    an idiotic and malicious pack,
Who all ungrateful, mad and heartless all, 64
    will act against you: but in short time they,
    not you, will have red temples. For the end
Will prove the madness of their beastlike way— 67
    so that it will appear a handsome deed
    to have made, of yourself, a party of one.
First place of refuge, first inn for your stay, 70
    will be the Ladder with the holy bird,°
    the house of the great Lombard's courtesy;
And he will have such kind regard for you 73
    he will act first, before you should request,
    when among others it's the deed that's slow.
With him you'll see that man° who was impressed 76
    so firmly by this planet at his birth,
    he'll win renown upon the field of war.

°*he'll … long:* Pope Boniface VIII, in Rome (cf. *Inf.* 19.52–57; John 2:13–17), whom Dante accuses of plotting his exile.

°*the Ladder with the holy bird:* the family Scaligeri, the "ladder bearers," upon whose coat of arms were blazoned a ladder and an eagle, symbol of the Roman Empire. The Scaligeri were Ghibelline lords of the Lombard city of Verona.

°*that man:* Dante's friend and patron Cangrande della Scala; see notes.

Non se ne son le genti ancora accorte
   per la novella età, ché pur nove anni
   son queste rote intorno di lui torte;
ma pria che 'l Guasco l'alto Arrigo inganni,
   parran faville de la sua virtute
   in non curar d'argento né d'affanni.
Le sue magnificenze conosciute
   saranno ancora, sì che ' suoi nemici
   non ne potran tener le lingue mute.
A lui t'aspetta e a' suoi benefici;
   per lui fia trasmutata molta gente,
   cambiando condizion ricchi e mendici;
e portera'ne scritto ne la mente
   di lui, e nol dirai"; e disse cose
   incredibili a quei che fier presente.
Poi giunse: "Figlio, queste son le chiose
   di quel che ti fu detto; ecco le 'nsidie
   che dietro a pochi giri son nascose.
Non vo' però ch'a' tuoi vicini invidie,
   poscia che s'infutura la tua vita
   via più là che 'l punir di lor perfidie".
Poi che, tacendo, si mostrò spedita
   l'anima santa di metter la trama
   in quella tela ch'io le porsi ordita,
io cominciai, come colui che brama,
   dubitando, consiglio da persona
   che vede e vuol dirittamente e ama:
"Ben veggio, padre mio, sì come sprona
   lo tempo verso me, per colpo darmi
   tal, ch'è più grave a chi più s'abbandona;
per che di provedenza è buon ch'io m'armi,
   sì che, se loco m'è tolto più caro,
   io non perdessi li altri per miei carmi.

79

82

85

88

91

94

97

100

103

106

109

They don't yet know about him on the earth,   79
   since he is still a lad; nine years alone
   have these wheels turned around him, but before
Emperor Henry's gulled by the Gascon,°   82
   he'll flash forth in his manhood, evident
   in scorning silver and accepting toil.
But men will know of his magnificent   85
   deeds in the end, and even his enemies
   will speak of them: their tongues will not be still.
Trust in him and his kindly offices.   88
   By him will affluence and beggary
   change places in the fate of many men,
And you'll bear graven in your memory   91
   more, that you will not tell," and he said things
   they won't believe who see them with the eye.
Then added: "Son, these are the glosses on   94
   what you've been told; behold the plots that wait
   concealed for a few turnings of these rings.
Don't look upon your neighbors, though, with hate.   97
   Your life will be enfutured far enough
   to see them punished for their broken faith."
In falling silent, that blest soul revealed   100
   that he had freely passed the shuttle over
   the loom upon whose works I'd set the thread,
So I began as one whose thoughts will waver,   103
   craving advice from him who sees things straight,
   who wills things straight, who loves. "Father, I see
Time digs its spurs to hasten in its gait   106
   against me, and to deal me such a blow,
   the more disarmed, the heavier the weight—
Then I should arm myself with prudence now,   109
   that if they take from me my dearest land,
   I won't lose all the rest by what I sing.

° *the Gascon:* scornful reference to Pope Clement V, who lured the young emperor Henry VII into Italy, then turned against him. Dante has reviled Clement and his Francophile politics before (*Inf.* 19.82–87).

Giù per lo mondo sanza fine amaro,   112
   e per lo monte del cui bel cacume
   li occhi de la mia donna mi levaro,
e poscia per lo ciel, di lume in lume,   115
   ho io appreso quel che s'io ridico,
   a molti fia sapor di forte agrume;
e s'io al vero son timido amico,   118
   temo di perder viver tra coloro
   che questo tempo chiameranno antico".
La luce in che rideva il mio tesoro   121
   ch'io trovai lì, si fé prima corusca,
   quale a raggio di sole specchio d'oro;
indi rispuose: "Coscïenza fusca   124
   o de la propria o de l'altrui vergogna
   pur sentirà la tua parola brusca.
Ma nondimen, rimossa ogne menzogna,   127
   tutta tua visïon fa manifesta;
   e lascia pur grattar dov' è la rogna.
Ché se la voce tua sarà molesta   130
   nel primo gusto, vital nodrimento
   lascerà poi, quando sarà digesta.
Questo tuo grido farà come vento,   133
   che le più alte cime più percuote;
   e ciò non fa d'onor poco argomento.
Però ti son mostrate in queste rote,   136
   nel monte e ne la valle dolorosa
   pur l'anime che son di fama note,
che l'animo di quel ch'ode, non posa   139
   né ferma fede per essempro ch'aia
   la sua radice incognita e ascosa,
né per altro argomento che non paia".   142

Down in the world that's bitter without end,°   112
   and on the mountain from whose lovely peak
   the eyes of my sweet Lady lifted me,
And then from light to light in Heaven I've learned   115
   of things which, if I told, many a mouth
   would find the flavor pungent as a leek,
But if I'm a too timid friend of truth,   118
   with those who'll call these days the days of old
   I fear I'll lose the fame that lengthens youth."
Like sunrays in a mirror made of gold,   121
   the light where laughed the jewel I found on high
   flashed in its joy at first, and then replied,
"A clouded conscience that is darkened by   124
   its own shame or the shame its kin may catch
   will indeed find your words too harsh, too brusque.
Nevertheless, with every falsehood scrapped,   127
   let everything you've seen be manifest,
   and where they've got the mange, let them go scratch.
For if your words are sharp at the first taste,   130
   they'll leave behind a living nourishment
   when they have been digested at the last.
This shout of yours will batter like a gale   133
   that pounds the tallest peaks with greatest force—
   and of its worth that's no small argument.
This is the reason why, within these spheres,   136
   upon the mount and in the sorrowing pit,
   you've been shown only souls whose names men know,
Because the mind that hears won't set one foot   139
   of faith in an example that presents
   a never-heard-of or a hidden root,
Nor in all but the clearest evidence."   142

° *the world that's bitter without end:* Hell; Purgatory is *the mountain.*

Già si godeva solo del suo verbo
    quello specchio beato, e io gustava
    lo mio, temprando col dolce l'acerbo;
e quella donna ch'a Dio mi menava   4
    disse: "Muta pensier; pensa chi'i' sono
    presso a colui ch'ogne torto disgrava".
Io mi rivolsi a l'amoroso suono   7
    del mio conforto; e qual io allor vidi
    ne li occhi santi amor, qui l'abbandono:
non perch' io pur del mio parlar diffidi,   10
    ma per la mente che non può redire
    sovra sé tanto, s'altri non la guidi.
Tanto poss' io di quel punto ridire,   13
    che, rimirando lei, lo mio affetto
    libero fu da ogne altro disire,
fin che 'l piacere etterno, che diretto   16
    raggiava in Bëatrice, dal bel viso
    mi contentava col secondo aspetto.
Vincendo me col lume d'un sorriso,   19
    ella mi disse: "Volgiti e ascolta;
    ché non pur ne' miei occhi è paradiso".
Come si vede qui alcuna volta   22
    l'affetto ne la vista, s'elli è tanto,
    che da lui sia tutta l'anima tolta,

CANTO EIGHTEEN

*Cacciaguida names for Dante the flames of other **warriors of God**. Then Dante and Beatrice ascend to **Jupiter, the sixth sphere**, where Dante sees stars form the constellation of **the Eagle of justice**.*

He was rejoicing in his word, alone,
    that blessed mirror, and I—tempering
    the bitter with the sweet—sipped of my own,
When she who'd led me unto God began,   4
    "Let your thought change, for I am near the Lord,
    the One who lifts the yoke of every wrong."
I turned unto my comfort when I heard   7
    her kindly voice, and saw such depth of love
    in her blest eyes, I give up, for no word
Can claim my confidence, and, even more,   10
    unless Another guides it, memory
    cannot return from heights so far above
Its power. But as I gazed, my soul was free   13
    of all its many cravings to possess
    anything else—for that much I can say,
Because the everlasting winsomeness   16
    shone upon Beatrice, from whose lovely eyes
    reflected radiance contented me.
Conquering with the flashing of a smile,   19
    she said to me, "Listen now, turn around—
    my eyes are not the only Paradise."
As sometimes here on earth the soul's held bound   22
    by a single sentiment so utterly
    you read it in the face, so I then turned

così nel fiammeggiar del folgór santo,   25
   a ch'io mi volsi, conobbi la voglia
   in lui di ragionarmi ancora alquanto.
El cominciò: "In questa quinta soglia   28
   de l'albero che vive de la cima
   e frutta sempre e mai non perde foglia,
spiriti son beati, che giù, prima   31
   che venissero al ciel, fuor di gran voce.
   sì ch'ogne musa ne sarebbe opima.
Però mira ne' corni de la croce: 34
   quello ch'io nomerò, lì farà l'atto
   che fa in nube il suo foco veloce".
Io vidi per la croce un lume tratto   37
   dal nomar Iosuè, com' el si feo;
   né mi fu noto il dir prima che 'l fatto.
E al nome de l'alto Macabeo   40
   vidi moversi un altro roteando,
   e letizia era ferza del paleo.
Così per Carlo Magno e per Orlando   43
   due ne seguì lo mio attento sguardo,
   com' occhio segue suo falcon volando.
Poscia trasse Guiglielmo e Rinoardo   46
   e 'l duca Gottifredi la mia vista
   per quella croce, e Ruberto Guiscardo.
Indi, tra l'altre luci mota e mista,   49
   mostrommi l'alma che m'avea parlato
   qual era tra i cantor del cielo artista.
Io mi rivolsi dal mio destro lato   52
   per vedere in Beatrice il mio dovere,
   o per parlare o per atto, segnato;

Back to the saintly thunderbolt to see   25
   in his bright flaring the desire in him
   to have a little longer talk with me.

And he began again: "On this fifth limb   28
   of the tree that takes its life from the crown,
   ever in fruit and not to lose one leaf,

Those spirits are blest who were of great renown   31
   on earth before they came to Paradise,
   leaving abundant spoils for poetry.

Therefore behold the two arms of the cross: 34
   for there the spirit I shall name will act
   like quickfire bursting from a thundercloud."

I saw the name of Joshua attract   37
   one light along the cross so suddenly
   that as I heard the word I saw the fact.

At the name of the greatest Maccabee°   40
   I saw another quick-revolving light—
   no other lash to spin the top but glee!

And so for Roland, so for Charles the Great,   43
   I followed flames with my attentive gaze,
   as a man's eye will follow his falcon's flight.

William and Reynard° came then, and the rays   46
   of the duke Godfrey° drew my sight along
   that starry cross, and Robert the Most Wise.°

Moving away, mingling his light among   49
   the other lights, the soul who'd talked with me
   showed what he was of artist in the throng

Of Heaven's singers. I turned right, to see   52
   whether what I should do now might appear
   sealed upon Beatrice by a sign or word,

°*the greatest Maccabee:* Judas Maccabeus; see notes.

°*William and Reynard:* William of Orange (d. 812), founder of a monastery and, like Charlemagne and *Roland* and the fictional Reynard, the hero of legends of Christian crusading.

°*duke Godfrey:* Godfrey of Bouillon (1058–1100), conqueror of Jerusalem in the First Crusade.

°*Robert the Most Wise:* Norman prince Robert (1015–85), surnamed Guiscard (source of our word "wizard") for his astute military tactics. He too was the hero of songs recounting his feats against the Saracens in southern Italy. Dante has alluded to his campaigns (*Inf.* 28.14).

e vidi le sue luci tanto mere,   55
    tanto gioconde, che la sua sembianza
    vinceva li altri e l'ultimo solere.
E come, per sentir più dilettanza   58
    bene operando, l'uom di giorno in giorno
    s'accorge che la sua virtute avanza,
sì m'accors' io che 'l mio girare intorno   61
    col cielo insieme avea cresciuto l'arco,
    veggendo quel miracol più addorno.
E qual è 'l trasmutare in picciol varco   64
    di tempo in bianca donna, quando 'l volto
    suo si discarchi di vergogna il carco,
tal fu ne li occhi miei, quando fui vòlto,   67
    per lo candor de la temprata stella
    sesta, che dentro a sé m'avea ricolto.
Io vidi in quella giovïal facella   70
    lo sfavillar de l'amor che lì era
    segnare a li occhi miei nostra favella.
E come augelli, surti di rivera,   73
    quasi congratulando a lor pasture,
    fanno di sé or tonda or altra schiera,
sì dentro ai lumi sante creature   76
    volitando cantavano, e faciensi
    or *D,* or *I,* or *L* in sue figure.
Prima, cantando, a sua nota moviensi;   79
    poi, diventando l'un di questi segni,
    un poco s'arrestavano e taciensi.
O diva Pegasëa che li 'ngegni   82
    fai glorïosi e rendili longevi,
    ed essi teco le cittadi e ' regni,
illustrami di te, sì ch'io rilevi   85
    le lor figure com' io l'ho concette:
    paia tua possa in questi versi brevi!

And saw her brilliant shining eyes so clear,   55
   so filled with joy, the beauty of that sight
   defeated all the rest I'd had of her.
And as you feel the surging of delight   58
   in doing well, and come to understand
   your virtue is advancing day by day,
So I could sense that in my sweeping round   61
   to higher Heaven there came a widening bow,
   seeing that wondrous lady grown more grand.
As in a moment's leap will fade the glow   64
   of blushing from a girl whose skin is fair,
   once she's relieved of what has shamed her so,
Such a change met my vision, turning there   67
   to gaze upon the light that welcomed me,
   the candor of the sixth—and tempered—star.
And in that Jovial torchlight I could see   70
   the flames of love in characters of flame
   spell out our human speech before my eye.
And as birds rising flapping from a stream   73
   as if applauding for their feeding well,
   fly in a circling flock or other form,
So in those lights the saintly creatures flew,   76
   and as they flew about they sang for joy
   and formed the figures D and I and L.
First they sang, moving to the melody,   79
   but when they'd formed a letter, in that sign
   they settled for a moment and were still.
O divine Pegasean,° you who bring   82
   man's inborn powers to glory and long life
   as they their cities and their empires, rain
Your light upon me, that in high relief   85
   I sculpt what I remember of that heaven.
   Show forth your power, though the verse is brief!

°*divine Pegasean:* the Muse. A kick from the winged horse Pegasus caused the stream Hippocrene to burst forth from Helicon, the mountain sacred to the Muses.

JUPITER

Mostrarsi dunque in cinque volte sette   88
    vocali e consonanti; e io notai
    le parti sì, come mi parver dette.
'*DILIGITE IUSTITIAM*', primai   91
    fur verbo e nome di tutto 'l dipinto;
    '*QUI IUDICATIS TERRAM*', fur sezzai.
Poscia ne l'emme del vocabol quinto   94
    rimasero ordinate; sì che Giove
    pareva argento lì d'oro distinto.
E vidi scendere altre luci dove   97
    era il colmo de l'emme, e lì quetarsi
    cantando, credo, il ben ch'a sé le move.
Poi, come nel percuoter d'i ciocchi arsi   100
    surgono innumerabili faville,
    onde li stolti sogliono agurarsi,
resurger parver quindi più di mille   103
    luci e salir, qual assai e qual poco,
    sì come 'l sol che l'accende sortille;
e quïetata ciascuna in suo loco,   106
    la testa e 'l collo d'un'aguglia vidi
    rappresentare a quel distinto foco.
Quei che dipinge lì, non ha chi 'l guidi;   109
    ma esso guida, e da lui si rammenta
    quella virtù ch'è forma per li nidi.
L'altra bëatitudo, che contenta   112
    pareva prima d'ingigliarsi a l'emme,
    con poco moto seguitò la 'mprenta.
O dolce stella, quali e quante gemme   115
    mi dimostraro che nostra giustizia
    effetto sia del ciel che tu ingemme!

And so they showed themselves in five times seven   88
    vowels and consonants, and I noted them
    in order, as the signs appeared to me.
At first DILIGITE IUSTITIAM—   91
    these were the letters and the words portrayed,
    concluding with QUI IUDICATIS TERRAM.°
And then they held the pattern they'd arrayed   94
    in the last M, and made Jupiter seem
    silver studded with gold. And I beheld
Descending on the summit of that M°   97
    more lights that moved, and came to rest, and sang,
    I believe sang the Goodness drawing them
Unto Himself. You shake a half-scorched stock   100
    and hosts of sparkles spray before your eyes,
    whence silly folks once tried to tell their luck,°
So more than a thousand stars appeared to rise,   103
    all surging to the heights, some more, some less,
    just as the Sun that kindles them allots.
When each had settled quietly in place,   106
    in that night-piercing bonfire I descried
    the figure of an eagle's neck and head.
He who paints there has no one for a guide;   109
    He is his Guide, in Him we trace the power
    that shapes the form wherein a being nests.
The other spirits in beatitude   112
    seemed happily enlilied in the M,
    yet moved a bit to make the sign complete.
Sweet star, how many jewels of what bright gleam   115
    showed me that all man's justice is the far
    influence of that heaven you engem!

°*DILIGITE ... TERRAM:* "Love justice, ye who judge the earth" (Wis. 1:1).

°*the summit of that M:* The medieval capital M had three vertical strokes. When the stars descend upon the central stroke they turn the M into the shape of a heraldic lily. Soon after, they shift a little at the top to make the letter look like an eagle; see notes.

°*silly ... luck:* Country folk in Italy believed that the number of sparks would correspond to the number of whatever object they wished to possess.

Per ch'io prego la mente in che s'inizia   118
    tuo moto e tua virtute, che rimiri
    ond' esce il fummo che 'l tuo raggio vizia;
sì ch'un'altra fiata omai s'adiri   121
    del comperare e vender dentro al templo
    che si murò di segni e di martìri.
O milizia del ciel cu' io contemplo,   124
    adora per color che sono in terra
    tutti svïati dietro al malo essemplo!
Già si solea con le spade far guerra;   127
    ma or si fa togliendo or qui or quivi
    lo pan che 'l pïo Padre a nessun serra.
Ma tu che sol per cancellare scrivi,   130
    pensa che Pietro e Paulo, che moriro
    per la vigna che guasti, ancor son vivi.
Ben puoi tu dire: "I' ho fermo 'l disiro   133
    sì a colui che volle viver solo
    e che per salti fu tratto al martiro,
ch'io non conosco il pescator né Polo".   136

So I beseech the Mind wherein your power   118
    and motion has its source, that you may turn
    to see the smoke that has obscured your fire,

And one more time grow angry and not brook   121
    selling and buying within that Temple° gate—
    that Temple bricked with miracles and blood!

O army of the heaven I contemplate,   124
    pray for the soldiers who have lost their road
    with such a twisted chief° to imitate!

Time was, they used to wage war with the sword—   127
    but now it's used to chop and portion out
    the bread the loving Father bars from none.

You who write "interdict" to rub it out,   130
    remember, Peter and Paul are living yet,
    who died to tend the vines you've stripped and picked.

Well may you say, "My heart's so firmly set   133
    on him° who chose to live his life alone,
    whom a dance dragged to martyrdom, I don't

Know that Paul fellow, or the Fisherman."°   136

°*that Temple:* the Church.

°*twisted chief:* the pope (here, anachronistically, John XXII), who, Dante asserts, extorts money by the frequent and frivolous issuance of interdicts. The people of a nation or a city under interdict may not receive the sacraments except at the brink of death.

°*him:* John the Baptist (cf. Matt. 3:1–4; 14:1–13), whose image was stamped on the gold florin.

°*the Fisherman:* Saint Peter.

Parea dinanzi a me con l'ali aperte
la bella image che nel dolce *frui*
liete facevan l'anime conserte;
parea ciascuna rubinetto in cui   4
raggio di sole ardesse sì acceso,
che ne' miei occhi rifrangesse lui.
E quel che mi convien ritrar testeso,   7
non portò voce mai, né scrisse incostro,
né fu per fantasia già mai compreso;
ch'io vidi e anche udi' parlar lo rostro,   10
e sonar ne la voce e "io" e "mio",
quand' era nel concetto e 'noi' e 'nostro'.
E cominciò: "Per esser giusto e pio   13
son io qui essaltato a quella gloria
che non si lascia vincere a disio;
e in terra lasciai la mia memoria   16
sì fatta, che le genti lì malvage
commendan lei, ma non seguon la storia".
Così un sol calor di molte brage   19
si fa sentir, come di molti amori
usciva solo un suon di quella image.
Ond' io appresso: "O perpetüi fiori   22
de l'etterna letizia, che pur uno
parer mi fate tutti vostri odori,

Canto Nineteen

*The Eagle addresses Dante's unspoken question on **the fate of the virtuous pagans,** insisting upon **the inscrutability of divine providence** and decrying **the wickedness of rulers** in Christendom in Dante's day.*

There shone before me now with widespread wings
    the lovely image which in their delight
    the spirits had sewn up in unity,
And each a little ruby where the bright   4
    flame of the Sun burned with so strong a ray
    I saw that Sun by the reflected light.
And what I am now summoned to portray   7
    no ink's been known to write, or voice to speak,
    or any fantasy to comprehend,
For I heard and I saw the Eagle's beak   10
    express itself in words like "I" and "mine"
    when "we" and "ours" were in its mind's intent.
"For being just and pious," it began,   13
    "I am exalted here unto this glory
    unconquerable by any wish of man,
Leaving behind on earth a memory   16
    even the wicked people there commend,
    while never following the history."
As flames of many built-up embers send   19
    one warmth, one light, so came one sound alone
    from all the many loves that image penned,
And I replied, "O everlasting blooms   22
    of the eternal happiness, who make
    your many fragrances appear as one,

solvetemi, spirando, il gran digiuno   25
    che lungamente m'ha tenuto in fame,
    non trovandoli in terra cibo alcuno.
Ben so io che, se 'n cielo altro reame   28
    la divina giustizia fa suo specchio,
    che 'l vostro non l'apprende con velame.
Sapete come attento io m'apparecchio   31
    ad ascoltar; sapete qual è quello
    dubbio che m'è digiun cotanto vecchio".
Quasi falcone ch'esce del cappello,   34
    move la testa e con l'ali si plaude,
    voglia mostrando e faccendosi bello,
vid' io farsi quel segno, che di laude   37
    de la divina grazia era contesto,
    con canti quai si sa chi là sù gaude.
Poi cominciò: "Colui che volse il sesto   40
    a lo stremo del mondo, e dentro ad esso
    distinte tanto occulto e manifesto,
non poté suo valor sì fare impresso   43
    in tutto l'universo, che 'l suo verbo
    non rimanesse in infinito eccesso.
E ciò fa certo che 'l primo superbo,   46
    che fu la somma d'ogne creatura,
    per non aspettar lume, cadde acerbo;
e quinci appar ch'ogne minor natura   49
    è corto recettacolo a quel bene
    che non ha fine e sé con sé misura.
Dunque vostra veduta, che convene   52
    essere alcun de' raggi de la mente
    di che tutte le cose son ripiene,
non pò da sua natura esser possente   55
    tanto, che suo principio non discerna
    molto di là da quel che l'è parvente.
Però ne la giustizia sempiterna   58
    la vista che riceve il vostro mondo,
    com' occhio per lo mare, entro s'interna;

Breathe upon me and free me, help me break   25
   the long fast and the hunger of my heart,
   finding for it no earthly food to take:
I'm well aware that though some other part   28
   may mirror the justice of the Deity,
   your heaven apprehends it through no veil.
You know how I am set attentively   31
   to hear the truth—you know what healing food
   one doubt so old has made me hunger for."
As when the falconer lifts the falcon's hood—   34
   with a head toss and with his wings' applause
   he puts himself in handsome trim to hunt—
So did I see that symbol sewn with praise   37
   of grace divine a-ruffling with the sound
   of songs they know in Heaven who rejoice.
Then it said, "He who swung the sextant round   40
   the limits of the world, and marked a line
   between the manifest and too profound,
Could never stamp the seal of His design   43
   through the whole world, but that His Word must bide
   in infinite excelling, past all things.
And this shows why the first who fell for pride,°   46
   he of created things the pinnacle,
   fell unripe, since he would not wait for light;
Clearly, then, lesser natures are but small   49
   vessels to hold the Good that knows no ground
   and only by Itself is measurable.
Therefore your human vision, which is bound   52
   to be a single one of the rays shot
   from the all-filling Mind of the divine,
By its own nature, its own power, cannot   55
   discern much more than anyone might see
   before his eyes about his origin.
So in the justice of eternity   58
   the vision of your world can plumb no more
   than can the eye that stares into the sea,

°*the first who fell for pride:* Satan.

che, ben che da la proda veggia il fondo,   61
   in pelago nol vede; e nondimeno
   èli, ma cela lui l'esser profondo.

Lume non è, se non vien dal sereno   64
   che non si turba mai; anzi è tenèbra
   od ombra de la carne o suo veleno.

Assai t'è mo aperta la latebra   67
   che t'ascondeva la giustizia viva,
   di che facei question cotanto crebra;

ché tu dicevi: "Un uom nasce a la riva   70
   de l'Indo, e quivi non è chi ragioni
   di Cristo né chi legga né chi scriva;

e tutti suoi voleri e atti buoni   73
   sono, quanto ragione umana vede,
   sanza peccato in vita o in sermoni.

Muore non battezzato e sanza fede: 76
   ov' è questa giustizia che 'l condanna?
   ov' è la colpa sua, se ei non crede?".

Or tu chi se', che vuo' sedere a scranna,   79
   per giudicar di lungi mille miglia
   con la veduta corta d'una spanna?

Certo a colui che meco s'assottiglia,   82
   se la Scrittura sovra voi non fosse,
   da dubitar sarebbe a maraviglia.

Oh terreni animali! oh menti grosse!   85
   La prima volontà, ch'è da sé buona,
   da sé, ch'è sommo ben, mai non si mosse.

Cotanto è giusto quanto a lei consuona: 88
   nullo creato bene a sé la tira,
   ma essa, radïando, lui cagiona".

Quale sovresso il nido si rigira   91
   poi c'ha pasciuti la cicogna i figli,
   e come quel ch'è pasto la rimira;

cotal si fece, e sì leväi i cigli,   94
   la benedetta imagine, che l'ali
   movea sospinte da tanti consigli.

Seeing the bottom when you're near the shore 61
    but not on the high main; and nonetheless,
    hidden in its profundity, the floor
Lies there below. All light is from the peace 64
    that never is disturbed; but darkness is
    the shadow, or the poison, of the flesh.
The covert's now revealed that made you miss 67
    the living justice huddled up in night
    when pressed with doubt you kept on posing this:
'Upon the Indus' banks a man is born, 70
    and in that country no one's there to preach
    on Christ, no one to read of Him, or write;
And all his actions and desires are good, 73
    as far as human reason can perceive,
    without a sin in either deed or speech.
He dies unbaptized and without the faith. 76
    Where is the justice that condemns the man?
    Where is his fault, if he does not believe?'
Now who are you, to perch upon your bench 79
    and judge of things a thousand miles away,
    who can't see any farther than a span?
That man who would contest with me, I say, 82
    were Scripture not above you to assist,
    would find good cause for doubting every day.
O living souls of earth! Minds thick with mist! 85
    What in Itself is good, the primal Will,
    never moves from Itself, the highest Good.
All things are just, as chiming with this Will. 88
    It's drawn by no created good, but brings
    that very good to being by its rays."
As having fed her chicks the mother stork 91
    will flutter a turn for joy about the nest,
    while one who's fed will gaze on her in wonder,
So did I raise my lashes, so that blest 94
    image revolved about me on the wing,
    moved by so many wills in unity,

Roteando cantava, e dicea: "Quali   97
   son le mie note a te, che non le 'ntendi,
   tal è il giudicio etterno a voi mortali".
Poi si quetaro quei lucenti incendi   100
   de lo Spirito Santo ancor nel segno
   che fé i Romani al mondo reverendi,
esso ricominciò: "A questo regno   103
   non salì mai chi non credette 'n Cristo,
   né pria né poi ch'el si chiavasse al legno.
Ma vedi: molti gridan 'Cristo, Cristo!',   106
   che saranno in giudicio assai men *prope*
   a lui, che tal che non conosce Cristo;
e tai Cristian dannerà l'Etïòpe,   109
   quando si partiranno i due collegi,
   l'uno in etterno ricco e l'altro inòpe.
Che poran dir li Perse a' vostri regi,   112
   come vedranno quel volume aperto
   nel qual si scrivon tutti suoi dispregi?
Lì si vedrà, tra l'opere d'Alberto,   115
   quella che tosto moverà la penna,
   per che 'l regno di Praga fia diserto.
Lì si vedrà il duol che sovra Senna   118
   induce, falseggiando la moneta,
   quel che morrà di colpo di cotenna.
Lì si vedrà la superbia ch'asseta,   121
   che fa lo Scotto e l'Inghilese folle,
   sì che non può soffrir dentro a sua meta.
Vedrassi la lussuria e 'l viver molle   124
   di quel di Spagna e di quel di Boemme,
   che mai valor non conobbe né volle.

And as it wheeled in flight I heard it sing.   97
  "As my song is unfathomable to you,
   so too to man, the judgments of the King."
Then those flames kindled by the Holy Ghost   100
  settled again to rest within that sign
   that made the Romans reverend below,
And thus resumed: "Never unto this reign   103
  climbs any man without belief in Christ,
   before nor since they nailed Him to the wood.
But here, behold: many now cry, 'Christ, Christ!'   106
  who'll be less near to Him on Judgment Day
   than will the one who never knew of Christ.
Such Christians the Ethiopian will decry   109
  at the division of the flocks that brings
   man to eternal wealth or poverty.
What may a Persian say about your kings,°   112
  when in that open register he reads
   all they have done to earn the Lord's dispraise?
There he will see, writ among Albert's deeds,°   115
  evil that soon enough will move the pen,
   leaving the reign of Prague a land of weeds.
There he will see the sorrow upon the Seine°   118
  brought by the one whose coins were falsified,
   who perished from the blow of a boar's skin.
There he will see what kingdom-thirsty pride   121
  made each, the Scot and Englishman,° a fool,
   too proud to live behind a boundary!
There will be seen the soft lascivious rule   124
  of him of Spain° and him of the Boheme,°
   who never knew true worth, nor wished to know.

°*your kings:* For more on the Christian rulers the Eagle condemns, see notes.
°*Albert's deeds:* Albert was the Holy Roman Emperor; see notes.
°*the sorrow upon the Seine:* the actions of Philip IV (the Fair), king of France; see notes.
°*Englishman:* probably Edward I (d. 1307), who fought many battles against the insurgent Scots under Robert Bruce.
°*him of Spain:* Ferdinand IV (1286–1312).
°*him of the Boheme:* Wenceslaus IV, king of Bohemia (cf. *Purg.* 7.101–2).

Vedrassi al Ciotto di Ierusalemme   127
   segnata con un i la sua bontate,
   quando 'l contrario segnerà un emme.
Vedrassi l'avarizia e la viltate   130
   di quei che guarda l'isola del foco,
   ove Anchise finì la lunga etate;
e a dare ad intender quanto è poco,   133
   la sua scrittura fian lettere mozze,
   che noteranno molto in parvo loco.
E parranno a ciascun l'opere sozze   136
   del barba e del fratel, che tanto egregia
   nazione e due corone han fatte bozze.
E quel di Portogallo e di Norvegia   139
   lì si conosceranno, e quel di Rascia
   che male ha visto il conio di Vinegia.
O beata Ungheria, se non si lascia   142
   più malmenare! e beata Navarra,
   se s'armasse del monte che la fascia!
E creder de' ciascun che già, per arra   145
   di questo, Niccosïa e Famagosta
   per la lor bestia si lamenti e garra,
che dal fianco de l'altre non si scosta".   148

There seen the Cripple of Jerusalem,°
   marked with an I to note the generous deed,
   while all the opposite require an M.

There will be seen the cowardice and greed
   of the custodian° of the isle of flame,
   where the years of Anchises found their end,

And to show just how meager he became,
   his entry's all in chopped abbreviation,
   noting much in the small space by his name.

The squalid stuff will show, the degradation
   wrought by the brother and the unk° who made
   bastards of two crowns and one storied nation.

And they of Norway and of Portugal°
   will there be noted, and the Serbian° too,
   who envied the Venetian currency.

Fortunate Hungary, if you don't allow
   further misguidance! Fortunate Navarre,
   had you armed with the alps° that swaddle you!

But trust this as a sign of how you'll fare:
   Cyprus now bears a beast° upon her back
   that makes the people cry in agony

And runs with all the others of its pack."

127

130

133

136

139

142

145

148

° *the Cripple of Jerusalem:* Charles II of Anjou; see notes.
° *the custodian:* Frederick II of Aragon, king of Sicily (r. 1296–1337), *the isle of flame* where Anchises died.
° *the brother and the unk:* James, king of Aragon, brother of Frederick II of Aragon; James, king of Majorca, uncle of Frederick II.
° *they of Norway and of Portugal:* Haakon VII (r. 1299–1319) and Diniz (r. 1261–1325).
° *the Serbian:* literally, "he of Rascia," Stephen Uros II (1282–1321), who decreed that Venetian coins, or dishonestly light copies thereof, would be currency for his realm. Dante condemns the decree, but it helped bring prosperity to Stephen's people.
° *the alps:* the Pyrenees, separating Navarre from France (and French kings) to the north.
° *a beast:* Henry II of Lusignan, French king of Cyprus. Dante predicts similar misfortune for Navarre, about to suffer likewise under French rule.

Quando colui che tutto 'l mondo alluma
    de l'emisperio nostro sì discende,
    che 'l giorno d'ogne parte si consuma,
lo ciel, che sol di lui prima s'accende,   4
    subitamente si rifà parvente
    per molte luci, in che una risplende;
e questo atto del ciel mi venne a mente,   7
    come 'l segno del mondo e de' suoi duci
    nel benedetto rostro fu tacente;
però che tutte quelle vive luci,   10
    vie più lucendo, cominciaron canti
    da mia memoria labili e caduci.
O dolce amor che di riso t'ammanti,   13
    quanto parevi ardente in que' flailli,
    ch'avieno spirto sol di pensier santi!
Poscia che i cari e lucidi lapilli   16
    ond' io vidi ingemmato il sesto lume
    puoser silenzio a li angelici squilli,
udir mi parve un mormorar di fiume   19
    che scende chiaro giù di pietra in pietra,
    mostrando l'ubertà del suo cacume.
E come suono al collo de la cetra   22
    prende sua forma, e sì com' al pertugio
    de la sampogna vento che penètra,
così, rimosso d'aspettare indugio,   25
    quel mormorar de l'aguglia salissi
    su per lo collo, come fosse bugio.

CANTO TWENTY

*The Eagle names the most exalted spirits in its sphere. These include, as amazing instances of the unknowability of God's plan, the pagans **Trajan** and **Ripheus**.*

When he that brightens all the world with light
   passes below our hemisphere, and day
   in all directions dwindles into night,
Where once there was one fire to light the sky   4
   it reappears for vision instantly
   in many lights resplendent with his one:
Phenomenon of Heaven that came to me   7
   when in the blessed beak the banner sign
   of the world and its generals fell still,
And all those living stars began to shine   10
   in brighter splendor, caroling the while
   what fades from any memory of mine.
Sweet love, whose mantle is a radiant smile!   13
   How ardent, you whose flutes will only sing
   with holy thoughts that breathe upon the soul!
And when the precious gems enjeweling   16
   that star imposed a silence, and the gleam
   was stilled of its angelic shimmering,
I thought I heard the rushing of a stream   19
   splashing in open sky from stone to stone,
   showing the plenty of its spilling spring.
And as the music will assume its tone   22
   at the neck of a lute, and wind will play
   as it sings whistling through the bagpipes' stops,
Setting aside all waiting and delay,   25
   the whooshing climbed up through the Eagle's neck
   as in a hollow pipe, assumed a voice,

THE EAGLE

Fecesi voce quivi, e quindi uscissi   28
   per lo suo becco in forma di parole,
   quali aspettava il core ov' io le scrissi.
"La parte in me che vede e pate il sole   31
   ne l'aguglie mortali", incominciommi,
   "or fisamente riguardar si vole,
perché d'i fuochi ond' io figura fommi,   34
   quelli onde l'occhio in testa mi scintilla,
   e' di tutti lor gradi son li sommi.
Colui che luce in mezzo per pupilla,   37
   fu il cantor de lo Spirito Santo,
   che l'arca traslatò di villa in villa:
ora conosce il merto del suo canto,   40
   in quanto effetto fu del suo consiglio,
   per lo remunerar ch'è altrettanto.
Dei cinque che mi fan cerchio per ciglio,   43
   colui che più al becco mi s'accosta,
   la vedovella consolò del figlio:
ora conosce quanto caro costa   46
   non seguir Cristo, per l'esperïenza
   di questa dolce vita e de l'opposta.
E quel che segue in la circunferenza   49
   di che ragiono, per l'arco superno,
   morte indugiò per vera penitenza:
ora conosce che 'l giudicio etterno   52
   non si trasmuta, quando degno preco
   fa crastino là giù de l'odïerno.
L'altro che segue, con le leggi e meco,   55
   sotto buona intenzion che fé mal frutto,
   per cedere al pastor si fece greco:

And in the form of words rushed through the beak,   28
   stilling the expectation of my heart,
   wherein I wrote them. It began to speak:
"Now you must fix your eyes upon the part   31
   of me which in an eagle born to die
   sees and endures the brilliance of the sun.°
See the flames in the twinkling of my eye!   34
   These of all souls by whom my figure beams
   enjoy my vision most exaltedly.
He in the center,° as the pupil, gleams   37
   who was the singer of the Holy Spirit,
   the king who moved the Ark from house to house;
Now does he understand his songs have merit   40
   insofar as they spring from his own will,
   by the concordant blessings they inherit.
The spirit° who stands nearest to my bill   43
   of the five in the ring that forms the brow
   consoled the widow with the murdered son;
Now does he understand what debt you owe   46
   not following Christ, by the experience
   of this sweet life, and the opposite below.°
The following soul° in this circumference,   49
   where the arch rises, gained a long delay,
   and stayed his death by genuine penitence;
Now does he understand, when just men pray,   52
   eternal judgment does not change, deferring
   until tomorrow what's decreed today.
The next soul bore me off with all the laws   55
   and made us Greek, to grant the Shepherd Rome,
   a good intent° that sprouted up bad fruit;

°*the part ... sun:* the eye (cf. 1.48 and note).

°*He in the center:* King David, singer of the Psalms, who danced before the *Ark* of the Covenant as it was brought to Jerusalem (2 Sam. 6; cf. *Purg.* 10.55–69). For a discussion of these souls and this passage, see introduction.

°*The spirit:* the emperor Trajan; see notes. For his dealing justice to the *widow,* see *Purg.* 10.73–93.

°*the opposite below:* that of Hell.

°*The following soul:* King Hezekiah (cf. 2 Kings 20:1–11).

°*The next soul ... good intent:* Emperor Constantine, thought to have conceded to the papacy control over central Italy.

ora conosce come il mal dedutto 58
    dal suo bene operar non li è nocivo,
    avvegna che sìa 'l mondo indi distrutto.
E quel che vedi ne l'arco declivo, 61
    Guiglielmo fu, cui quella terra plora
    che piagne Carlo e Federigo vivo:
ora conosce come s'innamora 64
    lo ciel del giusto rege, e al sembiante
    del suo fulgore il fa vedere ancora.
Chi crederebbe giù nel mondo errante 67
    che Rifëo Troiano in questo tondo
    fosse la quinta de le luci sante?
Ora conosce assai di quel che 'l mondo 70
    veder non può de la divina grazia,
    ben che sua vista non discerna il fondo".
Quale allodetta che 'n aere si spazia 73
    prima cantando, e poi tace contenta
    de l'ultima dolcezza che la sazia,
tal mi sembiò l'imago de la 'mprenta 76
    de l'etterno piacere, al cui disio
    ciascuna cosa qual ell' è diventa.
E avvenga ch'io fossi al dubbiar mio 79
    lì quasi vetro a lo color ch'el veste,
    tempo aspettar tacendo non patio,
ma de la bocca, "Che cose son queste?", 82
    mi pinse con la forza del suo peso:
    per ch'io di coruscar vidi gran feste.
Poi appresso, con l'occhio più acceso, 85
    lo benedetto segno mi rispuose
    per non tenermi in ammirar sospeso:
"Io veggio che tu credi queste cose 88
    perch' io le dico, ma non vedi come;
    sì che, se son credute, sono ascose.

Now does he understand the plagues that come 58
    from his good deed will never harm his soul,
    even should they destroy all Christendom.
The spirit at the semicircle's fall 61
    was William,° whom they weep for in that land
    that weeps for Charles and Frederick living still;
Now does he understand how deeply Heaven 64
    loves a just king, and in his lightning blaze
    he shows it still, for all to understand.
Who would believe, down in the world that errs, 67
    that Ripheus the Trojan in this round
    would be the fifth among the holy flares?
Far more he understands of grace divine 70
    than all the world can see, although his eye
    can still not plumb the depth of the profound."
As a lark wheeling in the open sky, 73
    first twittering, then quietly content
    with the last sweetness of her melody,
So seemed to me the symbol, the imprint 76
    of the eternal pleasure, at whose will
    all things become what they were meant to be.
And though my doubt was plainly visible, 79
    like colors mantled by a pane of glass,
    I couldn't bear the waiting longer still
But broke forth, uttering, "What things are these!" 82
    driven by urgency; and I could see
    the glittering of their grand festivities.
And then, more flickers kindling in the eye, 85
    not to suspend me in my wonderings,
    the blessed symbol made me this reply:
"I clearly see that you believe these things 88
    because I say them, but you don't see how;
    believed they are, but still they lie concealed.

° *William:* William the Good, king of Sicily (r. 1166–89), far superior to *Charles* II of Anjou and *Frederick* II of Aragon.

Fai come quei che la cosa per nome   91
    apprende ben, ma la sua quiditate
    veder non può se altri non la prome.

Regnum celorum vïolenza pate   94
    da caldo amore e da viva speranza,
    che vince la divina volontate:

non a guisa che l'omo a l'om sobranza,   97
    ma vince lei perché vuole esser vinta,
    e, vinta, vince con sua beninanza.

La prima vita del ciglio e la quinta   100
    ti fa maravigliar, perché ne vedi
    la regïon de li angeli dipinta.

D'i corpi suoi non uscir, come credi,   103
    Gentili, ma Cristiani, in ferma fede
    quel d'i passuri e quel d'i passi piedi.

Ché l'una de lo 'nferno, u' non si riede   106
    già mai a buon voler, tornò a l'ossa;
    e ciò di viva spene fu mercede:

di viva spene, che mise la possa   109
    ne' prieghi fatti a Dio per suscitarla,
    sì che potesse sua voglia esser mossa.

L'anima glorïosa onde si parla,   112
    tornata ne la carne, in che fu poco,
    credette in lui che potëa aiutarla;

e credendo s'accese in tanto foco   115
    di vero amor, ch'a la morte seconda
    fu degna di venire a questo gioco.

L'altra, per grazia che da sì profonda   118
    fontana stilla, che mai creatura
    non pinse l'occhio infino a la prima onda,

tutto suo amor là giù pose a drittura: 121
    per che, di grazia in grazia, Dio li aperse
    l'occhio a la nostra redenzion futura;

ond' ei credette in quella, e non sofferse   124
    da indi il puzzo più del paganesmo;
    e riprendiene le genti perverse.

You're like a person who has come to know 91
    what a thing's called, but does not know its essence,
    unless another draws it out for you.

The kingdom of Heaven suffers violence 94
    from living hope and burning charity
    that overcome the will of the divine,

Not as a man will overcome a man— 97
    the divine wins because it would be won,
    and won, it wins with its benignity.

The first and fifth lives° of the eyebrow stun 100
    your eyes with wonder, for you see the seat
    of angels here embellished with their souls.

They did not leave their bodies (as you suppose) 103
    Gentiles, but Christians of firm faith, each one
    believing in the suffering of those feet

To come, or having passed. To flesh and bone 106
    the one returned from never-repenting Hell,
    and that was the reward of living hope,

Of living hope, with power to impel 109
    prayers to God that he might rise once more,
    and live, and so be moved to willing well.

Returned unto his flesh the briefest hour, 112
    the glorious spirit I've been speaking of
    believed in Him and sought His help and power,

And in believing, kindled into love 115
    so true, the second time he fell asleep
    he merited his coming to this joy.

By grace that showers from a spring so deep 118
    no creature's sight can penetrate into
    its first upwelling wave, the other soul

Placed all his love in righteousness below; 121
    for which, grace upon grace, God raised his eye
    and showed him our redemption yet to come,

And he believed in it, and from that day 124
    he could not bear the stink of paganism,
    and he reproached the people gone awry.

° *The first and fifth lives:* Trajan and Ripheus, to all appearances pagans.

Quelle tre donne li fur per battesmo   127
   che tu vedesti da la destra rota,
   dinanzi al battezzar più d'un millesmo.

O predestinazion, quanto remota   130
   è la radice tua da quelli aspetti
   che la prima cagion non veggion *tota!*

E voi, mortali, tenetevi stretti   133
   a giudicar: ché noi, che Dio vedemo,
   non conosciamo ancor tutti li eletti;

ed ènne dolce così fatto scemo,   136
   perché il ben nostro in questo ben s'affina,
   che quel che vole Iddio, e noi volemo".

Così da quella imagine divina,   139
   per farmi chiara la mia corta vista,
   data mi fu soave medicina.

E come a buon cantor buon citarista   142
   fa seguitar lo guizzo de la corda,
   in che più di piacer lo canto acquista,

sì, mentre ch'e' parlò, sì mi ricorda   145
   ch'io vidi le due luci benedette,
   pur come batter d'occhi si concorda,

con le parole mover le fiammette.   148

Those Ladies° were his sponsors at baptism,   127
    the three at the right wheel of the chariot,
    a thousand years before the Baptist came.
O predestination, how remote   130
    your root is from those sights that cannot see
    the fullness of the primal cause! And you
Mortals, withhold your judgment: even we   133
    who see the face of God do not yet know
    the number chosen from eternity—
And it is sweet, such lack in what we know,   136
    because in this good is our good made fine,
    that what the Lord may will, we too will so."
So was I given soothing medicine   139
    to clear the haze from vision all too near,
    by that bright icon, seal of the divine.
And as an expert hand on the guitar   142
    follows the singer with a trembling chord,
    lending a greater pleasure to the air,
So while the Eagle spoke I can recall   145
    those two blest gleams of light, that I could see
    flashing their happy flames at every word,
Like eyes that blink in perfect harmony.   148

° *Those Ladies:* Faith, Hope, and Charity, who danced beside *the chariot* of the Griffin in the mystical procession in Earthly Paradise (*Purg.* 29.121–29).

Già eran li occhi miei rifissi al volto
  de la mia donna, e l'animo con essi,
  e da ogne altro intento s'era tolto.
E quella non ridea; ma "S'io ridessi",   4
  mi cominciò, "tu ti faresti quale
  fu Semelè quando di cener fessi:
ché la bellezza mia, che per le scale   7
  de l'etterno palazzo più s'accende,
  com' hai veduto, quanto più si sale,
se non si temperasse, tanto splende,   10
  che 'l tuo mortal podere, al suo fulgore,
  sarebbe fronda che trono scoscende.
Noi sem levati al settimo splendore,   13
  che sotto 'l petto del Leone ardente
  raggia mo misto giù del suo valore.
Ficca di retro a li occhi tuoi la mente,   16
  e fa di quelli specchi a la figura
  che 'n questo specchio ti sarà parvente".
Qual savesse qual era la pastura   19
  del viso mio ne l'aspetto beato
  quand' io mi trasmutai ad altra cura,

CANTO TWENTY-ONE

*Dante and Beatrice rise to **Saturn, the seventh sphere,** the sphere of **the con-**
templatives, who scale a **ladder** to and from the heaven of heavens. **Peter**
Damian descends to greet Dante and speak of **the degeneracy of the monas-**
tic orders.*

Upon my Lady's countenance once more
    I'd fixed my eyes, and with my eyes, my soul;
    and every other thought was swept aside.
She was not smiling, but, "If I should smile,"   4
    she began, "you'd become like Semele
    reduced to ashes by the power of Jove,
Because my beauty, as you doubtless see,   7
    kindles the more the higher we scale the flight
    that scales the palace of eternity.
If it's not tempered, it will grow so bright,   10
    your mortal power would be a branch destroyed
    by a thunderbolt before its radiant might.
We've risen to the seventh splendor now,   13
    that sends its rays commingled with the bold
    fire of the Lion's heart° to earth below.
Let your mind follow fast what you behold: 16
    make your eyes into mirrors for the sign
    that in *this* mirror will appear to you."
Who knew the feeding of these eyes of mine   19
    upon the sweetness of her blessed face,
    might well imagine, when I turned them then

°*fire of the Lion's heart:* Saturn is in conjunction with Leo and its bright heart star, Regulus.

conoscerebbe quanto m'era a grato   22
   ubidire a la mia celeste scorta,
   contrapesando l'un con l'altro latø.
Dentro al cristallo che 'l vocabol porta,   25
   cerchiando il mondo, del suo caro duce
   sotto cui giacque ogne malizia morta,
di color d'oro in che raggio traluce   28
   vid' io uno scaleo eretto in suso
   tanto, che nol seguiva la mia luce.
Vidi anche per li gradi scender giuso   31
   tanti splendor, ch'io pensai ch'ogne lume
   che par nel ciel, quindi fosse diffuso.
E come, per lo natural costume,   34
   le pole insieme, al cominciar del giorno,
   si movono a scaldar le fredde piume;
poi altre vanno via sanza ritorno,   37
   altre rivolgon sé onde son mosse,
   e altre roteando fan soggiorno;
tal modo parve me che quivi fosse   40
   in quello sfavillar che 'nsieme venne,
   sì come in certo grado si percosse.
E quel che presso più ci si ritenne,   43
   si fé sì chiaro, ch'io dicea pensando:
   'Io veggio ben l'amor che tu m'accenne.
Ma quella ond' io aspetto il come e 'l quando   46
   del dire e del tacer, si sta; ond' io,
   contra 'l disio, fo ben ch'io non dimando'.
Per ch'ella, che vedëa il tacer mio   49
   nel veder di colui che tutto vede,
   mi disse: "Solvi il tuo caldo disio".
E io incominciai: "La mia mercede   52
   non mi fa degno de la tua risposta;
   ma per colei che 'l chieder mi concede,
vita beata che ti stai nascosta   55
   dentro a la tua letizia, fammi nota
   la cagion che sì presso mi t'ha posta;

Unto another duty, what great grace,　　　　　　　　　22
　　what joy it was to heed my heavenly guide,
　　a joy that tipped the other in the scales!

Within that crystal ring around the world　　　　　25
　　which bears the name of its beloved king,°
　　under whose reign all evil-will lay dead,

In gold enlaced with sunlight shimmering,　　　　28
　　I saw a ladder heavenward-tall extend
　　its rungs so high, my own light could not bring

The summit to me: on those rungs descend　　　　31
　　so many splendors that I thought the sky
　　had spilled its wealth of stars upon this sign.

And as, by natural proclivity,　　　　　　　　　　34
　　the flocked rooks at the dawning of the day
　　ruffle their feathers to grow warm again,

Then without turning back some fly away,　　　　37
　　others return to where they'd raised the wing,
　　and others fly in easy wheels and stay,

So seemed to me the manner in that ring　　　　40
　　as soon as each light reached a certain grade
　　among those sparking flames. The glimmering

That stopped his turning nearest to us made　　43
　　himself so brilliant that I said in thought,
　　"I see your love for me is well portrayed!

But she is silent, she from whom I've sought　　46
　　the how and when to speak or to be still.
　　I wish to ask—it's better I do not."

Whereupon she who saw my silent will　　　　　49
　　through the sight of the One all-seeing said,
　　"Now set your warm desire at liberty."

And I began: "All I have merited　　　　　　　　52
　　can't make me worthy of your least reply,
　　but for her sake who grants that I may ask,

Fortunate life remaining hidden by　　　　　　　55
　　your happiness, give me to know, reveal
　　the reason why you have approached me here,

° *its beloved king:* Saturn, mythical ruler of the world in its early Golden Age.

SATURN

e dì perché si tace in questa rota   58
   la dolce sinfonia di paradiso,
   che giù per l'altre suona sì divota".
"Tu hai l'udir mortal sì come il viso",   61
   rispuose a me; "onde qui non si canta
   per quel che Bëatrice non ha riso.
Giù per li gradi de la scala santa   64
   discesi tanto sol per farti festa
   col dire e con la luce che mi ammanta;
né più amor mi fece esser più presta,   67
   ché più e tanto amor quinci sù ferve,
   sì come il fiammeggiar ti manifesta.
Ma l'alta carità, che ci fa serve   70
   pronte al consiglio che 'l mondo governa,
   sorteggia qui sì come tu osserve".
"Io veggio ben", diss' io, "sacra lucerna,   73
   come libero amore in questa corte
   basta a seguir la provedenza etterna;
ma questo è quel ch'a cerner mi par forte,   76
   perché predestinata fosti sola
   a questo officio tra le tue consorte".
Né venni prima a l'ultima parola,   79
   che del suo mezzo fece il lume centro,
   girando sé come veloce mola;
poi rispuose l'amor che v'era dentro: 82
   "Luce divina sopra me s'appunta,
   penetrando per questa in ch'io m'invento,
la cui virtù, col mio veder congiunta,   85
   mi leva sopra me tanto, ch'i' veggio
   la somma essenza de la quale è munta.
Quinci vien l'allegrezza ond' io fiammeggio;   88
   per ch'a la vista mia, quant' ella è chiara,
   la chiarità de la fiamma pareggio.
Ma quell' alma nel ciel che più si schiara,   91
   quel serafin che 'n Dio più l'occhio ha fisso,
   a la dimanda tua non satisfara,

And say why you are silent in this wheel 58
  of the sweet symphony of Paradise
  when all below resound devotedly."
"Your hearing is as mortal as your eyes," 61
  he answered me, "so now we've ceased to sing,
  for the same reason Beatrice does not smile.
Only to bring you cause for reveling 64
  in my replies and in my robe of light
  have I come down the ladder, rung to rung;
Nor is it greater love that wings my flight. 67
  The same or greater bubbles up above,
  as manifest in flames that burn more bright.
Deep charity makes us ready servants of 70
  the Wisdom that steers the world—the charity
  that sorts our places here as you observe."
I answered, "Sacred lamp, well do I see 73
  how in this court free acts of love suffice
  for following the eternal destiny,
But what is hard for me to see is this: 76
  why among your companions you alone
  should be predestined for this duty now."
I'd not reached the last word when he'd begun 79
  to make his center radiate and spin
  as swiftly as a mill will spin the stone,
And then replied the love that dwelt therein: 82
  "I feel divine light like a lance's point
  piercing this womb of light I'm swaddled in.
Its power, with my power of sight conjoint, 85
  lifts me so high above myself I see
  the pinnacle of Being, its bursting fount.
Thence burns the flame of my felicity— 88
  and measured is the brightness of my flame
  to what my sight enjoys of clarity.
Not even the heavenly soul of clearest gleam 91
  could satisfy your question, not the most
  God-contemplating of the Seraphim,

però che sì s'innoltra ne lo abisso 94
    de l'etterno statuto quel che chiedi,
    che da ogne creata vista è scisso.

E al mondo mortal, quando tu riedi, 97
    questo rapporta, sì che non presumma
    a tanto segno più mover li piedi.

La mente, che qui luce, in terra fumma; 100
    onde riguarda come può là giùe
    quel che non pote perché 'l ciel l'assumma".

Sì mi prescrisser le parole sue, 103
    ch'io lasciai la quistione e mi ritrassi
    a dimandarla umilmente chi fue.

"Tra ' due liti d'Italia surgon sassi, 106
    e non molto distanti a la tua patria,
    tanto che ' troni assai suonan più bassi,

e fanno un gibbo che si chiama Catria, 109
    di sotto al quale è consecrato un ermo,
    che suole esser disposto a sola latria".

Così ricominciommi il terzo sermo; 112
    e poi, continüando, disse: "Quivi
    al servigio di Dio mi fe' sì fermo,

che pur con cibi di liquor d'ulivi 115
    lievemente passava caldi e geli,
    contento ne' pensier contemplativi.

Render solea quel chiostro a questi cieli 118
    fertilemente; e ora è fatto vano,
    sì che tosto convien che si riveli.

In quel loco fu' io Pietro Damiano, 121
    e Pietro Peccator fu' ne la casa
    di Nostra Donna in sul lito adriano.

Poca vita mortal m'era rimasa, 124
    quando fui chiesto e tratto a quel cappello,
    che pur di male in peggio si travasa.

For what you've asked so fathoms the abyss   94
    of law established from eternity,
    it is cut off from all created eyes.
Returning to the world of things that die,   97
    bring back this truth, so men will not presume
    to move their feet to reach a goal so high.
Here your mind shines, there it is smoke and gloom.   100
    Figure, then, how—down there—they can surpass
    in vision those the heavenly spheres assume!"
His words thus settled things; I must not pass.   103
    I left the question and restrained my course
    and humbly asked the spirit who he was.
"Mountains surge up between the Italian shores   106
    not too far distant from your fatherland,
    with ridges higher than the thunder's roars,
And form Catria, a humpback of the land.   109
    Below it stands a consecrated house,
    a hermitage once given utterly
To honoring the Lord." He raised his voice   112
    a third time, adding, "At the service of God
    I was so firm and settled in that place,
With olive oil alone to dress my food,   115
    easily I endured the heat and cold,
    contented in my contemplating thought.
That cloister used to render a rich yield   118
    to Heaven; now a barren, dry terrain,
    as shall before much longer be revealed.
In that place I was Peter Damian,   121
    Peter the Sinner so named in the house
    of Our Lady on the Adriatic Main.
Little of mortal life was left to me   124
    when I was called and dragged to don the hat°
    that passes from bad vessels into worse.

°*don the hat:* of the cardinalate, in 1057; yet the red hat was not adopted until 1252.

Venne Cefàs e venne il gran vasello 127
    de lo Spirito Santo, magri e scalzi,
    prendendo il cibo da qualunque ostello.
Or voglion quinci e quindi chi rincalzi 130
    li moderni pastori e chi li meni,
    tanto son gravi, e chi di rietro li alzi.
Cuopron d'i manti loro i palafreni, 133
    sì che due bestie van sott' una pelle:
    oh pazïenza che tanto sostieni!".
A questa voce vid' io più fiammelle 136
    di grado in grado scendere e girarsi,
    e ogne giro le facea più belle.
Dintorno a questa vennero e fermarsi, 139
    e fero un grido di sì alto suono,
    che non potrebbe qui assomigliarsi;
né io lo 'ntesi, sì mi vinse il tuono. 142

Shoeless and gaunt came Cephas,° came the great 127
    vessel of the Holy Spirit, lodging where
    they could, eating what they were given to eat—
But now our modern shepherds won't appear 130
    unless they're led and propped on either side
    and their grave persons boosted from the rear.
Their robes cover their palfreys when they ride. 133
    Infinite patience, so much do you bear!
    Two beasts that go under a single hide!"
Upon these words I saw from stair to stair 136
    more flames descend and spin themselves about,
    and every spinning made them lovelier.
Round him they came and stopped and gave a shout 139
    so deep, no roar on earth I've ever heard
    compares: the crack of thunder overcame me
And in the shock I did not hear a word. 142

°*Cephas:* Aramaic: "Rock," Peter. The *vessel of the Holy Spirit* is Saint Paul (cf. *Inf.* 2.28).

Oppresso di stupore, a la mia guida
  mi volsi, come parvol che ricorre
  sempre colà dove più si confida;
e quella, come madre che soccorre   4
  sùbito al figlio palido e anelo
  con la sua voce, che 'l suol ben disporre,
mi disse: "Non sai tu che tu se' in cielo?   7
  e non sai tu che 'l cielo è tutto santo,
  e ciò che ci si fa vien da buon zelo?
Come t'avrebbe trasmutato il canto,   10
  e io ridendo, mo pensar lo puoi,
  poscia che 'l grido t'ha mosso cotanto;
nel qual, se 'nteso avessi i prieghi suoi,   13
  già ti sarebbe nota la vendetta
  che tu vedrai innanzi che tu muoi.
La spada di qua sù non taglia in fretta   16
  né tardo, ma' ch'al parer di colui
  che disïando o temendo l'aspetta.
Ma rivolgiti omai inverso altrui;   19
  ch'assai illustri spiriti vedrai,
  se com' io dico l'aspetto redui".
Come a lei piacque, li occhi ritornai,   22
  e vidi cento sperule che 'nsieme
  più s'abbellivan con mutüi rai.

Canto Twenty-two

*Still in the sphere of **Saturn**, Dante speaks with **Saint Benedict**, who decries the corruption of the Benedictines. Then Dante and Beatrice ascend to **the eighth sphere**, that of **the fixed stars**.*

I turned—oppressed with wonder, stupefied,
    exactly as a little child will run
    back to the one he trusts most—to my guide,
And as a mother comes to help her son,   4
    who, pale and breathless, hears her ready voice
    that always seems to make him strong again,
"Didn't you know that you're in Paradise?"   7
    she said. "Didn't you know that everything
    in Heaven is holy, and all our acts arise
From righteous zeal? Then think how changed you'd be,   10
    having been overcome by the mere cry,
    if I should smile, and if these souls should sing;
Yet had you understood their shouted prayer,   13
    the divine vengeance had been known to you.
    But you will see it strike before you die.
A man may think the sword of Heaven too slow   16
    or quick, as he may wish or fear its fall:
    yet it will cut when it is destined to.
But turn around and look on someone else,   19
    for if you heed me and you turn your gaze,
    you will see many an illustrious soul."
And as she pleased I turned my eyes and saw   22
    a hundred little globes in unison
    adorning one another with their rays.

Io stava come quei che 'n sé represse   25
    la punta del disio, e non s'attenta
    di domandar, sì del troppo si teme;
e la maggiore e la più luculenta   28
    di quelle margherite innanzi fessi,
    per far di sé la mia voglia contenta.
Poi dentro a lei udi': "Se tu vedessi   31
    com' io la carità che tra noi arde,
    li tuoi concetti sarebbero espressi.
Ma perché tu, aspettando, non tarde   34
    a l'alto fine, io ti farò risposta
    pur al pensier, da che sì ti riguarde.
Quel monte a cui Cassino è ne la costa   37
    fu frequentato già in su la cima
    da la gente ingannata e mal disposta;
e quel son io che sù vi portai prima   40
    lo nome di colui che 'n terra addusse
    la verità che tanto ci soblima;
e tanta grazia sopra me relusse,   43
    ch'io ritrassi le ville circunstanti
    da l'empio cólto che 'l mondo sedusse.
Questi altri fuochi tutti contemplanti   46
    uomini fuoro, accesi di quel caldo
    che fa nascere i fiori e ' frutti santi.
Qui è Maccario, qui è Romoaldo,   49
    qui son li frati miei che dentro ai chiostri
    fermar li piedi e tennero il cor saldo".
E io a lui: "L'affetto che dimostri   52
    meco parlando, e la buona sembianza
    ch'io veggio e noto in tutti li ardor vostri,
così m'ha dilatata mia fidanza,   55
    come 'l sol fa la rosa quando aperta
    tanto divien quant' ell' ha di possanza.

I stood as one who in his heart holds down 25
    the goad of his desire, and out of fear
    to annoy with his questions, does not try,

When of the pearls that dwell within that sphere 28
    the largest and most lightsome jewel came
    to make my will content. For I could hear

From the light's heart, "If you could see the flame 31
    of charity we burn in, as I do,
    you'd have expressed your thoughts and felt no shame.

I would not have your pilgrimage be slow: 34
    that waiting may not hold you from the goal,
    I'll reply to the thought you've guarded so.

That mountain with Cassino° on its spur 37
    was thronged with worshipers in pagan time,
    people disposed to evil and deceived

By cheating gods. I am he, first to climb 40
    that peak to bring His name who brought the earth
    the truth that raises us to the sublime;

With radiant grace so far above my worth, 43
    I drew each of the villages around
    from the impious cult that had seduced

The whole world. All these other flames were bound 46
    in contemplation, kindled by the heat
    engendering the flowers and holy fruit:

Romualdus and Macarius° are here, 49
    and my good brothers who, within the close,
    held their hearts steadfast where they held their feet."

"The love that your conversing with me shows," 52
    said I, "and signs of kindness so intense
    I see your blazes brightening, every one,

Have swelled in me as rich a confidence 55
    as does the sunshine when it brings to light
    the fullest flowering of the open rose.

°*Cassino:* The speaker is Saint Benedict, who founded his first monastery at Monte Cassino, near Naples, in the sixth century.

°*Romualdus and Macarius:* Romualdus founded the Camaldolese order in 1018; Macarius may be either of two Egyptian hermits, disciples of Saint Anthony of Egypt in the fourth century.

Però ti priego, e tu, padre, m'accerta   58
    s'io posso prender tanta grazia, ch'io
    ti veggia con imagine scoverta".

Ond' elli: "Frate, il tuo alto disio   61
    s'adempierà in su l'ultima spera,
    ove s'adempion tutti li altri e 'l mio.

Ivi è perfetta, matura e intera   64
    ciascuna disïanza; in quella sola
    è ogne parte là ove sempr' era,

perché non è in loco e non s'impola;   67
    e nostra scala infino ad essa varca,
    onde così dal viso ti s'invola.

Infin là sù la vide il patriarca   70
    Iacobbe porger la superna parte,
    quando li apparve d'angeli sì carca.

Ma, per salirla, mo nessun diparte   73
    da terra i piedi, e la regola mia
    rimasa è per danno de le carte.

Le mura che solieno esser badia   76
    fatte sono spelonche, e le cocolle
    sacca son piene di farina ria.

Ma grave usura tanto non si tolle   79
    contra 'l piacer di Dio, quanto quel frutto
    che fa il cor de' monaci sì folle;

ché quantunque la Chiesa guarda, tutto   82
    è de la gente che per Dio dimanda;
    non di parenti né d'altro più brutto.

La carne d'i mortali è tanto blanda,   85
    che giù non basta buon cominciamento
    dal nascer de la quercia al far la ghianda.

Pier cominciò sanz' oro e sanz' argento,   88
    e io con orazione e con digiuno,
    e Francesco umilmente il suo convento;

Therefore assure me, Father, if I might   58
    receive so great a grace—I beg of you,
    unveil your human image to my sight."
"Brother, your deep desire shall be fulfilled,"   61
    said he, "only within the final sphere,°
    where are fulfilled my own and others' too.
Entire and sweetly ripe and perfect there   64
    is every longing; only in that place
    does every part stand where it ever has.
It turns upon no pole nor stands in space.   67
    Unto that height our ladder scales the skies,
    and so its end is stolen from your gaze.
Unto that height he saw this ladder rise,   70
    patriarch Jacob, with its topmost parts,
    and angels swift to duty. But these days
No one wishes to climb it, no one starts   73
    one foot from off the earth, and so my rule's
    nothing but parchment fit to throw away.
Where there was once a chapel, now the halls   76
    are dens for thieves; and sacks of wormy grain,
    sacks brimming over, are the brothers' cowls.
And yet the heaviest usury men maintain   79
    grieves not the will of God as does that fruit°
    that makes the monkish hearts such fools for gain,
For all the Church is guardian of belongs   82
    to those who in the Lord's name ask and seek—
    not kin, not those of uglier repute.
The flesh of mortal beings is so weak,   85
    on earth a good beginning may not hold
    long enough to bring acorns from the oak.
Peter began without silver and gold;   88
    with prayer and with fasting I began;
    and Francis gathered with humility.

° *the final sphere:* the Empyrean; cf. 32.35.
° *that fruit:* money given to monasteries for the poor; cf. 12.93.

e se guardi 'l principio di ciascuno,   91
  poscia riguardi là dov' è trascorso,
  tu vederai del bianco fatto bruno.

Veramente Iordan vòlto retrorso   94
  più fu, e 'l mar fuggir, quando Dio volse,
  mirabile a veder che qui 'l soccorso".

Così mi disse, e indi si raccolse   97
  al suo collegio, e 'l collegio si strinse;
  poi, come turbo, in sù tutto s'avvolse.

La dolce donna dietro a lor mi pinse   100
  con un sol cenno su per quella scala,
  sì sua virtù la mia natura vinse;

né mai qua giù dove si monta e cala   103
  naturalmente, fu sì ratto moto
  ch'agguagliar si potesse a la mia ala.

S'io torni mai, lettore, a quel divoto   106
  trïunfo per lo quale io piango spesso
  le mie peccata e 'l petto mi percuoto,

tu non avresti in tanto tratto e messo   109
  nel foco il dito, in quant' io vidi 'l segno
  che segue il Tauro e fui dentro da esso.

O glorïose stelle, o lume pregno   112
  di gran virtù, dal quale io riconosco
  tutto, qual che si sia, il mio ingegno,

con voi nasceva e s'ascondeva vosco   115
  quelli ch'è padre d'ogne mortal vita,
  quand' io senti' di prima l'aere tosco;

e poi, quando mi fu grazia largita   118
  d'entrar ne l'alta rota che vi gira,
  la vostra regïon mi fu sortita.

A voi divotamente ora sospira   121
  l'anima mia, per acquistar virtute
  al passo forte che a sé la tira.

If you compare the first springs of each one 91
    with where it's gone astray, you will soon see
    that what was white is now a murky brown.

But truly the retreat of the Red Sea° 94
    and Jordan flowing backward at God's will
    were greater wonders than the help will be."

So saying, to his brotherhood he turned, 97
    and, merged in unity, the brothers rose
    swift as a whirlwind—yet in union still.

The gentle lady moved me with a sign 100
    to climb the stairs behind them; that was all,
    so did her nature overmaster mine.

Nor ever on earth where men may mount or fall 103
    by natural force is any motion fast
    enough to match the swiftness of my wing.

Reader, may I return to that devout 106
    triumphal march that makes me weep in shame
    for all my sins and often beat my breast;

You couldn't have stuck your finger in a flame 109
    and whipped it back before I saw—and was
    within—the sign that follows on the Bull.°

O light bursting with virtue, glorious stars, 112
    unto whose influence, as I see, is due
    whatever I possess of native powers,

The sun was born with you and hid with you 115
    when first I felt the air of Tuscany,
    the sun, the father of all mortal life;

And when the grace was richly granted me, 118
    I was assigned your region of the skies
    for entering your high wheel. Devotedly

Unto you starry Twins my spirit sighs 121
    to gain the strength to master the hard test
    that draws on all my force. "You are so near

°*the retreat of the Red Sea:* at Moses' command (Ex. 14:21). The *Jordan* held back its upper waters to allow Joshua and the Hebrews to cross to Jericho (Josh. 3:15–17).

°*the sign that follows on the Bull:* Gemini (following Taurus), zodiacal sign thought propitious for artists and poets.

"Tu se' sì presso a l'ultima salute",   124
    cominciò Bëatrice, "che tu dei
    aver le luci tue chiare e acute;
e però, prima che tu più t'inlei,   127
    rimira in giù, e vedi quanto mondo
    sotto li piedi già esser ti fei;
sì che 'l tuo cor, quantunque può, giocondo   130
    s'appresenti a la turba trïunfante
    che lieta vien per questo etera tondo".
Col viso ritornai per tutte quante   133
    le sette spere, e vidi questo globo
    tal, ch'io sorrisi del suo vil sembiante;
e quel consiglio per migliore approbo   136
    che l'ha per meno; e chi ad altro pensa
    chiamar si puote veramente probo.
Vidi la figlia di Latona incensa   139
    sanza quell' ombra che mi fu cagione
    per che già la credetti rara e densa.
L'aspetto del tuo nato, Iperïone,   142
    quivi sostenni, e vidi com' si move
    circa e vicino a lui Maia e Dïone.
Quindi m'apparve il temperar di Giove   145
    tra 'l padre e 'l figlio; e quindi mi fu chiaro
    il varïar che fanno di lor dove;
e tutti e sette mi si dimostraro   148
    quanto son grandi e quanto son veloci
    e come sono in distante riparo.
L'aiuola che ci fa tanto feroci,   151
    volgendom' io con li etterni Gemelli,
    tutta m'apparve da' colli a le foci;
poscia rivolsi li occhi a li occhi belli.   154

The ultimate perfection of the blest,"   124
   so Beatrice began, "you must possess
   clear eyes and keener vision. So, before
Further in-selving in this blessedness,   127
   gaze down and see how much of the world below
   you have already set beneath your feet,
So that, all that it can, your heart will go   130
   gladly along with the triumphing band
   that in this ring of ether march with joy."
I turned and looked on all the space that spanned   133
   the seven spheres, and saw this globe so small
   I smiled to see how paltry it appeared;
And I approved that counsel best of all   136
   that scorns it—but to think of something higher
   truly bespeaks a spirit brave and tall.
I saw Latona's daughter° bright with fire—   139
   but all the shadows on her face were gone
   that made me think of matter dense and rare.
The countenance of your son, Hyperion,°   142
   I could sustain, and saw the motions of
   Dione and Maia round about his sphere.
Then there appeared the tempering light of Jove   145
   between his father and his ardent son,°
   and then the variation as they move,
Shifting their places; then the seven were shown   148
   each in its size, in its velocity,
   and in the distances of every den.
I turned with the eternal Twins to see   151
   what fires our rage, that little winnowing floor°
   between the hills and rivers by the sea;
Then turned my eyes to the lovely eyes once more.   154

° *Latona's daughter:* the moon. For the spots on the moon, see 2.49–148.
° *Hyperion:* father of Helios, the sun. *Dione and Maia* are, respectively, the mothers of Mercury and Venus.
° *his father and his ardent son:* Saturn and Mars.
° *that little winnowing floor:* the little habitable land on this little earth (cf. Boethius, *Cons. Phil.* 2 pr. 7).

Come l'augello, intra l'amate fronde,
   posato al nido de' suoi dolci nati
   la notte che le cose ci nasconde,
che, per veder li aspetti disïati   4
   e per trovar lo cibo onde li pasca,
   in che gravi labor li sono aggrati,
previene il tempo in su aperta frasca,   7
   e con ardente affetto il sole aspetta,
   fiso guardando pur che l'alba nasca;
così la donna mïa stava eretta   10
   e attenta, rivolta inver' la plaga
   sotto la quale il sol mostra men fretta:
sì che, veggendola io sospesa e vaga,   13
   fecimi qual è quei che disïando
   altro vorria, e sperando s'appaga.
Ma poco fu tra uno e altro quando,   16
   del mio attender, dico, e del vedere
   lo ciel venir più e più rischiarando;
e Bëatrice disse: "Ecco le schiere   19
   del trïunfo di Cristo e tutto 'l frutto
   ricolto del girar di queste spere!".
Pariemi che 'l suo viso ardesse tutto,   22
   e li occhi avea di letizia sì pieni,
   che passarmen convien sanza costrutto.

CANTO TWENTY-THREE

*Dante witnesses **the triumph of Christ** and the blessing of the souls in Heaven, irradiated by His light. After **the coronation of Mary**, Christ and the Blessed Mother return to the Empyrean.*

A little bird among beloved boughs
    nestling with her sweet offspring through the night,
    when darkness hides away all things from us,
To see her chicks again, a longed-for sight,   4
    and find the food she feeds them in the day,
    a heavy labor but a sweet delight,
In earliest morn and on an open spray   7
    waits for the sun with yearning in her heart,
    gazing to catch the newborn dawn's first ray,
So did my Lady stand erect, intent,   10
    turning her eyes toward the noonday dome
    where the sun's sweep is least precipitant,
And when I saw her longing in suspense,   13
    I was as one allaying his desire
    with a delightful hope for things to come,
But it was not so long from here to there—   16
    I mean from expectation to the sight
    of Heaven blazing with a clearer fire—
When Beatrice said to me, "Behold the hosts   19
    of the triumph of Christ, behold the grain
    gathered from all the turning spheres of light!"
Within her countenance flames seemed to burn   22
    and in her eyes such brimming gladness shone
    I have to let it go, and not explain.

Quale ne' plenilunïï sereni   25
   Trivïa ride tra le ninfe etterne
   che dipingon lo ciel per tutti i seni,
vid' i' sopra migliaia di lucerne   28
   un sol che tutte quante l'accendea,
   come fa 'l nostro le viste superne;
e per la viva luce trasparea   31
   la lucente sustanza tanto chiara
   nel viso mio, che non la sostenea.
Oh Bëatrice, dolce guida e cara!   34
   Ella mi disse: "Quel che ti sobranza
   è virtù da cui nulla si ripara.
Quivi è la sapïenza e la possanza   37
   ch'aprì le strade tra 'l cielo e la terra,
   onde fu già sì lunga disïanza".
Come foco di nube si diserra   40
   per dilatarsi sì che non vi cape,
   e fuor di sua natura in giù s'atterra,
la mente mia così, tra quelle dape   43
   fatta più grande, di sé stessa uscìo,
   e che si fesse rimembrar non sape.
"Apri li occhi e riguarda qual son io;   46
   tu hai vedute cose, che possente
   se' fatto a sostener lo riso mio".
Io era come quei che si risente   49
   di visïone oblita e che s'ingegna
   indarno di ridurlasi a la mente,
quand' io udi' questa proferta, degna   52
   di tanto grato, che mai non si stingue
   del libro che 'l preterito rassegna.

As in the silent nights of the full moon   25
    Diana° smiles among her maiden stars
    who spangle every bosom of the sky,
Above the thousand thousand lights I saw   28
    one Sun that set them all to kindle, as
    the lights above the earth are lit by ours,
And through the living light appeared to pass   31
    one light-filled Being° radiantly clear
    and brighter than my vision could endure.
O Beatrice, my gentle guide and dear!   34
    She said to me, "What overwhelms your sight
    is power from which no power can repair.
Within it dwells the wisdom and the might   37
    that opened up the road to Heaven from earth,
    the peace so long awaited." Just as fire
Trammeled up in a thundercloud bursts forth   40
    by swelling broader than the cloud can seize,
    and, opposite its nature, smites the earth,
My mind, grown great among those delicacies,   43
    burst itself and its limits like that flame.
    Of what it did, I have no memories.
"Open your eyes, behold how I've become,   46
    for by the power of the things you've seen
    you now may bear the glory of my smile."
And I was as a man who feels again   49
    a trace of a lost dream, and strains to ply
    his powers to bring it back to mind—in vain—
When I heard what she offered to my eye,   52
    worthy of thanks that nothing will expunge
    out of the register of things gone by.

° *Diana:* goddess of the moon; the Italian reads "Trivia," the goddess of the three roads, as the same goddess was said to be manifest as Phoebe in the heavens, as Diana on earth, and as Hecate under the earth.

  ° *Being:* the risen Christ.

Se mo sonasser tutte quelle lingue   55
  che Polimnïa con le suore fero
  del latte lor dolcissimo più pingue,
per aiutarmi, al millesmo del vero   58
  non si verria, cantando il santo riso
  e quanto il santo aspetto facea mero;
e così, figurando il paradiso,   61
  convien saltar lo sacrato poema,
  come chi trova suo cammin riciso.
Ma chi pensasse il ponderoso tema   64
  e l'omero mortal che se ne carca,
  nol biasmerebbe se sott' esso trema:
non è pareggio da picciola barca   67
  quel che fendendo va l'ardita prora,
  né da nocchier ch'a sé medesmo parca.
"Perché la faccia mia sì t'innamora,   70
  che tu non ti rivolgi al bel giardino
  che sotto i raggi di Cristo s'infiora?
Quivi è la rosa in che 'l verbo divino   73
  carne si fece; quivi son li gigli
  al cui odor si prese il buon cammino".
Così Beatrice; e io, che a' suoi consigli   76
  tutto era pronto, ancora mi rendei
  a la battaglia de' debili cigli.
Come a raggio di sol, che puro mei   79
  per fratta nube, già prato di fiori
  vider, coverti d'ombra, li occhi miei;
vid' io così più turbe di splendori,   82
  folgorate di sù da raggi ardenti,
  sanza veder principio di folgóri.
O benigna vertù che sì li 'mprenti,   85
  sù t'essaltasti per largirmi loco
  a li occhi lì che non t'eran possenti.

If now were singing every richest tongue 55
    fed by Polymnia and her sisters° with
    their sweetest milk, to help me in my song,

They'd never reach one thousandth of the truth 58
    about the holy smile and how it brought
    serenest radiance to the holy face;

Yet as a man who finds his path is cut, 61
    so must the sacred poem overleap
    in finding signs to render Paradise.

But if my shoulders tremble, they that keep 64
    the ponderous theme and my mortality
    in mind will never blame me for the slip;

Not for a little raft, this stretch of sea 67
    my bold prow furrows, nor for pilots of
    weak heart, who spare themselves. She said to me,

"Why does my face hold you so bound in love 70
    that you don't turn to see the lovely garden,
    the flowers the rays of Christ have brought to bloom?

Here is the rose° wherein the Word divine 73
    was made incarnate, here the lilies° blow
    whose fragrance leads men on the righteous way."

So Beatrice—and I, most prompt to follow 76
    according to her counsel, once again
    prepared to battle with my feeble brow.

As my eyes have beheld a sunlit plain 79
    unveiled of shade, when from a broken cloud
    one pure ray shines upon a sweep of flowers,

So did I see those splendors crowd on crowd 82
    struck from above with burning shafts of light,
    but did not see the wellspring of their fire.

O power benign, whose seal is printed bright, 85
    you rose into the heavens to give room
    to eyes too weak to bear your radiant sight.

°*Polymnia and her sisters:* Polymnia, or Polyhymnia, is the muse of lyric poetry; *her sisters* are the other muses. For their *milk* of inspiration, cf. *Purg.* 22.101–2.
    °*rose:* Mary.
    °*lilies:* the apostles.

Il nome del bel fior ch'io sempre invoco 88
    e mane e sera, tutto mi ristrinse
    l'animo ad avvisar lo maggior foco;
e come ambo le luci mi dipinse 91
    il quale e il quanto de la viva stella
    che là sù vince come qua giù vinse,
per entro il cielo scese una facella, 94
    formata in cerchio a guisa di corona,
    e cinsela e girossi intorno ad ella.
Qualunque melodia più dolce suona 97
    qua giù e più a sé l'anima tira,
    parrebbe nube che squarciata tona,
comparata al sonar di quella lira 100
    onde si coronava il bel zaffiro
    del quale il ciel più chiaro s'inzaffira.
"Io sono amore angelico, che giro 103
    l'alta letizia che spira del ventre
    che fu albergo del nostro disiro;
e girerommi, donna del ciel, mentre 106
    che seguirai tuo figlio, e farai dia
    più la spera supprema perché lì entre".
Così la circulata melodia 109
    si sigillava, e tutti li altri lumi
    facean sonare il nome di Maria.
Lo real manto di tutti i volumi 112
    del mondo, che più ferve e più s'avviva
    ne l'alito di Dio e nei costumi,
avea sopra di noi l'interna riva 115
    tanto distante, che la sua parvenza,
    là dov' io era, ancor non appariva:
però non ebber li occhi miei potenza 118
    di seguitar la coronata fiamma
    che si levò appresso sua semenza.

Morning and evening I invoke the name°   88
   of the sweet bloom that held my mind intent
   to gaze in wonder at the greatest flame,

And when that living star had touched my eyes   91
   with tinting to reveal its brilliancy,
   its magnitude that conquers in those skies

As once it did below, across that heaven   94
   a torch descended like a garland crown
   that wheeled and turned about her in a ring.

The earthly melody of sweetest tone,   97
   pulling the human soul with fullest power,
   would seem the thunder of a flattened cloud

Compared against the sounding of that lyre   100
   whereby the lovely sapphire there is crowned,
   sapphiring Heaven with the clearest fire.

"I am the angel love° who circles round   103
   the deep gladness that breathes forth from the womb
   that was the dwelling place of our desire,

Turning, Lady of Heaven, till what time   106
   you follow your Son and make more heavenly
   the splendor of highest Heaven when you come."

So did the ever-circling melody   109
   seal up its song, and all the other gleams
   made Mary's name resound in every sky.

The royal mantle° binding all the reams   112
   that constitute the world, most fervent, most
   alive in the divine Breath and Its decrees,

At such great distance arched its inner coast   115
   no sight of it had made its way indeed
   down to where I was standing far below,

So my eyes lacked the power to proceed   118
   following ever higher the crowned flame
   that rose behind the rising of her Seed.

° *the name:* of Mary.
° *the angel love:* Gabriel; cf. 32.103–14.
° *The royal mantle:* the Primum Mobile.

E come fantolin che 'nver' la mamma 121
    tende le braccia, poi che 'l latte prese,
    per l'animo che 'nfin di fuor s'infiamma;
ciascun di quei candori in sù si stese 124
    con la sua cima, sì che l'alto affetto
    ch'elli avieno a Maria mi fu palese.
Indi rimaser lì nel mio cospetto, 127
    'Regina celi' cantando sì dolce,
    che mai da me non si partì 'l diletto.
Oh quanta è l'ubertà che si soffolce 130
    in quelle arche ricchissime che fuoro
    a seminar qua giù buone bobolce!
Quivi si vive e gode del tesoro 133
    che s'acquistò piangendo ne lo essilio
    di Babillòn, ove si lasciò l'oro.
Quivi trïunfa, sotto l'alto Filio 136
    di Dio e di Maria, di sua vittoria,
    e con l'antico e col novo concilio,
colui che tien le chiavi di tal gloria. 139

And as a little baby lifts his arms   121
    to mama when he's filled with milk, and shows
    the kindling of the love within his soul,
So did those splendors stand with wings that rose   124
    pointing their flames unto the highest height
    and making manifest how great their love
For Mary was. They stood before my sight,   127
    singing the "Queen of Heaven" with sound so sweet,
    my memory yet treasures the delight.
O what a fertile harvest of fine wheat   130
    is crammed into those bins in richest measure,
    who here on earth were such good fields to sow!
Here do they live, here they enjoy the treasure   133
    they won with tears they wept in Babylon,°
    in exile, when they left the gold in scorn.
Here triumphs under the exalted Son   136
    of God and Son of Mary, for his victory,
    with both the ancient council and the new,°
The one who keeps the keys° to such great glory.   139

°*Babylon:* their place of exile; this world with all its worldly goods (cf. Rev. 17:4–6; Ps. 137).
  °*the ancient council and the new:* saints who believed in Christ to come and saints who believed in Christ after he had come.
  °*The one who keeps the keys:* Saint Peter (cf. Matt. 16:19).

"O sodalizio eletto a la gran cena
del benedetto Agnello, il qual vi ciba
sì, che la vostra voglia è sempre piena,
se per grazia di Dio questi preliba   4
di quel che cade de la vostra mensa,
prima che morte tempo li prescriba,
ponete mente a l'affezione immensa   7
e roratelo alquanto: voi bevete
sempre del fonte onde vien quel ch'ei pensa".
Così Beatrice; e quelle anime liete   10
si fero spere sopra fissi poli,
fiammando, volte, a guisa di comete.
E come cerchi in tempra d'orïuoli   13
si giran sì, che 'l primo a chi pon mente
quïeto pare, e l'ultimo che voli;
così quelle carole, differente-   16
mente danzando, de la sua ricchezza
mi facieno stimar, veloci e lente.
Di quella ch'io notai di più carezza   19
vid' ïo uscire un foco sì felice,
che nullo vi lasciò di più chiarezza;
e tre fïate intorno di Beatrice   22
si volse con un canto tanto divo,
che la mia fantasia nol mi ridice.

CANTO TWENTY-FOUR

Saint Peter examines Dante on faith.

"O brotherhood elected for the great
    feast of the blessed Lamb, who is the food
    that ever fills your wish to take and eat,
If this man here is given the grace of God,   4
    before death's etched his final day in ink,
    to taste a little of the crumbs that fall
From your table, shed some dew upon him, think   7
    of his immeasurable desire, his mind
    attentive to the fountain whence you drink
Eternally." So Beatrice; and those souls,   10
    flaring in joy like comets, whirled in reels
    of spheres and every sphere whirled round its poles.
And as an orologe's ordered wheels°   13
    will spin so that you watch the first one go
    and it seems quiet, while the last wheel flies,
So did those dancers all in caroling   16
    lead me to judge the richness of their joy
    according to their motion, quick or slow.
A flame came forth of such felicity   19
    out of the circle of the dearest price,
    it left behind none of such clarity,
And turning in three turns round Beatrice,   22
    it sang a song so radiant and divine,
    my fancy can't repeat the hymn to me.

°*an orologe's ordered wheels:* An orologe was a medieval clock. The gears turned wheels of various sizes at various speeds.

Però salta la penna e non lo scrivo: 25
   ché l'imagine nostra a cotai pieghe,
   non che 'l parlare, è troppo color vivo.
"O santa suora mia che sì ne prieghe   28
   divota, per lo tuo ardente affetto
   da quella bella spera mi disleghe".
Poscia fermato, il foco benedetto   31
   a la mia donna dirizzò lo spiro,
   che favellò così com' i' ho detto.
Ed ella: "O luce etterna del gran viro   34
   a cui Nostro Segnor lasciò le chiavi,
   ch'ei portò giù, di questo gaudio miro,
tenta costui di punti lievi e gravi,   37
   come ti piace, intorno de la fede,
   per la qual tu su per lo mare andavi.
S'elli ama bene e bene spera e crede,   40
   non t'è occulto, perché 'l viso hai quivi
   dov' ogne cosa dipinta si vede;
ma perché questo regno ha fatto civi   43
   per la verace fede, a gloriarla,
   di lei parlare è ben ch'a lui arrivi".
Sì come il baccialier s'arma e non parla   46
   fin che 'l maestro la question propone,
   per approvarla, non per terminarla,
così m'armava io d'ogne ragione   49
   mentre ch'ella dicea, per esser presto
   a tal querente e a tal professione.
"Dì, buon Cristiano, fatti manifesto: 52
   fede che è?". Ond' io levai la fronte
   in quella luce onde spirava questo;
poi mi volsi a Beatrice, ed essa pronte   55
   sembianze femmi perch' ïo spandessi
   l'acqua di fuor del mio interno fonte.

I cannot write—it skips, this pen of mine;   25
    our glaring images, much less what we say,
    can never paint those folds of bliss so fine.
"My holy sister! So devotedly   28
    do you beseech, so ardent is your will,
    it has unbound me from that lovely sphere!"
For when the blessed soul of fire was still,   31
    thus did he send his voice to greet my Lady,
    breathing the words as I have given them.
"Eternal light of the great man," said she,   34
    "into whose keeping our Lord left the keys
    He'd brought to earth, keys to this wondrous joy,
Try this man on the faith as you may please,   37
    on any point, the weighty or the light,
    the faith whereby you walked upon the sea.
If he loves well and hopes well and believes,   40
    it can't be hid from you, for you maintain
    your watch where everything is painted truly,
But since what makes a citizen of this reign   43
    is the true faith, it's well, for glory's sake,
    that what he knows of it, he now make plain."
A bachelor° arms his wits and will not speak   46
    until the master gives the proposition,
    not to decide it but to show forth proof;
So while she spoke I mustered every reason,   49
    ready in arms for such a questioner
    and such a declaration. "Speak, make clear,
Good Christian man, that *that* is what you are: 52
    tell, what is faith?" At that I raised my brow
    unto the light that breathed this question forth,
Then glanced at Beatrice, who let me know   55
    with a prompt look that I should free the waters
    and let the well within me overflow.

°*bachelor:* candidate for the baccalaureate, about to answer aloud the questions put to him publicly by his master.

"La Grazia che mi dà ch'io mi confessi",   58
    comincia' io, "da l'alto primipilo,
    faccia li miei concetti bene espressi".

E seguitai: "Come 'l verace stilo   61
    ne scrisse, padre, del tuo caro frate
    che mise teco Roma nel buon filo,

fede è sustanza di cose sperate   64
    e argomento de le non parventi;
    e questa pare a me sua quiditate".

Allora udi': "Dirittamente senti,   67
    se bene intendi perché la ripuose
    tra le sustanze, e poi tra li argomenti".

E io appresso: "Le profonde cose   70
    che mi largiscon qui la lor parvenza,
    a li occhi di là giù son sì ascose,

che l'esser loro v'è in sola credenza,   73
    sopra la qual si fonda l'alta spene;
    e però di sustanza prende intenza.

E da questa credenza ci convene   76
    silogizzar, sanz' avere altra vista:
    però intenza d'argomento tene".

Allora udi': "Se quantunque s'acquista   79
    giù per dottrina, fosse così 'nteso,
    non lì avria loco ingegno di sofista".

Così spirò di quello amore acceso;   82
    indi soggiunse: "Assai bene è trascorsa
    d'esta moneta già la lega e 'l peso;

ma dimmi se tu l'hai ne la tua borsa".   85
    Ond' io: "Sì ho, sì lucida e sì tonda,
    che nel suo conio nulla mi s'inforsa".

Appresso uscì de la luce profonda   88
    che lì splendeva: "Questa cara gioia
    sopra la quale ogne virtù si fonda,

onde ti venne?". E io: "La larga ploia   91
    de lo Spirito Santo, ch'è diffusa
    in su le vecchie e 'n su le nuove cuoia,

"Grace given me to declare what I believe   58
   unto the high centurion," I began,
   "may my words well express what I conceive.

Father, as it was written by the true pen   61
   of your beloved brother Paul, who joined
   your work in setting Rome on the good line,

Faith is the substance of things hoped for and   64
   the argument of things not come to light.
   This is its essence, as I understand."

At that I heard, "Your thoughts are just and right,   67
   if you can tell me why he posits it
   as substance first, then as an argument."

And I responded, "The profundities   70
   of Heaven I have been generously shown
   are so deeply concealed from human eyes,

Their essence is a matter of faith alone,   73
   whereon our high hope builds its testament,
   so 'substance' is a proper term, for one;

And from the tenets of this faith we draw   76
   conclusions—with no other sight to see.
   Thus it is justly called an 'argument.' "

"If men could understand so perfectly   79
   the truths that teaching wins them down on earth,
   their wit would have no place for sophistry."

So did that love-enkindled fire breathe forth,   82
   then added, "You have thus far run the course
   to try this coin, its metal and the weight,

But tell me if you have it in your purse."   85
   "I do—with such a luster and so round,
   I have no maybes that the coin rings true."

"This precious jewel," came from the profound   88
   splendor that shone before me, "on whose gain
   is founded every other virtue—whence

Did you receive it?" "From the generous rain,"   91
   I answered, "of the Holy Spirit, shed
   on the old parchment and the new: its train

è silogismo che la m'ha conchiusa   94
  acutamente sì, che 'nverso d'ella
  ogne dimostrazion mi pare ottusa".

Io udi' poi: "L'antica e la novella   97
  proposizion che così ti conchiude,
  perché l'hai tu per divina favella?".

E io: "La prova che 'l ver mi dischiude,   100
  son l'opere seguite, a che natura
  non scalda ferro mai né batte incude".

Risposto fummi: "Dì, chi t'assicura   103
  che quell' opere fosser? Quel medesmo
  che vuol provarsi, non altri, il ti giura".

"Se 'l mondo si rivolse al cristianesmo",   106
  diss' io, "sanza miracoli, quest' uno
  è tal, che li altri non sono il centesmo:

ché tu intrasti povero e digiuno   109
  in campo, a seminar la buona pianta
  che fu già vite e ora è fatta pruno".

Finito questo, l'alta corte santa   112
  risonò per le spere un 'Dio laudamo'
  ne la melode che là sù si canta.

E quel baron che sì di ramo in ramo,   115
  essaminando, già tratto m'avea,
  che a l'ultime fronde appressavamo,

ricominciò: "La Grazia, che donnea   118
  con la tua mente, la bocca t'aperse
  infino a qui come aprir si dovea,

sì ch'io approvo ciò che fuori emerse;   121
  ma or convien espremer quel che credi,
  e onde a la credenza tua s'offerse".

"O santo padre, e spirito che vedi   124
  ciò che credesti sì, che tu vincesti
  ver' lo sepulcro più giovani piedi",

Of reasoning has so convinced my mind,   94
    conclusions clear and sharp as any sword,
    all other proofs seem blunted at the end."
"The ancient and the new," at that I heard,   97
    "those premises that led you to this faith—
    why do you take them for God's holy word?"
"The works° that followed have disclosed the truth,"   100
    said I, "for Nature never forged the steel
    or banged the anvil to accomplish those."
"What makes you sure they really happened? Tell.   103
    They alone testify," he answered me.
    "You call to witness what you seek to prove."
"Had the world turned to Christianity   106
    without a single wonder, this alone
    would outweigh all the rest a hundredfold,
For you were poor and hungry, entering on   109
    the field to sow the holy seed," said I,
    "which once gave wine and now is turned to thorn."
When that was done, the holy court on high   112
    from all their rings resounded, "God we praise,"
    singing in Paradise's melody.
That baron who had tested my belief,   115
    leading me from one branch to that above
    until we neared the crown and highest leaf,
Resumed, "The Lady Grace that whispers love   118
    into your mind has opened your lips till now
    to speak what you should speak—so I approve
What you've brought forth. But now it's time to say   121
    what you believe: profess it openly,
    and tell us also whence your faith has come."
"O holy Father, spirit who now see   124
    what once you held by a belief so strong
    you conquered younger feet to be the first

°*works:* miracles.

comincia' io, "tu vuo' ch'io manifesti   127
  la forma qui del pronto creder mio,
  e anche la cagion di lui chiedesti.

E io rispondo: Io credo in uno Dio   130
  solo ed etterno, che tutto 'l ciel move,
  non moto, con amore e con disio;

e a tal creder non ho io pur prove   133
  fisice e metafisice, ma dalmi
  anche la verità che quinci piove

per Moïsè, per profeti e per salmi,   136
  per l'Evangelio e per voi che scriveste
  poi che l'ardente Spirto vi fé almi;

e credo in tre persone etterne, e queste   139
  credo una essenza sì una e sì trina,
  che soffera congiunto 'sono' ed 'este'.

De la profonda condizion divina   142
  ch'io tocco mo, la mente mi sigilla
  più volte l'evangelica dottrina.

Quest' è 'l principio, quest' è la favilla   145
  che si dilata in fiamma poi vivace,
  e come stella in cielo in me scintilla".

Come 'l segnor ch'ascolta quel che i piace,   148
  da indi abbraccia il servo, gratulando
  per la novella, tosto ch'el si tace;

così, benedicendomi cantando,   151
  tre volte cinse me, sì com' io tacqui,
  l'appostolico lume al cui comando

io avea detto: sì nel dir li piacqui!   154

Entering the tomb,° you want me to declare,"   127
    said I, "the essence of my ready faith,
    and whence I have received what I profess.
And I respond: I believe in one God,   130
    sole and eternal, who was never moved
    but moves all Heaven with love and with desire;
Physics and metaphysics have not proved,   133
    alone, such faith for me: it also comes
    given me by the truth that rained from Heaven
Through Moses, through the prophets, through the Psalms,   136
    the evangelists, and you whose fostering words
    the Holy Ghost inspired; and I believe
In three eternal Persons, and in these   139
    one essence, so completely one and three,
    they suffer in conjunction 'are' and 'is.'
Of this deep truth of the divinity   142
    I touch on now, my mind has borne the seal
    the gospel teaching has impressed on me.
This is the spark, this is the principle   145
    that spills out into such a living flame
    it glitters like a star within my soul."
When a lord listens to what pleases him,   148
    soon as his servant finishes he'll fling
    his arms around him for the happy news—
So did he bless me now, so did he sing   151
    three times encircling me with happy light,
    that apostolic lamp at whose command
I'd spoken what had brought him such delight!   154

°*conquered ... tomb:* On Easter morning Peter and John ran to Jesus' tomb to see whether the women had spoken the truth. John arrived first, but the impetuous fisherman rushed past him to enter the tomb (John 20:1–9).

Se mai continga che 'l poema sacro
    al quale ha posto mano e cielo e terra,
    sì che m'ha fatto per molti anni macro,
vinca la crudeltà che fuor mi serra   4
    del bello ovile ov' io dormi' agnello,
    nimico ai lupi che li danno guerra;
con altra voce omai, con altro vello   7
    ritornerò poeta, e in sul fonte
    del mio battesmo prenderò 'l cappello;
però che ne la fede, che fa conte   10
    l'anime a Dio, quivi intra' io, e poi
    Pietro per lei sì mi girò la fronte.
Indi si mosse un lume verso noi   13
    di quella spera ond' uscì la primizia
    che lasciò Cristo d'i vicari suoi;
e la mia donna, piena di letizia,   16
    mi disse: "Mira, mira: ecco il barone
    per cui là giù si vicita Galizia".
Sì come quando il colombo si pone   19
    presso al compagno, l'uno a l'altro pande,
    girando e mormorando, l'affezione;

CANTO TWENTY-FIVE

Saint James examines Dante on *hope*. After the appearance of *Saint John*, Dante is struck blind.

If it should happen that this sacred song
  to which both Heaven and earth have set the hand—
  toil that has left me leaner for so long—
May quell the cruelty that has shut me out   4
  of the sweet sheepfold° where I slept, a lamb,
  foe to the wolves that brought it strife and war,
With other vellum then and other fame   7
  I will return a poet, and take my crown
  at my baptismal spring: for there I came
Into the faith whereby a soul is known   10
  by God as His; and for that faith my brow
  was garlanded by Peter up above.
And then in our direction surged a glow   13
  out of the ring whence came the primacy°
  of all the vicars whom Christ left below,
And full of joy my Lady said to me,   16
  "Behold in wonder! See the baron° come
  at whose Galician tomb the pilgrims pray."
As when a dove that flutters to his home   19
  settles beside his fellow and each shows
  love in his coos and primping all around,

°*sheepfold:* Florence (cf. 16.25).

°*the primacy:* Peter, chief of the apostles.

°*the baron:* the apostle James the Greater, brother of John, reputed to have been buried in Galicia in northeastern Spain. The church of Saint James of Compostela was one of the chief destinations of pilgrims in the Middle Ages.

così vid' ïo l'un da l'altro grande   22
  principe glorïoso essere accolto,
  laudando il cibo che là sù li prande.
Ma poi che 'l gratular si fu assolto,   25
  tacito *coram me* ciascun s'affisse,
  ignito sì che vincëa 'l mio volto.
Ridendo allora Bëatrice disse: 28
  "Inclita vita per cui la larghezza
  de la nostra basilica si scrisse,
fa risonar la spene in questa altezza: 31
  tu sai, che tante fiate la figuri,
  quante Iesù ai tre fé più carezza".
"Leva la testa e fa che t'assicuri: 34
  ché ciò che vien qua sù del mortal mondo,
  convien ch'ai nostri raggi si maturi".
Questo conforto del foco secondo   37
  mi venne; ond' io leväi li occhi a' monti
  che li 'ncurvaron pria col troppo pondo.
"Poi che per grazia vuol che tu t'affronti   40
  lo nostro Imperadore, anzi la morte,
  ne l'aula più secreta co' suoi conti,
sì che, veduto il ver di questa corte,   43
  la spene, che là giù bene innamora,
  in te e in altrui di ciò conforte,
dì quel ch'ell' è, dì come se ne 'nfiora   46
  la mente tua, e dì onde a te venne".
  Così seguì 'l secondo lume ancora.
E quella pïa che guidò le penne   49
  de le mie ali a così alto volo,
  a la risposta così mi prevenne:
"La Chiesa militante alcun figliuolo   52
  non ha con più speranza, com' è scritto
  nel Sol che raggia tutto nostro stuolo:

So did I see those great and glorious   22
  princes give welcome, each unto his friend,
  praising the feast they find in Paradise.
Their bright felicitations at an end,   25
  each stood before me, silently awaiting,
  burning too brilliantly for me to face.
Beatrice smiled, beholding them, and said,   28
  "O renowned spirit who were moved to write
  about the bounty of our basilica,
Let hope resound its praises in this height.   31
  You know, you were its emblem, times untold
  when Jesus held the three° at dearest price."
"Lift up your head, be confident and bold,   34
  for everything must ripen in our rays
  that rises up here from your mortal world."
This strength and comfort from the second blaze   37
  came to me, whence I raised my eyes unto
  those mountains that had bowed them. "Since, by grace,
The Emperor of Heaven has willed for you   40
  to come into this court before you die,
  and meet His nobles in His inmost halls,
And, seeing the truth about this company,   43
  comfort yourself and others with hope's power,
  hope, that on earth stirs love for the true good,
Say what hope is, say how it's come to flower   46
  within your mind, and say what was the spring
  whence you received it." So the second light.
That guide who'd led the feathers of my wing   49
  to so soaring a flight, that pious one
  anticipated me by answering,
"The Church Militant does not have a son   52
  of greater hope; as is written in the tome
  of the Sun that sheds His rays on all our host;

° *the three:* Peter, James, and John, to whom Christ sometimes showed special favor: they alone were present at the transfiguration (Matt. 17:1–9).

però li è conceduto che d'Egitto 55
vegna in Ierusalemme per vedere,
anzi che 'l militar li sia prescritto.

Li altri due punti, che non per sapere 58
son dimandati, ma perch' ei rapporti
quanto questa virtù t'è in piacere,

a lui lasc' io, ché non li saran forti 61
né di iattanza; ed elli a ciò risponda,
e la grazia di Dio ciò li comporti".

Come discente ch'a dottor seconda 64
pronto e libente in quel ch'elli è esperto,
perché la sua bontà si disasconda,

"Spene", diss' io, "è uno attender certo 67
de la gloria futura, il qual produce
grazia divina e precedente merto.

Da molte stelle mi vien questa luce; 70
ma quei la distillò nel mio cor pria
che fu sommo cantor del sommo duce.

'Sperino in te', ne la sua tëodia 73
dice, 'color che sanno il nome tuo':
e chi nol sa, s'elli ha la fede mia?

Tu mi stillasti, con lo stillar suo, 76
ne la pistola poi; sì ch'io son pieno,
e in altrui vostra pioggia repluo".

Mentr' io diceva, dentro al vivo seno 79
di quello incendio tremolava un lampo
sùbito e spesso a guisa di baleno.

Indi spirò: "L'amore ond' ïo avvampo 82
ancor ver' la virtù che mi seguette
infin la palma e a l'uscir del campo,

vuol ch'io respiri a te che ti dilette 85
di lei; ed emmi a grato che tu diche
quello che la speranza ti 'mpromette".

E io: "Le nove e le scritture antiche 88
pongon lo segno, ed esso lo mi addita,
de l'anime che Dio s'ha fatte amiche.

Therefore it has been granted him to come,   55
    before his discharge from his earthly band,
    from Egypt to behold Jerusalem.

As for the other two points you demand   58
    (not for your own sake, but that he report
    how much this virtue pleases you), to him

I leave them, for he will not find them hard,   61
    nothing to boast of. Let him speak, and may
    the grace of God grant him his hopes in fact!"

Just as a pupil quick and willingly   64
    revealing what he's studied and learned well,
    follows his teacher's questions with reply,

"Hope," said I, "is the certain expectation   67
    of future glory, and is born in us
    by divine grace and merits we have won.

This light has come to me from many stars,   70
    but first was rained into my heart by him,
    the sovereign singer° of the sovereign Guide.

'Let them have hope in You who know Your name,'   73
    he declares in his theody—and who
    can fail to know His name, who shares my faith?

Then did you shed your rain upon me too   76
    in your epistle, and my well's so full,
    for other men I spill the overflow."

While I was speaking, from the living bosom   79
    of that great flame there trembled suddenly
    a flash that shivered like a lightning bolt,

And he breathed forth, "The love that kindles me   82
    even now for the hope that held me near,
    until I gained the palm of victory

And left the field, desires that I say more   85
    to you who cherish it, and would delight
    to hear you tell what hope has promised you."

"The new and the old Scriptures set the goal   88
    that indicates the promises to me,
    and to each soul whom God has made His friend.

° *sovereign singer:* David, singer of the Psalms (cf. 20.38).

Dice Isaia che ciascuna vestita   91
   ne la sua terra fia di doppia vesta:
   e la sua terra è questa dolce vita;
e 'l tuo fratello assai vie più digesta,   94
   là dove tratta de le bianche stole,
   questa revelazion ci manifesta".
E prima, appresso al fin d'este parole,   97
   'Sperent in te' di sopr' a noi s'udì;
   a che rispuoser tutte le carole.
Poscia tra esse un lume si schiarì   100
   sì che, se 'l Cancro avesse un tal cristallo,
   l'inverno avrebbe un mese d'un sol dì.
E come surge e va ed entra in ballo   103
   vergine lieta, sol per fare onore
   a la novizia, non per alcun fallo,
così vid' io lo schiarato splendore   106
   venire a' due che si volgieno a nota
   qual conveniesi al loro ardente amore.
Misesi lì nel canto e ne la rota;   109
   e la mia donna in lor tenea l'aspetto,
   pur come sposa tacita e immota.
"Questi è colui che giacque sopra 'l petto   112
   del nostro pellicano, e questi fue
   di su la croce al grande officio eletto".
La donna mia così; né però piùe   115
   mosser la vista sua di stare attenta
   poscia che prima le parole sue.
Qual è colui ch'adocchia e s'argomenta   118
   di vedere eclissar lo sole un poco,
   che, per veder, non vedente diventa;
tal mi fec' ïo a quell'ultimo foco   121
   mentre che detto fu: "Perché t'abbagli
   per veder cosa che qui non ha loco?

Isaiah says that the elect shall be 91
    robed with a double robe in their true land,
    the land of this sweet life, their Paradise;
Truth made far easier to understand 94
    by your own brother,° where he writes about
    the white-robed saints of Revelation's band."
At the end of these words immediately 97
    we heard above us, "Let them hope in you,"
    and all the rings of dancers gave reply.
Among those carolers shone so bright a glow, 100
    had Cancer a crystal of such radiance,
    winter would be one monthlong day below.
As a glad maiden rises for the dance, 103
    to give due honor to the new-made bride
    and not for any fault or arrogance,
So did I see that splendor magnified 106
    come to the two who danced in harmony
    to notes most fitting for their fire of love.
Into the wheel and singing entered he: 109
    my Lady like a still and silent spouse
    now held her gaze upon them steadily.
"This is the man° who lay upon the breast 112
    of Christ our Pelican; who was chosen for
    the glorious duty from the very Cross."
So did my Lady speak, and evermore 115
    she gazed upon them with attentive mind,
    as still, while she was speaking, as before.
As one who squints and tries his wits to find 118
    a way to catch an eclipse of the sun,
    and sees it partly hidden, and goes blind
From seeing—so I strained to look upon 121
    the final flame. "Why daze yourself," said he,
    "to see what has no place in Heaven here?

°*your own brother:* Saint John (cf. Rev. 7:9).
°*the man:* John, who reclined upon Jesus' breast at the Last Supper (John 13:23) and who was chosen to care for Mary as her adopted son (John 19:26–27).

In terra è terra il mio corpo, e saragli   124
    tanto con li altri, che 'l numero nostro
    con l'etterno proposito s'agguagli.
Con le due stole nel beato chiostro   127
    son le due luci sole che saliro;
    e questo apporterai nel mondo vostro".
A questa voce l'infiammato giro   130
    si quïetò con esso il dolce mischio
    che si facea nel suon del trino spiro,
sì come, per cessar fatica o rischio,   133
    li remi, pria ne l'acqua ripercossi,
    tutti si posano al sonar d'un fischio.
Ahi quanto ne la mente mi commossi,   136
    quando mi volsi per veder Beatrice,
    per non poter veder, benché io fossi
presso di lei, e nel mondo felice!   139

My body is earth in earth, and so shall be   124
    with all the rest, until our number's grown
    to equal the eternal destiny.
The two lights who ascended°—they alone—   127
    wear two robes in this blessed garden. Bring
    this truth back to your world." As he began,
A stillness fell upon the fiery ring;   130
    from his first word they quieted the swell
    of their three voices raised in caroling,
Just as the bosun's whistle sounds, to quell   133
    labor, or danger, and the oars aligned
    to smite the water rest in unison.
How deeply I was troubled in my mind   136
    when I turned round to look on Beatrice
    and could not see—for I was dazzled blind,
Though near her, in a world of happiness!   139

° *The two lights who ascended:* Christ and Mary, who was granted the immediate grace of the glorification of her body.

Mentr' io dubbiava per lo viso spento,
  de la fulgida fiamma che lo spense
  uscì un spiro che mi fece attento,
dicendo: "Intanto che tu ti risense   4
  de la vista che haï in me consunta,
  ben è che ragionando la compense.
Comincia dunque; e dì ove s'appunta   7
  l'anima tua, e fa ragion che sia
  la vista in te smarrita e non defunta:
perché la donna che per questa dia   10
  regïon ti conduce, ha ne lo sguardo
  la virtù ch'ebbe la man d'Anania".
Io dissi: "Al suo piacere e tosto e tardo   13
  vegna remedio a li occhi, che fuor porte
  quand' ella entrò col foco ond' io sempr' ardo.
Lo ben che fa contenta questa corte,   16
  Alfa e O è di quanta scrittura
  mi legge Amore o lievemente o forte".
Quella medesma voce che paura   19
  tolta m'avea del sùbito abbarbaglio,
  di ragionare ancor mi mise in cura;

CANTO TWENTY-SIX

Saint John examines Dante on love. When Dante answers appropriately, he finds himself before the spirit of Adam, who answers four of Dante's questions regarding his life in Eden.

While I was faltering from extinguished sight
    there came a breath that held my spirit tense,
    attending to that blinding blaze of light,
As it said, "While we're waiting till you sense   4
    the power of vision you consumed in me,
    let conversation be our recompense.
Begin, and tell to what felicity   7
    your soul aspires as to its single end.
    It's well your sight has only gone astray,
Not died; for she who leads you through this land   10
    of godlike light possesses in her eyes
    the power that dwelt in Ananias' hand."°
"Let it come fast or slow as she may please,"   13
    said I, "to heal my vision, once the gate
    she entered with the fire that ever burns
Within my heart. The good that brings this court   16
    its peace is Alpha and Omega of
    all that with gentle or insistent voice
Is read to me by my instructor, Love."   19
    The voice that stilled my fears for my lost sight
    imposed on me the task to speak some more:

°*Ananias' hand:* When Saint Paul was stricken blind on his way to Damascus, Christ instructed him in a vision to proceed to the house of Ananias, a disciple. When Ananias laid his hands on Paul's head and prayed, Paul recovered his sight (Acts 9:8–18).

THE HEAVEN OF THE FIXED STARS

e disse: "Certo a più angusto vaglio
    ti conviene schiarar: dicer convienti
    chi drizzò l'arco tuo a tal berzaglio".

                   22

E io: "Per filosofici argomenti
    e per autorità che quinci scende
    cotale amor convien che in me si 'mprenti:

                   25

ché 'l bene, in quanto ben, come s'intende,
    così accende amore, e tanto maggio
    quanto più di bontate in sé comprende.

                   28

Dunque a l'essenza ov' è tanto avvantaggio,
    che ciascun ben che fuor di lei si trova
    altro non è ch'un lume di suo raggio,

                   31

più che in altra convien che si mova
    la mente, amando, di ciascun che cerne
    il vero in che si fonda questa prova.

                   34

Tal vero a l'intelletto mïo sterne
    colui che mi dimostra il primo amore
    di tutte le sustanze sempiterne.

                   37

Sternel la voce del verace autore,
    che dice a Moïsè, di sé parlando:
    'Io ti farò vedere ogne valore'.

                   40

Sternilmi tu ancora, incominciando
    l'alto preconio che grida l'arcano
    di qui là giù sovra ogne altro bando".

                   43

E io udi': "Per intelletto umano
    e per autoritadi a lui concorde
    d'i tuoi amori a Dio guarda il sovrano.

                   46

Ma dì ancor se tu senti altre corde
    tirarti verso lui, sì che tu suone
    con quanti denti questo amor ti morde".

                   49

Non fu latente la santa intenzione
    de l'aguglia di Cristo, anzi m'accorsi
    dove volea menar mia professione.

                   52

"Now you must set things in a clearer light,"
    said he, "and spread a finer sieve, to say
    who aimed your bow and arrow at that mark." 22

"Arguments of philosophy," said I,
    "and heavenly authority that descends
    to men on earth, have stamped such love on me; 25

For good, as it is good, and known as good,
    enkindles love, and lights love all the more
    according to the good it comprehends. 28

So toward that Being, so superior
    that every other good a man may find
    is only a reflection of His splendor, 31

More than toward any others the keen mind
    must move in love—when once it should detect
    the truth whereon this argument is built. 34

He° lays this bare before my intellect
    who demonstrates to me the primal love
    of all the everlasting substances. 37

The voice of the true Author, speaking of
    Himself to Moses, also lays it bare,
    saying, "I shall reveal all worth to you." 40

And you in your proemion° with the blare
    of trumpets cry these mysteries aloud,
    clearer than any calls the earth can hear." 43

"By proofs from human intellect," I heard,
    "and authors who confirm those reasonings,
    the highest of your love yet turns to God. 46

But declare if you feel still other strings
    whizzing the arrow of your soul His way—
    how many teeth of Love, how many stings!" 49

I saw what he was leading me to say;
    Christ's eagle° hardly had withheld from me
    his holy meaning—what I must declare. 52

°*He:* We are not sure to whom Dante refers; see notes.
°*your proemion:* the beginning of the gospel of John.
°*Christ's eagle:* John, whose symbol in Christian art was the eagle (cf. Rev. 4:7).

Però ricominciai: "Tutti quei morsi   55
  che posson far lo cor volgere a Dio,
  a la mia caritate son concorsi:
ché l'essere del mondo e l'esser mio,   58
  la morte ch'el sostenne perch' io viva,
  e quel che spera ogne fedel com' io,
con la predetta conoscenza viva,   61
  tratto m'hanno del mar de l'amor torto,
  e del diritto m'han posto a la riva.
Le fronde onde s'infronda tutto l'orto   64
  de l'ortolano etterno, am' io cotanto
  quanto da lui a lor di bene è porto".
Sì com' io tacqui, un dolcissimo canto   67
  risonò per lo cielo, e la mia donna
  dicea con li altri: "Santo, santo, santo!".
E come a lume acuto si disonna   70
  per lo spirto visivo che ricorre
  a lo splendor che va di gonna in gonna,
e lo svegliato ciò che vede aborre,   73
  sì nescïa è la sùbita vigilia
  fin che la stimativa non soccorre;
così de li occhi miei ogne quisquilia   76
  fugò Beatrice col raggio d'i suoi,
  che rifulgea da più di mille milia:
onde mei che dinanzi vidi poi;   79
  e quasi stupefatto domandai
  d'un quarto lume ch'io vidi tra noi.
E la mia donna: "Dentro da quei rai   82
  vagheggia il suo fattor l'anima prima
  che la prima virtù creasse mai".
Come la fronda che flette la cima   85
  nel transito del vento, e poi si leva
  per la propria virtù che la soblima,
fec' io in tanto in quant' ella diceva.   88
  stupendo, e poi mi rifece sicuro
  un disio di parlare ond' ïo ardeva.

So I resumed, "All of the teeth, the spurs   55
    that lead a man to turn to the Divine,
    converge to call my heart to charity,
For this world's very being, and my own,   58
    the death He suffered so that I might live,
    the joy that I and all believing men
Hope for, with that sure knowledge° ever alive,   61
    have drawn me from the ocean that deceives
    and set me on the shores of the true love.
I love the green and vine-adorning leaves   64
    of the eternal Master of the vine,
    according to the good each leaf receives."
When I fell still, there came the sweetest song   67
    of "Holy, holy, holy" through the heavens,
    my Lady singing with the sounding throng.
And as the power of eyesight shakes off sleep,   70
    hastening to accost a lance of light
    that penetrates the lids and pierces deep,
And he who's wakened startles at the sight,   73
    ignorant in the unexpected blaze
    until perception helps him see things right—
So all the dust and chaff that filmed my eyes   76
    the eyes of Beatrice swept away, with more
    than thousand thousand of her flashing rays,
And I saw clearer than I'd seen before,   79
    and asked my Lady—nearly stupefied—
    about another light, for there were four.
"He dwells within that radiance," she replied,   82
    "and looks on his Creator lovingly,
    who was the first soul whom the First Power made."
And as the crowning branches of a tree   85
    bow in the passing wind, and then arise
    by their own power that lifts them naturally,
So while she spoke to me I dropped my eyes   88
    in wonder, till again I felt secure,
    reassured by my burning wish to speak.

°*that sure knowledge:* mentioned above (lines 28–30), that God is the most desirable good.

E cominciai: "O pomo che maturo   91
   solo prodotto fosti, o padre antico
   a cui ciascuna sposa è figlia e nuro,

divoto quanto posso a te supplìco   94
   perché mi parli: tu vedi mia voglia,
   e per udirti tosto non la dico".

Talvolta un animal coverto broglia,   97
   sì che l'affetto convien che si paia
   per lo seguir che face a lui la 'nvoglia;

e similmente l'anima primaia   100
   mi facea trasparer per la coverta
   quant' ella a compiacermi venìa gaia.

Indi spirò: "Sanz' essermi proferta   103
   da te, la voglia tua discerno meglio
   che tu qualunque cosa t'è più certa;

perch' io la veggio nel verace speglio   106
   che fa di sé pareglio a l'altre cose,
   e nulla face lui di sé pareglio.

Tu vuogli udir quant' è che Dio mi puose   109
   ne l'eccelso giardino, ove costei
   a così lunga scala ti dispuose,

e quanto fu diletto a li occhi miei,   112
   e la propria cagion del gran disdegno,
   e l'idïoma ch'usai e che fei.

Or, figliuol mio, non il gustar del legno   115
   fu per sé la cagion di tanto essilio,
   ma solamente il trapassar del segno.

Quindi onde mosse tua donna Virgilio,   118
   quattromilia trecento e due volumi
   di sol desiderai questo concilio;

e vidi lui tornare a tutt' i lumi   121
   de la sua strada novecento trenta
   fïate, mentre ch'ïo in terra fu'mi.

"O apple who alone were formed mature,   91
   O ancient Father Adam," I began,
    "whose daughters are the wives of all your sons,

I beg you as devoutly as I can,   94
   speak to me, tell me, for you know my will—
   unspoken will, that I may hear you soon!"

Sometimes the rustling of an animal   97
   shivers his hidden warren and you see
   whatever fear or longing stirs his soul;

That first of human spirits similarly   100
   showed to me through the covert of his flame
   how merry he became in pleasing me,

And breathed these words, "Although you do not name   103
   your wish, I hold it clearer in my sight
   than you can hold your clearest certainty,

Because I see it in the glass that gives   106
   the truth, the mirror of the universe,
   while nothing else can wholly mirror it.

You want to know the number of the years   109
   since the Lord set me on that garden's height
   whence she prepared you for so long a climb;°

And for how long it was my eyes' delight;   112
   the true cause of the great antipathy;°
   and what speech I invented, and employed.

My son, it wasn't tasting from the tree   115
   that led me into exile, but alone
   my trespassing the mark set down for me.

In Limbo where your Lady ventured down   118
   to entreat Virgil, for four thousand and
   three hundred and two turnings of the sun

I longed for this assembly, and saw it turn   121
   nine hundred thirty times along its road
   through all the zodiac, while I lived on earth.

°*that garden's height . . . climb:* Earthly Paradise, atop the Mountain of Purgatory, whence
Beatrice led Dante to Heaven.

°*the great antipathy:* God's wrath against Adam.

La lingua ch'io parlai fu tutta spenta   124
  innanzi che a l'ovra inconsummabile
  fosse la gente di Nembròt attenta:
ché nullo effetto mai razïonabile,   127
  per lo piacere uman che rinovella
  seguendo il cielo, sempre fu durabile.
Opera naturale è ch'uom favella;   130
  ma così o così, natura lascia
  poi fare a voi secondo che v'abbella.
Pria ch'i' scendessi a l'infernale ambascia,   133
  I s'appellava in terra il sommo bene
  onde vien la letizia che mi fascia;
e *El* si chiamò poi: e ciò convene,   136
  ché l'uso d'i mortali è come fronda
  in ramo, che sen va e altra vene.
Nel monte che si leva più da l'onda,   139
  fu' io, con vita pura e disonesta,
  da la prim' ora a quella che seconda,
come 'l sol muta quadra, l'ora sesta".   142

Before the people heeded Nimrod's word
   to build the work° they never could perfect,
   the language I first spoke was spent, was dead,
For never was a rational effect
   that could outlast the shifts of human pleasure,
   renewing customs as the stars direct.
That man has language is the work of Nature,
   but that his language should be thus or so,
   she leaves to you to choose it as you wish.
Before I went to banishment below
   I was the name on earth for the high Good
   that now has clothed me in the robe of joy;
And then they called it *El*—right that they should,
   for mortal use is like a branch's leaves:
   where one may fall, another springs to bud.
On that mount rising highest from the waves
   I lived, pure or dishonest, from first dawn
   till the sun changed its quadrant in the sky—
Six hours, that ended with the passing noon."

124

127

130

133

136

139

142

°*the work:* the Tower of Babel, believed to have been begun by *Nimrod* (Gen. 11:1–9; cf. *Inf.* 31.77–78, *Purg.* 12.34–36).

'Al Padre, al Figlio, a lo Spirito Santo',
    cominciò, 'gloria!', tutto 'l paradiso,
    sì che m'inebrïava il dolce canto.
Ciò ch'io vedeva mi sembiava un riso   4
    de l'universo; per che mia ebbrezza
    intrava per l'udire e per lo viso.
Oh gioia! oh ineffabile allegrezza!   7
    oh vita intègra d'amore e di pace!
    oh sanza brama sicura ricchezza!
Dinanzi a li occhi miei le quattro face   10
    stavano accese, e quella che pria venne
    incominciò a farsi più vivace,
e tal ne la sembianza sua divenne,   13
    qual diverrebbe Iove, s'elli e Marte
    fossero augelli e cambiassersi penne.
La provedenza, che quivi comparte   16
    vice e officio, nel beato coro
    silenzio posto avea da ogne parte,
quand' ïo udi': "Se io mi trascoloro,   19
    non ti maravigliar, ché, dicend' io,
    vedrai trascolorar tutti costoro.
Quelli ch'usurpa in terra il luogo mio,   22
    il luogo mio, il luogo mio che vaca
    ne la presenza del Figliuol di Dio,

Canto Twenty-seven

Saint Peter denounces the corruption of the papacy and the Church. After he instructs Dante to tell what he has heard, the poet and Beatrice rise to the ninth sphere, the Primum Mobile.

"To Father and to Son and Holy Ghost,"
    sang all the heavens, "glory!"—filling me
    with drunken joy; it seemed what I beheld
Was laughter of the universe, the glee   4
    of laughter whose inebriating swell
    enters by what you hear and what you see.
O joy! O happiness ineffable!   7
    O riches safe, no worry of desire!
    O life of love and peace, perfect and full!
Before me the four torches stood afire,   10
    and he° the spirit who was first to move
    to speak to me, surged in his fiery life,
Becoming in his countenance as Jove   13
    if he and Mars (if he and Mars were birds)
    could trade their plumage. And the Providence
That orders all in Heaven and divides   16
    the times and offices, imposed a due
    silence on that blest choir, and on all sides,
When I heard Peter: "If I change my hue,   19
    don't be amazed—for when I speak, you'll see
    all of these others changing color too.
He° who usurps on earth my Holy See,   22
    my Holy See, my Holy See, which sits
    empty in the presence of God's Son, he

°*he:* Peter, flushing with righteous anger.
°*He:* Pope Boniface VIII.

fatt' ha del cimitero mio cloaca   25
    del sangue e de la puzza; onde 'l perverso
    che cadde di qua sù, là giù si placa".
Di quel color che per lo sole avverso   28
    nube dipigne da sera e da mane,
    vid' ïo allora tutto 'l ciel cosperso.
E come donna onesta che permane   31
    di sé sicura, e per l'altrui fallanza,
    pur ascoltando, timida si fane,
così Beatrice trasmutò sembianza;   34
    e tale eclissi credo che 'n ciel fue
    quando patì la supprema possanza.
Poi procedetter le parole sue   37
    con voce tanto da sé trasmutata,
    che la sembianza non si mutò più:
"Non fu la sposa di Cristo allevata   40
    del sangue mio, di Lin, di quel di Cleto,
    per essere ad acquisto d'oro usata;
ma per acquisto d'esto viver lieto   43
    e Sisto e Pïo e Calisto e Urbano
    sparser lo sangue dopo molto fleto.
Non fu nostra intenzion ch'a destra mano   46
    d'i nostri successor parte sedesse,
    parte da l'altra del popol cristiano;
né che le chiavi che mi fuor concesse,   49
    divenisser signaculo in vessillo
    che contra battezzati combattesse;
né ch'io fossi figura di sigillo   52
    a privilegi venduti e mendaci,
    ond' io sovente arrosso e disfavillo.
In vesta di pastor lupi rapaci   55
    si veggion di qua sù per tutti i paschi:
    o difesa di Dio, perché pur giaci?

Has made my sacred cemetery a sewer   25
   of blood and filth, to please the twisted one
   who fell from here to misery below."
Think of the tint that shades the dusk or dawn   28
   when the sun slants its light upon a cloud—
   with such a flush all Paradise now shone;
A lady, dignified and self-assured,   31
   will so remain, but casts a timid glance,
   merely to hear of someone else's fault;
So Beatrice was transformed in countenance,   34
   and I believe just such an eclipse then
   darkened the heavens when Omnipotence
Suffered upon the Cross. His words went on,   37
   his voice so changed from what it was at first,
   even his countenance had not altered more:
"The Bride of Christ was never raised and nursed   40
   by my blood, Linus' blood, the blood of Cletus,
   to be put out to use to pocket gold!
No, Sixtus, Pius, Urban, and Calixtus,°   43
   to gain the glad life of this blessed state,
   spilled their blood after shedding many tears.
It was not our intent to separate   46
   the Christian people, part to left, to right,
   sitting at our successor's either hand,
Nor that the keys I was conceded might   49
   blazon the banners of some new Crusade
   for sallying forth to battle the baptized,
Nor that my face should mark a seal, to trade   52
   in cheating privileges bought and sold,
   that make my flames so often blush and fade.
We see rapacious wolves in every fold   55
   garbed as the men who lead the sheep to graze.
   Defending arm of God, why do you sleep?

°*Linus, Cletus, Sixtus, Pius, Urban, Calixtus:* early popes martyred for the faith.

Del sangue nostro Caorsini e Guaschi   58
   s'apparecchian di bere: o buon principio,
   a che vil fine convien che tu caschi!

Ma l'alta provedenza, che con Scipio   61
   difese a Roma la gloria del mondo,
   soccorrà tosto, sì com' io concipio;

e tu, figliuol, che per lo mortal pondo   64
   ancor giù tornerai, apri la bocca,
   e non asconder quel ch'io non ascondo".

Sì come di vapor gelati fiocca   67
   in giuso l'aere nostro, quando 'l corno
   de la capra del ciel col sol si tocca,

in sù vid' io così l'etera addorno   70
   farsi e fioccar di vapor trïunfanti
   che fatto avien con noi quivi soggiorno.

Lo viso mio seguiva i suoi sembianti,   73
   e seguì fin che 'l mezzo, per lo molto,
   li tolse il trapassar del più avanti.

Onde la donna, che mi vide assolto   76
   de l'attendere in sù, mi disse: "Adima
   il viso e guarda come tu se' vòlto".

Da l'ora ch'ïo avea guardato prima   79
   i' vidi mosso me per tutto l'arco
   che fa dal mezzo al fine il primo clima;

sì ch'io vedea di là da Gade il varco   82
   folle d'Ulisse, e di qua presso il lito
   nel qual si fece Europa dolce carco.

Cahors and Gascony° are set to swill   58
  our Roman blood—O good beginning, how
  filthy your end is, how contemptible!
But that deep providence will aid us now—   61
  I see it nearing—that defended Rome
  for the world's glory, raising Scipio.°
And you, my son, returning from this wheel   64
  with mortal weight, open your lips and speak!
  Do not conceal what I do not conceal."
As frozen vapor in our skies will flake   67
  and fall to earth in winter, when the horn
  of Heaven's Goat° is nudging on the sun,
So did I see those rising flakes adorn   70
  ethereal Heaven in triumphant flight,
  the spirits that had stayed with us awhile.
I followed their appearance with my sight,   73
  followed them till the atmosphere between
  had grown so vast, I could no longer pass
Beyond. And then my Lady, having seen   76
  that I was free from gazing up on high,
  said, "Lower your eyes and see how far you've turned."
From the hour when I'd last beheld the earth,   79
  I saw I'd turned along the whole arc's way
  from the first climate's noon to setting sun;
Saw where Ulysses' foolish passage° lay   82
  there past Cadiz, while, here, I saw the shore°
  Europa walked when she was made a sweet

°*Cahors and Gascony:* Cahors (by repute a nest of usurers, *Inf.* 11.50) was the fatherland of John XXII (r. 1305–34; see 18.126 and note); Gascony, that of Clement V (r. 1305–14), the pope who moved the papal offices from Rome to Avignon, because, as Dante saw it, he was toadying to the French king Philip the Fair (cf. *Inf.* 19.82–87).

°*Scipio:* the victor over Hannibal in the Second Punic War; see 6.52–4 and note.

°*Heaven's Goat:* Capricorn.

°*Ulysses' foolish passage:* sailing through the Straits of Gibraltar into the Atlantic (cf. *Inf.* 26.125).

°*the shore:* on the eastern Mediterranean. In mythology, Jupiter fell in love with *Europa* and, in the form of a bull, swept her away (Ovid, *Met.* 2.858–75).

E più mi fora discoverto il sito   85
    di questa aiuola; ma 'l sol procedea
    sotto i mie' piedi un segno e più partito.

La mente innamorata, che donnea   88
    con la mia donna sempre, di ridure
    ad essa li occhi più che mai ardea;

e se natura o arte fé pasture   91
    da pigliare occhi, per aver la mente,
    in carne umana o ne le sue pitture,

tutte adunate, parrebber nïente   94
    ver' lo piacer divin che mi refulse,
    quando mi volsi al suo viso ridente.

E la virtù che lo sguardo m'indulse,   97
    del bel nido di Leda mi divelse
    e nel ciel velocissimo m'impulse.

Le parti sue vivissime ed eccelse   100
    sì uniforme son, ch'i' non so dire
    qual Bëatrice per loco mi scelse.

Ma ella, che vedëa 'l mio disire,   103
    incominciò, ridendo tanto lieta,
    che Dio parea nel suo volto gioire:

"La natura del mondo, che quïeta   106
    il mezzo e tutto l'altro intorno move,
    quinci comincia come da sua meta;

e questo cielo non ha altro dove   109
    che la mente divina, in che s'accende
    l'amor che 'l volge e la virtù ch'ei piove.

Luce e amor d'un cerchio lui comprende,   112
    sì come questo li altri; e quel precinto
    colui che 'l cinge solamente intende.

Non è suo moto per altro distinto,   115
    ma li altri son mensurati da questo,
    sì come diece da mezzo e da quinto;

Burden. More of this little threshing floor   85
    had been revealed to me, but that the sun
    had walked before my feet one sign and more.°
My enamored mind that ever gazed upon   88
    my Lady in the obedience of love
    now burned to turn my eyes to her again,
And all that art or Nature ever gave   91
    as bait to catch the eyes and take the mind,
    whether in human flesh or portraiture,
Were all these beauties in one sight combined,   94
    it would be nothing to the rare delight
    that flashed upon me when I turned to see
Her laughing eyes—granting me such great might,   97
    I ripped my roots from Leda's lovely nest°
    and swept on to the heaven of swiftest flight.
So uniform are all those liveliest   100
    and highest of the highest realms, what place
    Beatrice chose for me I can't attest,
But she, who saw what I desired to know,   103
    began to speak with such a happy smile,
    I seemed to see God's gladness in her face:
"The nature of the universe, the soul   106
    that stills the center and sweeps all things around,
    begins here, from its origin and goal;
And for this heaven° no place is to be found   109
    but in the mind of God, wherein take wing
    the love that turns it, and the power it rains.
Light and love comprehend it one ring   112
    as it rings all the rest: and he alone
    comprehends this girdling ring, who girdles it.
The motion of this sphere derives from none—   115
    its motion rather measures all the rest,
    as two and five combine to measure ten;

°*one sign and more:* of the zodiac. The sun stands at between two and four hours' declination from the zenith above Dante's position.

°*Leda's lovely nest:* Gemini. Enamored of Leda, Jupiter made love to her in the form of a swan. From the resulting egg came the Twins, Castor and Pollux (Ovid, *Met.* 6.109).

°*this heaven:* the Primum Mobile.

e come il tempo tegna in cotal testo 118
   le sue radici e ne li altri le fronde,
   omai a te può esser manifesto.

Oh cupidigia, che i mortali affonde 121
   sì sotto te, che nessuno ha podere
   di trarre li occhi fuor de le tue onde!

Ben fiorisce ne li uomini il volere; 124
   ma la pioggia continüa converte
   in bozzacchioni le sosine vere.

Fede e innocenza son reperte 127
   solo ne' parvoletti; poi ciascuna
   pria fugge che le guance sian coperte.

Tale, balbuzïendo ancor, digiuna, 130
   che poi divora, con la lingua sciolta,
   qualunque cibo per qualunque luna;

e tal, balbuzïendo, ama e ascolta 133
   la madre sua, che, con loquela intera,
   disïa poi di vederla sepolta.

Così si fa la pelle bianca nera 136
   nel primo aspetto de la bella figlia
   di quel ch'apporta mane e lascia sera.

Tu, perché non ti facci maraviglia, 139
   pensa che 'n terra non è chi governi;
   onde sì svïa l'umana famiglia.

Ma prima che gennaio tutto si sverni 142
   per la centesma ch'è là giù negletta,
   raggeran sì questi cerchi superni,

che la fortuna che tanto s'aspetta, 145
   le poppe volgerà u' son le prore,
   sì che la classe correrà diretta;

e vero frutto verrà dopo 'l fiore". 148

And now to you it should be manifest,   118
    time grips its roots into this vase, unseen,
    while in the rest breaks into leaf and crown.

Cupidity! You who drown mortal men   121
    so far beneath you, no one has the power
    to lift his eyes out of your waves again!

Goodwill in man is born and comes to flower,   124
    but the rains ever battering the ground
    swell the true plums and turn them soft and sour.

For faith and innocence are only found   127
    among the children—but they flee at last,
    even before the down is on the cheek.

The baby babbler here still keeps the fast,   130
    who'll gobble down, soon as his tongue is freed,
    in any month, what food may meet his taste.

The baby babbler here still loves and heeds   133
    his mother, who'll desire, when he can talk
    grown-up, to see her dead and in her tomb.

So does a fair complexion turn to black   136
    in the direct light of the lovely daughter
    of him who brings the dawn and leaves the dusk.°

This should not be a great surprise to you.   139
    Think that on earth nobody rules and steers—
    and so the human family goes astray.

But the neglected hundredths of your years   142
    won't make your January start in spring°
    before these highest rings will shed such rays

As will storm down the fortune you await,   145
    turning the prow and aft wholly about,
    so that the fleet a-sea will furrow straight,

And, from the flower, the tree will bear good fruit."   148

°*So ... dusk:* a vexed tercet. The general suggestion is of human corruption; see notes.

°*hundredths ... spring:* The discrepancy between the Julian calendar year and the slightly shorter solar year would cause January, eventually, to begin in spring.

Poscia che 'ncontro a la vita presente
    d'i miseri mortali aperse 'l vero
    quella che 'mparadisa la mia mente,
come in lo specchio fiamma di doppiero   4
    vede colui che se n'alluma retro,
    prima che l'abbia in vista o in pensiero,
e sé rivolge per veder se 'l vetro   7
    li dice il vero, e vede ch'el s'accorda
    con esso come nota con suo metro;
così la mia memoria si ricorda   10
    ch'io feci riguardando ne' belli occhi
    onde a pigliarmi fece Amor la corda.
E com' io mi rivolsi e furon tocchi   13
    li miei da ciò che pare in quel volume,
    quandunque nel suo giro ben s'adocchi,
un punto vidi che raggiava lume   16
    acuto sì, che 'l viso ch'elli affoca
    chiuder conviensi per lo forte acume;
e quale stella par quinci più poca,   19
    parrebbe luna, locata con esso
    come stella con stella si collòca.
Forse cotanto quanto pare appresso   22
    alo cigner la luce che 'l dipigne
    quando 'l vapor che 'l porta più è spesso,

CANTO TWENTY-EIGHT

*Dante is granted a distant vision of the cosmos: a single brilliant **point of light** surrounded by the nine heavenly spheres, whence comes the song of **the angelic hosts,** whose hierarchies Beatrice enumerates.*

When she'd laid bare the truth of this poor life
    of miserable and mortal humankind,
      she who exalts my mind to Paradise—
As when a torchlight shimmers from behind   4
    upon a man who sees it in a glass
      before he grasps it in his sight or mind,
He turns around to see if it's the case   7
    and sees the glass has spoken in accord
      with what is true, as notes of music pace
With measure—so my memory will record   10
    I turned to look into her lovely eyes
      where Love once set the snare and drew the cord.
My own were seized then by a wondrous thing,   13
    by what that scroll of Heaven reveals to sight
      whenever you gaze deep into this ring:
I saw a point that shot out rays of light   16
    so keen, you have to shut your eyes before
      the searing brilliance of its radiant might.
The star that looks the tiniest from here   19
    would seem a moon if placed beside that point,
      as when you see a star beside a star.
As when a starlight in the misty sky   22
    will tint the gathering vapor, rendering
      a colored halo like a sash nearby,

distante intorno al punto un cerchio d'igne   25
    si girava sì ratto, ch'avria vinto
    quel moto che più tosto il mondo cigne;
e questo era d'un altro circumcinto,   28
    e quel dal terzo, e 'l terzo poi dal quarto,
    dal quinto il quarto, e poi dal sesto il quinto.
Sopra seguiva il settimo sì sparto   31
    già di larghezza, che 'l messo di Iuno
    intero a contenerlo sarebbe arto.
Così l'ottavo e 'l nono; e ciascheduno   34
    più tardo si movea, secondo ch'era
    in numero distante più da l'uno;
e quello avea la fiamma più sincera   37
    cui men distava la favilla pura,
    credo, però che più di lei s'invera.
La donna mia, che mi vedëa in cura   40
    forte sospeso, disse: "Da quel punto
    depende il cielo e tutta la natura.
Mira quel cerchio che più li è congiunto;   43
    e sappi che 'l suo muovere è sì tosto
    per l'affocato amore ond' elli è punto".
E io a lei: "Se 'l mondo fosse posto   46
    con l'ordine ch'io veggio in quelle rote,
    sazio m'avrebbe ciò che m'è proposto;
ma nel mondo sensibile si puote   49
    veder le volte tanto più divine,
    quant' elle son dal centro più remote.
Onde, se 'l mio disir dee aver fine   52
    in questo miro e angelico templo
    che solo amore e luce ha per confine,
udir convienmi ancor come l'essemplo   55
    e l'essemplare non vanno d'un modo,
    ché io per me indarno a ciò contemplo".

About so near the point a fiery ring
    revolved so rapidly it would defeat
    the swiftest girdling of the universe.°   25

And this was girdled by a second ring,
    that by a third, the third then by ring four,
    and likewise four by five, and five by six.   28

As for the following seventh's vast domain,
    only if Iris' bow° were fully drawn
    could it embrace it with the tightest strain.   31

So too for eight and nine, and each ring spun
    more slowly than the ring that came before,
    according to their distance from the One;   34

And the least distant from that purest fire
    shone with the clearest flame, I think because
    the point entruthed itself most fully there.   37

My Lady saw how hesitant I was,
    how deeply in suspense. "That is the point,"
    said she, "whence Heaven and all things depend.   40

Gaze at the ring that's nearest to the light.
    Know that the love that stings it into flame
    makes it revolve with such a headlong speed."   43

"Now, if the world were ordered with the same
    order I see within these wheels," said I,
    "what you've set forth would satisfy my mind.   46

But in the world that we can sense, we see
    those turning rings grow ever more divine
    the farther from the center.° So to lend   49

Peace and fulfillment to this wish of mine,
    here in this wondrous and angelic temple
    whose whirling only love and light confine,   52

I need to hear some more—why the example
    and the exemplar vary in their plan.
    Myself, I dwell upon it, all in vain."   55

°*the swiftest girdling of the universe:* the Primum Mobile.

°*Iris' bow:* the rainbow.

°*the center:* in Dante's mind, the earth. Dante wonders why, in the physical cosmos—*the example*—the earth stands at the center, while in this vision located in the mind of God—in this *exemplar*—the earth is farthest from the center.

"Se li tuoi diti non sono a tal nodo   58
  sufficïenti, non è maraviglia:
  tanto, per non tentare, è fatto sodo!".

Così la donna mia; poi disse: "Piglia   61
  quel ch'io ti dicerò, se vuo' saziarti;
  e intorno da esso t'assottiglia.

Li cerchi corporai sono ampi e arti   64
  secondo il più e 'l men de la virtute
  che si distende per tutte lor parti.

Maggior bontà vuol far maggior salute;   67
  maggior salute maggior corpo cape,
  s'elli ha le parti igualmente compiute.

Dunque costui che tutto quanto rape   70
  l'altro universo seco, corrisponde
  al cerchio che più ama e che più sape:

per che, se tu a la virtù circonde   73
  la tua misura, non a la parvenza
  de le sustanze che t'appaion tonde,

tu vederai mirabil consequenza   76
  di maggio a più e di minore a meno,
  in ciascun cielo, a süa intelligenza".

Come rimane splendido e sereno   79
  l'emisperio de l'aere, quando soffia
  Borea da quella guancia ond' è più leno,

per che si purga e risolve la roffia   82
  che pria turbava, sì che 'l ciel ne ride
  con le bellezze d'ogne sua paroffia;

così fec'ïo, poi che mi provide   85
  la donna mia del suo risponder chiaro,
  e come stella in cielo il ver si vide.

E poi che le parole sue restaro,   88
  non altrimenti ferro disfavilla
  che bolle, come i cerchi sfavillaro.

L'incendio suo seguiva ogne scintilla;   91
  ed eran tante, che 'l numero loro
  più che 'l doppiar de li scacchi s'inmilla.

"No cause for wonder if your fingers fail
    to find the skill for solving such a knot.
      So taut it's grown, from never being tried!"

                                      58

Thus from my Lady; then she said, "Take what
    I'll tell you now, if you'd be satisfied,
      and hone your understanding over it.

                                      61

These corporeal rings are narrow or wide
    as there is less or greater power diffuse
      through all their parts. Their influence for good

                                      64

Is greater, as the power is bounteous;
    greater the good, greater the body's size,
      if all its parts are equally complete.

                                      67

And so this heaven that seizes, as it flies,
    all of the other heavens, corresponds
      to the ring that loves most fully and most knows;

                                      70

So if you gird your measure to the bounds
    of actual power, and not the mere appearance
      of substances that look like rings of flame,

                                      73

You'll see the just and wondrous consequence:
    more power, more speed and size; less power, less;
      fitting for every sphere's intelligence."

                                      76

As from the softer cheek of Boreas°
    there comes a breeze upon a cloudy day
      that leaves the dome of air in lucent peace

                                      79

When it has scoured the ruffled clouds away
    and melted all the trouble from a sky
      laughing with loveliness on every hand—

                                      82

So when my Lady gave me her reply
    I saw the truth, beheld it like a star
      shining in brightness and serenity.

                                      85

And when she finished, as an iron bar
    thrust in the forge will fling out glints of flame,
      so were those circles glittering in fire.

                                      88

Turning within its blaze each sparkle came—
    more numerous in their enthousanding
      than the redoubling of a chessboard's squares!

                                      91

° *softer cheek of Boreas:* the gentle wind from the northwest.

CRYSTALLINE HEAVEN

Io sentiva osannar di coro in coro   94
   al punto fisso che li tiene a li *ubi,*
   e terrà sempre, ne' quai sempre fuoro.
E quella che vedëa i pensier dubi   97
   ne la mia mente, disse: "I cerchi primi
   t'hanno mostrato Serafi e Cherubi.
Così veloci seguono i suoi vimi,   100
   per somigliarsi al punto quanto ponno;
   e posson quanto a veder son soblimi.
Quelli altri amori che 'ntorno li vonno,   103
   si chiaman Troni del divino aspetto,
   per che 'l primo ternaro terminonno;
e dei saper che tutti hanno diletto   106
   quanto la sua veduta si profonda
   nel vero in che si queta ogne intelletto.
Quinci si può veder come si fonda   109
   l'esser beato ne l'atto che vede,
   non in quel ch'ama, che poscia seconda;
e del vedere è misura mercede,   112
   che grazia partorisce e buona voglia:
   così di grado in grado si procede.
L'altro ternaro, che così germoglia   115
   in questa primavera sempiterna
   che notturno Arïete non dispoglia,
perpetüalemente *'Osanna'* sberna   118
   con tre melode, che suonano in tree
   ordini di letizia onde s'interna.
In essa gerarcia son l'altre dee: 121
   prima Dominazioni, e poi Virtudi;
   l'ordine terzo di Podestadi èe.
Poscia ne' due penultimi tripudi   124
   Principati e Arcangeli si girano;
   l'ultimo è tutto d'Angelici ludi.
Questi ordini di sù tutti s'ammirano,   127
   e di giù vincon sì, che verso Dio
   tutti tirati sono e tutti tirano.

And choir to choir I heard hosannaing
    to the fixed Point that held them to their *where,*
    and will hold ever, where they ever were.
And when she saw my thoughts begin to veer,
    "The inmost of the rings," she said to me,
    "show you the Seraphim and Cherubim
Slung by the vine with such velocity
    as to be like that point as best they can,
    and can, as they are made sublime to see.
Around them go the Thrones of sight divine,
    the loves that are the seat of those above
    and make the inner ternion complete.
And know that all those angels take delight
    insofar as their sight can plumb the flood
    of truth, where every intellect may rest.
Hence you can see that our beatitude
    is founded on the act of mind that sees,
    and not on love, which follows afterward;
Our vision measured to the merits grace
    has brought to birth, along with virtuous will;
    so we proceed by stages and degrees.
The second ternion, sprouting from the soil
    that is this first and everlasting Spring
    that no night-starry Aries° shall despoil,
In their perpetual unwintering
    ring out Hosanna in three melodies,
    for in this hierarchy angels sing
As their felicity resounds in threes:
    the first are Dominations, Virtues next,
    and the Powers' order is the third of these.
The two penultimate rings of all the dance
    are where the Princes and Archangels turn;
    the last is filled with Angels as they feast.
On high do all these orders gaze and yearn;
    as they are bound with bonds to those below,
    so all are drawn, and draw in turn, toward God.

94

97

100

103

106

109

112

115

118

121

124

127

°*Aries:* Aries is a ram, after all.

E Dïonisio con tanto disio   130
    a contemplar questi ordini si mise,
    che li nomò e distinse com' io.
Ma Gregorio da lui poi si divise;   133
    onde, sì tosto come li occhi aperse
    in questo ciel, di sé medesmo rise.
E se tanto secreto ver proferse   136
    mortale in terra, non voglio ch'ammiri:
    ché chi 'l vide qua sù gliel discoperse
con altro assai del ver di questi giri".   139

So passionately did Dionysius° ply
    his heart to dwell upon these hierarchies,
      he named them and distinguished them as I.   130
Afterward Gregory parted from his ways,
    but when he arrived here with open eyes   133
      he laughed at his mistake. Nor gape in wonder
That a mere mortal man on earth was given
    to know this truth about such secret things,   136
      for he who saw,° when he was swept to Heaven,
Told him much more besides about these rings."

          139

°*Dionysius:* Dionysius the Areopagite, to whom was attributed the *Celestial Hierarchies* (cf. 10.115–17 and note). *Gregory* the Great divided the nine angelic orders slightly differently.

°*he who saw:* Saint Paul. Dionysius was converted by Paul in Athens (Acts 17:34); it was thought that Paul then told him what he saw when he was swept up to the third heaven (2 Cor. 12:1–5).

Quando ambedue li figli di Latona,
    coperti del Montone e de la Libra,
    fanno de l'orizzonte insieme zona,
quant' è dal punto che 'l cenìt inlibra   4
    infin che l'uno e l'altro da quel cinto,
    cambiando l'emisperio, si dilibra,
tanto, col volto di riso dipinto,   7
    si tacque Bëatrice, riguardando
    fiso nel punto che m'avëa vinto.
Poi cominciò: "Io dico, e non dimando,   10
    quel che tu vuoli udir, perch' io l'ho visto
    là 've s'appunta ogne *ubi* e ogne *quando*.
Non per aver a sé di bene acquisto,   13
    ch'esser non può, ma perché suo splendore
    potesse, risplendendo, dir *'Subsisto,'*
in sua etternità di tempo fore,   16
    fuor d'ogne altro comprender, come i piacque,
    s'aperse in nuovi amor l'etterno amore.
Né prima quasi torpente si giacque;   19
    ché né prima né poscia procedette
    lo discorrer di Dio sovra quest' acque.

CANTO TWENTY-NINE

*Beatrice reveals to Dante various truths about **the angels**: their creation, their powers, their number, and the fall of the rebels. She rebukes **errant philosophers on earth** who pretend to know more than they do about heavenly things.*

When both Latona's children, sun and moon,
    one in the Scales, the other in the Ram,
    share one horizon like a girdling zone,
From the point where the zenith dangles them
    in equal balance, till they both break free,
    trading their hemispheres by fall and rise°—   4
For such an instant, smiling rosily,
    was Beatrice silent as she gazed upon
    the point of light that had defeated me.   7
"I say, I do not ask you," she began,
    "what you would like to hear, which I have seen
    within this terminus of *where* and *when*.   10
Not (for it cannot be) that He should gain
    good for Himself, but that resplendence of
    His light should utter, 'I exist,' beyond   13
All time in His eternity, beyond
    confining space, according to His will,
    into new loves burst the Eternal Love.   16
Before, he did not lie adrowse and still—
    neither 'before' nor 'after' can precede
    the hovering of God above these waters.   19

°*trading . . . by fall and rise:* Since Libra and Aries stand opposite each other, for an instant the *sun and moon* share one horizon, till one enters the northern and the other enters the southern hemisphere.

Forma e materia, congiunte e purette,
    usciro ad esser che non avia fallo,
    come d'arco tricordo tre saette.   22

E come in vetro, in ambra o in cristallo
    raggio resplende sì, che dal venire
    a l'esser tutto non è intervallo,   25

così 'l triforme effetto del suo sire
    ne l'esser suo raggiò insieme tutto
    sanza distinzïone in essordire.   28

Concreato fu ordine e costrutto
    a le sustanze; e quelle furon cima
    nel mondo in che puro atto fu produtto;   31

pura potenza tenne la parte ima;
    nel mezzo strinse potenza con atto
    tal vime, che già mai non si divima.   34

Ieronimo vi scrisse lungo tratto
    di secoli de li angeli creati
    anzi che l'altro mondo fosse fatto;   37

ma questo vero è scritto in molti lati
    da li scrittor de lo Spirito Santo,
    e tu te n'avvedrai se bene agguati;   40

e anche la ragione il vede alquanto,
    che non concederebbe che ' motori
    sanza sua perfezion fosser cotanto.   43

Or sai tu dove e quando questi amori
    furon creati e come: sì che spenti
    nel tuo disïo già son tre ardori.   46

Né giugneriesi, numerando, al venti
    sì tosto, come de li angeli parte
    turbò il suggetto d'i vostri alimenti.   49

L'altra rimase, e cominciò quest' arte
    che tu discerni, con tanto diletto,
    che mai da circüir non si diparte.   52

Matter and form, combined or pure indeed,   22
   came into faultless being by His act,
     as from a three-cord bow three arrows speed;
And as in crystal, amber, or in glass,   25
   a ray reflects as fast as it has come—
     from "be" to "shine" is not a moment's space—
So did the Sire's effect of triple form   28
   ray forth in being, simultaneously,
     and not drawn out from an exordium.
All these were ordered when they came to be: 31
   their order and their essence, one creation.
     Those at the summit of the world, pure act;
Pure potency retains the lowest part;   34
   between them, act and potency are bound
     with bonds that never can be torn apart.
Jerome wrote how the centuries went round   37
   in a long train from when the angel hosts
     were made to the creation of the world,
And yet the writers of the Holy Ghost   40
   have set this truth in many passages,
     which you will notice if you study well;
And something of it even reason sees,   43
   for reason does not grant that that which moves
     should long exist without its proper end,
To move.° Now you know where and when these loves   46
   were made, and how: and so three flames are quenched
     that burned in your desire. And in less time
Than it takes to reach twenty when you count,   49
   part of the angels fell away, and brought
     trouble into your world of elements.
The rest remained, and they began this art   52
   you now behold, dwelling with such delight
     they'll never leave the circling of their thought.

° *To move:* to move the planets, that is. Beatrice argues that the angelic intelligences were not
created long before the planets they were destined to move.

Principio del cader fu il maladetto   55
    superbir di colui che tu vedesti
    da tutti i pesi del mondo costretto.
Quelli che vedi qui furon modesti   58
    a riconoscer sé da la bontate
    che li avea fatti a tanto intender presti:
per che le viste lor furo essaltate   61
    con grazia illuminante e con lor merto,
    sì c'hanno ferma e piena volontate;
e non voglio che dubbi, ma sia certo,   64
    che ricever la grazia è meritorio
    secondo che l'affetto l'è aperto.
Omai dintorno a questo consistorio   67
    puoi contemplare assai, se le parole
    mie son ricolte, sanz' altro aiutorio.
Ma perché 'n terra per le vostre scole   70
    si legge che l'angelica natura
    è tal, che 'ntende e si ricorda e vole,
ancor dirò, perché tu veggi pura   73
    la verità che là giù si confonde,
    equivocando in sì fatta lettura.
Queste sustanze, poi che fur gioconde   76
    de la faccia di Dio, non volser viso
    da essa, da cui nulla si nasconde:
però non hanno vedere interciso   79
    da novo obietto, e però non bisogna
    rememorar per concetto diviso;
sì che là giù, non dormendo, si sogna,   82
    credendo e non credendo dicer vero;
    ma ne l'uno è più colpa e più vergogna.
Voi non andate giù per un sentiero   85
    filosofando: tanto vi trasporta
    l'amor de l'apparenza e 'l suo pensiero!
E ancor questo qua sù si comporta   88
    con men disdegno che quando è posposta
    la divina Scrittura o quando è torta.

The prime cause of the fall was the accursed   55
   pride of the angel whom you saw beneath
   all the weight of the cosmos, crushed and pressed;

But these kept humble tenor, knew themselves   58
   as rising from the generosity
   that made them quick to understand so much,

So were their eyes exalted, raised thus high   61
   by merit and illuminating grace,
   and now their will is firm and full and free.

Nor would I have you falter, but believe   64
   receiving grace is meritorious
   so far as will is open to receive.

Gather up what I say and you will come   67
   to contemplate far more about these halls
   and not need my assistance. But because

Down there on earth in all your many schools   70
   they teach that the angelic nature is
   one that remembers, understands, and wills,

I'll say a little more, that you may see   73
   the pure truth of what they confound below,
   in teachings that must speak equivocally.

These substances, once they had known their joy   76
   looking upon the face of God, did not
   turn from Him, from whose vision nothing hides,

And so they never have their vision cut   79
   by sight of something new; no need to keep
   in memory the divisions of their thought.

So that, down there, they° dream who do not sleep,   82
   with some believing that they speak the truth,
   some not; the latter bear more fault and blame.

You don't philosophize on a single path—   85
   you're so in love with how you look, so vain,
   you're carried wide. Even this love of show

We here in Heaven can bear with less disdain   88
   than when you make the Scripture halt behind
   your reasonings, or you twist it to sustain

°*they:* vain speculators on the angelic nature.

Non vi si pensa quanto sangue costa   91
   seminarla nel mondo e quanto piace
   chi umilmente con essa s'accosta.
Per apparer ciascun s'ingegna e face   94
   sue invenzioni; e quelle son trascorse
   da' predicanti e 'l Vangelio si tace.
Un dice che la luna si ritorse   97
   ne la passion di Cristo e s'interpuose,
   per che 'l lume del sol giù non si porse;
e mente, ché la luce si nascose   100
   da sé: però a li Spani e a l'Indi
   come a' Giudei tale eclissi rispuose.
Non ha Fiorenza tanti Lapi e Bindi   103
   quante sì fatte favole per anno
   in pergamo si gridan quinci e quindi:
sì che le pecorelle, che non sanno,   106
   tornan del pasco pasciute di vento,
   e non le scusa non veder lo danno.
Non disse Cristo al suo primo convento: 109
   'Andate, e predicate al mondo ciance';
   ma diede lor verace fondamento;
e quel tanto sonò ne le sue guance,   112
   sì ch'a pugnar per accender la fede
   de l'Evangelio fero scudo e lance.
Ora si va con motti e con iscede   115
   a predicare, e pur che ben si rida,
   gonfia il cappuccio e più non si richiede.
Ma tale uccel nel becchetto s'annida,   118
   che se 'l vulgo il vedesse, vederebbe
   la perdonanza di ch'el si confida:
per cui tanta stoltezza in terra crebbe,   121
   che, sanza prova d'alcun testimonio,
   ad ogne promession si correrebbe.

Falsehoods. They don't consider how much blood 91
    it cost to sow it in the world, or how
    deeply the humble man delights the Lord
When he stands by it. For show, each man will use 94
    all of his mother wit to chatter on—
    such fables preachers preach, while the Good News
Is left in silence. This one says the moon 97
    retreated at Christ's passion on the Cross,
    and so it blocked the shining of the sun,
But he lies: for the light was its own cause 100
    of hiding, so the Spaniards saw the eclipse,
    and Indians, as clearly as the Jews.
Florence has not so many Jacks and Jips 103
    as there are fables cried up everywhere
    and bound in parchment every year—so many,
The little sheep who hear them unaware 106
    turn from their pasture having fed on wind,
    and that they see no harm is no excuse.
Christ did not say to his first brotherhood, 109
    'Go and preach silly tales to all the earth,'
    but founded all their preaching on the truth,
And from their cheeks the truth alone blared forth: 112
    only to kindle faith they went to war,
    girt with the shield and lance of gospel truth.
Now they go forth to preach with jests galore 115
    and tricksy words—and if the people howl,
    their caps swell up and they don't ask for more!
But nesting in the funnel of the cowl 118
    is such a bird° that if the folks could see,
    they'd see what 'pardon' they were trusting in,
Sprouting upon the earth the idiocy 121
    of running off for promises so big
    without the proof or witness of the Church.

°*a bird:* a demon, not an angel (cf. *Inf.* 34.47).

Di questo ingrassa il porco sant' Antonio,   124
    e altri assai che sono ancor più porci,
    pagando di moneta sanza conio.
Ma perché siam digressi assai, ritorci   127
    li occhi oramai verso la dritta strada,
    sì che la via col tempo si raccorci.
Questa natura sì oltre s'ingrada   130
    in numero, che mai non fu loquela
    né concetto mortal che tanto vada;
e se tu guardi quel che si revela   133
    per Danïel, vedrai che 'n sue migliaia
    determinato numero si cela.
La prima luce, che tutta la raia,   136
    per tanti modi in essa si recepe,
    quanti son li splendori a chi s'appaia.
Onde, però che a l'atto che concepe   139
    segue l'affetto, d'amar la dolcezza
    diversamente in essa ferve e tepe.
Vedi l'eccelso omai e la larghezza   142
    de l'etterno valor, poscia che tanti
    speculi fatti s'ha in che si spezza,
uno manendo in sé come davanti".   145

This is the stuff that stuffs Saint Anthony's pig°
    and others who are bigger porkers yet,
    who pay in plugs and not in genuine coin.

124

But since we've been so long digressing, set
    your mind again upon our conversation
    and let our way be straight, as time is short.

127

The angels so surpass all numeration
    in rungs of blessedness, your speech must yield,
    nor can a mortal thought proceed so far.

130

And if you study what has been revealed
    by Daniel, in his 'thousands' you will see
    that any finite number is concealed.

133

The primal light is taken differently
    by all the various splendors; each receives
    the radiance in its own and single way.

136

Because love follows what the mind perceives,
    love's sweetness to a varying degree
    bubbles or rests the cooler in their souls.

139

Now you can see the liberality
    and high magnificence of the eternal Power,
    pieced out among so many mirrors made,

142

Remaining in Himself One, as before."

145

° *Saint Anthony's pig:* probably the Antonian friars, who had a habit of raising hogs and letting them run at will, and who were reputed to abuse the country folk by their tall tales. The *bigger porkers* may be other friars or the bedmates and bastards of the Antonians.

Forse semilia miglia di lontano
    ci ferve l'ora sesta, e questo mondo
    china già l'ombra quasi al letto piano,
quando 'l mezzo del cielo, a noi profondo,   4
    comincia a farsi tal, ch'alcuna stella
    perde il parere infino a questo fondo;
e come vien la chiarissima ancella   7
    del sol più oltre, così 'l ciel si chiude
    di vista in vista infino a la più bella.
Non altrimenti il trïunfo che lude   10
    sempre dintorno al punto che mi vinse,
    parendo inchiuso da quel ch'elli 'nchiude,
a poco a poco al mio veder si stinse: 13
    per che tornar con li occhi a Bëatrice
    nulla vedere e amor mi costrinse.
Se quanto infino a qui di lei si dice   16
    fosse conchiuso tutto in una loda,
    poca sarebbe a fornir questa vice.
La bellezza ch'io vidi si trasmoda   19
    non pur di là da noi, ma certo io credo
    che solo il suo fattor tutta la goda.
Da questo passo vinto mi concedo   22
    più che già mai da punto di suo tema
    soprato fosse comico o tragedo:

CANTO THIRTY

*Dante and Beatrice rise to **the Empyrean, the tenth circle.** Here all Heaven is revealed as a **river of light,** and as a **celestial rose.***

Maybe six thousand miles away the noon
    burns, while the shadow of the world is thrown
    near the horizon at the brink of dawn,
When the deep middle air of Heaven has grown   4
    so light that here and there the stars begin
    to fade from us down on that ocean's floor;
And as the brightest handmaid of the sun°   7
    advances in the sky, the sky will douse
    even its loveliest lanterns one by one;
So too the triumph of the choirs who feast   10
    forever about the point that conquered me,
    that seems embraced by what it has embraced,
Vanished from my vision gradually,   13
    so that I turned my eyes to Beatrice,
    compelled by love, and by no more to see.
If all I've said about her until this   16
    were comprehended in a single praise,
    now it would be too little to suffice.
I saw her beauty passing all our ways   19
    of understanding, and believe indeed
    that He alone who fashioned her enjoys
Its fullness. From this pass I must concede   22
    myself more overcome than ever was
    tragedian or comic at the peak

°*handmaid of the sun:* the dawn.

ché, come sole in viso che più trema,   25
   così lo rimembrar del dolce riso
   la mente mia da me medesmo scema.

Dal primo giorno ch'i' vidi il suo viso   28
   in questa vita, infino a questa vista,
   non m'è il seguire al mio cantar preciso;

ma or convien che mio seguir desista   31
   più dietro a sua bellezza, poetando,
   come a l'ultimo suo ciascuno artista.

Cotal qual io la lascio a maggior bando   34
   che quel de la mia tuba, che deduce
   l'ardüa sua matera terminando,

con atto e voce di spedito duce   37
   ricominciò: "Noi siamo usciti fore
   del maggior corpo al ciel ch'è pura luce:

luce intellettüal, piena d'amore;   40
   amor di vero ben, pien di letizia;
   letizia che trascende ogne dolzore.

Qui vederai l'una e l'altra milizia   43
   di paradiso, e l'una in quelli aspetti
   che tu vedrai a l'ultima giustizia".

Come sùbito lampo che discetti   46
   li spiriti visivi, sì che priva
   da l'atto l'occhio di più forti obietti,

così mi circunfulse luce viva,   49
   e lasciommi fasciato di tal velo
   del suo fulgor, che nulla m'appariva.

"Sempre l'amor che queta questo cielo   52
   accoglie in sé con sì fatta salute,
   per far disposto a sua fiamma il candelo".

Non fur più tosto dentro a me venute   55
   queste parole brievi, ch'io compresi
   me sormontar di sopr' a mia virtute;

Of difficulty: as the sun in eyes   25
   that tremble weakly, so my memory
   of her sweet smile now robs the intellect
And leaves me at a loss. From the first day   28
   I saw her face until this vision now,
   my road to song has not been cut away,
But here, as every artist, I must bow   31
   to my last power, and cease to follow on
   her loveliness by signs in poetry.
Such beauty I must leave to a clarion   34
   more brilliant than my trumpet to unite
   clear words and arduous truth. Then with the tone
And manner of a guide with goal in sight   37
   she recommenced: "We're on the outside of
   the highest body,° in the purest light,
In intellectual light, light filled with love,   40
   love of the true good, filled with happiness,
   happiness that surpasses all things sweet.
The first and second host of Paradise°   43
   you will see here, and one of these will bear
   the form you will behold on Judgment Day."
Just as a sudden lightning flash will scare   46
   away the power of vision and deprive
   one's sight of things made brilliant in the glare,
So I was now enveloped in a live   49
   gleaming of light that veiled me in a veil
   so vivid all around, I lost all sight.
"The love that soothes this heaven has power to heal   52
   the souls it takes unto itself, with grace
   to make the little candle fit to feel
His flame." Soon as these brief words found their place   55
   within my understanding, I became
   aware I had surpassed my former might:

°*the highest body:* the Empyrean, whose location is solely the mind of God in its stable unity; see notes.

°*first and second host of Paradise:* those who held the faith before, and after, the Incarnation. The first host is complete, and thus is the same as that which Dante *will behold on Judgment Day.*

e di novella vista mi raccesi   58
    tale, che nulla luce è tanto mera,
    che li occhi miei non si fosser difesi;
e vidi lume in forma di rivera   61
    fulvido di fulgore, intra due rive
    dipinte di mirabil primavera.
Di tal fiumana uscian faville vive,   64
    e d'ogne parte si mettien ne' fiori,
    quasi rubin che oro circunscrive;
poi, come inebrïate da li odori,   67
    riprofondavan sé nel miro gurge,
    e s'una intrava, un'altra n'uscia fori.
"L'alto disio che mo t'infiamma e urge,   70
    d'aver notizia di ciò che tu vei,
    tanto mi piace più quanto più turge;
ma di quest' acqua convien che tu bei   73
    prima che tanta sete in te si sazi":
    così mi disse il sol de li occhi miei.
Anche soggiunse: "Il fiume e li topazi   76
    ch'entrano ed escono e 'l rider de l'erbe
    son di lor vero umbriferi prefazi.
Non che da sé sian queste cose acerbe;   79
    ma è difetto da la parte tua,
    che non hai viste ancor tanto superbe".
Non è fantin che sì sùbito rua   82
    col volto verso il latte, se si svegli
    molto tardato da l'usanza sua,
come fec' io, per far migliori spegli   85
    ancor de li occhi, chinandomi a l'onda
    che si deriva perché vi s'immegli;
e sì come di lei bevve la gronda   88
    de le palpebre mie, così mi parve
    di sua lunghezza divenuta tonda.
Poi, come gente stata sotto larve,   91
    che pare altro che prima, se si sveste
    la sembianza non süa in che disparve,

And a new power of vision burst aflame—   58
    nor is there light too radiant and pristine
    for sight so strong. And I beheld a stream,
A river of flashing light that flowed between   61
    two shores the spring had touched with wondrous hues,
    dappled with glimmerings of a golden sheen.
And from that river living glints arose   64
    to settle on the banks with stippling blooms
    like rubies in a rounding ring of gold.
As if inebriated with perfumes   67
    those jewels vanish deep into the well,
    and when one vanishes, another comes.
"The flames of longing, flames that now impel,   70
    urging you on to learn of what you see,
    delight me all the more the more they swell,
But such a thirst you cannot satisfy   73
    before you've drunk the water of this spring."
    So said the sunlight of my eyes to me.
"The stream and every topaz you behold   76
    diving and rising, and the laughing flowers,
    are prefaces to truth, foreshadowing
Things that have ripened in their fullness: yours   79
    and none of theirs is the deficiency,
    for they are higher than your vision soars."
Never a newborn babe so suddenly   82
    leapt for his mother's milk should he awake
    much later than he's used to in the day,
As I rushed to the riverside to make   85
    a better mirror of my eyes, and leaned
    over the rippling waves where man is meant
To grow in grace; and as my lash's end   88
    sipped of the stream, it seemed to me it made
    its flowing long become a flowing round,
And then, as revelers at a masquerade   91
    seem other than they were if they divest
    the guise wherein their own was held in shade,

così mi si cambiaro in maggior feste   94
  li fiori e le faville, sì ch'io vidi
  ambo le corti del ciel manifeste.

O isplendor di Dio, per cu' io vidi   97
  l'alto trïunfo del regno verace,
  dammi virtù a dir com' ïo il vidi!

Lume è là sù che visibile face   100
  lo creatore a quella creatura
  che solo in lui vedere ha la sua pace.

E' si distende in circular figura,   103
  in tanto che la sua circunferenza
  sarebbe al sol troppo larga cintura.

Fassi di raggio tutta sua parvenza   106
  reflesso al sommo del mobile primo,
  che prende quindi vivere e potenza.

E come clivo in acqua di suo imo   109
  si specchia, quasi per vedersi addorno,
  quando è nel verde e ne' fioretti opimo,

sì, soprastando al lume intorno intorno,   112
  vidi specchiarsi in più di mille soglie
  quanto di noi là sù fatto ha ritorno.

E se l'infimo grado in sé raccoglie   115
  sì grande lume, quanta è la larghezza
  di questa rosa ne l'estreme foglie!

La vista mia ne l'ampio e ne l'altezza   118
  non si smarriva, ma tutto prendeva
  il quanto e 'l quale di quella allegrezza.

Presso e lontano, lì, né pon né leva: 121
  ché dove Dio sanza mezzo governa,
  la legge natural nulla rileva.

Nel giallo de la rosa sempiterna,   124
  che si digrada e dilata e redole
  odor di lode al sol che sempre verna,

So to my vision now in fuller feast 94
    the flowers and flashes changed, so that I saw
    both of the courts of Heaven manifest.°

O great splendor of God, by whom I saw 97
    the true reign in its lofty triumph ride,
    grant me the power to speak of what I saw!

There is a lamp above that makes the Lord 100
    visible to the creature He has made
    to find his only peace in seeing Him.

This light wells out into a ring so wide 103
    that its circumference would be too great
    a sash to hold the circle of the sun:

An ocean filled by one reflecting ray 106
    that strikes the arch of the first moving ring,°
    then radiates in life and potency.

And as above the lakeside mirroring, 109
    a slope will seem to view itself adorned
    in green and all the gayest flowers of spring,

Standing above the light surrounding me 112
    I saw in far more than a thousand rows
    the mirroring of the souls that had returned

To Paradise: and if the lowest sill 115
    drinks in so great a light, how grand must be
    the utmost petals of the heavenly rose!

Neither the height nor vastness swept away 118
    my clear perception, for I saw that joy
    in all its quantity and quality.

Nearness gives nothing, distance is no thief: 121
    for where God rules without a second cause,
    physical laws set nothing in relief.

Into the yellow of the perpetual rose 124
    that opens row to row, and to the sun
    ever in springtime sends its fragrant praise,

° *both of the courts of Heaven manifest:* not as flowers or jewels of light, but as saints and angels.
° *the first moving ring:* the Primum Mobile.

qual è colui che tace e dicer vole,   127
    mi trasse Bëatrice, e disse: "Mira
    quanto è 'l convento de le bianche stole!
Vedi nostra città quant' ella gira;   130
    vedi li nostri scanni sì ripieni,
    che poca gente più ci si disira.
E 'n quel gran seggio a che tu li occhi tieni   133
    per la corona che già v'è sù posta,
    prima che tu a queste nozze ceni,
sederà l'alma, che fia giù agosta,   136
    de l'alto Arrigo, ch'a drizzare Italia
    verrà in prima ch'ella sia disposta.
La cieca cupidigia che v'ammalia   139
    simili fatti v'ha al fantolino
    che muor per fame e caccia via la balia.
E fia prefetto nel foro divino   142
    allora tal, che palese e coverto
    non anderà con lui per un cammino.
Ma poco poi sarà da Dio sofferto   145
    nel santo officio: ch'el sarà detruso
    là dove Simon mago è per suo merto,
e farà quel d'Alagna intrar più giuso".   148

Beatrice led me, for I was as one   127
    who yearns to speak yet holds his peace at last.
    "Behold the council of the robes of white!
Look on our city and its ring so vast!   130
    Look on the saints so many, hardly a throne
    remains among us for the saints to come!
And that great throne you fix your eyes upon,   133
    seeing the diadem that's set on it,
    before you banquet at this wedding feast,
Is where the soul, august on earth, will sit,   136
    the glorious Henry,° come to Italy
    to steer her right, before she's fit for it.
Your fascination, blind cupidity,   139
    has made you like a little child who'll die
    starving, and yet will push the pap away.
And such a prefect will soon occupy   142
    the divine forum, that his plain-faced and
    his secret plans won't walk down the same way.
Not long will God suffer that one to stand   145
    in the holy office: he'll be trodden under
    where Simon Magus° earns his place, to force
Him of Anagni deeper down his hole."
                                                                            148

°*Henry:* young Henry VII of Luxembourg, crowned emperor in Rome in 1313 but opposed by the Guelph party, by the French, and by Pope Clement V (the *prefect* who betrayed him); Henry died the same year.

°*Simon Magus:* Simon attempted to purchase the gifts of the Holy Spirit from the apostles (Acts 8:17–24), thus lending his name to the sin of simony, the use of ecclesiastical goods for personal profit (cf. *Inf.* 19.1–6). Such sinners are punished in *Inferno* 19 by being thrust upside down into holes in the earth, their soles slicked with oil and set afire. Clement, says Beatrice, will be thrust into the hole that crams the simoniac popes, forcing *Him of Anagni,* Boniface VIII, *deeper down his hole* (*Inf.* 19.82–87). These are Beatrice's last words in the poem; see notes.

In forma dunque di candida rosa
    mi si mostrava la milizia santa
    che nel suo sangue Cristo fece sposa;
ma l'altra, che volando vede e canta   4
    la gloria di colui che la 'nnamora
    e la bontà che la fece cotanta,
sì come schiera d'ape che s'infiora   7
    una fïata e una si ritorna
    là dove suo laboro s'insapora,
nel gran fior discendeva che s'addorna   10
    di tante foglie, e quindi risaliva
    là dove 'l süo amor sempre soggiorna.
Le facce tutte avean di fiamma viva   13
    e l'ali d'oro, e l'altro tanto bianco,
    che nulla neve a quel termine arriva.
Quando scendean nel fior, di banco in banco   16
    porgevan de la pace e de l'ardore
    ch'elli acquistavan ventilando il fianco.
Né l'interporsi tra 'l disopra e 'l fiore   19
    di tanta moltitudine volante
    impediva la vista e lo splendore:
ché la luce divina è penetrante   22
    per l'universo secondo ch'è degno,
    sì che nulla le puote essere ostante.

CANTO THIRTY-ONE

*Beatrice takes her place again in the celestial rose, and Dante is now led by the mystic **Bernard of Clairvaux**.*

In the form of a white and lucent rose
    the holy soldiers were revealed to me,
    the saints whom by His blood Christ took to spouse;
Meanwhile the second host° who fly, and see   4
    and sing the glory of Him who stirs their love,
    and sing their Maker's liberality
Who made them for such glory, as a drove   7
    of bees enflower themselves again, again,
    returning where their labor is made sweet,
Into the many-petaled flower come down,   10
    and from its leaves they rise again and go
    where their Love dwells in day forevermore.
With living flame their countenances glow;   13
    their wings are golden, and the rest so white,
    they far excel the purity of snow.
Falling into the flower from height to height   16
    they brush them with the peace and ardent love
    they've gleaned from God, with wings swept back in flight.
Although between the flower and Sun above   19
    the angels flew in all their plenitude,
    they cast no haze upon the splendid sight:
For the world is penetrated by the light of God,   22
    all things according to their dignity.
    Nothing can stand against its piercing might.

°*second host:* the angels.

The Empyrean

Questo sicuro e gaudïoso regno,   25
    frequente in gente antica e in novella,
    viso e amore avea tutto ad un segno.
Oh trina luce che 'n unica stella   28
    scintillando a lor vista, sì li appaga!
    guarda qua giuso a la nostra procella!
Se i barbari, venendo da tal plaga   31
    che ciascun giorno d'Elice si cuopra,
    rotante col suo figlio ond' ella è vaga,
veggendo Roma e l'ardüa sua opra,   34
    stupefaciensi, quando Laterano
    a le cose mortali andò di sopra;
ïo, che al divino da l'umano,   37
    a l'etterno dal tempo era venuto,
    e di Fiorenza in popol giusto e sano,
di che stupor dovea esser compiuto!   40
    Certo tra esso e 'l gaudio mi facea
    libito non udire e starmi muto.
E quasi peregrin che si ricrea   43
    nel tempio del suo voto riguardando,
    e spera già ridir com' ello stea,
su per la viva luce passeggiando,   46
    menava ïo li occhi per li gradi,
    mo sù, mo giù e mo recirculando.
Vedëa visi a carità süadi,   49
    d'altrui lume fregiati e di suo riso,
    e atti ornati di tutte onestadi.
La forma general di paradiso   52
    già tutta mïo sguardo avea compresa,
    in nulla parte ancor fermato fiso;
e volgeami con voglia rïaccesa   55
    per domandar la mia donna di cose
    di che la mente mia era sospesa.

This kingdom free of care and filled with joy,   25
   crowded with citizens of the Old and New,
   turned all its love and vision to one goal.
O great delight that glittered for their view,   28
   O threefold light within an only Star,
   look on our battering tempest here below!
If the barbarians° swarming from the far   31
   shore where the Bear looks down all day and night,
   turning beside the cub she holds so dear,
Seeing Rome's labors risen to such height,   34
   went dumb with wonder, when the Lateran
   surpassed all works achieved by mortal might,
So I, who rose to the divine from man,   37
   to the eternal from the passing hour,
   from Florence to a people just and sane,
Filled must I be with what a speechless awe!   40
   Surely, between the wonder and the bliss,
   it pleased me to hear nothing, and be still.
And as a pilgrim takes refreshing ease   43
   glancing about the temple of his vow,
   hoping to tell of all the things he sees,
So did I search through all the levels now,   46
   taking my way in living light on high,
   above, below, and circling round. I saw
Faces persuasive in their charity;   49
   Another's light and smile adorn their eyes;
   their acts are graced with every dignity.
I'd seen the general form of Paradise—   52
   my gaze had grasped the pattern of the whole
   without yet fixing on a certain place,
And I turned with a fresh fire in the soul   55
   to ask my Lady of those things I see
   that hold my intellect in some suspense.

°*the barbarians:* probably Gauls, from the north, where the constellations of the Bears stand high in the sky.

Uno intendëa, e altro mi rispuose: 58
   credea veder Beatrice e vidi un sene
   vestito con le genti glorïose.
Diffuso era per li occhi e per le gene   61
   di benigna letizia, in atto pio
   quale a tenero padre si convene.
E "Ov' è ella?", sùbito diss' io.   64
   Ond' elli: "A terminar lo tuo disiro
   mosse Beatrice me del loco mio;
e se riguardi sù nel terzo giro   67
   dal sommo grado, tu la rivedrai
   nel trono che suoi merti le sortiro".
Sanza risponder, li occhi sù levai,   70
   e vidi lei che si facea corona
   reflettendo da sé li etterni rai.
Da quella regïon che più sù tona   73
   occhio mortale alcun tanto non dista,
   qualunque in mare più giù s'abbandona,
quanto lì da Beatrice la mia vista;   76
   ma nulla mi facea, ché süa effige
   non discendëa a me per mezzo mista.
"O donna in cui la mia speranza vige,   79
   e che soffristi per la mia salute
   in inferno lasciar le tue vestige,
di tante cose quant' i' ho vedute,   82
   dal tuo podere e da la tua bontate
   riconosco la grazia e la virtute.
Tu m'hai di servo tratto a libertate   85
   per tutte quelle vie, per tutt' i modi
   che di ciò fare avei la potestate.
La tua magnificenza in me custodi,   88
   sì che l'anima mia, che fatt' hai sana,
   piacente a te dal corpo si disnodi".
Così orai; e quella, sì lontana   91
   come parea, sorrise e riguardommi;
   poi si tornò a l'etterna fontana.

I expect one, another answers me.

   Not Beatrice do I find but an old man

   robed like the glorious nation of the blessed.

In light that bathed his eyes and cheeks there shone

   a benign happiness, a piety

   befitting a kind father for his son.

And suddenly I burst out, "Where is she?"

   "Beatrice stirred me from my place to bring

   your hungering to its end," responded he.

"Here, look up at the third-to-highest ring:

   there you will see your Lady on the throne

   Heaven assigns her for her meriting."

Silently then I raised my eyes alone

   and saw her wreathed with the eternal rays

   reflecting all around her like a crown.

The farthest straining of our mortal gaze

   to see the realm of thunders at its height,

   to the most abandoned bottom of the seas,

Is not so far as Beatrice was from sight,

   but that had no effect, since it was through

   no medium that her form came down to me.

"Lady in whom my hope is green anew,

   who suffered for my healing, and who deigned

   to leave your footprints in the lands below,°

It was your power and excellence that sustained

   my pilgrimage to see all I have seen;

   to you I owe the grace and strength I've gained.

I was a slave; you brought me liberty,

   through every road I walked, by every means

   you had within your power to succor me.

Preserve in me your work's magnificence

   so that my soul, which you have healed, one day

   will please you when it slips the body's bands."

I prayed—and she, who was as far away

   as she appeared, yet smiled and looked at me;

   then turned again to the eternal Spring.

58

61

64

67

70

73

76

79

82

85

88

91

°*the lands below:* in Hell.

E 'l santo sene: "Acciò che tu assommi   94
   perfettamente", disse, "il tuo cammino,
   a che priego e amor santo mandommi,
vola con li occhi per questo giardino;   97
   ché veder lui t'acconcerà lo sguardo
   più al montar per lo raggio divino.
E la regina del cielo, ond' ïo ardo   100
   tutto d'amor, ne farà ogne grazia,
   però ch'i' sono il suo fedel Bernardo".
Qual è colui che forse di Croazia   103
   viene a veder la Veronica nostra,
   che per l'antica fame non sen sazia,
ma dice nel pensier, fin che si mostra: 106
   'Segnor mio Iesù Cristo, Dio verace,
   or fu sì fatta la sembianza vostra?';
tal era io mirando la vivace   109
   carità di colui che 'n questo mondo,
   contemplando, gustò di quella pace.
"Figliuol di grazia, quest'esser giocondo",   112
   cominciò elli, "non ti sarà noto,
   tenendo li occhi pur qua giù al fondo;
ma guarda i cerchi infino al più remoto,   115
   tanto che veggi seder la regina
   cui questo regno è suddito e devoto".
Io levai li occhi; e come da mattina   118
   la parte orïental de l'orizzonte
   soverchia quella dove 'l sol declina,
così, quasi di valle andando a monte   121
   con li occhi, vidi parte ne lo stremo
   vincer di lume tutta l'altra fronte.
E come quivi ove s'aspetta il temo   124
   che mal guidò Fetonte, più s'infiamma,
   e quinci e quindi il lume si fa scemo,

"That you may sum your journey perfectly,"
  then said the holy elder, "to which end
    I pray, and holy love commissions me,   94

Fly with your gaze through all this garden round:
  looking on this felicity will hone
    your sight for climbing to the rays of God.   97

The Queen of Heaven, for whom I wholly burn
  in love, will grant us every grace we need.
    I am Bernard, her faithful champion."   100

A pilgrim from Croatia, far indeed,
  comes to view our Veronica,° and cannot
    fulfill so long a hunger for that food   103

But while the relic's shown he says, in thought,
  "And did you look like this, was this your face,
    O Jesus Christ my Lord and very God?"   106

So was I, marveling at the leaping blaze
  of charity in him who, in our world,
    by contemplating, tasted Heaven's peace.   109

"O son of grace, you never will find out,"
  he thus began, "this life of endless joy
    if still your vision gazes here below.   112

Then scan the rings unto the most remote
  until you see, upon her throne, the Queen°
    to whom this reign is subject, and devout."   115

I raised my eyes: as in the morning sheen
  the eastern swell of the horizon will
    vanquish the west, where daylight's last hours lean,   118

So from the valley to the highest hill
  my eyes climbed to the limit of that realm
    and saw its light, that was inconquerable.   121

On earth where we expect the dawning helm°
  Phaëthon could not guide, the flames increase
    but fade away in brilliance to each side;   124

°*Veronica:* the relic of the face of Christ, miraculously depicted on the veil with which a woman wiped him as he carried the Cross to Calvary. The name derives from the Latin *vera icon,* "true image." The relic was shown periodically for pilgrims at Saint Peter's (cf. *Vita nuova* 40.1).

°*the Queen:* Mary.

°*the dawning helm:* the chariot of the sun (see 17.1 and note).

così quella pacifica oriafiamma 127
    nel mezzo s'avvivava, e d'ogne parte
    per igual modo allentava la fiamma;
e a quel mezzo, con le penne sparte, 130
    vid' io più di mille angeli festanti,
    ciascun distinto di fulgore e d'arte.
Vidi a lor giochi quivi e a lor canti 133
    ridere una bellezza, che letizia
    era ne li occhi a tutti li altri santi;
e s'io avessi in dir tanta divizia 136
    quanta ad imaginar, non ardirei
    lo minimo tentar di sua delizia.
Bernardo, come vide li occhi miei 139
    nel caldo suo caler fissi e attenti,
    li suoi con tanto affetto volse a lei,
che ' miei di rimirar fé più ardenti. 142

So was that golden oriflamme of peace
    bright with life in the center, while each part
    saw the flame soften, equal in decrease.

127

And in that center, pennons spread apart,
    I saw millions of angels reveling,
    each one distinct in splendor and in art.

130

And as they play in Heaven and as they sing,
    such Beauty° smiles upon them, that for each
    saint to behold is utter ravishing,

133

Had I as rich a bounty in my speech
    as in imagination, I'd not dare
    give but a grace note of her sweet delight.

136

When Bernard saw my eyes intent to stare
    upon the warmth that warmed them with her rays,
    so lovingly he turned his own to her,

139

He made me the more ardent in my gaze.

142

°*Beauty:* Mary.

Affetto al suo piacer, quel contemplante
    libero officio di dottore assunse,
    e cominciò queste parole sante:
"La piaga che Maria richiuse e unse,   4
    quella ch'è tanto bella da' suoi piedi
    è colei che l'aperse e che la punse.
Ne l'ordine che fanno i terzi sedi,   7
    siede Rachel di sotto da costei
    con Bëatrice, sì come tu vedi.
Sarra e Rebecca, Iudìt e colei   10
    che fu bisava al cantor che per doglia
    del fallo disse 'Miserere mei',
puoi tu veder così di soglia in soglia   13
    giù digradar, com' io ch'a proprio nome
    vo per la rosa giù di foglia in foglia.
E dal settimo grado in giù, sì come   16
    infino ad esso, succedono Ebree,
    dirimendo del fior tutte le chiome;
perché, secondo lo sguardo che fée   19
    la fede in Cristo, queste sono il muro
    a che si parton le sacre scalee.

CANTO THIRTY-TWO

*Bernard names for Dante the various souls in tiers along the petals of the rose. He ends by urging Dante to pray with him for the intercession of **Mary**, that Dante may be able to see the highest Good.*

Rapt in delight, that man of contemplation
    still freely assumed the teacher's role,
    beginning thus his holy revelation:
"Recall the wound that Mary closed with oil: 4
    that lovely woman° sitting at her feet
    is she who opened it, who pierced the soul.
In the third rank of thrones behold the seat   7
    of Rachel, who is sitting, as you see,
    with Beatrice, beneath the feet of Eve.
Sarah then, and Rebecca, Judith, and she,°   10
    twice-grandmother of the singer who in grief
    for his sin cried, "Have mercy upon me"—
These you can see descending down each reef   13
    in order as I name them, while I go
    proceeding through the rose from leaf to leaf.
And from the seventh level and below,   16
    just as above, are women of the Jews,
    dividing all the petals of the flower.
They are the wall that parts the sacred stairs   19
    according as souls kept the faith in time,
    turning their eyes to Christ: for near to us,

°*lovely woman:* Eve.

°*she:* Ruth, great-grandmother of the psalmist, King David (Ruth 4:17). The *sin* is his adultery with Bathsheba, wife of Uriah, whose death in the front lines of battle David cunningly arranged (2 Sam. 11:2–16). The psalm Dante quotes is the well-known *Miserere* (Ps. 51; cf. *Inf.* 1.65).

Da questa parte onde 'l fiore è maturo
   di tutte le sue foglie, sono assisi
   quei che credettero in Cristo venturo;   22
da l'altra parte onde sono intercisi
   di vòti i semicirculi, si stanno
   quei ch'a Cristo venuto ebber li visi.   25
E come quinci il glorïoso scanno
   de la donna del cielo e li altri scanni
   di sotto lui cotanta cerna fanno,   28
così di contra quel del gran Giovanni,
   che sempre santo 'l diserto e 'l martiro
   sofferse, e poi l'inferno da due anni;   31
e sotto lui così cerner sortiro
   Francesco, Benedetto e Augustino
   e altri fin qua giù di giro in giro.   34
Or mira l'alto proveder divino:
   ché l'uno e l'altro aspetto de la fede
   igualmente empierà questo giardino.   37
E sappi che dal grado in giù che fiede
   a mezzo il tratto le due discrezioni,
   per nullo proprio merito si siede,   40
ma per l'altrui, con certe condizioni:
   ché tutti questi son spiriti asciolti
   prima ch'avesser vere elezïoni.   43
Ben te ne puoi accorger per li volti
   e anche per le voci püerili,
   se tu li guardi bene e se li ascolti.   46
Or dubbi tu e dubitando sili;
   ma io discioglierò 'l forte legame
   in che ti stringon li pensier sottili.   49
Dentro a l'ampiezza di questo reame
   casüal punto non puote aver sito,
   se non come tristizia o sete o fame: 52
ché per etterna legge è stabilito
   quantunque vedi, sì che giustamente
   ci si risponde da l'anello al dito;   55

Where the flower is mature and in full bloom 22
    up to the utmost frond, are seated those
    who held their firm belief in Christ to come,
But they upon the far half of the rose, 25
    in the half rings with gaps among the places,
    believed in Christ already come, and fixed
Their gaze upon Him. And as, on this side, 28
    the Lady of Heaven holds her glorious throne
    and the other thrones beneath form a divide,
Facing hers is the throne of the great John,° 31
    who ever holy bore the desert land,
    martryrdom, and—two years—the realm below.
Then under him in the dividing strand 34
    come Francis, Benedict, and Augustine,
    and others down to here from band to band.
Behold the depths of providence divine: 37
    behold in wonder, for this garden shall
    be filled with both the visions of the faith,
And equally. Know, too, below the sill 40
    that cuts in half each of the two divisions,
    no spirits sit by merits of their own
But by another's—under some conditions, 43
    for all of these, before they had true choice,
    were liberated from the bonds of flesh.
And by the childlike piping of the voice 46
    and by their faces you can make them out
    easily, if you listen and look close.
You waver and are silent in your doubt, 49
    but I shall now ungrapple the tough bands
    that hold you in the grip of subtle thought.
Not one point, not one place is there for chance 52
    in all this kingdom's fullness broad and vast,
    as there is none for hunger, thirst, or grief:
For an eternal law has made steadfast 55
    all that you see, exactly as a ring
    fits on a finger, when the fit is just.

°*John:* the Baptist, who died two years before Christ and thus had to wait in *the realm below.*

e però questa festinata gente
   a vera vita non è *sine causa*
   intra sé qui più e meno eccellente.

Lo rege per cui questo regno pausa
   in tanto amore e in tanto diletto,
   che nulla volontà è di più ausa,

le menti tutte nel suo lieto aspetto
   creando, a suo piacer di grazia dota
   diversamente; e qui basti l'effetto.

E ciò espresso e chiaro vi si nota
   ne la Scrittura santa in quei gemelli
   che ne la madre ebber l'ira commota.

Però, secondo il color d'i capelli,
   di cotal grazia l'altissimo lume
   degnamente convien che s'incappelli.

Dunque, sanza mercé di lor costume,
   locati son per gradi differenti,
   sol differendo nel primiero acume.

Bastavasi ne' secoli recenti
   con l'innocenza, per aver salute,
   solamente la fede d'i parenti;

poi che le prime etadi fuor compiute,
   convenne ai maschi a l'innocenti penne
   per circuncidere acquistar virtute;

ma poi che 'l tempo de la grazia venne,
   sanza battesmo perfetto di Cristo
   tale innocenza là giù si ritenne.

Riguarda omai ne la faccia che a Cristo
   più si somiglia, ché la sua chiarezza
   sola ti può disporre a veder Cristo".

58

61

64

67

70

73

76

79

82

85

Then, for these souls of infants hurrying
    to their true life, it's not without a cause
    that they're exalted less, or more. The King 58

In whom this kingdom finds its sweet repose,
    the peace of so much love, so much delight,
    that no will is so bold to beg for more, 61

Formed all Heaven's minds before His happy sight,
    and at His pleasure showered His gifts of grace
    diversely: the effect must here suffice. 64

Clearly expressed you'll find it in the place
    in Holy Scripture, by the twins° who were
    angry with one another in the womb. 67

So it is just, this highest light should bear
    an aureole of grace about each one
    according to the color of the hair! 70

Therefore, without reward for what they've done,
    they're placed in different levels, differing
    in their inborn acuity alone. 73

Faith of the parents was the only thing
    required, with innocence, to win salvation,
    and be made whole in the first age of man;° 76

But from the closing of that generation,
    males had to lend their innocence more strength,
    raising the harmless quill by circumcision, 79

But now the age of grace has come at length;
    without the full baptism conferred by Christ,
    such innocence must be retained below. 82

Into the face° that most resembles Christ
    now look: for by her radiance only she
    can render you prepared for seeing Christ." 85

° *the twins:* red-haired Esau and black-haired Jacob (Gen. 25:22). Their rivalry began early: Esau came from the womb first, with Jacob clutching his brother's foot. Though twins, they did not receive the same grace from God, nor did they respond equally to the grace given (cf. Mal. 1:2–3, Rom. 9:11–13).

° *the first age of man:* from Adam to Abraham. The second age extended from Abraham to Christ.

° *the face:* that of Mary.

Io vidi sopra lei tanta allegrezza   88
 piover, portata ne le menti sante
 create a trasvolar per quella altezza,
che quantunque io avea visto davante,   91
 di tanta ammirazion non mi sospese,
 né mi mostrò di Dio tanto sembiante;
e quello amor che primo lì discese,   94
 cantando 'Ave, Maria, gratïa plena',
 dinanzi a lei le sue ali distese.
Rispuose a la divina cantilena   97
 da tutte parti la beata corte,
 sì ch'ogne vista sen fé più serena.
"O santo padre, che per me comporte   100
 l'esser qua giù, lasciando il dolce loco
 nel qual tu siedi per etterna sorte,
qual è quell' angel che con tanto gioco   103
 guarda ne li occhi la nostra regina,
 innamorato sì che par di foco?".
Così ricorsi ancora a la dottrina   106
 di colui ch'abbelliva di Maria,
 come del sole stella mattutina.
Ed elli a me: "Baldezza e leggiadria   109
 quant' esser puote in angelo e in alma,
 tutta è in lui; e sì volem che sia,
perch' elli è quelli che portò la palma   112
 giuso a Maria, quando 'l Figliuol di Dio
 carcar si volse de la nostra salma.
Ma vieni omai con li occhi sì com' io   115
 andrò parlando, e nota i gran patrici
 di questo imperio giustissimo e pio.
Quei due che seggon là sù più felici   118
 per esser propinquissimi ad Agusta,
 son d'esta rosa quasi due radici:

I saw a rain of such felicity   88
   showered upon her by the holy minds°
   fashioned for crossing that exalted sea,

That all the wondrous things I'd seen before   91
   had not so left my vision stunned, suspended,
   nor shown me so much of the face of God,

And the love that, to greet her, first descended,   94
   singing, "Hail, Mary, virgin full of grace,"
   now stood before her with his wings extended.

The blessed court responded to his song,   97
   singing the antiphon on every side,
   and radiant peace shone forth in every face.

"Holy Father, who for my sake abide   100
   coming down here and leaving the sweet place
   where you are seated by eternal lot,

Who is that angel of such joyous gaze   103
   looking into the eyes of our sweet Queen—
   so deeply in love, he seems to be ablaze?"

So to his doctrine once again I run: 106
   that man who was adorned by Mary's ray
   as star of morning by the rising sun.

And he: "Whatever grace and gallantry   109
   can dwell in angel or in blessed soul
   dwells all in him: as we desire should be,

For that is he who bore the palm below   112
   to Mary, when the Son of God would take
   upon Himself the burden of our flesh.

But let your eyes now follow in my wake   115
   as I point out the great patricians of
   this clement and most just empire. Those two

Who sit in greatest happiness above   118
   for being nearest to Augusta° are,
   as you might say, the two roots of this rose:

°*the holy minds:* the angels.
°*Augusta:* Mary. The title is imperial, and means "she who gives increase."

colui che da sinistra le s'aggiusta
   è 'l padre per lo cui ardito gusto
   l'umana specie tanto amaro gusta;
dal destro vedi quel padre vetusto
   di Santa Chiesa a cui Cristo le chiavi
   raccomandò di questo fior venusto.
E quei che vide tutti i tempi gravi,
   pria che morisse, de la bella sposa
   che s'acquistò con la lancia e coi clavi,
siede lungh' esso, e lungo l'altro posa
   quel duca sotto cui visse di manna
   la gente ingrata, mobile e retrosa.
Di contr' a Pietro vedi sedere Anna,
   tanto contenta di mirar sua figlia,
   che non move occhio per cantare osanna;
e contro al maggior padre di famiglia
   siede Lucia, che mosse la tua donna
   quando chinavi, a rovinar, le ciglia.
Ma perché 'l tempo fugge che t'assonna,
   qui farem punto, come buon sartore
   che com' elli ha del panno fa la gonna;
e drizzeremo li occhi al primo amore,
   sì che, guardando verso lui, penètri
   quant' è possibil per lo suo fulgore.
Veramente, *ne* forse tu t'arretri
   movendo l'ali tue, credendo oltrarti,
   orando grazia conven che s'impetri
grazia da quella che puote aiutarti;
   e tu mi seguirai con l'affezione,
   sì che dal dicer mio lo cor non parti".
E cominciò questa santa orazione:

121

124

127

130

133

136

139

142

145

148

151

The one who justly sits to left of her,
    he is the father° for whose brazen taste
    the race of man must taste such bitter fare;   121

On her right, he into whose hands Christ placed
    the keys° that open to this winsome flower:
    the ancient father of the Holy Church.   124

And he who witnessed° every heavy hour,
    before he died, to fall upon the Spouse,
    the lovely Bride won by the nails and lance,   127

Sits next to him; beside the other one
    now rests that chief° whose people fed on manna—
    nation of ingrates, fickle and rebellious.   130

Opposite Peter see the throne of Anna;°
    she gazes on her daughter, nor will move
    her blissful eyes all while she sings hosanna;   133

And opposite the highest father of
    the family of man sits Lucy, she
    who moved your Lady when your glances strove   136

Toward ruin. But since your hour of sleep flies by
    we will stop here, as a good tailor tries
    to cut the gown to fit the cloth he has;   139

And to the first Love let us turn our eyes,
    so that in gazing you may penetrate
    His rays, as far as human sight complies.   142

But truly, lest perhaps you should retreat,
    attempting to soar high by your own wing,
    it's fit that when you pray for grace, you entreat   145

The Lady who can help you by her favor:
    follow me now with all the love you bear;
    let your heart not depart from what I say."   148

And he began to speak this holy prayer: 151

° *the father:* Adam.

° *he ... the keys:* Saint Peter (Matt. 16:19), the root of all who believe.

° *he who witnessed:* Saint John, whose Apocalypse foretells the tribulation to be suffered by the Church.

° *that chief:* Moses, for whose ungrateful people God rained down manna (Ex. 16:13–15; see also Num. 11).

° *Anna:* mother of Mary.

"Vergine Madre, figlia del tuo figlio,
    umile e alta più che creatura,
    termine fisso d'etterno consiglio,
tu se' colei che l'umana natura   4
    nobilitasti sì, che 'l suo fattore
    non disdegnò di farsi sua fattura.
Nel ventre tuo si raccese l'amore,   7
    per lo cui caldo ne l'etterna pace
    così è germinato questo fiore.
Qui se' a noi meridïana face   10
    di caritate, e giuso, intra ' mortali,
    se' di speranza fontana vivace.
Donna, se' tanto grande e tanto vali,   13
    che qual vuol grazia e a te non ricorre,
    sua disïanza vuol volar sanz' ali.
La tua benignità non pur soccorre   16
    a chi domanda, ma molte fïate
    liberamente al dimandar precorre.
In te misericordia, in te pietate,   19
    in te magnificenza, in te s'aduna
    quantunque in creatura è di bontate.
Or questi, che da l'infima lacuna   22
    de l'universo infin qui ha vedute
    le vite spiritali ad una ad una,

CANTO THIRTY-THREE

*Saint Bernard entreats the intercession of **the Virgin Mary** that Dante may behold **the beatific vision**. The great journey and the poem end with the vision of the three great mysteries: **the Creation, the Trinity, and the Incarnation of Christ**.*

"Virgin Mother, daughter of your Son,
    humbler and loftier past creation's measure,
    the fulcrum of the everlasting plan,
You are she who ennobled human nature   4
    so highly, that its Maker did not scorn
    to make Himself the Creature of His creature.
In your womb was the flame of love reborn,   7
    in the eternal peace of whose warm ray
    this flower has sprung and is so richly grown.
For us you are the torch of the noonday   10
    of charity; below, you are the spring
    of ever-living hope for men that die.
Lady, so great you are, such strength you bring,   13
    who does not run to you and looks for grace,
    his wish would seek to fly without a wing.
Not only does your kindness come to brace   16
    our courage when we beg: often your free
    favor arrives before our prayer's race.
In you is mercy, in you is piety,   19
    in you magnificence, in you the sum
    of excellence in all things that come to be.
This pilgrim who has witnessed, coming from   22
    the lowest pool of all the universe,
    the lives of soul and soul in every realm,

supplica a te, per grazia, di virtute 25
   tanto, che possa con li occhi levarsi
   più alto verso l'ultima salute.

E io, che mai per mio veder non arsi 28
   più ch'i' fo per lo suo, tutti miei prieghi
   ti porgo, e priego che non sieno scarsi,

perché tu ogne nube li disleghi 31
   di sua mortalita co' prieghi tuoi,
   sì che 'l sommo piacer li si dispieghi.

Ancor ti priego, regina, che puoi 34
   chò che tu vuoli, che conservi sani,
   dopo tanto veder, li affetti suoi.

Vinca tua guardia i movimenti umani: 37
   vedi Beatrice con quanti beati
   per li miei prieghi ti chiudon le mani!".

Li occhi da Dio diletti e venerati, 40
   fissi ne l'orator, ne dimostraro
   quanto i devoti prieghi le son grati;

indi a l'etterno lume s'addrizzaro, 43
   nel qual non si dee creder che s'invii
   per creatura l'occhio tanto chiaro.

E io ch'al fine di tutt' i disii 46
   appropinquava, sì com' io dovea,
   l'ardor del desiderio in me finii.

Bernardo m'accennava e sorridea 49
   perch' io guardassi suso; ma io era
   già per me stesso tal qual ei volea:

ché la mia vista, venendo sincera, 52
   e più e più intrava per lo raggio
   de l'alta luce che da sé è vera.

Da quinci innanzi il mio veder fu maggio 55
   che 'l parlar mostra, ch'a tal vista cede,
   e cede la memoria a tanto oltraggio.

Qual è colüi che sognando vede, 58
   che dopo 'l sogno la passione impressa
   rimane, e l'altro a la mente non riede,

Now bends his knee to you, to gain such force   25
 by grace, that he may lift his eyes the higher
 unto his final healing and its source.

And I who never burned in such a fire   28
 for my own vision, all I can I pray,
 and hope my prayers suffice for his desire,

That by your prayers you melt the mist away   31
 that clouds the intellects of mortal men,
 in order that the highest bliss display

Himself to him. Also I beg you, Queen,   34
 who can do what you will, that his affection
 may remain pure after what he has seen.

Let human passions yield to your protection.   37
 See Beatrice, see how many of the blest
 now fold their hands to second my intention!"

The eyes beloved of God and honored best,   40
 fixed on the man who prayed, showed her delight
 in prayers that rise from a devoted breast,

And then they turned to the eternal Light,   43
 wherein, we trust, no creature else can send
 created vision with such perfect sight.

And I who now was drawing near the end   46
 of all desires, as it behooved me, to
 the summit let my leaping flames ascend;

Bernard smiled, motioned me to turn my view   49
 upward—but I had turned it on my own,
 was doing what he wanted me to do,

For as my sight grew pure and whole, alone   52
 it plumbed more and more deeply into the ray
 of Truth, the utmost Light. From this point on

Whatever human language can convey   55
 must yield to vision, passing the extreme—
 to such great prowess memory must give way.

As one who sees a vision in a dream,   58
 after the dream the passion so impressed
 lingers, though nothing else comes back to him,

cotal son io, ché quasi tutta cessa   61
   mia visïone, e ancor mi distilla
   nel core il dolce che nacque da essa.

Così la neve al sol si disigilla;   64
   così al vento ne le foglie levi
   si perdea la sentenza di Sibilla.

O somma luce che tanto ti levi   67
   da' concetti mortali, a la mia mente
   ripresta un poco di quel che parevi,

e fa la lingua mia tanto possente,   70
   ch'una favilla sol de la tua gloria
   possa lasciare a la futura gente;

ché, per tornare alquanto a mia memoria   73
   e per sonare un poco in questi versi,
   più si conceperà di tua vittoria.

Io credo, per l'acume ch'io soffersi   76
   del vivo raggio, ch'i' sarei smarrito,
   se li occhi miei da lui fossero aversi.

E' mi ricorda ch'io fui più ardito   79
   per questo a sostener, tanto ch'i' giunsi
   l'aspetto mio col valore infinito.

Oh abbondante grazia ond' io presunsi   82
   ficcar lo viso per la luce etterna,
   tanto che la veduta vi consunsi!

Nel suo profondo vidi che s'interna,   85
   legato con amore in un volume,
   ciò che per l'universo si squaderna:

sustanze e accidenti e lor costume   88
   quasi conflati insieme, per tal modo
   che ciò ch'i' dico è un semplice lume.

La forma universal di questo nodo   91
   credo ch'i' vidi, perché più di largo,
   dicendo questo, mi sento ch'i' godo.

So am I, for the sight is all but lost,   61
    and yet, born from that vision, to this day,
    droplets of sweet distill into my breast.

So in the sun the snow dissolves away;   64
    so did they lose the Sibyl's prophecy°
    when the wind blew the weightless leaves astray.

Summit of light that lift yourself so high   67
    above the mind of mortal man, restore
    some slightest shade of your theophany,

And grant then to my tongue sufficient power   70
    to leave the palest flicker of your glory
    to readers of a later day and hour,

For should something return to memory   73
    and sound but faintly in my verses here,
    the clearer will they see your victory.

Should I have turned my vision anywhere   76
    but to the living Ray, I'd have gone blind,
    so piercing was the power I had to bear;

Thus was I bolder—this I call to mind—   79
    to bear the mighty radiance that bloomed,
    till my might and Omnipotence were joined.

O overbrimming grace whence I presumed   82
    to gaze upon the everlasting Light
    so fully that my vision was consumed!

I saw the scattered elements unite,   85
    bound all with love into one book of praise,
    in the deep ocean of the infinite;

Substance and accident and all their ways   88
    as if breathed into one: and, understand,
    my words are a weak glimmer in the haze.

The universal Being of this band   91
    I think I saw—because when that is said,
    I feel the bliss within my heart expand.

°*the Sibyl's prophecy:* In the *Aeneid*, Aeneas is instructed to request that the Sibyl tell him her prophecy aloud, since when she writes it down a wind comes to scatter the leaves irretrievably (*Aen.* 3.443–51).

Un punto solo m'è maggior letargo 94
    che venticinque secoli a la 'mpresa
    che fé Nettuno ammirar l'ombra d'Argo.
Così la mente mia, tutta sospesa, 97
    mirava fissa, immobile e attenta,
    e sempre di mirar faceasi accesa.
A quella luce cotal si diventa, 100
    che volgersi da lei per altro aspetto
    è impossibil che mai si consenta;
però che 'l ben, ch'è del volere obietto, 103
    tutto s'accoglie in lei, e fuor di quella
    è defettivo ciò ch'è lì perfetto.
Omai sarà più corta mia favella, 106
    pur a quel ch'io ricordo, che d'un fante
    che bagni ancor la lingua a la mammella.
Non perché più ch'un semplice sembiante 109
    fosse nel vivo lume ch'io mirava,
    che tal è sempre qual s'era davante;
ma per la vista che s'avvalorava 112
    in me guardando, una sola parvenza,
    mutandom' io, a me si travagliava.
Ne la profonda e chiara sussistenza 115
    de l'alto lume parvermi tre giri
    di tre colori e d'una contenenza;
e l'un da l'altro come iri da iri 118
    parea reflesso, e 'l terzo parea foco
    che quinci e quindi igualmente si spiri.
Oh quanto è corto il dire e come fioco 121
    al mio concetto! e questo, a quel ch'i' vidi,
    è tanto, che non basta a dicer 'poco'.
O luce etterna che sola in te sidi, 124
    sola t'intendi, e da te intelletta
    e intendente te ami e arridi!

One instant sees more of my memories fade 94
    than two millenia fade the bravery
    that made the sea god gape at *Argo*'s shade.°
And so my mind, suspended utterly, 97
    held its gaze still immobile and intent,
    and ever kindled was my wish to see.
Before that Light one's will to turn is spent: 100
    one is so changed, it is impossible
    to shift the glance, for one would not consent,
Because all good—the object of the will— 103
    is summed in it, for it alone is best:
    beyond, defective; there, whole, perfect, still.
Even for these few memories I've confessed, 106
    my words are less than what a baby says
    who wets his tongue still at his mama's breast.
Not that I saw more than a single face 109
    as I was gazing into the living glow,
    for it is ever as it ever was,
But in my vision winning valor so, 112
    that sole appearance as I changed by seeing
    appeared to change and form itself anew.
Within that brilliant and profoundest Being 115
    of the deep light three rings° appeared to me,
    three colors and one measure in their gleaming:
As rainbow begets rainbow in the sky, 118
    so were the first two, and the third, a flame
    that from both rainbows breathed forth equally.
Alas how feeble language is, how lame 121
    beside my thought!—and, for what I was shown,
    to call thought "small" would be too great a claim.
O Light that dwell within Thyself alone, 124
    who alone know Thyself, are known, and smile
    with Love upon the Knowing and the Known!

°*sea god*…*Argo's shade:* Neptune, amazed to see his seas furrowed by the first ship, the *Argo*,
commanded by Jason in his quest for the golden fleece.
    °*three rings:* the Trinity.

Quella circulazion che sì concetta   127
   pareva in te come lume reflesso,
   da li occhi miei alquanto circunspetta,
dentro da sé, del suo colore stesso,   130
   mi parve pinta de la nostra effige:
   per che 'l mio viso in lei tutto era messo.
Qual è 'l geomètra che tutto s'affige   133
   per misurar lo cerchio, e non ritrova,
   pensando, quel principio ond' elli indige,
tal era io a quella vista nova: 136
   veder voleva come si convenne
   l'imago al cerchio e come vi s'indova;
ma non eran da ciò le proprie penne: 139
   se non che la mia mente fu percossa
   da un fulgore in che sua voglia venne.
A l'alta fantasia qui mancò possa;   142
   ma già volgeva il mio disio e 'l *velle,*
   sì come rota ch'igualmente è mossa,
l'amor che move il sole e l'altre stelle.   145

That circle° which appeared—in my poor style— 127
    like a reflected radiance in Thee,
      after my eyes had studied it awhile,
Within, and in its own hue, seemed to be 130
    tinted with the figure of a Man,
      and so I gazed on it absorbedly.
As a geometer struggles all he can 133
    to measure out the circle by the square,°
      but all his cogitation cannot gain
The principle he lacks: so did I stare 136
    at this strange sight, to make the image fit
      the aureole, and see it enter there:
But mine were not the feathers for that flight, 139
    Save that the truth I longed for came to me,
      smiting my mind like lightning flashing bright.
Here ceased the powers of my high fantasy. 142
    Already were all my will and my desires
      turned—as a wheel in equal balance—by
The Love that moves the sun and the other stars. 145

° *That circle:* the second, a reflection of the first: Christ, the Second Person of the Trinity.
  ° *measure . . . square:* to construct, with compass and straightedge alone, a square whose area is equal to that of a given circle. For the import of this insoluble geometric problem, see notes.

Appendix A

Dante, Letter to Cangrande della Scala

This remarkable letter to Dante's patron and the man to whom he dedicated the *Paradise* is priceless both for the author's interpretation of his own work (I am assuming what is still a matter of some controversy, that Dante is the author) and for the insight it gives us into the medieval mind, its habit of reading the entire universe as a system of interrelated and coruscating signs, each pointing in its own fashion to the Creator of all. The translation is that of the Everyman edition of *The Latin Works of Dante* (London: J. M. Dent, 1904), revised for contemporary idiom.

To the magnificent and virtuous lord, Lord Cangrande della Scala, vicar general of the most sacred imperial princedom in the city of Verona and in the state of Vicenza, his most devoted servant Dante Alighieri, a Florentine by birth, not by character, wishes long-enduring life and felicity, and the perpetual growth of the glory of his name.

The illustrious praise of your munificence, which wakeful fame scatters abroad as she flies, draws various men in such various directions as to exalt some of them in the hope of prosperity and success and hurl others of them into the terror of destruction. Now, I used to think that this fame, exceeding all deeds of men in our age, was extravagant, stretching beyond the warrant of truth; but lest my continued doubt should keep me in suspense too long, I sought Verona, even as the queen of the south sought Jerusalem, to scrutinize what I had heard by the faithful testimony of my own eyes. And there I beheld your splendor, I beheld and at the same time enjoyed your bounty; and even as I had formerly suspected that the reports were excessive, so did I afterward recognize that it was rather the facts that exceeded. So it came to pass that, as the mere report had already secured my goodwill along with a certain submission of mind, at the sight of the source and origin itself I became your most devoted servant and friend.

Nor do I think I am laying myself open to a charge of presumption (as some might allege) by arrogating to myself the name of friend, since unequals no less than equals are united in the sacrament of friendship. For if one should care to examine those friendships from which delight and advantage have sprung, quite often will he discover on inspection that such have united preeminent persons to their inferiors. And if he then attends to the true friendship which exists for its own sake, will it not abundantly appear that the friends of illustrious and supreme princes have for the most part been men obscure in fortune but shining in integrity? Why not, since even the friendship of God and man is in no way hindered by disparity. But if anyone thinks my assertions too bold, let him heed the Holy Spirit, who declares that certain men share in his own friendship, for in Wisdom we read, concerning Wisdom, that "she is an infinite treasure to men, and they who use her are made partakers of the friendship of God." But the artlessness of the vulgar herd judges without discrimination, and even as it supposes the sun to be one foot across, so too does its vain credulity deceive it concerning the characters of men. But it is not fitting for us, to whom it has been granted to know the best that is in us, to follow the footprints of the herd. Rather are we enjoined to oppose its wanderings, for we of vigorous intellect and reason, endowed with a certain divine liberty, are not bound by precedents. And that is no wonder, for such men are not directed by the laws, but rather the laws are directed by them. It is clear, then, that what I said above, namely that I am your most devoted servant and friend, is in no way presumptuous.

Cherishing your friendship, then, as my dearest treasure, I wish to preserve it with loving forethought and considered care. And therefore, since in the teaching of ethics we are instructed that friendship is made equal and is preserved by what is proportionate, I have vowed to keep the path of proportion in my return for all the bounty I have received from you. And so I have often and eagerly examined such small gifts as I have, and have set them side by side, and have scanned them again, trying to decide which would be the more worthy and the more acceptable to you. And I have found nothing more suited to your preeminence than the sublime canticle of the *Comedy* which is adorned with the title of *Paradise*; which canticle, under cover of the present letter, as though dedicated under its own special heading, I inscribe, I offer, and conclusively commend to you.

Nor will my glowing affection permit me to pass over in silence the thought that in this dedication there may seem to be greater honor and fame conferred upon the patron than on the gift. And what wonder? In its very inscription I appeared, to those who looked closely, to have already uttered, with conscious purpose, a presage of the destined increase of the glory to your name. But now, zeal for your glory, for which I thirst, making little of my own, urges me forward to the goal set before me from the beginning.

And so, having brought to a close what I have written in the form of a letter, I will at once assume the office of lecturer and sketch in outline something by way of introduction to the work I offer you.

As the Philosopher said in the second book of the *Metaphysics*, "as a thing is related to existence, so is it related to truth," because the truth about a thing (which is established in the truth as in its subject) is a perfect likeness of the thing as it is. Now some things exist in such a way that they possess absolute being in themselves; others exist as to possess a being dependent upon something else, by some kind of relation, for example "being at the same time as," or "being related to"—as we see in the correlatives "father and son," "master and servant," "double and half," "whole and part," and suchlike. Because the being of these latter things depends upon something else, it follows that their truth also depends upon something else, for if we have no knowledge of "half" we can never understand "double," and likewise with all the rest.

So if we wish to provide some introduction to a part of any work, it behooves us to provide some knowledge of the whole of which it is a part. I too, then, desiring to provide something by way of introduction to the above-named portion of the *Comedy*, have thought that if something were prefaced concerning the whole work, it would make approaching the part easier and more complete. There are six things, then, that must be inquired into at the beginning of any work of instruction: the *subject, agent, form,* and *end,* the *title of the work,* and the *branch of philosophy* which it concerns. And there are three of these wherein this part which I purposed to design for you differs from the whole, namely the *subject, form,* and *title;* whereas in the other three it does not differ, as is plain upon inspection. And so I must begin an inquiry concerning these three, especially with reference to the work as a whole; that done, the way to introduce the part will have become clear. After that we shall examine the other three, not only with reference to the whole but also with reference to that special part which I am offering to you.

To clarify, then, what we have to say, let it be known that the meaning of this work is not simple. On the contrary, it may be called "polysemous," that is to say, "of more senses than one." For we derive one meaning from the letter and others from what the letter signifies; the first is called literal, but the second allegorical or mystic. The better to show this mode of treatment, we may consider this verse: "When Israel came out of Egypt, and the house of Jacob from a people of strange speech, Judea became his sanctification, Israel his power." If we examine the letter alone, the departure of the children of Israel from Egypt in the time of Moses is presented to us. If we examine the allegorical sense, it is our redemption wrought by Christ. If the moral sense, it is the conversion of the soul from the grief and misery of sin to the state of grace. If the anagogical sense, it is the departure of the holy soul from the slavery of this corruption to the liberty of eternal glory. And although each of these mystic senses has its special name, they may all in general be called allegorical, since they differ from the literal and the historical. For *allegory* is derived from *alleon*, in Greek, which means the same as Latin *alienum* or *diversum*.

When we understand this we see clearly that the *subject* round which the various senses play must be twofold. And we must therefore consider the subject of this work as literally understood, and then its subject as allegorically intended. The subject of the whole work, then, taken in the literal sense only, is *the state of souls after death*—without qualification, since the whole progress of the work hinges on it and about it. But if the work is interpreted allegorically the subject is *how man, as by good or ill deserts, in the exercise of the freedom of his choice, becomes liable to the justice that rewards or to the justice that punishes.*

Now the *form* is twofold, the form of the work and the form of its presentation. The form of the work, in turn, is threefold, according to its three manners of division. The first division is that by which the whole work is divided into three canticles; the second, that by whereby each canticle is divided into cantos; the third, that whereby each canto is divided into lines. The form or method of presentation is poetic, fictive, descriptive, digressive, and resumptive; and likewise it proceeds by definition, distinction, proof, refutation, and setting forth of examples.

The *title of the work* is "Here beginneth the *Comedy* of Dante Alighieri, a Florentine by birth, not by character." To understand this, let it be known that *comedy* is derived from *comus*, "village," and *oda*, "song," whence a comedy is as it were a "rustic song." Thus comedy is a certain kind of poetic narration differing from all others. It differs from tragedy in its content, in that tragedy begins admirably and tranquilly, whereas its end or exit is foul and terrible; and it derives its name from *tragus,* "goat," and *oda,* as though to say "goat song," that is, fetid like a goat, as appears from Seneca in his tragedies. But comedy introduces some harsh complication and then brings its matter to a prosperous end, as appears in the comedies of Terence. Hence certain writers, on introducing themselves, have made it their practice to give this salutation: "I wish you a tragic beginning and a comic end." Comedy and tragedy likewise differ in their mode of speech, tragedy exalted and sublime, comedy lax and humble, as Horace has it in his *Ars poetica,* where he gives comedians leave sometimes to speak like tragedians, and conversely:

> *Interdum tamen et vocem comoedia tollit,*
> *iratusque Chremes tumido delitigat ore;*
> *et tragicus plerumque dolet sermone pedestri.*

Sometimes Comedy herself raises her voice, wrathful Chremes denounces with puffed-out lips, while the tragedian will often lower his voice to grieve in the speech of the man on the street.

And hence it is evident that the title of the present work is the *Comedy.* For if we consider its content, at the beginning it is horrible and fetid, for it is Hell; and in the end it is prosperous, desirable, and gracious, for it is Paradise. If we consider the method of speech, it is lax and humble, for it is the same vernacular wherein even women communicate. There are also other kinds of poetic narration, such as the bucolic song, elegy, satire, and the utterance of prayer, as may also be seen from Horace in his *Ars poetica.* But at present nothing needs to be said about them.

There can be no difficulty in determining the *subject* of the part I am offering you, for if the subject of the whole, taken literally, is *the state of souls after death,* not limited but taken without qualification, it is then clear that in this part the subject is that same state thus qualified, *the state of blessed souls after death.* And if the subject of the whole work taken allegorically is *how man by good or ill deserts, in the exercise of the freedom of his choice, becomes liable to the justice that rewards or the justice that punishes,* it is clear that the subject in this part is contracted to *how man by good deserts becomes liable to the justice that rewards.*

And in like manner the *form* of the part is clear from the form assigned to the whole. For if the form of the work as a whole is threefold, in this part it is twofold only, namely, here we have a canticle divided into cantos, and cantos divided into lines. The first division, that of the work into canticles, cannot be a part of the special form of this canticle, since the canticle is itself a part by virtue of that first division.

The *title of the work* is also clear, for if the title of the whole is "Here beginneth the *Comedy*," and so forth as set out above, the title of this part will be "Here beginneth the third canticle of Dante's *Comedy*, which is entitled *Paradise*."

Having investigated the three things wherein the part differs from the whole, we must examine the other three, wherein there is no diverging from the whole. The *agent*, then, of the whole and of the part is the man already named, who is seen throughout to be such.

The *end* of the whole and of the part may be manifold, to wit, the proximate end and the ultimate end; but dropping all subtle investigation we may say briefly that the end of the whole and of the part is to remove those living in this life from misery and lead them to happiness.

But the *branch of philosophy* which regulates this work in its whole and in its parts is morals or ethics, because the whole was undertaken not for speculation but for practical results. For although in some parts or passages speculation predominates, this is not for the sake of speculation but for the sake of practical results; because, as the Philosopher says in the second book of the *Metaphysics*, "practical men sometimes speculate on things in their relative and temporal bearings."

These things then premised, we must now expound the letter, as by a kind of foretaste; but we must announce in advance that the exposition of the letter is nothing other than the unfolding of the form of the work. This part, then, namely the third canticle, which is called *Paradise*, falls by its main division into two parts, the *prologue* and the *execution*, which second part begins with the line *By various spills of light the sun will shine.*

Concerning the prologue, you should know that although it might, in the common way, be called an *exordium*, yet in strict propriety it should be called by no other name than *prologue*, which is what the Philosopher seems to touch upon in the third book of the *Rhetoric*, where he says that "the proem is the beginning of a rhetorical discourse, as a prologue is of a poetic one, and a prelude is in flute playing." It is further to be noted that the prefatory enunciation, commonly called an exordium, is conducted differently by poets and by orators, for orators are wont to give a foretaste of what they are about to utter, calculated to prepare the mind of the hearer, whereas poets not only do this, but also utter some certain invocation afterward. And this is to their purpose, for they have need of ample invocation, since they have to implore something above the common scope of man from the higher beings, as in some sort of divine gift. Therefore the present prologue is divided into two parts: the first of which premises what is to be said, and the second invokes Apollo. And the second part begins with this line: *O good Apollo, for this last work of art.*

As for the first part, note that a good exordium requires three things, as Cicero says in his *Orator:* that one render his hearer benevolent and attentive and tractable—especially in a matter worthy of admiration, as Cicero himself says. And since the matter with which the present work is concerned is marvelous, the intention is, at the beginning of the exordium or prologue, to excite the reader's dispositions in connection with the marvelous. For he says that he will tell such part as he could retain of what he saw in the first heaven—which utterance includes all of those three things. For the profit of the things to be said secures benevolence; their wondrous nature, attention; and their being possible, docility. He shows their profitableness when he declares that he is going to relate those things that chiefly attract the longing of mankind—that is, the joys of Paradise. He touches on their wondrous nature when he promises to tell of such lofty and sublime things, that is, of the conditions of the celestial kingdom. He shows that they are possible when he says that he will tell those things which he had power to retain in his mind—and if he had such power, others will have it too. All these things are indicated in those words wherein he says that he was in the first heaven, and that he wishes to tell about the celestial kingdom all that he had power to retain as a treasure in his mind. Having therefore taken note of the excellence and perfection of the first part of the prologue, let us proceed to the letter.

He says, then, that *the glory of the One who moves all things,* who is God, *penetrates the universe with light,* yet *more radiant in one part and elsewhere less.* That it glows everywhere is declared by reason and authority. Reason declares it thus. Everything that is has its being either from itself or from another. But it is obvious that to have being from oneself is possible only to one: namely to the first, or initial, being, God. And since to have being does not imply self-necessity of being, and since self-necessity of being is possible to one only, that is to the first or initial Being which is the Cause of all, therefore all things that exist, save that one itself, have their being from another. If, then, we take any one of the individual phenomena of

368 · Appendix A

the universe it must evidently have its existence from something; and that
from which it has its existence has its own existence in turn either from it-
self or from something else. If from something else, then that again must
have its existence from itself or from something else. And so we would
have to go on to infinity along a line of effective causes, as is proved in the
second book of the *Metaphysics;* and since this is impossible, we must at
last come to the prime existence, which is God, and thus mediately or im-
mediately everything which exists has its being from him, for it is by what
the second cause received from the first that it has influence upon that
which it, in turn, causes, after the fashion of a body that receives and re-
flects a ray of light. Thus the first cause is cause in a higher degree, and
this is what the book *On Causes* says: "Every primary cause is more influ-
ential on that which it causes, than is a universal secondary cause." So
much for being.

With regard to essence as such, I prove it thus. Every essence, except
the primary, is caused; otherwise there would be more than one existence
of self-necessity, which is impossible. What is caused is either of nature or
of intelligence; and what is of nature is in turn caused by intellect, since
nature is the work of intelligence. Everything, therefore, which is caused,
is caused by some intellect, mediately or immediately. Since, then, virtue
follows the essence whose virtue it is, if the essence is intellectual the
whole virtue is of one intelligence which causes it; and thus, as before we
had come to a first cause of being itself, so now we come to a first cause of
essence and virtue. Thus it is clear that every essence and virtue proceeds
from the primal one, and the lower intelligences receive it as from a radi-
ating source, and throw the rays of their superior upon their inferior, as
do mirrors. Which Dionysius, speaking of the celestial hierarchy, seems
to describe clearly enough, and so it is said in *On Causes* that "every intel-
ligence is full of forms." It is clear, then, how reason declares that the di-
vine light, that is, the divine excellence, wisdom, and virtue, penetrates
and glows everywhere.

Authority too does what science does, for the Holy Spirit says to Jere-
miah, "Do I not fill heaven and earth?" and in the psalm, "Whither shall I
go from thy spirit, and whither shall I flee from thy presence? If I ascend
into heaven thou art there; if I descend into hell thou art present. If I take
my wings," and the rest. And Wisdom says that "the spirit of the Lord filled
the whole world," and the forty-second chapter of Ecclesiasticus says, "His
work is full of the glory of the Lord." To this the writings of the pagans

bear witness, for Lucan in his ninth book says, *Juppiter est quodcumque vides quocumque moveris,* "Jupiter is whatever you see, wherever you go."

It is therefore well said when it says that the divine ray, or divine glory, *penetrates the universe with light.* It pierces as to its essence; it glows as to its being. And what he adds as to *more* and *less* is manifest truth, since we see that one thing has its being in a more exalted grade, and another in a lower, as is made evident by heaven and the elements, that incorruptible and these corruptible.

And having premised this truth, he proceeds with a circumlocution for Paradise, and says that he was *in that heaven he makes most bright.* By this you are to know that that heaven is the supreme heaven, containing all the bodies of the universe and itself contained by love, within which all bodies move (itself abiding in eternal rest), receiving its virtue from no corporeal substance. And it is called the *Empyrean,* which is the same as the heaven flaming with fire or heat, not because there is any material fire or heat in it, but spiritual, namely holy love, or charity.

Now, that it receives more of the divine light can be proved by two things. First, by its containing all things and being contained by none; second, by its eternal rest or peace. As to the first the proof is this. Whatever contains is related by natural position to that which it contains, as the formative is related to the formable, as is stated in the fourth book of the *Physics.* But in the natural position of the whole universe the first heaven contains all things; therefore it is related to all things as the formative to the formable, which is the same as being related by way of cause. And since every causative power is a certain ray emanating from the first cause, which is God, it is manifest that that heaven which partakes most of the nature of cause receives most of the divine light.

As to the second: Everything that moves, moves for the sake of something that it lacks, the goal of its motion; as the sphere of the moon moves because of some part of itself which has not the position toward which it is moving; and inasmuch as every part of it, not having attained every position (an impossibility), moves to some other, it follows that it always moves and never rests, in accordance with its appetite. And what I say of the sphere of the moon must be understood of all the rest except the first. Everything that moves, then, has some defect, and does not grasp its whole being at once. Therefore that heaven which is not moved by anything has in itself and in its every part, in perfect fashion, everything it is capable of having, so that it needs no motion for its perfecting. And since all perfection is a ray of the primal perfection, which realizes the highest degree of perfection, it is clear that the first heaven receives the most of the light of the primal being, which is God. It is true that this argument appears to proceed from the negation of the antecedent, which is not in itself conclusive as a form of argument; but if we consider its content, it is conclusive, because it refers to an eternal being, the defect in which would be susceptible of being eternalized. Thus if God gave it no movement it is clear that he did not give it material that was defective in anything; and on this supposition, by reason of its content, the argument holds. It is the same way of arguing as if I were to say, "If he is a man he is able to laugh," for in all analogies the like reasoning will hold, if the subjects are truly analogous. So it is evident that when he says, *in that heaven he makes most bright,* he means to describe, by circumlocution, Paradise, or the Empyrean.

And concordantly with all this the Philosopher declares in his first book *On Heaven* that heaven has matter more honorable than the things below it in proportion as it is more remote from the things here. We might further adduce what the Apostle says to the Ephesians concerning Christ, "who ascended above all the heavens, that he might fill all things." This is that heaven of the "delights of the Lord," concerning which delights Ezekiel says against Lucifer, "Thou, the seal of similitude, full of wisdom and perfect in beauty, wast in the delights of the Paradise of God."

And when he has said that he was in that place of Paradise, described by circumlocution, he goes on to say that he saw *things that neither mind can hold nor tongue utter,* and he tells why, saying that our minds *so plunge into the deep* of the very thing for which they long, which is God, that *memory cannot follow where they go.* To understand this, know that the human intellect, when it is exalted in this life, because of its being co-natural and having affinity with some separate intellectual substance, is so far exalted that after its return memory fails it, because it has transcended the measure of humanity. And this we are given to understand by the Apostle, speaking to the Corinthians, where he says, "I know such a man (whether in the body or out of the body I know not, God knoweth), who was rapt into Paradise and heard hidden words, which it is not lawful for a man to utter." Mark, when the intellect had transcended human measure in its ascent, it did not remember the things that took place beyond its own range. And this we are given to understand also in the gospel of Matthew, where the three disciples fell upon their faces, and record nothing thereafter, as if they had forgotten. And in Ezekiel it is written, "I saw and fell upon my face." And if all this is not enough for those who would carp, let them read Richard of Saint Victor in his book *On Contemplation,* let them read Bernard *On Consideration,* let them read Augustine *On the Capacity of the Soul,* and they will cease to carp. But if they yelp against the attribution of exaltation so great, because of the sin of the speaker, let them read Daniel, where they will find that Nebuchadnezzar, too, was divinely enabled to see certain things against sinners, and then dropped them into oblivion; for he "who makes his sun to rise upon the good and the evil, and sends his rain upon the just and the unjust," sometimes in compassion, for their conversion, sometimes in wrath, for their punishment, reveals his glory, in greater or less measure, as he wills, to those who live never so wickedly.

He saw, then, as he says, certain things *neither mind can hold nor tongue utter, when one returns from that great height,* and it must be noted carefully that he says he has neither knowledge nor power. He has not the knowledge, because he has forgotten; he has not the power, because even if he remembered and retained the matter, still language itself would fail, for we see many things by the intellect for which there are no vocal signs. Plato gives a sufficient hint of this truth in his works by turning to metaphors, for he saw many things by intellectual light which he could not express in direct speech.

Then he says that *what small part* he could keep *of that holy kingdom* would become the matter of his song; and the nature and extent of these things would be revealed in the execution of the work.

Then when he says, *O good Apollo,* and so forth, he makes his invocation. And that itself is divided into two parts: in the first he makes petition in his invocation; in the second he urges upon Apollo the petition he has made, announcing a kind of remuneration. And the second part begins, *Father, virtue divine.* The first part is divided into two parts, in the first of which he seeks the divine aid, and in the second touches upon his need to make the petition, which is its justification. And it begins here: *Until this hour one peak of twin Parnassus,* and so on.

This is the general purport of the second part of the prologue, but I will not now expound it in detail, for I am pressed by my narrow domestic circumstances, so that I must relinquish this and other matters profitable to the common good. But I hope from your munificence that I may have the opportunity, at some other time, to proceed to a profitable exposition.

Concerning the execution, which was paired with the prologue in the division of the whole, I will say nothing at present concerning either its divisions or its purport, save this, that there will be a process of ascending from heaven to heaven; and the narrative will tell of blessed souls discovered in each orb, and how true blessedness consists in the sense of the prime source of truth, as is made evident by this passage from the gospel of John: "This is true blessedness, to know thee, the true God," and the rest, and by Boethius in the third book of *The Consolation of Philosophy*, in the passage "to behold thee is the end." Whence it comes about that to make manifest the glory of blessedness in those souls, many things will be asked of them (as of those who look upon all truth) which have much profit and delight. And inasmuch as, when the source, or origin, has been found, namely God, there is nothing to seek beyond it, since he is Alpha and Omega, that is, the beginning and the end, as the vision of John calls him; the work ends in God himself, who is blessed *in secula seculorum*, for all eternity.

APPENDIX B

Dante, from the *Convivio*

The *Convivio*—which might be called, with an eye to the Greek philosophy from which it takes its inspiration, the *Symposium,* or with an eye to the Christian metaphor for that bliss whereto all human intellects aspire, the *Banquet*—is Dante's treatise, comprising both prose and poetry, on the natural human desire to know and the role of philosophy in the fulfillment of that desire. Along the way it treats of many of Dante's most empassioned interests: his defense of his native Italian as a worthy medium for poetry; his unjust exile from Florence; his evaluation of the relative merits of other contemporary poets writing in Italian and Provençal; the nature of the virtues and of the heavens to which they correspond; even the proper allegorical ways of understanding poetry. The following is the First Ode (cited by Charles Martel in *Paradise* 8), a poem that begins the Second Treatise of the *Convivio* and that describes, in retrospect, the poet's anguish at the loss of Beatrice and at her being supplanted, in his heart, by another love, namely philosophy. The translation is adapted from that of Frederick Goldin, *German and Italian Lyrics of the Middle Ages* (New York: Doubleday, 1973).

Voi che 'ntendendo il terzo ciel movete

You who by understanding move third heaven,
hear now the reasoning uttered in my heart—
to no one else would I know how to tell it,
it is so new, so strange. The heaven that follows
your power, noble creatures that you are,
draws me into this state I find I'm in,
and so it seems my speaking of such life
should be addressed most worthily to you.
I beg you, then, to listen to my words.

I'll tell you of the marvel in my heart,
how in its chamber does the sad soul weep,
and how a spirit disputes this grief with her,
arriving by the rays shed by your star.

It used to be a sweet and soothing thing,
life to my sorrowing heart, to send my thought
before the feet of our Lord, where it would see
my Lady in the glorying of joy,
of whom so sweetly would it speak to me
my soul would say, "I will arise and go."
But someone has appeared who makes it flee,
who with such power lords it over mine
that all may see the trembling of my heart.
This one has made me gaze upon a woman,
saying, "The man who longs to look on bliss,
let him behold this lady's eyes in wonder—
but fear not all the anguish of his sighs."

That lowly thought that used to speak to me
about the angel diademed in heaven
has met its foe—and this destroys the other.
The soul weeps, such the sorrow it still feels,
and says, "Alas, how it has fled from me,
the pitying thought that used to bring me solace!"
My sadness-wearied soul speaks of my eyes:
"When such a lady saw them, what a time!
Why would they not believe my testimony?
I said of her, 'Surely within her eyes
awaits such one as slays all eyes like mine.'
Nor did it help that I was watchful lest
I gaze on such another—but now I am dead."

"You are not dead, but you have lost your way,
O soul of ours, who so lament in sorrow,"
replies a little spirit of gentle love,
"for that most lovely lady whom you feel
drawing your love has so transformed your life,
you are afraid, you've grown so weak and timid!
Behold how lowly she is, how full of pity,
gracious and wise in her magnificence—

call her your lady now, from this time forth!
Unless you fool yourself, you can't but see
so high a wonder, so adorned in beauty,
that you will say, "Love, my truth-telling Lord,
I am your handmaid, do whatever you will."

Song, I believe that they who truly fathom
your meaning will be few—so difficult
your speech is, so much work to understand.
Then if it happens you should come before
people to whom your meaning is not clear,
who are not sharp in heeding what you say,
I beg you, find new comfort, garner strength
and tell them, O my new and strange delight,
"Behold at least how beautiful I am."

APPENDIX C

Thomas Aquinas, Eucharistic Hymns

Scholars know of Thomas as the great synthesizer of Aristotelian thought and Christian doctrine, but the heart of the Angelic Doctor lay in his mystical contemplation of the person of Christ, especially as at once hidden and made manifest in the bread and wine of the Eucharist, the meal for men on earth that is a foretaste of the meal that is Paradise. Since the translations are fairly loose (as is common in English hymns), I have provided the Latin texts for comparison.

Adoro te devote

Adoro te devote, latens Deitas,
quae sub his figuris vere latitas.
Tibi se cor meum totum subicit,
quia te contemplans totum deficit.

Visus, gustus, tactus in te fallitur;
sed auditu solo tuto creditur.
Credo quicquid dixit Dei Filius:
nil hoc Veritatis verbo verius.

In cruce latebat sola Deitas;
sed hic latet simul et humanitas.
Ambo tamen credens atque confitens,
peto quod petivit latro paenitens.

Plagas, sicut Thomas, non intueor;
Deum tamen meum te confiteor.
Fac me tibi semper magis credere,
in te spem habere, te diligere.

O memoriale mortis Domini,
panis veram vitam praestans homini,
praesta meae menti de te vivere,
et te illi semper dulce sapere.

Pie pellicane, Jesu Domine,
me immundum munda tuo sanguine,
cuius una stilla salvum facere
totum mundum quit ab omni scelere.

Jesu, quem velatum nunc aspicio,
oro fiat illud quod tam sitio:
ut te revelata cernens facie
visu sim beatus tuae gloriae. Amen.

God with hidden majesty lies in presence here,
I with deep devotion my true God revere:
Whom this outward shape and form secretly contains,
Christ in His divinity manhood still retains.

All my other senses cannot now perceive,
But my hearing, taught by faith, always will believe:
I accept whatever God the Son has said:
Those who hear the word of God, by the Truth are fed.

God lay stretched upon the cross, only man could die.
Here upon the altar God and man both lie.
This I firmly hold as true, this is my belief,
And I seek salvation, like the dying thief.

Wounds that doubting Thomas saw, I could never see,
But I still acknowledge you my true God to be;
Grant that I shall always keep strong in faith and trust,
Guided by my Savior, merciful and just.

Blest reminder of the death suffered for mankind,
Sacrament of living bread, health to every mind,
Let my soul approach you, live within your grace,
Let me taste the perfect joys time shall not efface.

O pelican of mercy, Jesus Lord and God,
Cleanse me of my uncleanness by your saving blood,
Whereof a single drop would evermore suffice
To heal the world and save it from all its wickedness.

Jesus whom I now behold veiled as by a glass,
O may what I so thirst for come at last to pass,
That to know your glory, I, blessed by your grace,
May look upon my Lord and see you face to face. Amen.

(Verses 1–5 translated by Anthony G. Petti)

Pange, lingua

Pange, lingua, gloriosi corporis mysterium,
sanguinisque pretiosi quem in mundi pretium
fructus ventris generosi Rex effudit gentium.

Nobis datus, nobis natus ex intacta Virgine
et in mundo conversatus sparso verbi semine
sui moras incolatus miro clausit ordine.

In supremae nocte cenae recumbens cum fratribus,
observata lege plenae cibis in legalibus,
cibum turbae duodenae se dat suis manibus.

Verbum caro panem verum verbo carnem efficit,
fitque sanguis Christi merum, et si sensus deficit,
ad firmandum cor sincerum sola fides sufficit.

Tantum ergo sacramentum veneremur cernui,
et antiquum documentum novo cedat ritui;
praestet fides supplementum sensuum defectui.

Genitori Genitoque laus et iubilatio,
salus, honor, virtus quoque sit et benedictio,
Procedenti ab utroque compar sit laudatio. Amen.

Now, my tongue, the mystery telling of the glorious body sing,
And the blood, all price excelling, which the gentiles' Lord and King,
once on earth among us dwelling, shed for this world's ransoming.

Given for us, and condescending to be born for us below,
He with men in converse blending dwelt, the seed of truth to sow,
Till he closed with wondrous ending his most patient life of woe.

That last night at supper lying mid the twelve, his chosen band,
Jesus, with the Law complying, keeps the feast its rites demand;
Then, more precious food supplying, gives himself with his own hand.

Word-made-flesh, true bread he maketh by his word his Flesh to be,
Wine his Blood; when man partaketh, though his senses fail to see,
Faith alone, when sight forsaketh, shows true hearts the mystery.

Therefore we, before him bending, this great Sacrament revere;
Types and shadows have their ending, for the newer rite is here;
Faith, our outward sense befriending, makes our inward vision clear.

Glory let us give and blessing to the Father and the Son,
Honor, thanks, and praise addressing while eternal ages run;
Ever too his love confessing who from both with both is One. Amen.

(Translation from the Episcopal Church's 1940 *Hymnal*)

Lauda, Sion, Salvatorem

Lauda, Sion, Salvatorem,
lauda ducem et pastorem
in hymnis et canticis:
quantum potes, tantum aude,
quia maior omni laude,
nec laudare sufficis.

Laudis thema specialis,
panis vivus et vitalis
hodie proponitur,
quem in sacrae mensa coenae
turbae fratrum duodenae
datum non ambigitur.

Sit laus plena, sit sonora,
sit iucunda, sit decora
mentis iubilatio;
dies enim sollemnis agitur,

*in qua mensae prima recolitur
huius institutio.*

*In hac mensa novi Regis
novum Pascha novae legis
phase vetus terminat;
vetustatem novitas,
umbram fugat veritas,
noctem lux eliminat.*

*Quod in coena Christus gessit,
faciendum hoc expressit
in sui memoriam;
docti sacris institutis,
panem, vinum in salutis
consecramus hostiam.*

*Dogma datur Christianis
quod in carnem transit panis
et vinum in sanguinem;
quod non capis, quod non vides
animos firmat fides
praeter rerum ordinem.*

*Sub diversis speciebus,
signis tantum et non rebus,
latent res eximiae;
caro cibus, sanguis potus,
manet tamen Christus totus
sub utraque specie.*

*A sumente non concisus,
non confractus, non divisus,
integer accipitur;
sumit unus, sumunt mille,
quantum isti, tantum ille,
nec sumptus consumitur.*

*Sumunt boni, sumunt mali,
sorte tamen inaequali
vitae vel interitus:*

mors est malis, vita bonis;
vide paris sumptionis
quam sit dispar exitus.

Fracto demum sacramento
ne vacilles, sed memento
tantum esse sub fragmento
quantum toto tegitur:
nulla rei fit scissura,
signi tantum fit fractura,
qua nec status nec statura
signati minuitur.

Ecce panis angelorum
factus cibus viatorum,
vere panis filiorum,
non mittendus canibus:
in figuris praesignatur,
cum Isaac immolatur,
agnus paschae deputatur,
datur manna patribus.

Bone pastor, panis vere,
Iesu, nostri miserere,
tu nos pasce, nos tuere,
tu nos bona fac videre
in terra viventium:
tu qui cuncta scis et vales,
qui nos pascis hic mortales,
tuos ibi commensales,
coheredes et sodales
fac sanctorum civium. Amen.

Praise your Redeemer, O Sion, praise your Lord and your shepherd in canticles and hymns, dare to praise him with all your might, for he is greater than all praise, nor will your praising ever suffice.

Today is proclaimed a theme of special praise, praise of the living and life-giving bread, which we declare was given on the table of the holy supper to the gathering of the twelve brothers.

Let our praise be full, let it resound, let our hearts rejoice in gladness fit for this day, for it is a solemn day we observe, the day whereon we recall the first institution of this feast.

At this table of the new King, the new paschal sacrifice of the new law has put the old to flight; the new drives away the old as truth dispels the shadows, as light drives darkness from its threshold.

What Christ performed at that supper he commanded us to do in memory of him, and thus taught by the sacred things he then established, we now consecrate as victim this bread and this wine for our salvation.

This is proclaimed for Christians to believe, that the bread passes into flesh and the wine into blood, not to be grasped or seen but affirmed by a spirit-filled faith beyond the natural order of things.

Under different guises, signs and not objects in themselves, the wondrous things lie hidden: flesh as food and blood as drink, while Christ in his fullness still dwells under each.

Not cut in pieces by him who eats, not broken, not divided, Christ is received whole; one receives him, a thousand receive him, yet as much for the one as for the thousand; nor, though he is received, is he consumed.

The good receive, the wicked receive, yet are allotted unequal destinies, to life or to condemnation, death for the wicked, life for the good: see how unequal are the results of the same reception of him.

When the sacrament at last is broken do not waver, but remember that under each fragment is veiled what is veiled in the whole; there is no cleaving of the thing itself, for though the sign is broken, the thing that it signifies, what it is and what it is to be, is not diminished.

Behold the bread of angels, made food for the wayfarer, true bread for the sons, not to be thrown before dogs! In figures it was foreshadowed, when Isaac was to be sacrificed as a burnt offering, when the paschal lamb was chosen and set aside, when manna was given to our forefathers.

O Jesus, good shepherd, true bread, have mercy upon us! May you feed us, may you watch over us, give us to see the good things in the land of the living; you who know all things and can do all things, you who here feed us though we are destined to die, make us there sharers in your banquet, fellow heirs and friends of the holy citizens above.

Verbum supernum prodiens

Verbum supernum prodiens,
nec Patris linquens dexteram,
ad opus suum exiens,
venit ad vitae vesperam.

In mortem a discipulo
suis tradendus aemulis,
prius in vitae ferculo
se tradidit discipulis,

Quibus sub bina specie
carnem dedit et sanguinem,
ut duplicis substantiae
totum cibaret hominem.

Se nascens dedit socium,
convescens in edulium;
se moriens in pretium,
se regnans dat in praemium.

O salutaris hostia,
quae caeli pandis ostium,
bella premunt hostilia,
da robur, fer auxilium.

Uni trinoque Domino
sit sempiterna gloria,
qui vitam sine termino
nobis donet in patria. Amen.

The Word now proceeding from the heavens above, nor ever leaving the right hand of the Father, coming forth to do his work arrives at the evening of his life.

About to be handed over by his disciple to those who envied him, he first gave himself to his disciples as sustenance for life; to them beneath a double guise he gave his flesh and blood, that he might feed the whole man, man of two substances, body and soul.

At his birth he gave himself as our friend; while supping with us he gave himself as our food; at his death he gave himself as our ransom; reigning in heaven he gives himself as our eternal reward.

O saving Victim, you who open wide the gates of heaven! Our foes press upon us; give us strength, give us your assistance!

To the Lord, the One and Three, be glory now and forever, who we pray shall give us life without end in our fatherland above. Amen.

Appendix D

Saint Francis of Assisi, "The Canticle of Brother Sun"

By his most beloved work, this poem of jubilant praise of God and his creation, Saint Francis intended to show his brothers how to revere the Lord through a humble appreciation of His earthly works. The little poor man of God who owned nothing gained the whole world, and he who thought himself unworthy to touch the body of Christ in the Eucharist is on intimate terms with the sun and moon, the water and the fire, the earth and bodily death. The translation is from Regis Armstrong, O.F.M. Cap., and Ignatius C. Brady, O.F.M., *Francis and Clare: The Complete Works* (New York: Paulist Press, 1982).

> Most High, all-powerful, good Lord,
> Yours are the praises, the glory, the honor, and all blessing.
>
> To You alone, Most High, do they belong,
> and no man is worthy to mention your name.
>
> Praised be You, my Lord, with all your creatures,
> especially Brother Sun,
> Who is the day and through whom You give us light.
>
> And he is beautiful and radiant with great splendor;
> and bears a likeness of You, Most High One.
>
> Praised be You, my Lord, through Sister Moon and the stars;
> in heaven You formed them clear and precious and beautiful.
>
> Praised be You, my Lord, through Brother Wind,
> and through the air, cloudy and serene, and every kind of weather
> through which You give sustenance to Your creatures.

Praised be You, my Lord, through Sister Water,
which is very useful and humble and precious and chaste.

Praised be You, my Lord, through Brother Fire,
through whom you light the night
and he is beautiful and playful and robust and strong.

Praised be You, my Lord, through our Sister Mother Earth,
who sustains and governs us,
and who produces varied fruits with colored flowers and herbs.

Praised be You, my Lord, through those who give pardon for Your love
and bear infirmity and tribulation.

Blessed are those who endure in peace
for by You, Most High, they shall be crowned.

Praised be You, my Lord, through our Sister Bodily Death,
from whom no living man can escape.

Woe to those who die in mortal sin.
Blessed are those whom death will find in Your most holy will,
for the second death shall do them no harm.

Praise and bless my Lord and give Him thanks
and serve Him with great humility.

APPENDIX E

Saint Bernard of Clairvaux, from *Commentary on the Song of Songs* and from a Sermon on the Virgin Mary

In his sustained meditation upon the erotic Song of Solomon, Bernard probes the mystery of divine love not with the analytic mind of a philosopher but with the burning intensity of a lover. The following excerpts from Bernard's *Commentary on the Song of Songs* show how man's highest bliss is literally an ecstasy, a being swept beyond oneself, which must ever be initiated by God but which responds to man's yearnings as fully as the groom's kiss responds to the yearnings of the bride. This union of the soul of man with God is enabled by and is brought to perfection in the person of the Bridegroom, Christ. The translation, lightly edited, is from Kilian Walsh, O.C.S.O., *On the Song of Songs I* (*The Works of Bernard of Clairvaux*, Vol. 1) (Kalamazoo, Mich.: Cistercian Publications, 1977).

FROM SERMON 2

During my frequent ponderings on the burning desire with which the patriarchs longed for the incarnation of Christ, I am stung with sorrow and shame. Even now I can scarcely restrain my tears, so filled with shame am I by the lukewarmness, the frigid unconcern of these miserable times. For which of us does the consummation of that event fill with as much joy as the mere promise of it inflamed the desires of the holy men of pre-christian times? Very soon now there will be great rejoicing as we celebrate the feast of Christ's birth. But how I wish it were inspired by his birth! All the more therefore do I pray that the intense longing of those men of old, their heartfelt expectation, may be enkindled in me by these words: "Let him kiss me with the kiss of his mouth" (Sg. 1:1). Many an upright man in those far-off times sensed within himself how profuse the graciousness that would be poured upon those lips (Ps. 44:3). And intense desire springing from that perception (Is. 26:8) impelled him to utter:

"Let him kiss me with the kiss of his mouth," hoping with every fiber of his being that he might not be deprived of a share in a pleasure so great.

The conscientious man of those days might repeat to himself: "Of what use to me the worldly effusions of the prophets? Rather let him who is the most handsome of the sons of men (Ps. 44:3), let him kiss me with the kiss of his mouth. No longer am I satisfied to listen to Moses, for he is a slow speaker and not able to speak well (Ex. 4:10). Isaiah is 'a man of unclean lips' (Is. 6:5), Jeremiah does not know how to speak, he is a child (John 1:6); not one of the prophets makes an impact on me with his words. But he, the one whom they proclaim, let him speak to me, 'let him kiss me with the kiss of his mouth.' I have no desire that he should approach me in their person, or address me with their words, for they are 'a watery darkness, a dense cloud' (Ps. 17:12); rather in his own person 'let him kiss me with the kiss of his mouth'; let him whose presence is full of love, from whom exquisite doctrines flow in streams, let him become 'a spring inside me, welling up to eternal life' (John 4:14). Shall I not receive a richer infusion of grace from him whom the Father has anointed with the oil of gladness above all his rivals (Ps. 44:8), provided that he will bestow on me the kiss of his mouth? For his living, active word (Heb. 4:12) is to me a kiss, not indeed an adhering of the lips that can sometimes belie a union of hearts, but an unreserved infusion of joys, a revealing of mysteries, a marvellous and indistinguishable mingling of the divine light with the enlightened mind, which, joined in truth to God, is one spirit with him (1 Cor. 6:17). With good reason then I avoid trucking with visions and dreams; I want no part with parables and figures of speech; even the very beauty of the angels can only leave me wearied. For my Jesus utterly surpasses these in his majesty and splendor (Ps. 44:5). Therefore I ask of him what I ask of neither man nor angel: that he kiss me with the kiss of his mouth.

"Note how I do not presume that it is with his mouth I shall be kissed, for that constitutes the unique felicity and singular privilege of the human nature he assumed. No, in the consciousness of my lowliness I ask to be kissed with the kiss of his mouth, an experience shared by all who are in a position to say: 'Indeed from his fullness we have, all of us, received' (John 1:16)."

I must ask you to try to give your whole attention here. The mouth that kisses signifies the Word who assumes human nature; the nature assumed receives the kiss; the kiss however, that takes its being both from the giver and the receiver, is a person that is formed by both, none other than "the one mediator between God and mankind, himself a man, Christ Jesus" (1 Tim. 2:5). It is for this reason that none of the saints dared say: "let him kiss me with his mouth," but rather, "with the kiss of his mouth." In this way they paid tribute to that prerogative of Christ, on whom uniquely and in one sole instance the mouth of the Word was pressed, that moment when the fullness of the divinity yielded itself to him (Col. 2:9) as the life of his body. A fertile kiss therefore, a marvel of stupendous self-abasement that is not a mere pressing of mouth upon mouth; it is the uniting of God with man. Normally the touch of lip on lip is the sign of the loving embrace of hearts, but this conjoining of natures brings together the human and divine, shows God reconciling "to himself all things, whether on earth or in heaven" (Col. 1:20). "For he is the peace between us, and has made the two into one" (Eph. 2:14). This was the kiss for which just men yearned under the old dispensation, foreseeing as they did that in him they would "find happiness and a crown of rejoicing" (Ecclus. 15:6), because in him were hidden "all the jewels of wisdom and knowledge" (Col. 2:3). Hence their longing to taste that fullness of his (John 1:16).

FROM SERMON 7

"Let him kiss me with the kiss of his mouth," she said. Now who is this "she"? The bride. But why bride? Because she is the soul thirsting for God. In order to clarify for you the characteristics of the bride, I shall deal briefly with the diverse loves between persons. Fear motivates a slave's attitude toward his master, gain that of the wage-earner to his employer, the pupil is attentive to his teacher, the son is respectful to his father. But the one who asks for a kiss, she is a lover. Among all the natural endowments of man love holds first place, especially when it is directed to God, who is the source whence it comes. No sweeter names can be found to embody that sweet interflow of affections between the Word and the soul, than bridegroom and bride. Between these all things are equally shared, there are no selfish reservations, nothing that causes division. They share the same inheritance, the same table, the same home, the same marriage-bed, they are flesh of each other's flesh. "This is why a man leaves his father and mother and joins himself to his wife, and they become one body" (Gen. 2:24). The bride for her part is bidden to "forget her nation and her ancestral home," so that the bridegroom may fall in love with her beauty

(Ps. 44:11). Therefore if love is the special and outstanding characteristic of the bride and groom, it is not unfitting to call the soul that loves God a bride. Now one who asks for a kiss is in love. It is not for liberty that she asks, nor for an award, not for an inheritance nor even knowledge, but for a kiss. It is obviously the request of a bride who is chaste, who breathes forth a love that is holy, a love whose ardor she cannot entirely disguise. For note how abruptly she bursts into speech. About to ask a great favor from a great personage, she does not resort, as others do, to the arts of seduction, she makes no devious or fawning solicitations for the prize that she covets. There is no preamble, no attempt to conciliate favor. No, but with a spontaneous outburst from the abundance of her heart (Mt. 12:34), direct even to the point of boldness, she says: "Let him kiss me with the kiss of his mouth."

Does not this seem to you to indicate that she wished to say: "Whom have I in heaven but you? And there is nothing upon earth that I desire besides you" (Ps. 72:25).

From a Sermon on the Virgin Mary

In Mary's acceptance of the will of God revealed to her by the angel Gabriel, Bernard sees the magnificence of both her humility and of her dignity in being chosen the mother of Jesus and, by adoption, the mother of all who believe in Jesus. The reader will note Bernard's direct influence upon *Paradise* 33 and upon, in the successive rings of the *Purgatory,* Dante's presentation of Mary as exemplar of every virtue. The translation is by S. J. Eales, from Dom J. Mabillon, ed., *The Life and Works of Bernard of Clairvaux* (London, 1896).

From Homily I on the Annunciation

To that city then was sent the Angel Gabriel by God; but to whom was he sent? "To a Virgin, espoused to a man whose name was Joseph." Who is this virgin so worthy of reverence as to be saluted by an Angel: yet so humble, as to be betrothed to a carpenter? A beautiful combination is that of virginity with humility. But of how great respect must she be thought worthy, in whom maternity consecrates virginity, and the splendor of a Birth exalts humility? You hear her, a virgin, and humble: if you are not able to imitate the virginity of that humble soul, imitate at least her humility. Virginity is a praiseworthy virtue, but humility is more necessary....

What say you to this, O virgin who art proud? Mary forgets her virginity and dwells only upon her humility; and you think only of flattering yourself about your virginity, while neglecting humility. "The Lord," said she, "has had regard to the humility of His handmaid." Who was she who speaks this? A virgin holy, prudent, and pious. Would you claim to be more chaste, more pious than she? Or do you think that your modesty is more acceptable than the purity of Mary, since you think that you are able by it to please God without humility, whilst she was not able? The more honorable you are by the singular gift of chastity, the greater is the injury you do to yourself by staining it with an admixture of pride. It were better for you not to be a virgin, than to grow haughty about virginity. It is not granted to all to live in virginity, but to many fewer to do so with humility....

There is something still more admirable in Mary: namely, her maternity joined with virginity. For from the beginning was never such a thing heard, as that one should be at the same time Mother and Virgin. If you consider also of whom she is the Mother, to what degree will not your admiration of such a marvelous advancement soar? Will you not feel that you can hardly admire it enough? Will not your judgment or rather that of Truth, be, that she whose Son is God is exalted even above the choirs of Angels? Is it not Mary who says boldly to God, the Lord of Angels, "Son, why hast thou thus dealt with us?" Who of the Angels would dare to speak thus? It is sufficient for them, and they count it a great thing, that they are spirits by nature, that they were made and called Angels by His grace, as David testifies: "Who makes his Angels spirits?" (Ps. 104:4). But Mary, knowing herself to be Mother, with confidence names Him Son, whom they obey with reverence. Nor does God disdain to be called by the name which He has deigned to assume. For a little after the Evangelist adds: "And He was subject to them" (Luke 2:51). Who, and to whom? God, to human beings; God, I say, to whom the Angels are subject, whom Principalities and Powers obey, was subject unto Mary; and to Joseph also for her sake. Admire then both the benign condescension of the Son and the most excellent dignity of the Mother; and choose whether of the two is more admirable. Each is a wonder, each a miracle. God is obedient to a woman, an unexampled humility! A woman is in the place of ancestor to God, a distinction without a sharer! When the praises of virgins are sung, it is said that they follow the Lamb whithersoever he goeth (Rev. 14:4). Of what praise shall she be thought worthy, who even goes before Him?

Learn, O man, to obey; learn, O dust and ashes, to abase thyself and submit. The Evangelist, speaking of thy Creator, says: "He was obedient unto them," that is, to Mary and Joseph. Blush then, O ashes, that dare to be proud! God humbles Himself, and dost thou raise thyself up? God submits Himself unto men, and dost thou lord it over thy fellow creatures, and prefer thyself to thy Creator? Would that God, if ever I should nourish such an inclination, would deign to reply to me as He once reproached His Apostle: "Get thee behind Me, Satan, for thou savor not the things which be of God" (Matt. 16:23)....

The verse of the Evangelist ends thus: "And the Virgin's name was Mary." Let us say a few words upon this name also. The word Mary means "Star of the Sea," which seems to have a wonderful fitness to the Virgin Mother. For she is fitly compared to a star; for just as a star sends forth its ray without injury to itself, so the Virgin, remaining a virgin, brought forth her Son. The ray does not diminish the clearness of the star, nor the Son of the Virgin her virginity. She is even that noble star risen out of Jacob, whose ray enlightens the whole world, whose splendor both shines in the Heavens and penetrates into Hell: and as it traverses the lands, it causes minds to glow with virtues more than bodies with heat, while vices it burns up and consumes. She, I say, is that beautiful and admirable star, raised of necessity above this great and spacious sea of life, shining with vitues and affording an illustrious example. Whosoever thou art who knowest thyself to be tossed about among the storms and tempests of this troubled world rather than to be walking peacefully upon the shore, turn not thine eyes away from the shining of this star, if thou wouldst not be overwhelmed with the tempest. If the winds of temptation arise, if you are driving upon the rocks of tribulation, look to the star, invoke Mary. If you are tossed upon the waves of pride, of ambition, of envy, or rivalry, look to the star, invoke Mary. If wrath, avarice, temptations of the flesh assail the frail skiff of your mind, look to Mary. If you are troubled by the greatness of your crimes, confessed by the foulness of your conscience, and desperate with the horror of judgment, you feel yourself drawn into the depth of sorrow and into the abyss of despair; in dangers, in difficulties, in perplexities, invoke and think of Mary. Let not the name depart from your heart and from your lips; and that you may obtain a part in the petitions of her prayer, do not desert the example of her life. If you think of and follow her you will not go wrong, nor despair if you beg of her. With her help you will not fall or be fatigued; if she is favorable you will be sure to arrive; and thus you will learn by your own experience how rightly it is said: "The Virgin's name was Mary."

NOTES

In the past I have tried to tailor my notes for that long-desired creature, the general reader; but in the case of Dante's *Paradise* I must do more. Even the general reader, should one happen to pick up the *Paradise,* must require a great deal of annotation, not for scholarly purposes, but merely to assist him in glimpsing the design and subtlety, along with the splendor and power, of this most demanding poem. I confess I am no expert in the secondary literature written about Dante, but I do know something of the theological and philosophical background to Dante's thought, and it is those that I emphasize in the notes to follow. Medieval theology is in its own right a vast domain of poetic brilliance, within whose constellations Dante's *Paradise* assumes its glorious place. I am, however, indebted to the translators and annotators who have preceded me, and in particular am grateful for the splendid edition by Umberto Bosco and Giovanni Reggio, sane and sensitive as they are to all the nuances of Dante's poetry, and especially, what is rare in literary work these days, to the human.

CANTO ONE

Where your treasure lies, said Jesus, there will your heart lie also. Dante had to fight against exhaustion in Hell and Purgatory, weighed down as he was by the flesh—that is, by sin. Near home now, and no longer burdened with sin, he rises with lightness in the heart—whether in the flesh or not in the flesh, he cannot tell, nor, as far as his speed is concerned, does it matter.

P. 3, L. 2. *light:* "God is light, and in him is no darkness at all" (1 John 1:5). Dante follows the long medieval and patristic tradition, whereof the work of Pseudo-Dionysius the Areopagite is the most notable example (see 10.115–17 and note), of holding that of all created things, light is the closest in nobility to God. This light is not merely physical, though it is at least that; it is also and more fundamentally intellectual light, a spiritual creation (cf. Augustine, *Confessions* 13.3). It is the light of God's glory that fills all things, that gives them their very being by filling them (Jer. 23:24). That the glory of God shines in varying degrees in various objects is a commonplace of medieval thought (cf. Pseudo-Dionysius, *Divine Names* 872A) and is one of Dante's most insistent themes, as he will assert that the structural complexity and inner harmony of the universe are expressed by means of these differences. That there is a hierarchy among the blessed is implied if not asserted by Christ himself: "In my Father's house there are many mansions" (John 14:2); "Whosoever therefore shall humble himself as this little child, the same is the greatest in the kingdom of heaven" (Matt. 18:4).

P. 3, LL. 5–6. *nor tongue / utter:* Dante begins by recalling the rapture of Saint Paul to the third heaven (defined by Bonaventure, *Breviloquium* 2.3, as the Empyrean): "And I knew such a man . . . how that he was caught up into paradise, and heard unspeakable words, which it is not lawful for a man to utter" (2 Cor. 12:3–4; cf. *Inf.* 2.28–30). This passage and the commentary upon it will be cited with some frequency in these notes; it is as central to *Paradise* as the *Aeneid* is to the *Inferno.*

P. 3, L. 9. *memory cannot follow where we go:* That is because memory must use images of finite things we can sense, or abstractions dependent upon language for their clarification in our own minds even before we try to express them to others. Memory is a faculty of beings that exist in time, a reflection of the Creator whose providence, omniscience, and memory are all one; but to enjoy a vision of Paradise is to be granted a glimpse of what surpasses our memory and our very dimensionality: "What then shall I do, O you who are my true life, my God? I will pass beyond even this power of mine which is called memory, desiring to reach you, where you may be reached, and to cling to you there where you can be clung to" (Augustine, *Conf.* 10.17). Failure of the human mind to retain a mystic revelation, compelling it to resort to bizarre imagery, as in the recorded dreams of Saint Hildegard's *Scivias* or in the mysterious allegories of the Apocalypse, will be one of the recurring motifs of *Paradise.* So will the limitations of human knowledge: our vision of God must be a "knowing through unknowing, in a union that passes all understanding" (Pseudo-Dionysius, *Div. Names* 872A).

P. 3, L. 13. *Apollo:* Dante's invocation beseeches not his own genius and memory (*Inf.* 2.7–9), nor the Muse of epic, Calliope (*Purg.* 1.7–12), but Apollo, the god of poetry himself. The language of the invocation derives from Virgil: "Grant to me, Arethusa, this last labor," the opening line of the Tenth Eclogue, written in honor of the shepherd Gallus, a poet and Apollo's favorite, who died of unrequited love. Allegorically, as son of Jove, Apollo stands for Christ, whose Spirit Dante invokes (line 19) to impart the *power* of the Father. One of the gifts of the Spirit is prophecy, especially the prophecy of the final days, as the world comes to its fulfillment: "And it shall come to pass in the last days, saith God, I will pour out of my Spirit upon all flesh: and your sons and your daughters shall prophesy, and your young men shall see visions, and your old men shall dream dreams; and on my servants and on my handmaidens I will pour out in those days of my Spirit; and they shall prophesy; and I will shew wonders in heaven above, and signs in the earth beneath" (Acts 2:17–19). That explains why Dante looks forward to a time when *better voices* will arrive, not a better poet but a more glorious prophet *praying for what Apollo shall proclaim.* Thus the opening of *Paradise* places Dante in the context of apocalyptic judgment against the culpable institutions of his day, while looking forward in hope to man's redemption. To wish to glean the leaves of the *beloved laurel* sacred to Apollo (Ovid, *Metamorphoses* 1.553–67; see also note at 25.8) is to strive in hope for true glory for one's nation, and, beyond that, for *the glory of the One who moves all things,* the source and end of all glory. To fail to strive for that glory is to fail in hope and love. It is to remain stolidly content with one's sinful self, one's corrupt city and failing Church. There is nothing high and noble in that, nothing that a true poet or Caesar may boast of, much less a follower of Christ.

The quest for glory, however, inevitably runs the risk of pride, of venturing on the same presumptuous journey that doomed Ulysses (*Inf.* 26.90–142). To guard against this sin, Dante refers to the example of the satyr *Marsyas,* flayed by Apollo after he lost the musical duel to which he had challenged the god (Ovid, *Met.* 6.382–91). Thus, as in *Purgatory* (1.11–12), Dante's invocation acknowledges his own powers, such as they are, while pleading that what is lacking in him be made up by the Muses—by, we should say, the Holy Spirit. Indeed, the tale of Marsyas illustrates, by a symbolic pun, not only what punishment Dante wishes to avert, but what grace he entreats. For he too wishes to be "unsheathed" from his own flesh, to see what, in the flesh, no man can see.

P. 5, L. 37. *spills of light:* "mouths" for the stream of sunlight at dawn, moving north or south from one day to the next, depending on the season.

P. 5, L. 41. *a more favorable time of year:* The astronomy has engendered some debate. Consider one circle (the celestial horizon at the latitude of the Mountain of Purgatory) intersecting three other circles at one point, and you will have four circles and, as far as your path is concerned, three crossings. If the three other circles are the celestial equator (the great circle perpendicular to the earth's axis and lying in the same plane with the earth's equator), the ecliptic (the apparent path of the sun at the equator—tilted at 23.5 degrees from the celestial equator, since the earth is tilted so on its axis), and the equinoctial colure (the great circle, perpendicular to the celestial equator, lying in the same plane with the earth's axis and intersecting the points at which the sun rises at the equinoxes), you will be describing the morning of the spring equinox, thought to be the moment when the physical world was created (cf. *Inf.* 1.38; *Paradise* 13.74). *Purgatory* began with a vision of four stars, representing the four cardinal virtues, those natural to man, and ended with Dante's baptism, witnessed by the three ladies of the chariot, representing faith, hope, and love, the three su-

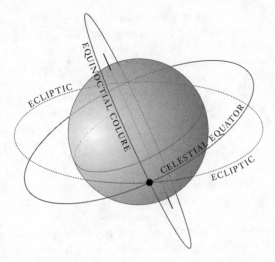

pernatural or theological virtues (*Purg.* 1.22–27; 31.109–11). It seems, then, that *Paradise* opens at that moment of pristine perfection, both origin and culmination of the world, when all these virtues are united.

P. 5, L. 51. *like a pilgrim:* Dante's simile is apt: from God shine forth all rays of being, and to God again are they meant to return. That is the *exitus et reditus* whereon, says Aquinas, the cosmos is based. That man is a pilgrim in this life, like Moses a "stranger in a strange land" (Ex. 2:22), was a medieval commonplace (Dante refers to pilgrims quite frequently, e.g., 25.18; 31.103–8), and remains central to Christian thought. Yet the modern reader should note that all of time and all of time's objects are on the road, so to speak—even the angels ascending and descending upon Jacob's ladder (cf. note at 21.29), doing the errands of the Lord.

P. 7, L. 52. *through my eyes:* It was through the eyes that Dante was first wounded by love for Beatrice, and it is through the eyes, windows and mirrors of the intellect, that Dante gains vision that supersedes the human. Throughout the *Comedy* the eyes of Beatrice, which see so much and which enable Dante to see, are the objects of the poet's devotion (cf. *Inf.* 2.116; *Purg.* 27.54). So it is that love for a beautiful woman and intellectual meditation upon what theology reveals to mortal eyes are woven effortlessly together in Dante's art.

P. 7, L. 70. *man's soaring beyond man:* Ital. *trasumanar,* "transhumaning," Dante's coinage (cf. 31.37). In Christian teaching, the promise of salvation is the promise of being taken up, without loss of individuality, into God. It is not merely a matter of seeing what one cannot otherwise see, but of dwelling in eternity and being what one cannot otherwise be, in the transforming light of God (for God shall be "all in all," 1 Cor. 15:28). Hence Dante's allusion to the apotheosis of *Glaucus* in the preceding lines.

P. 7, L. 75. *Love that steers the heavens:* Echoing Boethius: "Love which commands the heavens" (*Consolation of Philosophy* 2. m. 8); "O you who govern the world with perpetual reason" (3 m. 9). Ital. *governi* retains some of its etymological sense of ruling by giving direction, steering.

P. 7, L. 77. *wheel You have made eternal by desire:* The wheeling of the heavens and indeed the motion of all things, including human works, derives from the Creator, ever still and ever in motion (cf. Augustine, *Conf.* 13.37). The circular orbit of the spheres reflects both perfect stillness (since it is one simple and undecaying motion) and desire (since in its motion it strives to fulfill its Creator's will and in so moving returns to him).

P. 7, L. 78. *harmony:* the music of the spheres. Moving at different speeds, the spheres were thought to produce, in the "friction" of each against the one below and the one beneath, notes that composed an intellectual harmony of ultimate beauty.

P. 9, L. 92. *Lightning:* The realm of fire, in the upper atmosphere, at times produces lightning that strikes the earth, contrary to the proper motion of fire, which is to rise. Beatrice's point is that it is also and more preeminently man's nature to rise to his own realm: not earth or the upper atmosphere, but the very presence of God (Aquinas, *Summa contra gentiles* 4.87). She will make the same point below (1.136–41), asking the reader to consider the absurdity of *a still flame on earth.* That is the absurdity of intellectual blindness and hardness of heart—in a word, sin.

P. 9, L. 105. *resemble God:* The world is not a cascade of chances raining down upon the earth. It is a work of art, bearing, in its artistic order, the impress of its Maker (or as Bonaventure puts it, God is the efficient, exemplary, and final cause of all things: all things come from God, and all, in distinctive manner, return to him; *Brev.* 2.1). From that order a rational being can read *the trace / of that eternal Power.* Notice too that order of any complexity requires subordination, exactly as one cannot write a symphony wherein every instrument plays the same note with the same intensity. Thus it is one of the blessings of the Creator that some *approach more near and others less*—a point Beatrice makes at some length in Canto 2.

P. 11, L. 132. *to swerve away:* by free will. Sin is an unnatural (but, for free beings, possible) wrenching away from our proper motion, as unnatural as the freezing of fire: "There is naturally implanted in the minds of men the desire for the true good, even though foolish error draws them toward false goods" (Boethius, *Cons. Phil.* 3 pr. 2). In Dante's simile, it is the clay in the potter's hands (cf. Is. 64:8) that might be of poor quality—not created so, but become so by sin, having grown literally *deaf* or hard of hearing: "For this people's heart is waxed gross, and their ears are dull of hearing, and their eyes they have closed; lest at any time they should see with their eyes, and hear with their ears, and should understand with their heart, and should be converted" (Matt. 13:15).

CANTO TWO

Here shall thy proud waves be stayed, said the Lord, creating the seas and in the act of creation defining them, setting limits upon them, making them discrete from all other things. It is said that the greatest mystery of this universe is that there should be a universe at all; second to that, I believe, is that there should be discrete *things* in the universe, in harmony with yet separate from one another. Dante's discussion of the spots on the moon should be understood at the very least as a probing into the question of the separate identities of the various creatures in the universe, regardless of the fundamental matter that underlies them all.

P. 13, L. 1. *your shallops:* Dante is fond of using sailing as a metaphor for poetic enterprise (cf. *Purg.* 1.1–3), but this is not just a picturesque image. Following the suggestion of the New Testament, ancient Christians considered the ark of Noah to be a foreshadowing of the faith of the Church (Augustine, *City of God* 15.27; cf. Heb. 11:7; 2 Pet. 2:5), a faith to be tried during the dark and sinful days preceding the second coming of Christ: "And as it was in the days of Noe, so shall it be also in the days of the son of man. They did eat, they drank, they married wives, they were given in marriage, until the day that Noe entered the ark, and the flood came, and destroyed them all" (Luke 18:26–27). It is thus needful to get into that ark, and that is why baptismal fonts throughout Europe are octagonal: eight people were spared the great flood. But Dante suggests here that, for following his poem and the truths it reveals, it is not enough to be baptized; one needs a ship *of sturdy wood* (cf. Richard of Saint Victor, *The Mystical Ark* 2.2), provided by the contemplation of *the bread of angels,* the wisdom of God: "Come, eat of my bread, and drink of the wine which I have mingled" (Prov. 9:5).

P. 13, L. 12. *never fills them full:* The food satisfies but does not satiate; it fills at the same time as it whets the appetite for more.

P. 13, L. 15. *before the splashes settle evenly:* Those who do not lift their heads to look upon *the bread of angels* will instead have to settle for the vain and insubstantial: "What advantage hath the boasting of riches brought us? All those things are passed away like a shadow, and like a post that runneth on, and as a ship that passeth through the waves, whereof, when it is gone by, the trace cannot be found, nor the path of its keel in the waters" (Wis. 5:8–10).

P. 15, L. 24. *sunk...nock:* an example of the rhetorical device called hysteron proteron, wherein what one expects to come first comes second. Obviously, an arrow whistles off the nock before it is sunk in the target. Dante's odd inversion suggests that we are leaving behind us the iron bonds of space and time. Dante will refer to space and time, no doubt, when he beholds the earth beneath him, but here in Paradise there is not that clock-watching worry that is never far from Virgil's mind. For he will say, of Beatrice's ascent, *her act has no extent in time* (10.39). That is fitting, for Paradise is the realm where all times are present in the eternal mind of God.

P. 15, L. 37. *If I was body:* Again Dante adapts the words of Saint Paul, describing his own vision of Heaven (2 Cor. 12:1–5; cf. *Inf.* 2.28–30).

P. 15, LL. 38–39. *how ... body:* an impossibility, unless by the will of God; but the resurrected body will be such as to "pass through the celestial spheres without dividing them, not on account of its own subtlety, but by divine power" (Aquinas, *Summa theologiae* suppl. 83.2). The mystery touches upon that of the Trinity, three Persons in one God, on the indwelling of the Spirit within the human soul, on the union of God and man in Christ, and on man's being brought into union with God.

P. 15, L. 42. *how Godhead and our nature were made one:* As Dante enters the first sphere of Heaven, the moon, he broaches—almost casually, as if he were puzzling over the problem of lunar dimensionality—the central mystery of the Christian faith. To put it baldly, that mystery is this: how can God exist? By "God" we mean no abstract necessity or final plug for an extended equation, but a Being who creates, lovingly, that which is not God and, in the case of men and angels, that which is not God but which is like God. The Christian tradition Dante follows suggests that such a Creator makes sense only if, as it were, God himself embraces in himself the principles of multiplicity and loving relationship (otherwise God would need creatures to love—but no need is found in God); hence the Son is begotten of the Father and the Spirit is the Person of Love they breathe forth for each other. Then, if God is to create beings that are like God, he must also endow them with the capacity to love. God's "descent" into his creation, making what he loves and what is, in the case of rational beings, able freely to love him in return, is a mirroring of the Trinity and a universal sign of the Incarnation of Christ. For Christ is "incarnate" in the order of the world—the world is a foreshadowing or aftershadowing of Christ incarnate, Christ the "power of God, and the wisdom of God" (1 Cor. 1:24), humbly putting off his glory to take on flesh (Phil. 2:8)—long before Jesus ever walked the sands of Galilee. These mysteries, in the Christian faith, are bound inextricably: the world is the creation and mirroring of the Trinity, whose Second Person would become incarnate to redeem the world. It is no less than the mystery of the inner life of the Deity; yet for that mystery was man made. Dante asserts with magnificent boldness that when we see God face-to-face we will see—not theologize, not reason, but simply see—how Christ is both human and divine, as now we see—not philosophize—that a statement and its direct contradiction cannot both be true and cannot both be false. The Godhead will be axiomatic, the foundation and the ultimate object of thought; and indeed it is impossible to suppose that the Godhead could be otherwise.

P. 15, L. 49. *shadowy signs:* The modern reader must remember that Dante does in fact accept the foundational epistemology of our science: that, as Aquinas insisted, all knowledge comes to us *initially* through the senses. Dante really is interested in the problem of spots on a heavenly body—what are they, and why are they there? And he really is interested in rejecting the fanciful; hence his dismissal of folk legends about Cain and his dog and his thornbush. Thus Beatrice reasons with what a lazy reader might consider a clinical, investigative thoroughness. Are the spots on the moon caused by variations in the thickness of lunar matter? Our experience of the world, she argues—and we should pause to note that our allegory of theology is making this argument—allows us only two possibilities. Either the moon is translucent in the darker and presumably thinner areas, or the darker areas are made of thin matter overlaying the same thick matter that constitutes the brighter areas. But neither hypothesis works. If the dark areas possess thin matter, then the moon's translucence should be apparent during a solar eclipse—but no such translucence appears. On the other hand, if we try the mirror experiment Beatrice proposes (with astute empiricism), we will see that modest-to-large differences in distance will affect the size of the light but not its intensity. (That we should use mirrors in this experiment is especially fit: Bonaventure claims that the whole universe and all things therein are mirrors reflecting God; *Itinerarium mentis in Deum* prol. 4.) Beatrice's conclusion is thus based upon the lowest rung of contemplation, according to Richard of Saint Victor (*The Twelve Patriarchs* 5): beholding of and reasoning about objects around us. That leads her upward into the realm of theology proper: the moon is bright and less bright because of variations in the nobility of its matter—variations in its capacity to reflect the light of the sun, or the light of God. Dante thus returns to the first lines of *Paradise*, and prepares the reader to meet souls that are more and less endowed with beatitude.

P. 17, L. 57. *flaps with too short a wing:* The first two of the six wings of contemplation, says Richard of Saint Victor, are to cling in wonder to visible things and to reason the truths about them. These two wings will assist you in learning about the mutability of the things of earth, but that is about all they can do, alone: "For there are heavenly bodies and there are terrestrial bodies; and the glory of heavenly things is one thing, and the glory of terrestrial things is another. The brightness of the sun is one thing, and the brightness of the moon another, and star differs from star in brightness" (*Ark* 1.10; quoting 1 Cor. 15:40–41). Dante seems to have Richard's appraisal of reason in mind here as he discusses the brightness of the moon.

P. 19, L. 109. *to fill your intellect with light:* Dante will lose the accidents of ignorance and error; what will remain is what he essentially is.

P. 21, L. 123. *take from above, and set in act below:* The entire universe is a creature whose life consists in the transmission and diffusion of light (cf. Pseudo-Dionysus, *Div. Names* 693B, 821B).

P. 21, L. 132. *the seal:* This is one of the most important images used by Aquinas, and then by Dante, to describe God's act of creation. He seals it as if it were warm wax, stamping it with himself. So here he who is One creates a multiplicity of beings that in their degrees and kinds of nobility, and in the harmony among them, are stamped, not in identical fashion but ever to the same end, with his power and wisdom and love. The universe is not God's body, but it is a kind of body made by God and for God, with its various members serving various functions.

P. 21, L. 133. *your human dust:* a biblical epithet enjoining humility: "Dust thou art, and unto dust shalt thou return" (Gen. 3:19); "He remembereth that we are dust" (Ps. 103:14).

P. 21, L. 145. *not 'dense' and 'rare':* Distinctions between things lend beauty to the universe and are intended by God; that ordered beauty must be denied by any form of monism. So argued Aquinas: "Eliminated hereby is the opinion of the ancient natural philosophers who held that there was but one cause, a material one, from which all things were made by rarity and density. For these thinkers were obliged to say that the distinction of things which we observe in the universe resulted not from the ordering intention of some principle, but from the fortuitous movement of matter" (*Summa con. gen.* 2.39.9).

CANTO THREE

For he is our peace, said the apostle Paul of Christ, who reconciles Jew and gentile. The souls of the inconstant, desiring to remain true to Christ but also desiring peaceable lives, allowed their vows to be broken. Having kept their faith, if not their vows, to the end, they now see that only in their Redeemer is peace to be found, and only in his will are all the wills of men made one.

P. 23, L. 15. *trace of a pearl on a fair brow:* The delicately evocative and visually precise image reveals a deep truth about Paradise: it is the place where distinction and individuality are gained, not lost. The ascent to Heaven is no absorption and dissolution into the divine (think by contrast of the flattened namelessness of the traitors encased in the ice of Hell, *Inf.* 34.10–15), but an apotheosis of the unique and unrepeatable image of God that is most truly oneself. The faint visibility of Piccarda's face foreshadows the resurrection of the body (7.142–48) and the consummation of humanity that is body and soul united in bliss.

P. 27, L. 30. *failing to fulfill their vows:* The fault of inconstancy is aptly associated with the moon and its phases. More particularly, the *kind* of inconstancy shown here is significant. We do not see, for instance, those who were lacking in constant fortitude or constant temperance or constant love. Piccarda's is rather the fundamental inconstancy: that of giving up your will to God and then taking it back, not wholly, but a little bit, to flee harm or other trouble. It is the essence of the pardonable sin. The blessed saints of this sphere erred more fundamentally than did Peter, who in a moment of fear denied Christ; they allowed the course of their lives to be directed by a promise they did not exactly break, but were not ardently loving enough to suffer greatly to fulfill. They are like most good men and women, except that they are now absolutely innocent and ravishingly lovely.

P. 27, L. 39. *no one understands unless he tastes:* In the presence of the beautiful Piccarda, Dante recalls what he had long ago written in praise of Beatrice: "Her beauty entering the beholder's eye / Brings sweetness to the heart, all sweets above: / None comprehends who does not know this state" (*Vita Nuova* 26; tr. Barbara Reynolds). Here it is applied not to Piccarda's person but to the beatitude both she and Beatrice enjoy.

P. 27, L. 50. *Piccarda:* sister of Dante's friend and fellow poet Forese Donati (cf. *Purg.* 23–24). As a young girl Piccarda entered the convent of Saint Clare (see lines 97–99 below), but her violent and scheming brother Corso (cf. Forese's condemnation of him, *Purg.* 24.82–87) compelled her to leave the convent. Actually, he kidnapped her and made her marry a member of his Black faction among the Guelph partisans in Florence. Piccarda took ill shortly thereafter and died.

P. 29, L. 66. *see more, know more, and be held more dear:* "More" and "less" in Paradise must not be interpreted in a clumsy earthly sense, as Dante's character seems to want to do here. The souls of Paradise are not blessed equally, true; and it is inherent in our nature to desire to know more, or rather, to know all we can. But all the souls in Paradise enjoy the full beatific vision (4.27–36), are filled with it, and can enjoy no more. They differ in their capacity to be filled with it, just as unequal containers may be equally full. The souls desire no more than this all-filling will of God; hence the differences excite no envy (cf. Augustine, *City of God* 22.30) but are themselves a source of happiness. Piccarda's reply to Dante will draw the spiritual implication from the previous canto's discussion of the variations in the moon's brightness: we must not think her "low" level of blessedness a defect, but a part of God's design, reflected in creation: "The diversity and inequality in created things are not the result of chance, nor of a diversity of matter, nor of the intervention of certain causes or merits, but of the intention of God himself, who wills to give the creature such perfection as it is possible for it to have" (Aquinas, *Summa con. gen.* 2.45.9).

P. 29, L. 85. *In His will is our peace:* "For he is our peace" (Eph. 2:14). The peace that passeth understanding (Phil. 4:7) is to dwell in the will of God; it is a peace not of resignation but of fulfillment and, in Augustine's magnificent phrase, of "the tranquillity of order" (*City of God* 19.13). Always in Paradise we must guard against seeing blessed repose as a terminus: it is the serene dawn of a new heaven and a new earth (Rev. 21:1–6).

P. 29, L. 87. *fashioned by Nature or the hand of God:* As Beatrice will explain (7.130–48), God fashions some creatures without an intermediary: these include the human soul and, in the creation of Adam, the first human flesh. Those things created through an intermediary necessarily obey the providential will of God; those created directly are free to love and therefore free to disobey, but even their hardheartedness and disobedience are comprehended in that providential will.

P. 31, L. 107. *the sweet cloistered garden:* Piccarda touchingly recalls the peace of the nun's life she had chosen. The image of the cloister, or enclosed garden, is scriptural, referring to the womb of Mary and to the Church, the Bride of Christ: "A garden inclosed is my sister, my spouse; a spring shut up, a fountain sealed" (Sg. 4:12).

P. 31, L. 118. *Constance:* When Henry VI, son of Frederick I Barbarossa and thus heir to the German lands known as the Holy Roman Empire, married Constance (1154–1198), daughter of Roger I of Sicily and heiress to that island and to the kingdom of Puglia (southern Italy), it seemed as if the empire were about to be reestablished on solid footing, flanking the papal lands to north and south. Constance was the aunt of Manfred (cf. *Purg.* 3.113) and the mother of the talented and conceited Emperor Frederick II (cf. *Inf.* 10.119), so-called Stupor Mundi, or Wonder of the World, for his own intellectual achievements and his having surrounded himself with a court of able poets and thinkers and diplomats. Widowed in 1197, Constance named Pope Innocent III as Frederick's tutor; this resulted in a long history of cooperation and strife between the pope and the heterodox young emperor. The typically anti-imperial Guelphs spread a rumor, which Dante appears to accept, that Constance had been a nun and had been forced to renounce her vow in order to marry Henry. In his youth a Guelph, Dante now shows his adherence to the principle of empire, a power that, he was to insist in his late treatise *On Monarchy,* was ordained by God as equal with the papacy. He admires Constance for her bravery, and in Frederick II he sees not only the last king of *Swabia* but the last Roman emperor at least until his day, for the successors to Frederick's German realms, notably "German Albert" (*Purg.* 6.97), had not bothered to cross the Alps to be crowned in Rome.

CANTO FOUR

When I consider thy heavens, the work of thy fingers, the moon and the stars, which thou hast ordained, what is man—asks the psalmist—that thou art mindful of him? The ancients may have exalted heroes such as Hercules to the stars, and Plato may suggest that the souls of good men are reabsorbed into the star that once shed its influence upon them. Neither, asserts Dante, can match the claim of Scripture, that man, a little lower than the angels, is more to be esteemed than those spangled lights.

P. 35, L. 1. *Between...appetite:* At first glance Dante's simile appears to assert a determinism at odds with the doctrine of free will that he asserts in this very canto. The *free man* seems to choose according to the appeal and vicinity of the food, without possibility of independent judgment. Two points need to be made, however. First, those who believe in the freedom of the will do not claim, in man, an absolute arbitrariness, a freedom from being influenced by one's surroundings. Indeed, Aquinas fairly insists upon such influence, defining virtue as the acquired habit—the Aristotelian "second nature"—of choosing the good. Second, neither Dante nor Aquinas asserted the primacy of the will over the other faculties of the soul. That primacy belongs to intellect, which informs the will of the good or evil of a thing. The will that is formally free (that is, nothing compels it to act against its own desires) and free of sin (its desires are just) will act in accord with the intellect's judgment. But in Dante's deliberately absurd metaphor, the intellect's judgment is that the foods are exactly as far away and exactly as enticing, not a hair more or less, just as, varying the analogy, neither deer the dog sees is more catchable and neither wolf the sheep sees is more dangerous. The will obeys by resigning! Naturally, this is a comical way to describe Dante's hesitation as he grapples with two doubts, but we soon learn from Beatrice that the doubts are *not* equally worrisome, and in fact one of the doubts springs from the false assumption that one way to fulfill a vow might be just as valid as another. Aquinas held that such a dilemma was impossible, since in one respect or another, one of the choices would stand out (*Summa theol.* 2.1.13.6).

This canto also implicitly rejects any notion of stellar determinism, on grounds that are empirical as well as theological. Thus Aquinas seems to have Platonists in mind when he rebukes the folly of people ignorant of the causes of things: "Such is evidently the case with those who subject human wills to the stars...and this is likewise true of those who think that angels are the creators of souls, that human souls are mortal, and, generally, of persons who hold any similar views derogatory to the dignity of man" (*Summa con. gen.* 2.3.5; cf. also Augustine, *City of God* 5.2–7).

P. 35, L. 19. *If my good intent endures:* Dante wonders why Piccarda and Constance enjoy lesser merit, when they preserved the intent to keep their vows (3.117–118). The fact is that they did and did not preserve that intent; the conundrum is analogous to the hypothetical situation presented at the beginning of the canto. They willed two things: to stay in the cloister, and to avoid the suffering that staying in the cloister would bring upon them. Aquinas argued that one can, for instance in considering ends and means, will two things simultaneously (*Summa theol.* 2.1.12.3), and also that the action one yields to out of fear, though not willed absolutely, possesses more of the voluntary than of the involuntary (2.1.6.6).

P. 37, L. 24. *as Plato speculated:* Dante probably read Plato's *Timaeus;* in that work, as in the *Republic* and other works, Plato teaches that the soul is immortal, but he also says, with a certain whimsy, that the souls of men return to the planetary gods who were instructed by the great creating god to make them: "The part of them worthy of the name immortal, which is called divine and is the guiding principle of those who are willing to follow justice and you—of that divine part I will myself sow the seed, and having made a beginning, I will hand the work over to you. And do ye then interweave the mortal with the immortal and make and beget living creatures, and give them food and make them to grow, and receive them again in death" (41c–d). How close this is to Dante's Christian belief that God creates some things directly and some things by an intermediary! Yet to yield to it one must deny that the body is good and holy and is to be resurrected, and that a human being essentially is a union of body and soul. Indeed, Augustine saw that the Platonic understanding of celestial intelligences presupposed a belief that a mortal body is no better than a trap for the soul (*City of God* 13.16–17); it is carnal, he says, to despise the flesh (14.5)! Of Dante's two doubts, therefore, this is the more dangerous, and Beatrice addresses it first, revealing to him and to the reader that the souls do not dwell in the spheres (as Dante's poetic scheme is designed to have us believe, at first) but in the presence of God, all of them.

P. 37, LL. 27–28. *most / Endeitied of Seraphim:* Ital. *più s'india,* Dante's coinage. The Seraphim are afire for wisdom and behold God most deeply (28.98–102); *Moses* and *Samuel* are the greatest of the Old Testament prophets (Jer. 15:1); *John* the Baptist was graced with the vision of the coming of the Christ, and *John* the apostle was the visionary of the Apocalypse. None of these, not even Mary, endowed with the deepest sight of all created beings (33.43–45), dwells in a Heaven different from that wherein Piccarda and Constance dwell.

P. 37, L. 43. *why Holy Scripture condescends:* One error is to deny the body; another is to believe that images of bodies necessarily represent bodies as we know them. The principle here is ancient: Augustine clearly taught that sometimes the literal meaning of Scripture *is* the allegorical; otherwise phrases like "the arm of God" would be nonsense (*Christian Doctrine* 3.31). So too Richard of Saint Victor, asserting not merely that such images are necessary but that they are aids for us as we climb from imagination to contemplation (*Twelve Pat.* 15). Scripture must be adapted to the intellects that are to understand it, and thus must use "corporeal metaphors" (Aquinas, *Summa theol.* 1.1.9).

P. 39, L. 55. *Perhaps he can be read another way:* Perhaps Plato intends that we read him allegorically, as Scripture so requires. For the possibility of such a reading of Plato, Dante may be indebted to Aquinas's teacher Albert the Great (*On the Nature and Origin of the Soul* 2.7).

P. 39, L. 72. *proof:* In Canto 2, Beatrice argued by means of logical analysis (there can be only two ways in which variation of density can result in spots on the moon) and empirical observation (neither possibility stands the test of observed fact). Now she argues by observing and analyzing human faculties and actions, and by distinguishing terms. We know, she implies, what it is to be contingently unwilling—unwilling generally, but yielding to fear, given the circumstances. These two sorts of will must be distinguished. Since Piccarda and Constance gave themselves to the convent, it is not enough that they should wish they had been allowed to keep their vows. They must act as flame acts, immediately returning to the action of its proper nature, to rise, as soon as the interfering wind ceases to beat it aside. Even if we do something only out of fear, "the will of the one who fears contributes something to the act" (Aquinas, *Summa theol.* 2.1.6.6).

P. 39, L. 83. *Lawrence:* The martyred deacon (d. 258) was roasted on a gridiron. With his last words he instructed his tormentors to turn him over to make sure he was cooked evenly.

P. 39, L. 84. *Mucius:* Gaius Mucius Scaevola. When the Etruscan king Porsenna was laying siege to Rome, Mucius disguised himself, infiltrated the enemy camp, and slew the man he thought must be the king, but it was the king's secretary. Seized by the soldiers, Mucius was sentenced to be burnt alive; but he thrust his right hand into a fire and told Porsenna that even should he be slain, there were hundreds of youths in Rome who would attempt the same feat, one after the other. Amazed by the lad's courage, Porsenna set him free. From that day on, the self-maimed Mucius earned the nickname Scaevola, or Lefty (Livy, *History* 2.13).

P. 41, L. 103. *Alcmaeon:* son of Amphiaraus the prophet and Eriphyle. After Eriphyle betrayed her husband for a luxurious necklace, the ghost of Amphiaraus appeared to Alcmaeon and begged him to avenge his death (Statius, *Thebaid* 2.269–305; see *Purg.* 12.49–51; *Inf.* 20.31–36). Alcmaeon was conditionally unwilling to murder his mother—he would have preferred not to—but he did commit the deed.

P. 43, L. 127. *Like a beast in its den:* The charming metaphor suggests that, as a beast is home in its den, so man is at home in, finds his sweetest dwelling in, the truth. Man desires that truth, and it is a tenet of Aristotelian epistemology that just as in other living things there is no desire without an object of that desire (cf. Aquinas, *Summa theol.* 1.12.1), so in man the desire for truth implies the existence of truth. The doubts we experience are but the hesitation born from the impetuousness of that desire and the natural difficulty of comprehending certain truths. As in the give-and-take of the scholastic disputation, doubt is a necessary (we may say exciting) moment in the quest for truth.

CANTO FIVE

Let your yes be yes and your no be no, casting aside the ways of the double-dealer of old. Jesus' remarks on the swearing of oaths remind his listeners of the majesty of God and of his creation. With that majesty in mind, it becomes unthinkable that one could bandy terms with God, as if he were a fellow merchant in a fish market, since not only is all creation from God, so also is one's will. That freedom, says Beatrice in this canto, is our most precious gift next to existence itself.

P. 45, L. 11. *a faint glow:* According to Boethius, all vice can be described as the will's settling for a partial good instead of seeking the whole (*Cons. Phil.* 3 pr. 8). All created things are good, all are worthy of our love (cf. 26.64–66), but only the Creator is the worthy object of our ultimate desire.

P. 45, L. 22. *the will at liberty:* Virgil had said that Beatrice would wish to speak to Dante about the freedom of the will (*Purg.* 18.73–75). Free will is implied by our capacity to reason and love ("Reason also is choice," said Milton); that triad of power, wisdom, and love—without which a truly rational being is unimaginable—makes the soul reflect the triune God. If liberty of the will is the greatest gift God has conferred upon man (as Dante will repeat in *On Monarchy,* 1.12.6), then the free sacrifice of that liberty is the greatest sacrifice man can make. More: it makes man like Christ, who set aside his glory as God, the greatest act of humility logically and ontologically possible (Phil. 2:5–7). Consequently it is absurd to suppose that one can retract the sacrifice of will itself and substitute for it a mere object of the will. Aquinas treats the problem of dispensation or commutation of vows at great length (*Summa theol.* 2.2.88.10–12).

P. 47, L. 29. *sacrifice:* Ital. *vittima,* "victim." Dante is certainly alluding to the paschal sacrifices of the Hebrews (cf. Ex. 12:1–10), foreshadowing the paschal sacrifice of Christ, who came "to put away sin by the sacrifice of himself" (Heb. 9:26).

P. 47, L. 48. *in Leviticus:* not in the Italian, but Beatrice is referring to a passage in that book, which requires the addition of a fifth in the redemption of an altered vow (Lev. 27:15–27), while forbidding absolutely the redemption of anything that has been consecrated to the Lord (27:28–29).

P. 47, L. 57. *the silver and the yellow keys:* Man cannot alter the substance of a vow unless two conditions are met: he must take on an even heavier load, and he must gain permission to do so by the authority of a priest, who acts in the person of God. For the image of the silver and the golden keys, see *Purg.* 9.117–29.

P. 49, L. 69. *his stupidity:* Beatrice first warns Christians to keep the vows they make, then warns them against making stupid, rash, or immoral vows (like Jephthah's, which was not a vow to keep). They should not think that the failure to keep a vow can be washed away with a little sacramental confession, nor should they be impelled to make vows by their greed. The Jews living among them must take vows seriously, fulfilling them according to explicit laws; meanwhile the rash Christian is like a silly lamb butting against the air—easy prey for the wolf.

P. 49, L. 80. *not silly sheep:* "Be no more children, tossed to and fro, and carried about with every wind of doctrine" (Eph. 4:12).

P. 51, L. 105. *to make our friendships grow:* The exuberance of the souls in Paradise (contrast the taciturnity and surliness of those in Hell, and the tentative affability of those in Purgatory) shows the purity of their love. In them, love for the generous Creator spills forth into love for his creatures, and thus every new soul in Paradise brings an added reason for rejoicing. It is exactly as Virgil—who will never know such rejoicing—reasoned it must be (*Purg.* 15.67–76). Also apt is the charming image of the fishes flitting toward what they think is food. The feast here is love itself, in communion with Christ.

P. 51, L. 117. *the earth's platoons:* All believers on earth are considered soldiers in the Church Militant (cf. 25.52; also Job 7:1: "Man's life on earth is that of a soldier," Vulgate); the language is also appropriate to the speaker, who, as we will see, has a few things of his own to say about the warring eagle of the Roman Empire.

P. 51, L. 123. *deities:* Man's sin was in wanting to be a god (Gen. 3:5), on man's terms and by man's act; but God conforms his saints to himself, giving them deity as they abide in him: "I have said, Ye are gods; and all of you are children of the Most High" (Ps. 82:6), participating in the happiness that is God (cf. Boethius, *Cons. Phil.* 3 pr. 10).

CANTO SIX

All authority is of God. Dante thus has scriptural warrant, beyond the inclinations of his Aristotelian philosophy, to see providence at work in earthly rule, and in particular in the Roman rule that set the stage for the birth of Christ. The celebration of monarchy will sound strange to the modern reader, even the reader who claims to share Dante's faith. The latter might do well at least to reopen the question of whether on earth obedience to the king is a just image of obedience to the King.

P. 55, L. 1. *the eagle's wing:* The eagle was the symbol of Roman rule, and will return below in the sphere of Jupiter as the constellation sign of just rulership. Dante believed that monarchy was ordained by God as the most natural and fitting form of government for mankind, the most analogous to God's own rule and the most consonant with human freedom. In particular, he believed that the

Roman monarchy was the fit bringer of peace to the world at the time when Christ, the Prince of Peace, would be born, and that it was afterward the fit disseminator of true Christian law. By contrast with the souls in the sphere of the moon, the souls here in the sphere of Mercury kept their vows—not kept them too well (for to say that would be absurd) but concentrated on their duties of government and stewardship almost to the exclusion of the worship of God. Piccarda chose restfulness over glorious labor; we may say that Justinian, the speaker here and the recounter of the flight of the never-resting Roman eagle, chose labor over glorious repose.

Here is a summary of the eagle's career. It rises first near *the mountains* surrounding Troy. After Troy is sacked and burned, it flies west, following (astronomically and providentially) the course of Heaven, in the keeping of Aeneas, *him who made Lavinia queen* (cf. Virgil, *Aen.* 6.764–65; *Inf.* 4.125–26). In Italy, Aeneas had to fight for the right to settle his people and marry Lavinia, uniting his Trojans with some of the native Latins, in which war *Pallas died* fighting to set the eagle in its domain (*Aen.* 10.474–89). After Aeneas's death, his son Ascanius moved his seat of rule to *the Alban shore*, south of Rome, and there it remained until the feats of Romulus and his successors established it in what is now Rome. (From this point on, Dante largely follows the account of Roman history given by Livy.) The neighboring Sabines, rivals of Romulus and his men, struggled for mastery over Rome and its vicinity; they sought to deny the Romans the chance to produce heirs, but Romulus got the better of them. He invited the Sabines to celebrate the feast of the Lupercal with him and his men, and while the people were making merry the Romans absconded with the Sabine women (Livy, *Hist.* 1.9). The building of Rome brought the kings that followed Romulus into conflict with the relations living at Alba. To settle the dispute, Tullius Servius and the Alban king agreed to let mastery be decided by having *the three* battle *the three:* a contest between three Roman brothers and three Alban brothers. The Roman Horatii defeated the Alban Curiatii (*Hist.* 1.23–26). Rome continued, through the reigns of its *seven kings,* to conquer the small neighboring tribes. Then it threw off the yoke of its monarchy, which had passed into the keeping of Etruscan warlords. This revolution is told in the form of a romance, in the tale of *Lucretia's woe.* When Lucretia, wife of a Roman nobleman, was raped by the son of Tarquin the Proud, the last Etruscan king, the Roman nobles drove out the royal family and established an aristocratic, deeply conservative republic (*Hist.* 1.49–60).

From then on, the history of Rome is one of conquest of *kings and councils,* sometimes in aggressive wars against rivals, more often in wars against aggressors. Rome always wins. She defeats the Greek (*Pyrrhus,* in the so-called Pyrrhic War, 280–275 B.C.), the Gaul (*Brennus,* who in 390 B.C. sacked Rome, but who was then expelled by Camillus; *Hist.* 5.49–50), the Arab (*Hannibal,* who in the Second

Punic War, 218–202 B.C., was defeated by *Scipio*). Those ages produce many brave, sternly virtuous, self-denying heroes. Lucius *Quinctius* Cincinnatus was made dictator of Rome, with a term of six months, to repel the neighboring Aequi. He saved his city in fifteen days, resigned the dictatorship, and returned to his modest farm outside the city, which he worked with his own hands (*Hist.* 3.26–30). He was nicknamed Cincinnatus, or Curly, for what Dante calls *the careless shock of hair*; not preoccupied with wealth or the vanities, he. Titus Manlius *Torquatus* was a hero of Rome's early wars against the Gauls and the Latins; he was nicknamed the Necklaced One from his having run up to rip the *torqueum* off the neck of the opposing general. The *Decii*, father and son, were victors over the Samnites; the family of the *Fabii* distinguished themselves again and again in the early wars against the Gauls and against Rome's neighbor Veii (*Hist.* 5.36; 5.46); and its most illustrious scion, Quintus Fabius Maximus Cunctator (the Delayer) fought an unappreciated war of attrition against Hannibal in southern and central Italy. Publius *Scipio* Africanus, the noble, gentle, cultured young general who defeated Hannibal at Zama in 202 B.C. (*Hist.* 30.32–35), was revered as the greatest man Rome ever produced. Gnaeus Pompeius (*Pompey*) the Great was, with Crassus and Julius *Caesar*, a member of the First Triumvirate, who wrested effective control of Rome from the Senate in 59 B.C. He is paired with Scipio for his military exploits as a young man: in 83 B.C., when he was only twenty-three years old, he was awarded a triumphal march by the Roman state, an unprecedented distinction for a youth who had held no public office.

With Pompey we arrive at the threshold of Christianity. Dante sees the events that followed as comprehensible only in the context of God's redemptive plan. First, Gaius Julius Caesar *took up the flag*, assumed control of the Roman armies in the north, and defeated the Gauls, gaining the lands watered by the *the Rhône, / the Loire, the Yser, and the Saône*. Envious of his victories and fearing that he had grown too powerful, the Roman Senate ordered him to Rome to account for his tenure as general. By law, no one could lead an army into senatorial lands; so when Caesar crossed the boundary thereof, *the Rubicon*, he was declaring war against the corrupt Senate. Dante's brisk language suggests that it was no civil war, really, but the establishment of something glorious: Caesar took up the flag *at Rome's desire*. The eagle *swept its squadrons into Spain to fight*, defeating the officers of Caesar's onetime ally Pompey, now allied with the Senate against him; then it crushed Pompey's army at *Pharsalia* (even the *hot Nile*, across the Mediterranean, felt the pain—perhaps because Pompey had been the lover of Egypt's queen, Cleopatra). Then, according to Lucan's epic *Pharsalia*, Caesar took the eagle round about the East, seeing the Trojan rivers *Simoïs and Antandros*, and Hector's tomb. After that, the eagle seized *Ptolemy's* realm, Egypt, and pressed on against *Juba*—the Mauretanian king who had assisted Pompey—finally cleaning up the remnants of Pompey's troops in Spain.

Now under the *second steward,* Augustus Caesar, the eagle avenges the death of Julius Caesar and consolidates Caesar's empire by sacking *Perugia* and defeating Marc Antony at *Modena,* and seizing control of the land of *Cleopatra,* who *from the asp took swift and bitter death* rather than be led in triumph through Rome. Augustus's victories ushered in the Pax Romana, a period of about two hundred years of relative quiet in the Mediterranean world. Under the reign of his successor, Tiberius, *the third Caesar's hand,* Christ died to atone for the sins of men; then *Titus,* son of the emperor Vespasian and soon to become emperor himself, destroyed Jerusalem. But when the time of peace came to an end and it grew more and more difficult for the emperors to rule from Rome—for they were usually hurrying from one vulnerable frontier to the next, struggling against waves of Goths and other invaders—*Constantine* moved the capital *against the course of Heaven* (cf. 20.55–60), and indeed, unwittingly but probably against the will of Heaven, from Rome to Byzantium, where the eagle *nested on Europe's farthest coast* for two centuries, barely European, until it passed into the hands of *Justinian.*

P. 55, L. 10. *Justinian:* Justinian (r. 527–65) was the last emperor of Byzantium to try in earnest to regain control over the western lands of the empire, which in 476 had fallen into the hands of Arian (heretic) Goths. His wars against the Goths on the Italian peninsula and against the Vandals of North Africa, wars conducted by his *general,* the eunuch *Belisarius,* were temporarily successful, but incurred costs so large as to make it impossible for Byzantium to hold those lands after Justinian's death. His greatest work in preserving the Roman Empire, however, was not military but legal. Roman law had become a tangled monstrosity of traditions, cases, laws, and imperial decrees, often contradictory or obsolete. Justinian and his scholars *pruned the law of all rank and useless things,* removing what was merely confusing or unnecessary, resolving inconsistencies, and condensing it all into the last great works of classical antiquity, the *Corpus iuris civilis* and the *Institutiones.* Through these works the traditions of Roman government and law were bequeathed to the West, where, with a few exceptions such as Great Britain, they remain the basis of government throughout western Europe.

This is the only canto of the *Comedy* that is one uninterrupted speech; more remarkable, we are in Paradise and the speaker is not Beatrice. Dante's extraordinary decision illustrates his conviction that civil law and ecclesiastical discipline are coequal realms, the latter meant to lead us by showing us where the Highest Good may be sought, the former meant to lead us by encouraging virtue and correcting us when we stray (cf. 1 Pet. 2:13–14). As a representative of the Roman Empire, then, Justinian is the ideal choice, the one emperor whose very name is synonymous with the order, the sanctity, and the universality of law.

P. 55, L. 14. *one nature and not two:* Justinian says he followed the Monophysite

heresy favored by his wife, Theodora, until Pope *Agapetus* (r. 533–536) per-
suaded him otherwise. Historically, that is not so; Justinian was always ortho-
dox. Notably, only when he is converted, only when he believes in the
paradoxical double nature of Christ, does he see clearly enough to undertake
the labor of codifying one of the two realms of law, the civil.

P. 61, L. 103. *Ghibellines:* It is hard for the modern reader (and the modern transla-
tor!) to follow the swirls and riptides of medieval Italian politics. To oversim-
plify matters, the Ghibellines tended to favor the claims of the Holy Roman
Emperor—generally a German—to the lands in northern Italy, including Tus-
cany, and, after the marriage of Henry VI to Constance (see note at 3.118), to
Sicily and southern Italy. The *Guelphs* (whom Justinian castigates shortly) op-
posed such claims, supporting the papacy and, in effect, their own legal and
mercantile independence. But regional and familial rivalries played as great a
role as political philosophy in determining a man's party; and that is not even
to mention the confusion-stirring ambitions of France, naturally suspicious of
any strong German emperor to her east and herself covetous of Italian lands to
her south, yet often also desiring an independence from or even supremacy
over her strongest ally, the papacy. Dante was a member of the White party of
Florentine Guelphs, yet his philosophy with regard to papacy and empire grew
to be Ghibelline, the party of his patron Cangrande della Scala (cf. note at
17.76). But here Dante condemns both parties, since neither is really interested
in justice.

P. 61, L. 106. *this lad Charles:* as always, a scornful reference to Charles II, duke of
Anjou and king of Naples, who attempted to stir a revolt against Aragonese rule
to regain the lands lost in the Sicilian Vespers (cf. 8.76 and note). Charles's fa-
ther sings in Purgatory beside his old enemy Peter III of Aragon (*Purg.*
7.112–14); the lad Charles is lesser than the father, whose modicum of virility
is thus summed up by Sordello: "Him of manly nose" (7.113). The political
greed of Charles II in continually opposing the Roman eagle will be punished
in the defeats of his sons, as is decreed in Scripture: "We have given the hand to
the Egyptians, and to the Assyrians, to be satisfied with bread. Our fathers have
sinned, and are not; and we have borne their iniquities" (Lam. 5:6–7; cf. Ex.
20:5; Matt. 23:32).

P. 63, L. 129. *Romeo:* Romeo de Villeneuve (1170?–1250) was the chief steward of
the Provençal count *Raymond Berenguer* IV. History does not support the legend
Dante recounts; Romeo was not cast off by Raymond but survived him, raising
his daughter Beatrice, managing the lands, and finally marrying Beatrice to
Charles I of Anjou. But legend had it that Romeo (a nickname meaning "pil-
grim" or, as I have translated Dante's pun in line 135, *foreigner*) had managed
Raymond's estates at great profit to the count and had married Raymond's four
daughters to kings. Naturally, jealous courtiers began to backbite, and Romeo

was exiled from Provence. It is interesting that the canto ends with the example of a man who humbly sought renown not for himself but for his master and his master's family, and who was rewarded with scorn and beggary. The reader should compare Romeo's patient suffering with Pier della Vigna's decision to kill himself rather than endure similarly unjust accusations (*Inf.* 13.70–72).

CANTO SEVEN

He became obedient unto death. It is easy, if one wishes to evade the mystery of the atonement that is broached in this canto, to lapse into legalism: man sinned, therefore man should pay; but man has not the wherewithal to pay; therefore God must become man. And indeed Beatrice's reasoning on the matter might give one encouragement that way. It would, however, be a mistake, for Beatrice herself insists that the death of Christ is an act of love too glorious to fathom unless one's mind has been fostered in the fire of love. The death that was Adam's curse is now made Adam's redemption, and in imitation of Christ corporeal men can do at least one thing impossible even for the angels. They can die, and in dying be reborn.

P. 65, L. 6. *a double ray:* Critics disagree about the nature of these rays. My guess, for what it is worth, is that God favors the clear-sighted Justinian with the light of two kinds of law, ecclesiastical and civil, for the two realms of Church and empire (see note at 6.14).

P. 67, LL. 25–26. *a rein / upon his will:* True freedom in a finite creature can thrive only within boundaries. Adam's sin was thus to disobey the boundless God who made him what he was and who gave him all the good he had the capacity to enjoy. To reject all boundary is to try to usurp the place of God and thereby to injure one's own nature. For the rein as necessary for a free will, cf. *Purg.* 16.91–96. Saint Bonaventure argues that Adam's sin rendered man incapable of knowing the Trinity: "He could no longer imitate the divine power, behold divine light, or love divine goodness" (*Brev.* 4.1). Then only the work of the Trinity could redeem him—as Dante asserts below.

P. 67, L. 30. *the Word of God:* Christ: "In the beginning was the Word, and the Word was with God, and the Word was God" (John 1:1).

P. 67, L. 33. *His eternal love:* As so often in *Paradise,* the action of God, whether in creating the universe or in redeeming man or in simply and eternally being, is shown to be the act of the Trinity: here, of Christ uniting man to the Father through his Love, the Spirit.

P. 67, L. 39. *the way of truth and life:* "I am the way, the truth, and the life: no man cometh unto the Father, but by me" (John 14:6). Dante also returns to the image of going astray that began the entire *Comedy* (*Inf.* 1.3).

P. 67, L. 48. *the earth trembled:* An earthquake and darkness—a breaking of the elements of the world, we might say—marked the death of Christ: "And, behold, the veil of the temple was rent in twain from the top to the bottom; and the earth did quake, and the rocks rent; and the graves were opened; and many bodies of the saints which slept arose" (Matt. 27:51–52). That same quake shook the stony architecture of Hell (*Inf.* 12.31–45), releasing the souls of the faithful Jews from bondage and opening Paradise to them (4.52–63).

P. 67, L. 57. *in just this way:* Why was it most fitting—not exactly necessary, but most just—that God become man? Dante's reasoning, along with his stress on "fitness," derives from Saint Anselm's definitive treatise *Cur Deus homo.* Briefly, Anselm declared that man's sin incurred a debt, but since the debt was to the infinite and eternal God who had given him his very being, that debt must be infinite. But finite man, even if innocent, has not the means to pay an infinite debt. Therefore only God can pay it. But since man sinned, it is fitting that man pay. The only solution that satisfies justice is that God become man; yet it does more: it is an act of the overflowing generosity of God. In the beginning God made what was not God, imprinting it with himself; now, to redeem a part of that creation, he becomes man, setting aside his glory. Hence it is that this explanation, says Beatrice, can be comprehended only by one who has been *fostered* (Ital. *adulto*) *in the fire of love.* It is in fact a greater wonder of mercy, says Aquinas, "than if God had forgiven the sin without satisfaction" (*Summa theol.* 3.46.1).

P. 69, L. 65. *envy:* Dante is echoing Boethius, who asserts that God created out of sheer overflowing love, freely, according to the form that existed within him "without envy" (*Cons. Phil.* 3 m. 9).

P. 69, L. 68. *infinite:* "I know that, whatsoever God doeth, it shall be for ever" (Eccl. 3:14).

P. 69, L. 85. *in its seed:* In Adam all men have sinned: "Since by man came death, by man came also the resurrection of the dead" (1 Cor. 15:21).

P. 71, L. 100. *to mount high:* The point is Anselm's, but Dante's language derives from Richard of Saint Victor: "For the satisfaction [of this sin] it was fitting that there be as great humiliation in atonement as there was presumption in the untruth. But God of all rational beings holds the highest place, and man the lowest. When therefore man presumed to rise against God, it was the revolt of the lowest against the highest. Hence for the remediation and expiation it behooved that the highest be humbled to the lowest" (*On the Incarnation of the Word* 8; cf. also Augustine, *City of God* 7.33).

P. 71, L. 107. *his generous heart:* Ital. *bontà del core,* "the excellence of his heart," perhaps "the excellence of his intention." The redemption of man is portrayed as more than the satisfaction of a legal requirement. It is an act wholly in accord with the original act of love and wisdom that gave birth to the universe. It is, indeed, the masterpiece of love, wherein *earth's first day* and *earth's final night* meet and take their meaning from the loving sacrifice of Christ, redeeming man who would be God by making him like God: "The merit of Christ, then, is the root of all our merits, both those which offset penalties, and those which gain for us eternal life" (Bonaventure, *Brev.* 4.7).

P. 71, L. 120. *humbled Himself:* Cf. Phil. 2:8.

P. 73, L. 141. *out of the potencies of elements:* literally, "from power that has been created." All other living things are, we might say, wholly determined by natural causes. The elements of earth, air, water, and fire were thought, in their various combinations and separately, to possess potencies that might be set in action by the *revolving* of the heavenly spheres. This, says Aquinas, is not creation properly speaking, but the moving and altering of already created things (*Summa con. gen.* 2.20). But the human soul is brought into being through the creative action of God (*Summa con. gen.* 2.87).

P. 73, L. 144. *so enamoring it:* All rational souls by nature desire the Highest Good (cf. *Purg.* 18.19–33).

P. 73, L. 148. *your bodies shall arise:* In what must scandalize a Platonist or Buddhist, Christianity insists upon the holiness and the possible immortality of flesh. Here Dante claims that, were it not for sin, human flesh would not decay; with the redemption of Christ, human flesh will rise again, to bliss or to condemnation: "So also is the resurrection of the dead. It is sown in corruption; it is raised in incorruption: It is sown in dishonor; it is raised in glory: it is sown in weakness; it is raised in power. It is sown a natural body; it is raised a spiritual body.... And so it is written, The first Adam was made a living soul; the last Adam was made a quickening spirit" (1 Cor. 15:42–45).

CANTO EIGHT

For the body is not one member, but many. Unity in the body of Christ, and in such human reflections of that body as cities and states, must be provided by love. As Beatrice's justification of the atonement was really an invitation to dwell upon love, so in this canto Charles Martel's discussion of imperial and Italian politics presupposes a love that should but does not dwell among the people, a love that would cause each member to be content in his fit place, desiring no other, neither scorning those below nor envying those above.

P. 75, L. 1. *its perilous time:* in the days of the pagan gods. The time was perilous because people did not know the one true God; but Dante seems also to have in mind a belief, beginning in that pagan world and continuing in the Averroism of his own day, that the influences of the stars determine human behavior, particularly in matters of love. Augustine had exposed the pretensions of the astrologers (*Conf.* 4.3), but the popular seeking of causes in the stars remained, and in fact one of the commonplaces of the tradition of courtly love, whether intended ironically or seriously, was that man was helpless before the power of Eros (cf. *Inf.* 5.103). Star worship is but a sophisticated form of idolatry—a near miss, and an understandable miss, but still error (Wis. 13:1–9).

P. 77, L. 31. *one of them:* Charles Martel (1271–95), not the grandfather of Charlemagne but the son of Charles II of Anjou (*the Cripple of Jerusalem;* cf. 19.127–29 and note) and of Mary, princess of Hungary. Charles Martel passed through Florence for a brief time in 1294, when Dante—just six years older than the young titular king of Hungary—must have met him. Dante's judgment against the Angevin princes is relentless, yet here he casts the youthful Charles as a friend, a fellow believer in the just claims of empire, and a good man who would have saved the world from much evil—for Charles would have adjoined to Hungary the lands of Naples and Provence—had he not died so young.

P. 77, L. 37. O you who move third heaven by intelligence: Ital. *Voi che 'ntendendo il terzo ciel movete.* It is the first line of the poem that begins the second book of Dante's treatise on the beauties of philosophy, the *Convivio* (see Appendix B). This is the third and final time when Dante's own poetry will be quoted in the other world (*Purg.* 2.112; 24.51). It is instructive to see the three lines in order and together: *Amor che ne la mente mi ragiona,* "The Love that speaks its reasons in my mind"; *Donne ch'avete intelletto d'amore,* "Ladies who have intelligence of love"; *Voi che 'ntendendo il terzo ciel movete,* "O you who move third heaven [the sphere of Venus] by intelligence." Of course, it is not accidental that all three lines have to do with love, specifically with the connection between love and the vision of truth. Here in *Paradise* Dante consummates his life as a poet, seeing all that he had done before as corrected and redeemed by the intellectual and amatory revelation that the grace of God, through the lovely Beatrice, now provides. If, in his youthful life, his *vita nuova,* Dante had, without understanding the distinction between earthly and heavenly beauty, surrendered his will and his intellect to the overmastering loveliness of the young Beatrice, and if, in the *Convivio,* he seemed to reject that former love and to connect love only to the intellectual beauties of philosophy, the *Comedy* returns to him the love of Beatrice and the love of philosophical contemplation, as earthly and intellectual movements in the grand symphony of love, body and soul, matter and form, that God has created.

P. 79, L. 58. *on the left banks of the Rhône:* Provence. Charles Martel was crowned king of *Hungary* in 1292, and was heir by his father to Provence, Puglia, and Sicily (which latter, however, Charles I lost to the Aragonese in 1282, in the revolt called the Sicilian Vespers).

P. 79, L. 72. *Rudolph . . . Charles:* Rudolph of Hapsburg, Charles Martel's father-in-law, and Charles I of Anjou, Charles Martel's grandfather. Were it not for the *evil government* of Charles I, the Sicilian revolt would never have happened, and the union of two great kingdoms would have continued.

P. 79, L. 78. *the miser-hearted Catalonian greed:* Ital. *l'avara povertà di Catalogna;* the phrase may suggest that the Catalonians (ministers of Charles Martel's brother Robert, successor of Charles II as king of Naples; Robert had spent seven years in Spain as a royal hostage in exchange for the freedom of their father, and had established friendships with the Catalonians) are greedy, or, more likely, that in their or his own insatiable greed they always considered themselves poor, as misers do. Critics are not sure to which acts of greed Dante refers.

P. 83, L. 93. *How...appear:* Dante considers what Charles has said about his brother Robert of Naples, *a degenerate from a rich estate,* and asks how such degeneracy can be. After all, "every tree is known by his own fruit" (Luke 6:44); how, then, can good seed produce bitter fruit? Dante's question, which may seem fairly easy to answer, actually requires the drawing of three important distinctions. First, Christ's proverb applies to an individual, not to a family; second, the seed is not the same as the tree, which is an allegory of the heart of a man, its good or evil to be divined by the fruit it produces; third, to believe in the influence of the heavenly bodies (or of heredity or environment) is not to believe in compulsion by heavenly bodies. Thus for Dante the answer does not lie in either a radical individualism (as if parents, for instance, had no influence upon their children) or in one kind of determinism or another (as if children, for instance, were always quite like their parents). Each human being at the moment of his conception is sealed with the unique influence of the reigning heavenly bodies; we may call it the unique set of predispositions provided by deoxyribonucleic acids—the point is pretty much the same. He is also, however, provided with free will, and his character will be largely shaped by the habits of those around him. His natural gifts would suffice to make him *blest and whole* in this world, were it not for his own freely chosen sin, and, Charles Martel stresses, were it not for the stupidity of men, who fail to recognize the office fit for each person and instead confound talents and duties. They make kings out of those who should be priests and priests out of those who should be kings, putting in disarray the ranks and orders on earth that should correspond to the ranks and orders of Paradise. The bitter fruit, then, is partly a result of a perfectly good seed stupidly planted, placed in the wrong soil.

P. 83, L. 114. *what has to be:* By definition what is necessary cannot be otherwise; therefore Nature, as a personification of God's efficacy, *natura naturans,* cannot come up short in necessary things. Since an ordered cosmos whose stars are governed by random influences is unimaginable, says Charles Martel, those influences must necessarily be directed toward some providential end. The fault lies not in the stars.

P. 85, L. 116. *if he were not a citizen:* Aristotle saw the Greek state, the *polis,* as an institution naturally rising out of the family. Whereas Plato defined justice by abstracting a blueprint for the just state from the relationships of reason, spirit, and appetite in the just man, Aristotle suggested that the individual himself, rather, is something of an abstraction. Man is simply not meant to live alone: at best he can scratch together the bare minimum for survival. But, like all created things natural or artificial, man has an end, a telos, that informs the design of his being. That end, Aristotle asserts, is happiness, the one thing we seek for its own sake rather than for the sake of something else. Now it was clear to Aristotle that man, a rational being, cannot attain that end of happiness unless conditions allow what distinguishes him as a creature, namely his rational faculties, to thrive. Setting aside eternal beatitude—which Aristotle did not assert—man needs conversation, art, productive enterprise, and the pursuit of wisdom, all of which require the leisure and the community that only a civilization can provide. Further, there can be no leisure unless an efficient division of labor frees people from having to perform countless tasks ill-suited to their talents and inclinations. So it is, on a practical level, that man needs ordered community on earth if he is to attain anything close to contentment. But Dante's point gains power from the context of the *Paradise*. Why should a soul in Heaven care about cities? He must; since after all he dwells in the City of God, the heavenly Jerusalem (Rev. 21:2), a city wherein "various voices make the sweeter song" (6.124). If, in the heavenly city, blessings and offices vary and in their variety and their hierarchical order they produce harmony and joy, then something like that wise varying and ordering should obtain on earth. So Augustine quotes Scipio Nasica, grandson of Scipio Africanus, speaking in Cicero's *Republic:* "That agreeable harmony ... is produced by the modulations of tones that are very dissimilar.... What musicians call harmony in music, in the State is known as concord, the closest and strongest bond of security in any commonwealth, and which can in no way exist without justice" (*City of God* 2.21; cf. *Republic* 2.42).

P. 85, LL. 124–126. *Solon ... Xerxes ... Melchizedek:* Charles Martel names four men of very different offices. Solon was the great and wise legislator-poet of Athens in the sixth century B.C. His compromises between the aristocrats and the small artisans and farmers who had fallen into debt slavery helped the state avert civil war. Xerxes the Great (r. 486–465 B.C.) was the warrior king of Persia (cf. *Purg.* 28.71) who waged war by land and sea against the European Greeks. Melchizedek was the mysterious king of Salem, a high priest who blessed Abraham by offering to God a sacrifice of bread and wine (Gen. 14:18–20). *He who lost his son / While soaring through the air* is Daedalus, the mythological inventor of the labyrinth of Crete.

P. 85, LL. 130–131. *Esau ... Jacob:* twin sons of Isaac. The elder, Esau, was ruddy and impetuous, a lover of hunting, and his father's favorite; the younger, Jacob, was dark-haired and subtle, his mother Rebecca's favorite (cf. Gen. 25:25–34). In Esau's trading his birthright as elder son for a bowl of soup, the Fathers of the Church saw an allegory of man trading the promised blessings of God for the delusory and paltry goods of the world. Punishment for that redounds to Esau's house, as it has to the Angevin house: "And the house of Jacob shall be a fire, and the house of Joseph a flame, and the house of Esau for stubble, and they shall kindle in them, and devour them; and there shall not be any remaining of the house of Esau" (Ob. 18).

P. 87, L. 145. *you wrench someone to religious things:* Commentators argue that Charles Martel aims at the confusion in his own Angevin family: his brother Lodovico became a Franciscan friar, but would have made a better king than did his brother Robert, a man given to the arts and to theological disputation. Gregory the Great has the following to say about people who take on the duties of religious office seemingly by whim: "Moses trembled, though God urged him forward; and yet a man who is weak yearns after the burden of office, and one who is extremely likely to fall under his own burden is willing to be overwhelmed by putting his shoulders beneath the burdens of others!" (*Pastoral Care* 1.7).

CANTO NINE

She has loved much, said Jesus of the harlot weeping at his feet, and therefore her sins were forgiven. None of the saints in this canto were particularly calm, pleasant, and nice people; Folquet in fact became a fighter in the Albigensian Crusade. But great love has never exactly been tepid in its zeal; is not now, nor ever will be.

P. 89, L. 3. *the deceits your children would endure:* Dante may be referring to the naming of Robert, Charles Martel's brother, as successor of Charles II of Anjou to the throne of Naples, instead of Charles Martel's son Caroberto. The move, quite legal, was approved by Boniface VIII.

P. 91, L. 29. *a burning brand:* Ezzelino III da Romano, one of the bloody tyrants boiling in the Phlegethon in Hell (*Inf.* 12.109–10). Dante's imagery derives from the legend that just before her son was born Ezzelino's mother dreamed that she gave birth to a fiery torch. He and Cunizza are a stark example of the truth uttered by Charles Martel (8.127–29), that heavenly influence is no respecter of houses. In another sense, the ardor of the lover of Christ is the true fire whereof Ezzelino's wrath was a perversion.

P. 91, L. 32. *Cunizza:* Cunizza da Romano (1198–1279?), as a young woman, was married in a political arrangement to broker peace between her family and that of the San Bonifazio. When that peace fell apart, the da Romano family, probably with Cunizza's approval, arranged to have her kidnapped and brought home. This was accomplished by the efforts of the poet Sordello, poet of love and scourger of the cowardice of princes (whom Dante meets in Canto 6 of *Purgatory,* and who had long sung the praises of Cunizza's beauty). As for Cunizza's *old sin* of improper amorousness—well, lechery—we know nothing of any liaison with Sordello himself, but after she returned home she did run off with a judge of Treviso, with whom she lived for some time until her husband or her family had him killed. After the death of her husband she was married and widowed at least once more; when her family's fortunes fell apart she spent her declining years in Florence, where her deeds gained her the reputation of a pious and charitable woman.

The reader should compare the tart-tongued and onetime raffish Cunizza with the refined Francesca of *Inferno* 5; both were forced to marry, both took up a lover, and in both cases the lover was killed. But the grace of God, who knows the heart, spared Cunizza and did not spare Francesca. Cunizza acknowledges her sin, and her old zeal in loving the wrong is transformed into zeal in loving what is right; cf. Matt. 21:31.

P. 91, L. 43. *that rabble:* the people of the March of Treviso. The Paduans will be slaughtered in battle, turning their marshes as red as the Bacchiglione, the stream that flows through Vicenza (cf. *Inf.* 15.113), for having been too insolent to acknowledge their duty to the emperor. Here Cunizza refers to a massacre visited upon the Guelphs of Padua by the Ghibellines of Vicenza, spurred on by Cangrande della Scala, Dante's patron and the legate of the emperor Henry VII (see 17.76–93 and note).

P. 93, L. 73. *in-Hims:* Dante's coinage, *s'inluia,* seems motivated by the mystical tradition, which asserts that in the beatific vision man does not only see God but, as suggested by the title of Bonaventure's *Itinerarium mentis in Deum,* journeys into him.

P. 93, L. 78. *six wings:* so the Seraphim are represented in Isaiah (6:2). Dante is probably recalling the six wings of contemplation enumerated and discussed in *The Mystical Ark* of Richard of Saint Victor (cf. 10.131 and note) and adopted by Bonaventure in the *Itinerarium.* For the absolute height of contemplation, the beholding of truths that are not only beyond reason but appear even to violate reason, man needs all six wings.

P. 95, L. 93. *steamed hot with its own blood:* Brutus massacred the people of Marseilles during the civil war against Julius Caesar and his allies. Dante's line comes straight from Lucan (*Phars.* 3.572–73).

P. 95, L. 95. *Folquet:* Folquet de Marseilles (d. 1231) was a man whose life could only have been fashioned in the whirling world of the high Middle Ages. As a young man he gained renown for his poetry of love, particularly his poems written in praise of the wife of the viscount of Marseilles. After her death his passion did not cool—he directed it elsewhere, becoming a monk in the severe Cistercian order, and in 1201 he was raised to the abbacy of Torronet. A few years later he was appointed bishop of Toulouse, just when that city and its environs were rife with a recrudescence of the ancient Manichean heresy. Albigensianism, as it came to be called (taking its name from the French town of Albi), springing from disgust occasioned by wealthy and worldly clergy, rejected the material world as evil and polluted and went so far as to elevate to its supreme sacrament suicide by starvation. While some Albigensians, the "perfect," purified themselves in utter abstention from such hateful things as sex, others, less perfect but relying in faith upon the sanctifying works of their starving saints, abandoned themselves to happy lechery. Saint Dominic (see 11.34 and note) founded his mendicant Order of Preachers to combat this heresy, and Folquet assisted him in the founding of the order, and himself took the lead in a Crusade against the Albigensians. In addition, he was present at the Fourth Lateran Council—a council ranking with Nicaea, Chalcedon, and Trent as one of the most significant in the history of the Church, as it reaffirmed, against doubts raised by the students of the newly rediscovered works of Aristotle, the presence of Christ in the Eucharist, body, blood, soul, and divinity. In so doing it reaffirmed the natural goodness of creation in general and of the flesh in particular; in celebration of which eucharistic truth Pope Innocent III proclaimed the new feast day of Corpus Christi. As in Cunizza, in Folquet love is a burning zeal, affirming the beautiful and reprehending the foul.

P. 95, L. 97. *On me:* Folquet burned in love on earth, as did the mythical lovers he names: *Dido,* who loved Aeneas (Virgil, *Aen.* 4.54–55; *Sychaeus* was Dido's deceased husband, *Creusa* was Aeneas's deceased wife); Phyllis *of Rhodope,* who hanged herself when *Demophoön* left her (Ovid, *Heroides* 2); *Hercules,* who fell in love with *Iole* and died when, unwittingly, his jealous wife, Deianira, gave him as a love charm the poisoned shirt of the centaur Nessus (cf. *Inf.* 12.67; Ovid, *Met.* 9.101–58).

P. 95, L. 115. *Rahab:* The earliest Christians saw the harlot Rahab as one of the blessed; Saint Paul says that she assisted Joshua out of faith (cf. Heb. 11:31; also Jas. 2:25). That she was a type—a foreshadowing—of the Church is made more credible when one recalls that Joshua and Jesus are in fact the same Hebrew name. The point was common among the Church Fathers. Moses, representing the Old Law, could lead the people only to the brink of the Jordan, nor could he himself cross. It was Joshua, the foreshadowing of his namesake Jesus, who actually led the people to the Promised Land. Rahab's questionable past is no obstacle against the symbolism, since the Church is ever in need of reform: "I am black, but comely" (Sg. 1:5). Thus, like Cunizza and Folquet, Rahab—the Church—is a sinner redeemed and sacrificing herself in love for her Redeemer. And, like Folquet, Rahab assisted one Joshua in the conquest of the Holy Land—unlike the present pope and other leaders of the Church, who go about whoring for money while leaving the Holy Land in the grip of the Turk. For that sort of whoring and pimping, Dante shows no mercy (cf. *Inf.* 19.55–57; see also Hos. 1:2 and passim for whoring as an image of turning away from faith in God).

P. 97, L. 127. *Your city:* Florence, founded by Satan!

P. 97, L. 132. *turned their shepherd into a wolf:* "Beware of false prophets, which come to you in sheep's clothing, but inwardly they are ravening wolves" (Matt. 7:15).

CANTO TEN

For wisdom, says Solomon, is the splendor of eternal light. Wisdom is the light wherein things are beheld truly; yet for Dante, and for the mystics of the Middle Ages, it is more. It is the very beholding of the light, a beholding enabled by the light of Wisdom, transforming the beholder into light. This is the sphere of the wise, but, more properly, it is the sphere of souls whom the indwelling Spirit of Wisdom has made most bright.

P. 99, L. 1. *Power:* God the Father, looking upon *his begotten Son,* in their mutual Spirit of Love, who is breathed forth from both (Aquinas, *Summa theol.* 1.36.4; the word "both" is hotly disputed, however, by Eastern Orthodox Christians). The Trinity is the Power, Wisdom, and Love that creates, orders, and sustains all things; to the Father is attributed creation, not because the Son and the Spirit share no part in it, but because creation is his by "appropriation" to his person as Father (Aquinas, *Summa theol.* 1.45.6). Dante's doxology and his formal description of the heavens, followed by a direct address to the reader, mark a kind of division in Paradise. Just as Canto 10 of *Inferno* separated sinners who loved things that were good in themselves but who loved them inordinately and idolatrously from sinners who chose wickedness for its own sake, and as Canto 10 of *Purgatory* separated souls waiting to atone from those actually being purged, so Canto 10 of *Paradise* separates saints to whom attaches some lightest shadow for immoderate love or desire for glory or simply fear from those blessed absolutely according to the gifts they were given by God's grace: wisdom (the sun), courage (Mars), justice (Jupiter), contemplative vision (Saturn), and, summing them all, the theological virtues of faith, hope, and love (the fixed stars). All souls, it must be remembered, dwell in the Empyrean, but the souls we have seen thus far were justly allegorized by those lower planets across whose paths the shadow of the earth was thought to fall. Here, however, all is light and all is love, and the poet begins with a breathtaking call to the reader to behold with wonder the splendid artistry of the Creator of the heavens and the earth.

P. 101, L. 23. *whet the appetite:* The metaphor of eating is not to be taken merely symbolically. The whole of the *Paradise* can be conceived as a poetic attempt to describe the mystery of the Eucharist, wherein the blessed form the Body of Christ by being conformed to Christ, and are conformed to Christ in what Pseudo-Dionysius calls the sacrament of synaxis, of union in Christ, receiving the light who is Christ (*Ecclesiastical Hierarchy* 424C and passim).

P. 101, LL. 27–28. *to write / What I have seen:* Literally, Dante says that he must turn back to the material whereof he has been made a scribe. The idea that he is not a creator but an amanuensis of what is revealed to him runs throughout the *Comedy* (cf. *Purg.* 24.52–54; *Par.* 17.136–42; 27.64–66) and links Dante with the apostle of the Apocalypse (cf. Rev. 1:11; 1:19, and passim).

P. 101, L. 29. *whose light divides the day:* Cf. Gen. 1:14–18.

P. 101, L. 30. *heavenly power:* Until well beyond the Renaissance it was thought that the sun not only fostered life on earth but could bring it into being spontaneously, as in the fertile mud of the Nile, and that the sun was the ultimate source of the brightness of jewels and gold and of their particular "virtues," or properties.

P. 101, L. 39. *her act has no extent in time:* As Dante has already suggested, the transitions from sphere to sphere are instantaneous. We are in eternity, where "before" and "after" have reference only to our pilgrimage of knowledge, our minds illumined by grace.

P. 101, L. 42. *their own intensity of light:* "And they that shall be wise shall shine as the brightness of the firmament; and they that turn many to righteousness, as the stars for ever and ever" (Dan. 12:3).

P. 101, L. 51. *He breathes His spirit and begets His Son:* Ital. *spira* and *figlia,* "breathes" and "sons," the latter as a transitive verb. The life of the Trinity is the source of the saints' desire and the fulfillment of their hunger. The reader may note that from now on the souls with whom Dante speaks will often be said to "breathe" their words forth, imparting to him the knowledge that the Spirit has breathed upon them.

P. 103, L. 60. *forgotten in eclipse:* Forgotten, by the "shadow" of intense light! This is the first time Dante says he has momentarily forgotten about Beatrice, but it will not be the last. The theology she symbolizes is leading us into the presence of wonders for whose understanding theology is but instrumental, nor can theology steep us in the essence of those wonders.

P. 103, L. 72. *laden with them the memory cannot leave:* For the memory's incapacity to retain more than a trace of Paradise, see 1.10–12 and 33.67–75; that is different from Dante's boasting about its power to present Hell, *Inf.* 2.7–9.

P. 103, L. 74. *fashion yourself a wing:* of contemplation, which, according to the medieval mystics, is none other than the soul's rapt love for Christ. Cf. Is. 40:31: "But they that hope in the Lord shall mount, as on the wings of eagles."

P. 103, L. 87. *without climbing up anew:* Note the reversal of the threat of Hell (cf. Virgil, *Aen.* 6.128–29; *Inf.* 3.9; 3.85; 5.19–20; 8.91–92) and the waiving of the warning of Purgatory (*Purg.* 9.131–32). Hell is easy to enter but hard to leave; if you look back in Purgatory you are cast outside but you will reenter; once you have been graced to see Paradise, you will return, and no warning need be given.

P. 105, L. 89. *would not be free:* To deny Dante's thirst (cf. Matt. 25:35; Is. 55:1) would be to act against the nature of blessedness, which is, as Piccarda says, "to live in loving" (3.78); it would be, in fact, to sin, and thereby to lose both power and freedom. What satisfies thirst is Wisdom—Christ, the Wisdom of God: "[Wisdom] hath mingled her wine; she hath also furnished her table" (Prov. 9:2).

428 · Notes for Canto Ten

P. 105, L. 96. *where you can fatten well, if you don't rove:* The meaning of this colorful and enigmatic line will be revealed later (11.118–39). For now, the reader should mark how often in this canto and in the mouth of this speaker Dante uses images of eating and drinking. For eating and drinking were a source of innocent delight for this speaker when he dwelt within his cherubic body on earth; and they were the vehicles of the Eucharist, the sacrament of union with Christ, whereof this same speaker also sang (see Appendix C). He is the Angelic Doctor, the great theologian and philosopher, and the writer of the most deeply moving eucharistic hymns in the treasury of the Church, Saint Thomas Aquinas (1225–74; canonized in 1323, two years after the death of Dante). Against the worldly wishes of his family, Aquinas joined the new order of Dominican friars in 1243, moving from his home near Monte Cassino to study at Paris and Cologne under the greatest thinkers of his time. These included *Albert of Cologne,* or Saint Albert the Great, a theologian and scientist from whom Aquinas adopted the Aristotelian stance that all human knowledge has its beginning in the senses. After he had completed his studies and had taught for a few years in Cologne, Aquinas returned to Paris and produced his staggering compendia of theology, the *Summa theologiae* and the *Summa contra gentiles.*

P. 105, L. 98. *Albert of Cologne:* Saint Albert the Great (1197?–1280), Dominican friar and the teacher of Thomas Aquinas. As a philosopher, Albert was persuaded that Christianity and Aristotelianism were compatible. His comfort with the this-worldly epistemology of Aristotle is manifest in his encyclopedia of facts (or sometimes suppositions) about the properties of plants, animals, and minerals.

P. 105, L. 104. *Gratian:* The most important canon lawyer of the Middle Ages was the Camaldolese monk Francis Gratian, whose work, known as the *Decretals,* dates from the early to the middle twelfth century. This work is a digest of canon law, Scripture, and citations from the Church Fathers, and attempts to come to some clear synthesis on ecclesial matters. It merits praise regardless of the wicked use to which grasping churchmen may put it (9.133–38).

P. 105 L. 107. *his widow's mite:* Dante alludes to the prologue of Peter Lombard's *Sentences,* wherein he compares his offering of his work to the widow's giving her last little coin to the temple (Luke 21.1–4).

P. 105, L. 111. *gluttonous to hear of him:* The salvation of Solomon had been a subject of some doubt, since in his old age he allowed his foreign wives to build altars to their gods (1 Kings 11:4–12).

P. 107, L. 131. *Isidore . . . Bede . . . Richard:* Isidore of Seville (560?–636), theologian and collector of oddments of knowledge and folklore, whose *Sentences* and *Etymologies* enjoyed wide repute in the Middle Ages; the Venerable Bede (674–735), Augustinian monk at Jarrow, where he wrote works of theology and the great *Ecclesiastical History of the English People;* Richard of Saint Victor (fl.

twelfth century), mystic and author of works such as *The Twelve Patriarchs, The Mystical Ark,* and *The Trinity,* whose fusion of precise distinction and subdivision of categories of experience in the contemplative life, with far-ranging allegorical exegesis, exercised a profound influence upon Dante's *Paradise.*

P. 107, L. 136. *Siger:* Siger of Brabant (1225?–1281?), the center of a critical intellectual controversy. For some time, philosophers and theologians had been studying the works of Aristotle, reintroduced into Europe first through Arab and Jewish translators working in Spain and then through direct examination and translation of the Greek manuscripts. Harmonizing Aristotelianism with Christian thought would have been a challenge in any case, given Aristotle's doctrine of the eternity of the cosmos and the lack of any governing providence in his notion of the First Mover. This challenge was made more acute by the works of the great commentator upon Aristotle's works, the Spanish Arab Averroës (1126–98). Averroës taught that matter and form are both perpetual, and that God's creation consisted in combining the two so that the forms could become embodied and the potentialities of matter actualized. (This language of act and potency is central also to the thinking of Aquinas, but Christians, interpreting Gen. 1:1 and John 1:1, had always asserted that God himself was the Creator of that unformed matter; cf. Augustine, *Conf.* 12.20. Aquinas, in addition, asserted that the forms also did possess an existence apart from the matter that embodied them, not in a realm of Platonic ideas but in the mind of God.) If the ontology of Averroës posed problems, his epistemology made those problems more acute. Since the work of God is not to create matter and form but to embody form in matter, making the forms intelligible to our understanding, it seems that we are but passive receptacles for the light God shines upon us from without. God—or his function as what Averroës called the Active (Agent) Intellect—makes whatever strikes our senses and our imagination (our passive intellect). But since this passive intellect does not act on its own and is only individuated from other passive intellects by the sense impressions it experiences in its body, it seems that when the body dies the person dies too, for all that the intellect, or soul, as abstract and unindividuated form, may be immortal.

Siger, dean of the faculty of the University of Paris, was a man in love with controversy, and brought himself much renown (and caused himself much trouble) by his carefree Averroism. Against Siger, Aquinas wrote *On the Unity of the Intellect,* maintaining no cleft between passive and active intellect in the human soul (cf. *Purg.* 25.61–75). Then Siger was condemned in 1270 by the conservative archbishop of Paris, Stephen Tempier, who in the notorious Condemnation of 1277 forbade the teaching of various of Siger's doctrines. It should be noted that Tempier's reaction was not against Averroism merely. Many Christian thinkers, chief among them the Franciscans led by Saint Bonaventure (also a teacher at the University of Paris), were deeply suspicious of the latent atheism and patent materialism they thought they saw in Aristotle, and of the desiccation of piety, of contemplative wonder, they thought that Aristotelianism produced. Thus several of Aquinas's own teachings were condemned there, and for a short time, in some quarters, the thought of the Angelic Doctor himself fell under the suspicion of heresy. This may explain why Thomas so cheerfully approves of Siger here and (gently) reproves the condemnation. It will not be the only case of intellectual rivals uniting in the sphere of the wise: Thomas's friendship with Bonaventure, whom we will meet in Canto 12, is surely far warmer now than it ever was on earth.

CANTO ELEVEN

Blessed are the poor, for theirs is the kingdom of Heaven. How odd that perhaps the greatest theologian who ever lived should sing the praises of the simple man of God—Francis, the poor barefoot beggar who dashed off songs in Italian but was never reported to have read books. Francis's wisdom, though, is hard to gainsay: you give up the trifles of wealth and you follow Christ, and in following him you gain not only eternity but joy in the beauty of this small world too.

P. 111, L. 1. *O senseless strife of mortals:* The language and sentiment derive from the ancient satirist Persius: "O cares of mortal men, O what folly in all your affairs" (*Satires* 7.1). Wisdom consists, in the first instance, in turning away from trifles.

P. 111, LL. 2–3. *flap / your wings:* So Richard of Saint Victor describes those whose contemplation reaches only the consideration of earthly things: "In any case, they fly well on these wings who daily consider the deceitful nature of earthly mutability and, by continual reconsideration, separate themselves from the vain desire for it. Thus, although you may not be able to fly as far as heavenly things on these two wings, nevertheless perhaps by flapping them you will be able to find a safe and tranquil haven" (*Ark* 10). The people Dante describes do not even do so much. They have fallen to the lures of the world that cheats (cf. 10.126); the lesson of these lines derives directly from Boethius (cf. *Cons. Phil.* 3 m. 8).

P. 113, L. 33. *with a cry:* Cf. Mark 15:37: "And Jesus cried with a loud voice, and gave up the ghost."

P. 113, L. 40. *Of one I'll speak:* The Dominican Thomas's narrative of the life of Saint Francis of Assisi will be mirrored, in form and content, by the Franciscan Bonaventure's narrative of the life of Saint Dominic (12.31–105); to this day Franciscans and Dominicans continue the tradition, begun in the earliest days of the orders, of preaching the sermon on the feast day of the founder of the other order. This tradition bespeaks more than polite affection: from the first, the Franciscans tended to the mystical, preserving even in their university teachings something of the antiratiocinative suspicions of their founder, for whom ardor of love was the finest preaching, while the Dominicans tended to the rational and analytical, preserving the charism of their founder, Dominic, who was spurred by a desire to fight the Albigensian heresy (cf. note at 9.95), armed with a life of poverty and charity but also with every intellectual tool available. Of course, I speak of inclinations only: Aquinas's mystical zeal shines through in his eucharistic hymns, and Bonaventure was no mean philosopher.

The details of Francis's life derive from the stories told about him while he was alive and set down in writing afterward by several of his disciples, including Bonaventure himself. From that hagiography Dante has selected certain motifs. First, Francis was a lover. That ardor is evident in Francis's own poetry (see Appendix D), for the saint was the first great poet of the Italian vernacular, in love with all of God's creation and—like Dominic, but unlike the present Dominicans, says Thomas—in love with his lady, *Poverty.* Second, Francis was a fighter. This lover of peace had the soul of a Crusader: like a champion in a tournament he won the hand of Lady Poverty against his father's opposition. The story goes that the young Francis Bernardone had been having dreams in which he was instructed to rebuild Christ's Church. Taking the command literally—there was always a winning straightforwardness and practicality about the poor man of God—he attempted to repair some of the churches in Assisi, finally borrowing from the till of his merchant father, *Pietro Bernardone,* to purchase the materials. His father accused him of theft, in the market square of Assisi, before *the spiritual court*—that is, before the bishop. With brave panache Francis turned the tables on his father, disowning *him,* stripping himself and flinging his clothes at him, saying that he wanted none of them. Recognizing that Francis was moved by the Spirit, the bishop embraced the lad with his own cloak and claimed him for the Church. Such impetuosity characterized Francis's life: as when he stowed himself on a Crusader ship and marched, without arms, before the sultan Saladin, to preach the gospel. Finally, Francis was a father and a shepherd of his flock, inspiring men to follow him in his at once simple and outlandish life, teaching them by his humility and by the wisdom that humility brings, rebuking them for any sign of worldliness, and recommending to them his Lady Poverty when he lay dying (the worth of poverty was a vexed issue in Dante's day; see note at 12.124). Poverty *alone*—the humiliation of owning nothing, not so much as a rag to cover one's nakedness—remained beside Christ on the Cross, and in his embrace of humble poverty, being conformed to Christ the Bridegroom (cf. Luke 9:58), Francis was granted the grace also to bear in his own flesh the marks of Christ crucified.

P. 113, L. 53. Ascesi: Tuscan for Assisi, but the Italian word means also "I have arisen," and Dante catches the symbolism of it, saying that the proper name for the birthplace of Francis is *Oriente;* "I will bring my servant the Orient" (Zech. 3:8, Vulgate). That word, in Latin, means "in the east," the direction of rising; churches faced west to east so that the priest at the altar would face *ad Orientem,* to the Rising One, Christ. I have attempted to translate accordingly.

P. 115, L. 62. *before his father:* Lat. *coram patre.* The language is juridical, but derives also from the gospels and refers to God. Thus before his earthly father Francis gives himself wholly to his heavenly Father.

P. 115, L. 79. *Bernard:* Bernard of Quintavalle, Francis's first disciple, gave all his goods to the poor, and was, as Francis's eldest son and heir, soon to be followed by the young visionary *Egidio* and the parish priest *Silvestro.*

P. 115, L. 83. *doff their shoes:* This humble sign follows the command Christ gave to his disciples: "Provide neither gold, nor silver, nor brass in your purses, nor scrip for your journey, neither two coats, neither shoes, nor yet staves" (Matt. 10:10).

P. 117, L. 92. *Pope Innocent:* Remarkably, this is the only time Dante refers to the greatest and most powerful pope of the Middle Ages, Innocent III (1198–1216). Legend had it that Innocent, not knowing what to make of the uncouth-looking Francis, dreamed that the Lateran itself was toppling, until it was steadied again upon the back of the man of Assisi. Innocent agreed to sanction the Franciscan way of life, on condition—for Innocent was a shrewd man who well knew the peril of unreined enthusiasms—that Francis adopt a written rule for the brothers. This rule was then officially approved by Pope *Honorius* III in 1223.

P. 117, L. 107. *his final seal:* The details of the vision that preceded Francis's reception of the stigmata are interesting: Christ appeared to him as a six-winged Seraph, nailed to a cross. Not in intellectual endeavor but in ardent prayer and love, both for Christ and for man, Francis contemplated Christ; but to contemplate Christ fully is to receive Christ, to be conformed to Christ. Indeed, Saint Bonaventure (whom we meet in the next canto) links contemplation and love of Christ with both the rapture of Saint Paul—so often alluded to in these notes—and the stigmata of Saint Francis (*Itinerarium* prol. 3).

P. 117, L. 117. *no other bier:* Francis wanted to die as he had lived. Knowing that his death was near, he asked his brothers to strip him and lay him outside the town gate: so, says Dante, he died in the arms of the lady he loved so well.

CANTO TWELVE

How good and pleasant it is for brethren to dwell in unity! On earth, Franciscan strives against Franciscan, and Dominicans stray from their founder, and Franciscan and Dominican each look with suspicion upon the other. In Paradise they are one. That is not a testament to their complacency, but to the Wisdom wherein they are made one. Brotherhood is specious if not founded in truth—the truth to whose preaching Dominic gave his life.

P. 123, L. 14. *echoing:* The image is charged with theological significance: Pseudo-Dionysius uses it to discuss the means by which the light of God is passed along and diffused from one celestial hierarchy to that below, and Dante will use the image of the reflected rainbow again (33.118–20) when seeking an image of the

Trinity. Here it suggests intimacy and distinction between the two garlands. The first is Aristotelian, legal, philosophical, historical, Dominican; the second, Platonic, theological, prophetic, Franciscan—but the reader should not press the distinction too far.

P. 125, LL. 26–27. *twin eyelashes ... single flash:* another image of the duality and unity that characterize both the relationship between the two champions of the Church, Francis and Dominic, and the style and content of Cantos 10–13.

P. 125, L. 37. *so dear a price:* the blood of God made man; no price could be greater (cf. 1 Cor. 6:20).

P. 127, L. 55. *the amorous servant:* Ital. *l'amoroso drudo. Drudo* derives from late Latin *drudus,* "believer," "man of faith," and was used in the vernacular poetry merely to denote a paramour (cf. Cavalcante, *In un boschetto,* line 14). Thus the "Franciscan" virtue of love is bound with the "Dominican" virtue of faith, and just as Thomas had gone out of his way to call Francis a champion, Bonaventure now goes out of his way to call Dominic an ardent lover.

Saint Dominic de Guzmán (c. 1171–1221), born in Caleruega in Old Castile, was the founder of the order that bears his name. He assumed as his vocation the support of Catholic orthodoxy, and the combat against heresy, by means of charismatic preaching and by the embracing of poverty. In their very different ways, both Francis and Dominic had to face an issue of theology and culture that had become pressing as Europe, and the Church with it, grew prosperous: what do we make of material goods? The Waldensian sect of Lombardy and Switzerland preached community of goods, as among the early apostles (cf. Acts 2:44–45), but also abjured private property for all believers (as Saint Paul certainly did not do) and rejected the hierarchical Church. Francis's response to this, as it were, was to embrace poverty while accepting the discipline of the Church and affirming both the goodness of material creation and the need for some people to own things in order that man might live—to farm, to mine and quarry, to weave, to hew, to trade, and so on. Dominic's response to the more aristocratic and intellectual Albigensian heresy, with its elaborated theories on the evil of the material world, was also to live in poverty, not because material goods were in themselves evil, but to make himself a credible preacher of the truth. And credible he was, founding in his own lifetime four monasteries, twenty priories, and eight provinces, and sending his friars to work from Britain to Palestine. Bonaventure once described Francis as the "new athlete of Christ," but the word "athlete"—meaning at that time a champion defending the just cause—more fittingly describes the tactical, single-minded fighter Dominic, whose order was approved in 1216 by Honorius III but who had begged Innocent III as early as 1205 for permission to preach in Provence against the Albigensians.

P. 127, L. 60. *made his mother a prophet:* Legend had it that Dominic's mother, while bearing the child, dreamed of a black and white dog. The Dominicans wore (and still wear) black and white robes, and were nicknamed *Domini canes,* "dogs of the Lord."

P. 127, L. 71. *Christ:* The name above every other name (Phil. 2:9) cannot fittingly be rhymed with any other word: only Christ is like Christ. This marks the first of four instances in which Dante will employ the triple "rhyme" on the name of the Son (cf. 14.104–8; 19.104–8; 32.83–87).

P. 127, L. 78. *It is for this I've come:* In prayer Dominic puts on Christ, adopting Christ's words of evangelism: "Let us go into the next towns, that I may preach there also: for therefore came I forth" (Mark 1:38).

P. 129, L. 98. *apostolic duty:* Dominic's comrade and friend, later Pope Gregory IX (who canonized Dominic in 1234), said of the saint that he lived the apostolic life to perfection.

P. 131, L. 110. *Tom:* Ital. *Tomma,* a variant of Tommaso. I cannot help suspecting a familiar form here that can be rendered only by the diminutive. That is fitting, since the cantos in the sphere of the sun are filled with touches of the small and sweet and familiar (cf. 14.61–66 and note at 14.64).

P. 131, LL. 119–120. *weed…bin:* Bonaventure alludes to the admonitory parable of the tares (Matt. 13:24–30). The wheat and the tares are permitted to grow up together indiscriminately but will be separated at the Last Judgment, one for harvest and the other for the fire. I have translated to bring out the allusion, but the Italian *arca,* here rendered "bin," means "ark," in the sense of the biblical ship or, far more commonly, a treasure box; and that calls into play the typological association of Noah's ark with the Church (and being left out of the ark means to be denied salvation; cf. 1 Pet. 3:20–21), and also what Jesus has to say about poverty and treasure: "Sell what ye have, and give alms; provide yourselves bags which wax not old, a treasure in the heavens that faileth not, where no thief approacheth, neither moth corrupteth. For where your treasure is, there will your heart be also" (Luke 12:33–34).

P. 131, L. 124. *not from Acquasparta or Casal:* Saint Francis was a troubadour, a mystic, not an administrator. He had no desire to gather any very large following of "poor little brothers," nor would he have known what to do with them all. But as the Franciscans grew, and as it became clear that if they were to preach to the laity they must be at least as well educated as the laity, they saw the need to become involved in the new universities. That would have been impossible, however, if every friar had to beg for bread every day. Clearly, the charism of poverty had to be reconciled with the effective preaching of the gospel—these could not be at odds. Bonaventure himself, as head of the Franciscan order, steered the rule gently toward an accommodation that would make evangelical sense, given the circumstances, without violating the heart of Franciscan commitment to poverty. But factions divided the order in the late thirteenth century. Some verged upon the body-despising Manicheanism that the poor Saint Francis, who sang of Brother Fire and Sister Water, would have found appalling; Ubertino da Casale was a defender of these strict Franciscans, the so-called "spirituals," and was finally accused of heresy in 1325. The cardinal and theologian Matthew of Acquasparta (a friend of Dante's nemesis Boniface VIII and a furtherer of the pope's political designs in Florence) favored the gentler application of the rule and was closer in spirit to Bonaventure than Dante would like to admit.

P. 131, L. 127. *Bonaventure:* Saint Bonaventure (1221–74), born in *Bagnoregio,* near Bolsena, called the Seraphic Doctor; elected general of the Franciscan order in 1256 and made cardinal in 1272. Bonaventure was a contemporary of Aquinas at the University of Paris. The work of his that influenced Dante the most, especially in the *Paradise,* was his *Itinerarium mentis in Deum* (*The Journey of the Mind into God*). The mystical ascent Bonaventure outlines (as derived from *The Twelve Patriarchs* and *The Mystical Ark* of Richard of Saint Victor) fires Dante's imagination, in these realms, more than do the analyses and arguments of Aquinas.

P. 131, L. 129. *the left-hand bounty of the world:* the riches and honor that Wisdom deals out from her left hand (Prov. 3:16).

P. 131, L. 133. *Hugh of Saint Victor:* abbot of Saint Victor (1097?–1141), a monastery near Paris that in the twelfth century enjoyed a magnificent flowering of works of Christian philosophy and mysticism. The potent blend of careful, particular analysis (of words and symbols especially) and mystical imagination characteristic of the Victorine scholars was congenial to both Bonaventure and Dante. Hugh's most important works were *On the Sacraments of the Christian Faith* and *In Praise of Charity.*

P. 131, L. 136. *Nathan:* He is the prophet who rebuked David for his stealing Bathsheba, the wife of his loyal soldier Uriah (2 Sam. 11:2–12:14), but who also revealed to David the future of his house (2 Sam. 7:1–17), which he would establish forever. This promise was interpreted by the Jews as foretelling the everlasting reign of the Messiah (cf. John 12:34), and the New Testament accordingly sees it as the establishment of the Church, with Christ as its head.

P. 131, L. 137. *Chrysostom:* John Chrysostom, the Golden-Mouthed (345–407), one of the four eastern Fathers of the Church. His work was known to Dante only by citations of the western Fathers or by citations of those citations in the medieval theologies.

P. 131, L. 137. *Anselm:* Saint Anselm of Canterbury (1033–1109), called the first of the scholastics, used philosophy to try to clarify the truths of the revealed faith. Anselm described his attempts thus: *Credo ut intelligam,* "I believe, that I may understand." He is the author of the *Proslogion,* the treatise that presents the so-called ontological proof of the existence of God, a proof more famous than closely considered, rejected rather negligently by Aquinas (*Summa Theol.* 1.2.1) but taken up again by Descartes and Leibnitz and, more recently, by the mathematicians Kurt Goedel and Roger Penrose. For the influence upon Dante of Anselm's treatise on the Incarnation, *Cur Deus homo,* see note at 7.57.

P. 133, L. 140. *Joachim:* Joachim of Flora (1130?–1202), Cistercian monk who wrote apocalyptic works on the Church's present crisis and future restoration (as did Dante himself; cf. *Purg.* 32), and who both Franciscans and Dominicans claimed as having prophesied the institution of their orders. Joachim was what is now called a dispensationalist, preaching that the Church was verging upon a new dispensation, the age of the Holy Spirit, following the (lapsed) dispensations of Father and Son. Bonaventure opposed his ideas, as Aquinas opposed the ideas of Siger of Brabant (cf. note at 10.136).

P. 133, L. 142. *a paladin:* The word is normally used of the twelve peers who fought beside Charlemagne and who figure in so many Christian chivalric romances; here it resumes the motif of Dominic as champion of the Church.

CANTO THIRTEEN

Precept upon precept, line upon line, says the prophet, mocking the Israelites who were too weary at heart to acquire the wisdom of the Lord. Solomon begged for wisdom within his proper sphere as ruler, says Thomas in this canto; but most people, theological weaklings though they are, do the reverse, straying well beyond their sphere to muse upon matters hidden in the darkness of providence.

P. 137, L. 25. *Not Bacchus there, not Paean do they sing:* Bacchus and Apollo (Paean) are false gods, actually also false sons of gods; instead the souls sing of the triune God and the true Son of God.

P. 139, L. 52. *What has to die and what can never die:* The former are created by God through an intermediary cause, the latter directly (cf. 7.133–44). The entire universe is a reflection and diffusion of the light of the Trinity; not a reflection of that light upon things already existent, but as Etienne Gilson puts it, commenting upon the *Celestial Hierarchy* and the *Ecclesiastical Hierarchy* of Pseudo-Dionysius, "a gift of light which is their very being" (*History of Christian Philosophy in the Middle Ages* [New York, 1954], 83).

P. 139, L. 56. *dis-one:* Ital. *disuna,* Dante's coinage, as is the next line's *s'intrea,* "en-threes itself," *the threeing of their Love.* Dante's lines employ "improper rhyme" on the word for "one": *disuna, aduna,* and, climactically, *una,* with obvious intent to stress the nature of the Trinity, three Persons in one God.

P. 139, L. 72. *various gifts of ingenuity:* an issue already discussed by Charles Martel (8.124–33).

P. 139, L. 74. *at the peak:* as was the case at the first spring equinox, the moment of creation (cf. *Inf.* 1.37–40; *Par.* 1.37–43; and note at 1.41).

P. 141, L. 96. *not to muse:* Dante has adapted the words of the Lord to Solomon, expressing his pleasure in what Solomon did request and in what he did not request: "And God said unto him, Because thou hast asked this thing, and hast not asked for thyself long life; neither hast asked riches for thyself, nor hast asked the life of thine enemies; but hast asked for thyself understanding to discern judgment; behold, I have done according to thy words: lo, I have given thee a wise and understanding heart; so that there was none like thee before thee, neither after thee shall any arise like unto thee. And I have also given thee that which thou hast not asked, both riches, and honor: so that there shall not be any among the kings like unto thee all thy days" (1 Kings 3:11–13). Dante's point seems to be that the man who would be wise should first seek justice with a pure heart (Wis. 1:1), and then the other sort of wisdom, the philosophical wisdom here presented, may well be added unto it. And in fact to Solomon, who preferred wisdom to scepter and throne (Wis. 7:8), are attributed Proverbs, Wisdom, and the Song of Songs, works of practical, moral, theological, and even mystical wisdom. Solomon's prayer for wisdom acknowledges, moreover, the limitations of man, who dwells in the body (Wis. 9:13–18).

P. 141, L. 100. *whether an uncaused motion can exist:* One of the five ways of demonstrating the existence of God, according to Aquinas, is to prove that there cannot be a motion without a cause (*Summa theol.* 1.2.3; *Summa con. gen.* 1.13; Aristotle, *Prior Analytics* 1.16). Unless the term "motion" includes God's eternal creation, then the answer to this question is no.

P. 141, L. 102. *triangle:* The first three examples in this list of questions Solomon did not pose were philosophical; the last is mathematical, geometric to be precise, with suggestions, however, of the mysteries of Trinitarian theology (cf. 33.133–36 and note). On any circle (and only on a circle), any triangle with the diameter as its base must be a right triangle (Euclid, *Elements* 3.31).

P. 143, L. 117. *haste:* "Seest thou a man that is hasty in his words? There is more hope of a fool than of him" (Prov. 19:20).

P. 143, L. 125. *Melissus, Bryson, and Parmenides:* The Italian adds *e molti,* "and many." Parmenides and Melissus were philosophers who flourished in Greece in the fifth century B.C.; Parmenides was fascinated by ontology and argued that all things in the universe must be the manifestation of an eternal and changeless One. Plato was sympathetic to Parmenides' philosophy, but Aristotle, with his insight that change and growth are inseparable from a contingent being and from the realization of its end, or telos, criticized both with great severity: "Now to investigate whether Being is one and motionless is not a contribution to the science of Nature. For just as the geometer has nothing more to say to one who denies the principles of his science... so a man investigating *principles* cannot argue with one who denies their existence. For if Being is just one, and one in the way mentioned, there is a principle no longer, since a principle must be the principle of some things or others.... Their premises [those of Parmenides and Melissus, that the ground of all being must be one and motionless] are false and their conclusions do not follow. Or rather the argument of Melissus is gross and palpable and offers no difficulty at all: accept one ridiculous proposition and the rest follows—a simple enough proceeding" (*Physics* 1.2, 185a). Aristotle also refuted Bryson's attempts to square the circle. For a guess as to why Dante inveighs against these three in particular, see note at line 127 below.

P. 143, L. 127. *Sabellius, Arius:* Sabellius (d. 265) denied the Trinity; Arius (d. 336) denied that Christ was the only-begotten, coeternal Son of the Father. In Parmenides and Melissus we have a sense-violating denial of motion, which results in the confounding of Creator with creation, since all being is thought to be identical and one. It is a mistaking of plurality. In these heretics, rather, we have a denial of Trinity and Incarnation—of the Christian doctrines that assert the unity of three Persons in one Godhead and the unity of two natures in Christ. The errors misconstrue the three mysteries (creation, Trinity, and Incarnation) revealed to Dante in the beatific vision (33.85–141). Another way to think of it—a way that explains the inclusion of the mathematical Bryson here, and his counterpart circle-squaring geometer's inclusion at 33.133–36, is that the errors confound the meanings of one, two, and three (cf. 14.28–33), and that they misunderstand the distinctions between, and the relations between, what is infinite and changeless (the circle, symbolizing the eternal) and what is finite, plural, and subject to change (the square, symbolizing the world of the four elements). Dante's passage seems to echo Gregory the Great's condemnation of preachers who only think they know the Scripture: "The hearts of little ones, already big with conception of the Word, they cleave with the sword of error, and thereby make a reputation, as it were, for their teaching" (*Pastoral Care* 3.24).

P. 143, LL. 130–131. *too sure / of what they judge:* It is the beginning of wisdom to recognize one's boundaries, one's limitations; it is a reverence for God the Creator. Jesus' parables are full of such reversals of the smug man's expectations as Thomas presents (cf. Luke 12:16–20).

CANTO FOURTEEN

Have ye here any meat? asked Jesus, and the disciples gave him a piece of broiled fish and part of a honeycomb. Not remarkable—except that the event takes place after the resurrection. A good Platonist can believe in the immortality of the soul, as a good Hindu or Tibetan Buddhist can believe in the shifting of the soul from one state to another. That the flesh itself should be glorified is another matter. But if God made that flesh and declared it good, why should it not also take part in glory?

P. 147, L. 28. *One and Two and Three:* One God in three Persons, the Second combining two natures, divine and human; cf. note at 13.127.

P. 147, L. 31. *Three times:* In the liturgy, the content and form of prayers are constructed to express the Trinity: the *Agnus Dei*, the *Sanctus*, the *Gloria*, and the *Credo*. So the angels sang whom Isaiah saw in a vision: "And one cried unto another, and said, Holy, holy, holy, is the Lord of hosts: the whole earth is full of his glory" (Is. 6:3).

P. 147, L. 42. *grace:* Grace, the free gift of God, grants the vision; the vision (as Thomas asserted) stirs love, and the souls shine in intensity accordant with that love. This too is a Trinitarian effect: from the power of the Father comes the wisdom of the Son that shines forth in the Love that is the Spirit.

P. 147, L. 45. *lovelier for being whole:* The point has already been made in the *Inferno* by Virgil (6.106–11). Following Aristotle and rejecting Plato, Aquinas argued that the human being is a body-soul unity, not a soul imprisoned in a body (*Summa con. gen.* 2.57); there are no preexisting human souls in some immaterial garden waiting to be transplanted into corporeality (*Summa theol.* 1.90.4). This means that the perfection of human bliss requires that the soul be reunited with the body (*Summa theol.* suppl. 80.4). Bonaventure says that since man sinned in the body, and since man was redeemed in the bodily resurrection of Christ, and since after all man by nature is made of soul and body, then justice, grace, and nature all demand that man be punished or blessed not in the soul merely but also in the body (*Brev.* 7.5).

P. 147, L. 52. *a fiery coal:* So Ezekiel describes the angels: "Their appearance was like burning coals of fire" (Ezek. 1:13).

P. 147, L. 59. *strong enough:* The glorified body will be made fit for the light of Paradise: "There are also celestial bodies, and bodies terrestrial: but the glory of the celestial is one, and the glory of the terrestrial is another" (1 Cor. 15:40). On the glorious light of the resurrected bodies, cf. Aquinas, *Summa theol.* suppl. 85.1.

P. 149, L. 64. *their mamas:* The Italian is the familiar form *mamme*. The souls long to be able to see again, in glory, the faces they held dear. It is a sweet touch of the homely and particular, such as we find so often in *Paradise*, and implicit in the doctrine of the resurrection of the body is the blessedness and wonder of the particular: of this face and no other, of the young woman, the *mamma*, smiling upon her child.

P. 149, L. 76. *O the true shimmering of the Holy Ghost:* charity itself, dwelling within them.

P. 149, L. 90. *a holocaust to God:* a burnt offering of the sort God likes best, humility (cf. Ps. 51:16–17; Hos. 6:6; Mic. 6:6–8).

P. 151, L. 106. *takes up his cross and follows Christ:* as the warriors of God, the Crusaders, did; and in so doing they were conformed to Christ. Cf. Luke 9:23; Matt. 16:24; Mark 8:34.

P. 151, L. 122. *a melody:* Earlier, Dante had trouble recognizing the lineaments of the sweet Piccarda; now, for the first time in Paradise, he has trouble hearing and understanding language itself. The hymns of *Purgatory* (there is no music in *Inferno*) are the familiar prayers of the daily office or of the mass; the hymns of *Paradise* (except for the *Regina Coeli*, 23.128), have no words we know. Pseudo-Dionysius had shied away from asserting any capacity in human language to describe God (*Div. Names* 1.1.3); we could say that God is "supereminently wise," but we would not be able to specify just what that means. But Aquinas had reexamined the problem of using language to refer to the divine, arguing that such epithets as "wise," in referring to God, need be neither univocal nor equivocal, but analogical: our notion of wisdom is not the same as God's wisdom, nor utterly unlike it, but an image of it, analogous to it (*Summa theol.* 1.13.5).

P. 151, L. 126. *"You arise" and "Conquer"*: "And the Lord said unto Joshua, Fear not, neither be thou dismayed: take all the people of war with thee, and arise, go up to Ai: see, I have given into thy hand the king of Ai, and his people, and his city, and his land" (Jos. 8:1). Joshua is a foreshadowing of Christ (cf. note at 9.115), and his entry into the Holy Land a foreshadowing of Christ's victory upon the Cross. The words of the song, once spoken to Joshua, apply to the resurrection of Christ, and to the victories won by the souls in this sphere—those victorious souls who literally and spiritually fought under the standard of the Cross, and who now, in the brilliance of the constellation of the cross, beam forth Christ.

CANTO FIFTEEN

I have fought the good fight, I have run the race to the finish, writes Paul to Timothy, anticipating the execution that could not be but soon. So much for the martial imagery whereof Paul is fond; but he continues, saying that even now he is being poured out like a libation. And there is the key: his very life, his blood, is a drink offering, a sacrifice. He fights who surrenders to the will of God; and at times God's will may be that one give up home and hearth, and fight, as did Dante's proud ancestor Cacciaguida.

P. 157, L. 4. *set a silence on that gentle lyre*: With gracious love the souls pause in their singing, giving Dante the chance to ask what he wishes.

P. 157, LL. 11–12. *love / of things that do not last eternally*: essentially the Boethian definition of folly and vice (*Cons. Phil.* 2 pr. 8).

P. 159, L. 27. *Aeneas in Elysium*: "And when through the green he saw Aeneas coming his way, he ran to him with both arms wide and tears trickling upon his cheeks" (Virgil, *Aen.* 6.684–86). Dante's reference to Aeneas works on several levels. Most obviously, it casts the prophecy and the moral judgments of Cacciaguida (whose identity as Dante's great-great-grandfather we are about to learn) in the context of the scene from the *Aeneid*. Aeneas has gone to the underworld to learn what he must do, now that he has landed in Italy. He also wishes to learn from Anchises how to avert the force of the curses aimed against him and to soothe the wrath of the goddess Juno. For his own attempt to call his city back to its true old Roman virtue and its place in the empire, Dante has been banished from Florence, with only a bare hope of returning (cf. 25.1–12), a hope that, as it happens, was never realized, as the poet died in Ravenna in 1321, still an exile. Next, the allusion to Virgil also binds that natural law so insisted upon in the *Inferno* and the *Purgatory* with the soaring mysticism of the *Paradise:* Cacciaguida is close in manner and in advice to Virgil, to Brunetto Latini (*Inf.* 15), and to Mark the Lombard (*Purg.* 16), and in him we see that, just as individual personality persists in Paradise, so does love of one's native land, because it too is given by God. There is a harmony between strapping on the shield of the red Cross to fight for Christ and standing up to see that your city maintain justice and decency. Furthermore, we are meant to think again about Dante's hesitancy before entering Hell: "I'm not Aeneas, I'm not Saint Paul!" (*Inf.* 2.32). So he protested; yet the poet knows that his namesake must play the part of both Aeneas and Saint Paul, reminding his countrymen of the duty they must render to Caesar and bringing them, by his vision, strength to perservere in the faith, that they may also render to God what is God's. Finally, the sweet father, Virgil (cf. Dante's poignant cry when he sees that Virgil has disappeared, *Purg.* 30.50), is now replaced by Cacciaguida, a true father to Dante, both spiritually and physically: family relations do not disappear but are revealed. Other than Virgil and Beatrice, no other interlocutor in the entire *Comedy* is given so much time to instruct Dante.

The entire scene between Dante and Cacciaguida is also heavily indebted to Cicero's *Somnium Scipionis,* or *Dream of Scipio,* originally the sixth book of his largely lost *Republic* but preserved separately and commented upon by Macrobius. That work features a young Publius Cornelius Scipio Africanus the Younger, visited in a dream by his grandfather and elder namesake, the Scipio who defeated Hannibal and was hailed as the savior of Rome (cf. 6.52; 27.63). The wisdom the elder Scipio gives to the younger is that of the vision of a providentially ordered cosmos, wherein the best a man can do is give himself in defense of his country (*Dream* 26.29).

P. 161, L. 73. *Love and the intellect:* What follows is a difficult passage of highly wrought rhetoric, whose immediate dramatic function is to have Cacciaguida know that Dante is too overcome to speak with perfect rationality. But the rhetoric clothes one of the most important theological and anthropological issues of the *Comedy.* Virgil had many occasions to speak to Dante about reason—that more earthly sister of intellect—and about will, which is impelled by affections, though it is not always to be directed by them. But never in his instruction could Virgil imagine a state in which the will, far more than free and obedient, was in perfect equilibrium with intellect. For good reason: that state is unattainable by sinful, mortal man. It was an old principle of alchemy that inequality of ingredients produces instability in the concoction. To attain that in-finitesimal apex, the thin-as-zero line of absolute balance, is to attain immor-tality and eternity. But that comes only as a gift of God's grace. Dante's words look forward to the end of the poem, when his desire and intellect will finally be made just, equal, and in perfect balance, like the wheeling of the immortal stars (33.143–45).

P. 161, L. 88. *who brought delight to me:* "And lo a voice from heaven, saying, This is my beloved Son, in whom I am well pleased" (Matt. 3:17).

P. 161, L. 90. *the root:* The speaker is Dante's great-great-grandfather Cacciaguida, about whom we know little more than what Dante tells us. He was the father of Alighiero, *the man from whom* Dante takes his name. Cacciaguida died in the Holy Land while on the Second Crusade with Conrad III, in 1147 or 1148.

P. 163, L. 97. *Florence:* not the first allusion in *Paradise* to Dante's city, but the first ut-terance of its name. Here begins Cacciaguida's proud reminiscences of old Flor-ence: the city was much smaller then, and its very smallness allowed for a stability and coherence among the important families. Its virtues were like those of the old Roman Republic, so praised in the *Dream of Scipio* (and in fact Cac-ciaguida alludes to the republic): its women were chaste, sober, and thrifty, ply-ing the loom while teaching their children about the Rome of old; dress and manners were simple; men stayed at home rather than go off to France to amass money; clothing was modest and decent; marriages were not yet financial merg-ers; lasciviousness in the bedroom had not yet vitiated true manhood. The ac-count does repeat what Dante himself has said about Florence's being too big and too rich, with "outsiders and your sudden wash of wealth" (*Inf.* 16.73). Yet it throws the malaise of Florence into high relief by its stark juxtaposition against a Florence at peace, with scenes of tender, intimate life at home interspersed among evocations of the names of once-prominent families and memories of Florentines who followed and obeyed the emperor, whether Hugh or Conrad.

P. 163, L. 106. *vacant of its family:* either because of exile or, more likely, because of the decadence and prodigality that are the ruin of many a wealthy house, whose scions are too greedy to have children or too wasteful to leave anything to them.

P. 163, L. 112. *Bellincion Berti:* father of "the womanly Gualdrada" and thus great-grandfather of the noble Florentine Guido Guerra (*Inf.* 16.37–38). He and the heads of the *Nerli* and *Vecchietto* families are examples of a natural city aristoc-racy dwelling in modesty and simplicity.

P. 163, L. 117. *the wool and loom:* The women of Florence were once like the good woman praised in Scripture: "She layeth her hands to the spindle" (Prov. 31:19).

P. 163, L. 118. *Fortunate women:* The exclamation, and the moral emphasis upon simplicity, derive from Virgil's *Georgics*, from a famous passage exhorting farm-ers to know their own good and to avoid the desire for luxury: "Ah too fortunate the husbandmen, did they know their own felicity! on whom far from the clash

of arms Earth their most just mistress lavishes from the soil a plenteous suste-
nance. Though no high proud-portalled house pours forth the vast tide of
morning visitants that fill her halls; though they feed no gaze on doors inlaid
with lovely tortoise-shell or raiment tricked out with gold or bronzes of
Ephyre; though the fleece's whiteness is not stained with Assyrian dye nor the
clear olive-oil spoiled for use with cinnamon; but careless quiet and life igno-
rant of disappointment, wealthy in manifold riches, but the peace of broad
lands, caverns and living lakes, and cool pleasances and the lowing of oxen and
soft slumbers beneath the tree fail not there; there are the glades and covers of
game, and youth hardy in toil and trained to simplicity, divine worship and rev-
erend age; among them Justice set her last footprints as she passed away from
earth" (2.458–74; translated by J. W. Mackail).

Dante portrays the continuity of traditional virtues by looking tenderly at
the haven these provide for women—for wives and mothers. It is a great com-
fort for them not to have to be buried, because of exile or the family's collapse,
anywhere else besides where their people have always been buried. Their hus-
bands do not abandon their beds, whoring after wealth in France. The women
pass along the traditions of their elders in so simple and unconscious a thing as
using the *sweet lisping talk* they heard their own parents use; and they tell leg-
ends about old *Rome* and about the *Trojans* who founded *Fiesole* in the days after
Aeneas settled in Italy. The reader should note that in any culture the telling of
stories—by mothers to their toddlers, by fathers and old men to youths—is a
means of instruction in who the members of a family or a nation are, what they
believe, and where their duty lies.

P. 165, L. 127. *A Lapo or Cianghella:* In 1300 Lapo Salterello, a Florentine poet and
political figure, assisted Boniface VIII in denouncing several of his fellow citi-
zens. But when his opponents the Black Guelphs rose to power in 1302, he was
condemned for bribe taking and banished from the city. Assuming that the ac-
cusation was just, the contrast with *Cincinnatus* is severe. Whereas Lapo was a
meddler who used political office for personal gain, Cincinnatus had to be
begged to take upon himself the office of dictator in Rome's time of peril, and
once he had done his job, retreated to his small farm. Cianghella was a young
widow who returned to her home in Florence to lead a life of wealthy de-
bauchery; *Cornelia,* mother of the land-reforming patriots Tiberius and Gaius
Gracchus, was a model of womanly chastity and honesty who once said that her
virtuous sons were her greatest treasure.

P. 165, L. 134. *Baptistery:* of Saint John the Baptist. For that site of entry into the
Church, Dante appears to have had a special affection (cf. *Inf.* 19.16–18; *Par.*
25.8–9). The child there at the moment of baptism receives his name, his iden-
tity: his membership in the Church and in that part of it called Florence, "the
sheepfold of Saint John" (16.25).

P. 165, L. 136. *Moronto and Eliseo:* Of them we have no certain knowledge, as we have none of Cacciaguida's wife.

P. 165, L. 139. *emperor Conrad:* Conrad III of Hohenstaufen (r. 1138–52) took part in the failed Second Crusade (1147–49), which featured a massacre of Christians beaten back from the city of Damascus.

CANTO SIXTEEN

Glorious things are spoken of thee, O Zion. If the order of grace presupposes the order of nature, then earthly cities are to reflect, though dimly, the glorious harmony of the City of God. Cacciaguida here resumes a thread of discussion broached by Justinian and developed by Charles Martel: the problem of the earthly city, and how it can live in some foreshadowing of eternal peace.

P. 167, L. 10. *voi:* In much of Italy today, especially in the south, the honorific pronoun is the second person plural, analogous to French *vous* and early modern English "you." Dante's contemporaries believed that Latin *vos* was first so used to address Julius Caesar, along with a host of other honorific titles (see Lucan, *Phars.* 5.385ff.). It is an implicit judgment against Rome and the papacy that the Romans *do not persevere* in giving the honorific title, not even to their emperor.

P. 167, L. 14. *smiling:* There can be no sin in Heaven, so why Beatrice's seeming embarrassment? It is a grace note of levity, as when we smile upon the odd but not harmful hobbyhorse of a favorite uncle. For a similar note of lighthearted embarrassment, see 28.130–35.

P. 169, L. 41. *the sixth parish:* that of Porta San Pietro near the old market and within the city walls. The point is that Dante's family is not newly come to the city, unlike those that Cacciaguida is about to name.

P. 169, L. 47. *between Mars and the Baptist:* That is an interesting way to denominate Florence. In the *Inferno,* the unnamed Florentine suicide expressed disdain for Florence's having changed her patron from the god Mars to John the Baptist— that is, from the military virtues of Rome to the idolizing of money, since Florentine currency bore the image of John the Baptist (13.143–50). But in the ways of chivalry and in the person of the knightly Cacciaguida, the old fighting spirit is placed in the service of the Baptist and the Christian faith. The problem with his own Florence, Dante suggests, is that it no longer lies between Mars and the Baptist; it has neither the ardor of faith nor the discipline of Roman manhood.

P. 171, L. 56. *the plowboys of Signa and Aguglion:* Signa is a hamlet near Florence, Aguglion a fortress in the Val di Pesa. Cacciaguida is referring, with an old man's frankness, to two political players of Dante's day. One, the judge Baldo d'Aguglione, allowed his friend and ally Niccolo Acciaioli to tamper with the records in a case of *graft* that had been brought against him. The podesta of Florence, one Monfiorito di Coderda, deposed and tried in 1299, suborned false testimony to exonerate Acciaioli, who soon succeeded Monfiorito and, as a quid pro quo, tried to destroy the record of his predecessor's confession (cf. *Purg.* 12.104–5). When the emperor Henry VII of Luxembourg (see 30.137 and note) came to Florence in 1311, Baldo headed a council granting amnesty to many Florentines exiled in the city's long partisan strife; Dante's name was not on the list. The other player, Bonifazio dei Morubaldini da Signa, was a Black Guelph who had turned from the Whites and who was instrumental in ordering Dante's exile.

P. 171, L. 62. *Simifonti:* a fortress in the Valdelsa, razed by Florence in 1202 in an effort to resist the rule of the emperor.

P. 171, L. 64. *Montemurlo:* a castle between Prato and Pistoia. The counts of that fortress, the Guidi, were simply called "the Counts," Ital. *Conti,* by the Florentines.

P. 171, L. 65. *Cerchi:* a prominent merchant family, chief among the White Guelphs. *Acone* is a rural parish in the Val di Sieve.

P. 171, L. 66. *Valdigreve:* a small valley of the Greve River, south of Florence. The *Buondelmonti* were at the heart of a scandal that was thought to have begun the city's partisan division between Guelphs and Ghibellines (cf. lines 139–47, and *Inf.* 28.103–11). When in 1235 the Florentines took their castle from them, the Buondelmonti had to relocate—and did, in Florence.

P. 171, LL. 73–75. *Luni ... Orbisaglia ... Chiusi ... Sinigaglia:* Once an important port, the ancient Etruscan city of Luni had been sacked by Saracens; the port was finally filled in. By the fourteenth century it had become an uninhabitable ruin. Orbisaglia was an ancient Roman town destroyed by the Visigoths. Chiusi still exists. It once was a powerful Etruscan town, Clusium, rivaling Rome; in fact it was the capital city of King Porsenna, who wished to return Etruscan kings to rule in Rome; cf. Livy, *Hist.* 2.10. In the Middle Ages it suffered from the malarial swamp of the Chiana River (cf. *Inf.* 29.47; *Par.* 13.22). Sinigaglia in the Marches still exists; it too had been suffering the depredations of malaria and the Saracens.

P. 173, L. 88. *the Hughs:* The following are names of the Florentine families of old. Cacciaguida does not blame their decline on decadent morals, necessarily, for all human things, families as well as cities, have their rise and fall.

P. 173, L. 94. *the portage gate:* the Porta San Pietro. Cacciaguida alludes to the fact that the Cerchi family of merchants now own the houses there that the *Ravignani* (the family of Bellincion Berti, 15.112) and the Conti used to own, among the latter of whom was *Count Guido* Guerra (*Inf.* 16.34–39). What crimes the Cerchi are supposed to be guilty of, critics cannot specify.

P. 173, L. 109. *How I have seen them fall:* probably the Ghibelline family of the Uberti, whose part in Florence's civil war caused them to be banished forever (cf. *Inf.* 10.83–84). Cacciaguida is, as it were, the saintly counterpart of its noble but heretic chief, Farinata degli Uberti.

P. 173, L. 110. *house of golden balls:* the Lamberti, exiled with their allies the Uberti after the battle of Montaperti in 1276. Dante blames Mosca dei Lamberti for having stoked the wrath of his family when a young man of the Buondelmonti family jilted one of their young ladies (see note for line 134 below).

P. 175, L. 119. *Ubertin Donato:* son-in-law of Bellincion Berti (cf. lines 98–99).

P. 175, L. 126. *della Pera:* Historians are unsure whether the della Pera were already no more in Dante's day (in which case Cacciaguida's point is again that all human things come to an end) or Dante considers them the ancestors of the wealthy Peruzzi clan (in which case Cacciaguida contrasts the honor given the former with the decadence of the latter).

P. 175, L. 127. *Hugh the Great:* Ital. *gran barone,* "great baron," referring to Hugh, marquis of Tuscany and legate of the emperor Otto III. Hugh is buried in Florence, in the Badia (the "Abbey"), which he himself had built, and where a service in his honor was performed every year on *the feast of Saint Thomas,* December 21, the day of Hugh's death in 1001, almost three centuries before the putative time of Dante's vision. Those families that had been elevated to knighthood by Hugh, then, were no newcomers to the aristocracy. Still, one of those families, the *one who binds his flag with bands of gold,* has betrayed that privilege by trucking with the commoners. Cacciaguida alludes to the family of Giano della Bella, a nobleman who sided with the commons in the Ordinances of Justice in 1293—ordinances that allowed for participation in government by men like Dante who were not members of the most powerful families.

P. 175, L. 134. *Borgo:* The *Gualterotti* and *Importuni* lived in a neighborhood of Florence called Borgo Santi Apostoli, just outside the walls of Cacciaguida's old Florence. The *newcomers* that Borgo could well have spared were the Buondelmonti. As the story goes, Buondelmonte dei Buondelmonti was engaged to marry a young girl of the Amidei family, but broke the engagement and married a daughter of the Donati family instead. Avenging their family honor, the Amidei, at the suggestion of Mosca, the chief of their allied family the Lamberti (cf. *Inf.* 28.103–11), had Buondelmonti killed. The resulting feud persisted and ramified, becoming the seedbed of the strife between the Florentine Guelphs and Ghibellines.

P. 177, L. 153. *backward in the field:* Florence was often defeated in battle—but not in Cacciaguida's day. Worse, says the warrior, is that Florence now sees her flag, a white lily against a red field (but altered by the Guelphs to a red lily in a white field), soaked in the blood of her own countrymen dying in civil conflict.

CANTO SEVENTEEN

And they rejoiced that they were counted worthy to suffer shame for his name.
Whether Dante rejoiced in his exile is not clear, but it is certain that no single event in his life has gained for him such glory. Indeed, were it not for the unjust banish-

ment from his native land, and the seizing of his goods by a political enemy, and the foolish pride of those men banished with him—were it not, in short, for the hard look at human evil that Dante was forced to take—we might not have the *Comedy*. But He who can bring good out of evil can bring good out of Florence.

P. 179, L. 15. *one triangle:* Here we have another truth from geometry (cf. 13.101–102 and note at 13.102); this time, that the sum of the angles of any triangle is equal to two right angles—and so at most one angle of a triangle can be *obtuse*, or wider than a right angle. As we can prove this truth by reason, Dante says, so Cacciaguida can, by looking upon God, perceive things that are not even necessary (as geometric truths are necessary) but contingent, and even before the contingent things come to be. In the *Inferno* Virgil uttered predictions that appeared prophetic but were really the results of keen-eyed reason; Virgil told Dante not to fear prophecies that spelled trouble and gloom; Virgil said, reasonably enough, that Beatrice would tell Dante all he needed to know about his future on earth (cf. *Inf.* 10.121–32). The prophecy that disturbed Dante the most was, naturally, that of his banishment—a prophecy delivered, with a certain stern sadness, by Farinata (lines 79–81), who had spoken proudly of his heritage and who had asked Dante not for his name but for the name of his forebears (line 42). Here, one of those forebears in fact reveals that Farinata spoke truly, but that in his patient suffering of the unjust exile Dante would finally be vindicated.

P. 181, L. 21. *some things were said to me:* prophesying trouble for Dante; e.g., *Inf.* 10.79–81; 15.61–72; 24.140–51; *Purg.* 8.133–39.

P. 181, L. 27. *Arrows foreseen:* This is almost a direct quote of Aquinas, himself quoting Gregory the Great's Sermon 35 on the gospels: "Lances that are foreseen strike with less force" (*Summa theol.* 2.2.123.9). Aquinas's point is that fortitude consists not in rash action—such as that undertaken by Dante's erstwhile allies—but in consideration and patience.

P. 181, L. 33. *the Lamb of God ... away:* So said John the Baptist, seeing Jesus come to be baptized: "Behold the Lamb of God, which taketh away the sin of the world" (John 1:32); these words are repeated three times in the *Agnus Dei*.

P. 181, L. 37. *Contingency:* Paradoxically, it is part of God's providential plan that some things will occur by necessity and others by contingency (Aquinas, *Summa theol.* 1.22.4).

P. 181, L. 38. *foursquare elements:* Ital. *quaderno*, "volume." I am guessing that there is an etymological pun here, referring to the book of the universe constituted by four elements. Hence, four is the number of the body and of contingency, which affects bodily things.

P. 181, L. 46. *Hippolytus of Athens:* Dante probably intends that the whole of the story of Hippolytus be seen as corresponding to his own. After Hippolytus had been exiled by his stepmother with her false charge of rape, and had been dragged to death by his own horses on the beach, he was given life again by Aesculapius, the son of the god of poetry, Apollo. Clothed with his new life, he was sent not to Greece but to Italy, where he became a Roman tutelary god, Virbius, the god of the citizen (Ovid, *Met.* 15.544–46), dwelling in the grove near Rome.

P. 183, L. 52. *They'll rail against the beaten:* So complained Boethius, unjustly accused of treason against the emperor and the Senate: "Finally, and this is the last straw, the judgment of most people is based not on the merits of a case but on the fortune of its outcome; they think that only things which turn out happily are good. As a result, the first thing an unfortunate man loses is his reputation" (*Cons. Phil.* 1 pr. 4).

P. 183, L. 62. *the company:* the other Whites exiled with Dante. He and they attempted at least twice to reenter the city by force; they failed. When Dante then counseled better preparation for the next attempt, they turned on him. They went on to fight without him, bloodying their own temples in defeat.

P. 183, L. 76. *that man:* Cangrande della Scala (1291–1329), ruler of Verona, a man of intellectual and military distinction. Dante dedicated the *Paradise* to Cangrande, sending him cantos while the work was in progress; his letter to Cangrande applying the four levels of scriptural exegesis to the interpretation of the *Comedy* is a crucial document for understanding the assumptions of a medieval artist and his audience (see Appendix A).

P. 187, L. 130. *sharp at the first taste:* Cacciaguida does not recommend that Dante enjoy the invectives against his unrighteous enemies. He may, but that is not the point. One of the purposes in telling a harsh truth is that those who feel its harshness may repent. Such criticism is medicinal. Dante's words echo what Lady Philosophy says to Boethius: "You will find what I have yet to say bitter to the taste, but, once you have digested it, it will seem sweet" (*Cons. Phil.* 3 pr. 1). If, however, Dante fails to speak, he may find himself as one of the very hirelings he condemns, who "fear to speak freely of what is right, and, in the words of the Truth, do not exercise the zeal of shepherds caring for the flock," leaving them prey for the wolves (Gregory the Great, *Past. Care* 2.4).

P. 187, L. 142. *clearest evidence:* As Scripture condescends to human faculties and seems to attribute bodies to angels and to God, so now the grace of God stoops to men's weakness and allows Dante to persuade by showing his readers examples of damned and blessed people they have heard of or have known.

CANTO EIGHTEEN

They shall mount, as on wings of eagles. Renewed youth and vigor, says the prophet, will come to those souls who put their trust in the Lord. The joyful warring of the souls in the sphere of Mars thus leads naturally to an image of the Roman eagle, or rather that of which the Roman eagle was a reflection: the Eagle of Heaven, called upon to answer questions of ultimate justice.

P. 189, L. 6. *who lifts the yoke of every wrong:* Beatrice reminds Dante that the Lord will lift from him even the burden of exile. She is acting as his *comfort,* or strengthener, as did Virgil so often (cf. *Purg.* 3.22; 9.44).

P. 189, L. 21. *my eyes are not the only Paradise:* This is another touch of womanliness in Beatrice, as was her smile when Dante momentarily forgot her beauty, and her smile again when Dante and Cacciaguida took roosterlike pride in their family.

P. 191, L. 29. *that takes its life from the crown:* Bliss springs from God, not as from its hidden root but as from its culmination, its perfection. Dante's language is scriptural: "Herein is my Father glorified, that ye bear much fruit; so shall ye be my disciples" (John 15:8).

P. 191, L. 33. *spoils for poetry:* Once again (cf. 1.28–29) Dante associates poetry with the same sacrifice of the self that is demanded by participation in a just war; to fail to fight is akin to failing to sing. It bespeaks a small-souled man, one content with amassing money or prestige or power. "Our desires are mean," Dante says (1.30), contrasting the busy indolence of the world with true enterprise in song and valorous deed.

P. 191, L. 37. *Joshua:* The great leader of the Israelites into Canaan, the stormer of Jericho, and the first judge in Israel, was considered a forerunner of Christ, who by his victory upon the Cross won for mankind the Promised Land of Paradise. Joshua is therefore justly the first and most prominent warrior named here (cf. note at 14.126).

P. 191, L. 40. *the greatest Maccabee:* Judas Maccabeus (d. 160 B.C.) led the Jewish revolt against the Greeks under Antiochus Epiphanes IV. Antiochus was a modern, cosmopolitan ruler, his placement of a statue of Zeus in the Holy of Holies in Jerusalem (1 Macc. 1:41–63) meant to compel universality of worship throughout his realm, since, as he considered the matter, one god was as good as another. The Maccabeans did not buy, and in fighting for the purity of the Old Law fought, as Dante suggests, for the New Law and for Christ.

P. 191, L. 43. *Roland . . . Charles the Great:* On Christmas Day in 800, Charlemagne (742–814) was crowned emperor in Rome by Pope Leo III after his victorious campaign against the Lombards. Charlemagne spurred, if not a revival of classical learning, at least a determined preservation of it in the schools he established, particularly in the great school at his capital, Aachen. He is noted here not for his just rule, nor for his unification of much of western Europe into a federation of duchies and principalities answerable to emperor and pope, but for his fighting for Christendom. Invited by one Saracen prince in Spain to help him beat back a more powerful Saracen prince, Charlemagne crossed the Pyrenees with his army; when the campaign was over and as his army threaded the mountains back into France, his rear guard was ambushed by Basques at a mountain pass near Roncesvalles. From this incident sprange the popular legends of Charlemagne and his greatest peer, Roland, whose death at the hands of Saracens—not Basques—at Roncesvalles is the subject of the magnificent Old French *Chanson de Roland*. Dante knew the legend of Roland and his horn, the oliphant (cf. *Inf.* 31.16–18).

P. 193, L. 69. *candor...star:* Dante senses by the change in color that he has ascended from the red Mars to the glowing white Jupiter. The colors allegorize a change in the virtues associated with those planets: we have moved from zeal to that obedient temperance indispensable to the discerning and enacting of justice.

P. 193, L. 71. *the flames of love in characters of flame:* "The just shall shine, and shall run to and fro like sparks among the reeds" (Wis. 3:7). It is remarkable that the souls of the just, conformed to the Word of God through whom all things were made, themselves spell out a sentence, indeed a series of words from the word of God. The point is that the earthly virtue of justice is no other than the manifestation in temporal affairs of the changeless justice of the eternal Word. Even the words we use to understand the Word have a beginning, a middle, and an end, because we dwell in time and must therefore remember (cf. Augustine, *Conf.* 11.27). The eagle's serial spelling of the sentence from scripture therefore both embodies how we human beings come to know what we know, and reminds us of our reliance upon the providence of God, for whom there is no beginning, no middle, and no end.

P. 193, L. 82. *divine Pegasean:* Confronting so remarkable a vision, Dante again invokes the Muse, this time allegorizing poetic inspiration in the soaring of the winged horse, Pegasus. As in the sphere of Mars he associated poetry with the glory of fighting for the Cross, so now he associates it with the praise of justly governed empires and cities.

P. 197, L. 93. QUI IUDICTIS TERRAM: Dante quotes the opening of the Book of Wisdom, "Love justice, you that are judges of the earth." That sentence is immediately followed by an exhortation to humility: "Think of the Lord in goodness, and seek him in simplicity of heart. For he is found by them that tempt him not, and he showeth himself to them that have faith in him" (Wis. 1:1–2). That exhortation applies not only to earthly rulers but to all those who, like the pilgrim Dante, question the nature of God's justice. Humility is a prerequisite for the exalted vision.

P. 197, L. 97. *that M:* This part of the constellation is transformed thus:

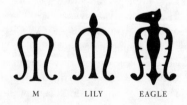

M   LILY   EAGLE

P. 197, L. 111. *wherein a being nests:* a lovely and apt metaphor for the relationship between form and the essence or substance of a thing. It is the power of God that allows the form, existent in his mind, to become the form of an actual object dwelling intimately *in* that form, as an eagle dwells in its nest.

P. 197, L. 113. *enlilied in the* M: By a slight movement of submission, the lights that form the heraldic lily, symbol of France, allow themselves to be transformed into the heraldic eagle, symbol of the Roman empire. The significance of the progression seems obvious, and helps explain Dante's launching into an invective against the pope—possibly, at least at this moment, thinking of Clement V, the man who truckled to the French king Philip IV (the Fair) in moving the papal curia from Rome to Avignon.

P. 199, L. 121. *one more time grow angry:* Dante wishes to see in his own time the zeal that moved Christ to drive the money changers out of the temple (cf. John 2:14–16, Ps. 69:9); the money changers profited from the "sacraments," as it were—from the sacrifices required under the Mosaic Law. The new money changers are viler, in that they use prohibitions of the sacrament to extort money. For similar cries to God for vengeance, cf. *Purg.* 6.118–23; 20.94–96.

P. 199, L. 123. *miracles and blood:* Ital. *di segni e di martìri,* "with 'signs' and with the 'testimonies' " of the martyrs. The language is scriptural: "And many wonders and signs were done by the apostles" (Acts 2:43). Dante has altered the phrase from "signs and wonders," to be found dozens of times in Scripture, to "signs and sufferings," or "signs and martyrdoms," stressing not the miracles the apostles performed but the blood they shed to build the Church.

P. 199, L. 124. *army of the heaven:* Ital. *milizia del ciel,* from Lat. *militia coeli;* it is a common scriptural image to describe the hosts of angels (cf. Deut. 17:3, Luke 2:13, Acts 7:42).

P. 199, L. 126. *a twisted chief to imitate:* Compare Dante's charge of self-seeking among the popes with Gregory the Great's warning to all prelates: "If a man vested with the appearance of holiness destroys others by word or example, it certainly were better for him that his earthly deeds, performed in a worldly guise, should press him to death, rather than that his sacred offices should have pointed him out to others for sinful imitation" (*Past. Care* 1.2; cf. Matt. 18:6). Nor does his malfeasance excuse the flock, who "are all gone out of the way" (Rom. 3:12).

CANTO NINETEEN

How unsearchable are his judgments! exclaims Saint Paul, observing the irony that the rejection of Christ by the Jews should result in bringing salvation to gentiles. In this canto and the next, Dante touches, in faith, upon such paradoxes of providence, believing in a justice that his mind, by the consequence of human limitations, cannot see in its entirety.

P. 201, L. 8. *no ink's been known to write:* The allusion is appropriate (and daring, as Dante applies it to his own work of imagination), given the mysteries of providence that the Eagle will discuss: "Eye hath not seen, nor ear heard, neither have entered into the heart of man, the things which God hath prepared for them that love him" (1 Cor. 2:9).

P. 201, L. 12. *"we" and "ours":* The Eagle speaks as a body, not because individuality is lost (it is not), but because the nature of justice is to sew a people up in unity as members of one body. The unifying harmony of the constellation—an imperial eagle rising out of words that identify the beginning of true wisdom, the fear of the Lord, with love of justice—is seen against the atomizing greed, ambition, and effeminate indolence that plague the Christian rulers of Dante's age. These may pretend to honor the glory of the one Church and of the one empire, but they act as if to ensure that neither will thrive again. The motif of the speaking eagle derives from the Apocalypse: "And I beheld, and heard the voice of an eagle flying across the heavens, crying aloud, 'Woe, woe, woe to the inhabitants of earth' " (Rev. 8:13, Vulgate).

P. 201, L. 13. *just and pious:* Ital. *giusto e pio,* "just and pious," but also "just and merciful"—and the reconciling of justice with mercy is precisely the problem which Dante will beg the Eagle to address.

P. 203, L. 26. *the hunger of my heart:* It is the great doubt of a good and unsentimentally honest Christian man, and it is the last great doubt that Dante's character will express. If faith is necessary for salvation, what happens to those virtuous men and women who did not know about Christ? If they had no opportunity to hear the word of God preached, how can they be punished for their lack of faith?

It appears to me that there are three ways to answer this question, and that Dante tentatively, and with great humility, approaches the third. The first way is that of Calvin, recalling that Augustine had called the virtues of the great republican Romans "splendid vices," or as Milton put it, "close ambition varnished o'er with zeal" (*Paradise Lost* 2.485). This is to grant only a specious virtue to the pagan (and Augustine himself was more generous than that; cf. *City of God* 5.11–14), to attribute selfish or at best quite impure motives to all those without the faith, regardless of whether they died horrible deaths for their countrymen, as did Regulus (*City of God* 1.15), or shared their last crusts with a neighbor. Strictly speaking, we need not worry about the virtuous pagans, since there are no virtuous pagans, or if there are virtuous pagans, their virtue is merely human and not in itself pleasing to God: "All our righteousnesses are as filthy rags" (Is. 64:6). But that is to universalize and absolutize what Isaiah says, taking it out of context; and it is an assertion flatly contradicted by the evidence of our senses and by the plain meaning of the word "virtue." Dante clearly did not accept it, as the presence in Limbo of the virtuous pagans shows.

The second way is that of modern man, who, if he is not busy denying the very possibility of salvation, is busy comfortably assuring himself that everyone (or at least everyone not below his own modest level of virtue) will be saved. Everyone will be saved, by that kind and loving God he keeps in an old chest of drawers along with a watch fob and a couple of silver dollars. The kindness of that God is attested by Scripture, the same Scripture that attests his justice and the reality of final alienation from him. But modern man is too lazily busy to think. So modern man is a soft Pelagian heretic. As long as we love one another (and by "love" we mean not the theological virtue nor even a good hearty pagan eros but the ability to get along passably well with the more likable of our fellows, an ability more due to a good diet than to any exercise of will), we will be saved. Therefore all the virtuous pagans will be saved, including the virtuous pagans who are ourselves.

The *third possibility* is that indeed some of the virtuous pagans may be saved, not by their own merits but by faith; while Calvin argued that the virtuous pagans only appeared virtuous, a holder of this third possibility would leave open the hope that some of the truly virtuous pagans only appeared pagan. When Jesus said, "I am the way, the truth, and the life; no one cometh to the Father but by me" (John 14:6), he may well be interpreted as saying, "All those who come to the Father do so by my work, my merits, my virtue infused into their hearts." What form this faith might take was left unclear by the Church Fathers. Augustine, for instance, said that the Hebrews who kept the faith believed in Christ to come, along with all those other individuals, perhaps far away, to whom this faith was mysteriously revealed (*City of God* 3.1). Aquinas attempted to specify what faith was sufficient for so mysterious a baptism. The testimony of reason assures a man that God exists and is a providential God; the testimony of the senses and of his conscience assures him that he is a sinner, unworthy of approaching a God most holy; by reason he therefore concludes that he needs a mediator, an intercessor, to approach God on his behalf (cf. *Summa theol.* 2.2.2.7). Elsewhere Aquinas states that at the dawn of the age of discretion, every human being faces a fundamental decision for good or for evil—for good, that is, enabled by the grace of God. If the person at that moment throws himself upon the mercy of God, he receives baptism, what is called the "baptism of desire," and on the day of doom will be judged accordingly. If, however, he does not do so, he rejects the assistance of faith and will inevitably fall into mortal sin. Thus Aquinas can argue that there is no unbaptized person beyond the age of discretion who is not in mortal sin; conversely, anyone who dies not in a state of mortal sin must have been baptized in one manner or another. Who is saved and who is not rests hidden in the secrets of divine providence, but that there might be Christians whom Christians do not recognize as such is suggested by

Christ himself: "And other sheep I have, which are not of this fold: them also must I bring, and they shall hear my voice; and there shall be one fold, and one shepherd" (John 10:16).

Catholic teaching in this matter suggests that the third way may be true, but the Church does not require believers to accept it (the second way is denounced as heretical). The reader should note that Dante approaches the third way but rejects, in part, Aquinas's analysis. For Dante has clearly maintained that there are many who are both unbaptized and virtuous, at least according to the four natural virtues of fortitude, prudence, temperance, and justice. Aquinas's analysis would clearly depopulate Dante's Limbo of all but, perhaps, the unbaptized infants. On the other hand, Dante does save three pagans, two of them named in the following canto; the third, Cato, we have met at the base of the Mountain of Purgatory. How he does this we shall see in the next canto.

I used to believe that all three cases were exceptional—like punctures of grace irrupting into an otherwise universal rejection of the unbaptized. Yet grace itself is exceptional, in that it is an unmerited and absolutely free gift of God. There is no predicting the acts of providence, and thus no predicting the gift of grace. The next canto will show that just as an awareness of providence should prevent us from judging God's sentences too hastily, so too it should prevent us from forgetting that we cannot know God's pardons, either. And finally we might remember the words of the eagle's Book of Wisdom: "For God made not death, neither hath he pleasure in the destruction of the living" (Wis. 1:13).

P. 203, L. 40. *the sextant:* Here God is the Ancient of Days, the providential Architect of the universe. The language and the essence of the argument derive from Job (cf. 38:4–11).

P. 203, L. 48. *would not wait for light:* Satan's sin is presented as an affront to providence. He wished to know (and God made him to wish to know), but on his own terms and in his own time, not God's.

P. 205, L. 66. *the shadow, or the poison, of the flesh:* The word "flesh" here is used equivocally. All created things are dark by comparison with the ineffable light of the Creator; in that sense, our being made of earth casts its shadow. But fallen man's disordered attachment to things of the flesh truly darkens his mind, and so it is that flesh or carnality is a poison: "They that are in the flesh cannot please God" (Rom. 8:8).

P. 205, L. 69. *pressed with doubt:* The Eagle now poses, in its strongest and most explicit form, the sadness that has weighed upon Dante's heart since the beginning of the *Comedy*. Dante has heard Virgil's plaintive exclamation of disappointment in never having known God (*Inf.* 1.124–29); has beseeched "the greater muse than ours" to assist him, "by that same God you did not know" (*Inf.* 1.131); has witnessed the Limbo of the virtuous pagans, and has heard the "everlasting tremble in the air" (*Inf.* 4.27) raised by the sighs of people who, unpunished, would yet never possess the end for which they were created; has heard Virgil remind him that there are wise men who now know that they will never find the knowledge they so ardently sought (*Purg.* 3.34–45); has heard Virgil confess—to lesser poets and lesser men—that he will never be saved (*Purg.* 7.7–8; 21.16–18); and has turned in astonishment at the approach of Beatrice to find that Virgil has vanished, has gone back to the edge of Hell forevermore (*Purg.* 30.49–51), "Virgil the sweetest father," the one who gave himself for Dante's healing. It is for Virgil above all that our narrator pleads.

P. 205, L. 75. *without a sin in either deed or speech:* The Eagle's language suggests that third way out of the dilemma, though that way is not examined explicitly in the poem. In some mysterious fashion Christ himself, "a prophet mighty in deed and word" (Luke 24:19), may reveal himself to people who are ignorant of their being within the Church, making them like unto him.

P. 205, L. 79. *Now who are you:* The Eagle's first reply is a rebuke, a reminder of the necessary limitations of our knowledge; it echoes that of God speaking to Job from the whirlwind: "Who is this that darkeneth counsel by words without knowledge? Gird up now thy loins like a man: for I will demand of thee, and answer thou me. Where wast thou when I laid the foundations of the earth? declare, if thou hast understanding" (Job 38:2–4; cf. also Rom. 9:20, Wis. 9:13–18).

P. 205, L. 88. *All . . . Will:* The Eagle's second reply sounds like the voluntarism of Duns Scotus and William of Ockham: God's will is not determined by what is just, rather justice is determined by God's will. I am not sure, however, that a voluntarist reading is correct here. First, it is certainly true that, in the analysis of Aquinas, all created goods are reflections of the divine Good; their very existence depends upon that Good. Second, to say that things are just insofar as they chime with the divine will (as Dante himself says in *On Monarchy* 2.2.4–6) is not to say that the divine reason, or Wisdom, is subordinate to that will. Dante here is talking about created things, not about the faculties of the Deity.

P. 207, L. 106. *many now cry, 'Christ, Christ!':* Dante adapts the words of Christ: "Not every one that saith unto me, Lord, Lord, shall enter into the kingdom of heaven; but he that doeth the will of my Father which is in heaven. Many will say to me in that day, Lord, Lord, have we not prophesied in thy name? and in thy name have cast out devils? and in thy name done many wonderful works? And then will I profess unto them, I never knew you; depart from me, ye that work iniquity" (Matt. 7:21–23). The third reply of the Eagle—a negative reply preparing for the hope presented in the next canto—is that the Christian who betrays the faith will find himself farther from Christ than will the man who never had the faith. What this distance implies, the Eagle does not and perhaps cannot specify; but it does echo what Christ says about impenitence in those to whom the faith has been preached, who will be judged by *the Ethiopian:* "The queen of the south shall rise up in the judgment with this generation, and shall condemn it: for she came from the uttermost parts of the earth to hear the wisdom of Solomon; and, behold, a greater than Solomon is here" (Matt. 12:42).

P. 207, L. 115. *There he will see, writ among Albert's deeds:* in the book of men's works, on the day of doom (Rev. 20:12). Emperor Albert of Austria (r. 1298–1308), against whose negligence of Italy Dante has inveighed (*Purg.* 6.97–117). Dante begins three tercets in a row with the hammering *Lì si vedrà,* "there he will see," followed by three beginning with *Vedrassi,* "there will be seen," and three beginning with *e,* "and." The set resembles the acrostic of *Purg.* 12.25–60, where Dante used initial letters of sets of tercets to spell VOM, *uom,* "man." Here the word is LVE, or *lue,* "plague." Critics who deny the acrostic here—who say that we are dealing with a happenstance—seem unaware that this is one of the most climactic moments in the whole *Comedy,* and that in fact it is akin to the devastating condemnation of human pride presented in that previous acrostic in the *Purgatory.* We have reached the culmination of the first movement of the Eagle's speech, a speech wholly devoted to answering the most pressing doubt Dante has ever had—a doubt, moreover, that Dante has woven into the fabric of the poem. This first movement sees the Roman eagle, chosen by God as both symbol and mediator of his justice, condemn the cowardice, sloth, greed, bestiality, and shortsighted pettiness of the men who are supposed to rule in the name of Christ. They are indeed a pestilence to their people, and the judgment against them is apocalyptic; cf. Wis. 6:3–7.

P. 207, L. 118. *the sorrow upon the Seine:* Or "the plague upon the Seine"; the plague is brought by—and is—Philip IV (the Fair), king of France (r. 1268?–1314). Dante alludes to the story that Philip died from a fall he suffered when the wild boar he was hunting gored his horse from beneath. Philip is often the object of Dante's revilement (*Inf.* 19.87; *Purg.* 20.85–93); modern historians consider him a strong medieval king who acquired wealth and territory, often by unscrupulous means, for France. When he levied taxes on the clergy to pay for his war with England, he found himself in conflict with Boniface VIII in another chapter in the medieval struggle to define the proper roles, and the proper subordination, of secular authority and church. The strife came to a head in 1303 with the so-called Anagni Outrage: Boniface's papal bull *Unam sanctam* had asserted the supremacy of the papacy (Dante bitterly attacks its arguments in his late work *On Monarchy*), and Philip had responded by sending henchmen to the pope's residence in Anagni to arrest him for heresy and to use rather physical persuasion to change the octogenarian pontiff's mind. Boniface died shortly thereafter, and in two years Philip managed to secure the election of a Frenchman, Clement V, as pope. Clement moved the papal see to Avignon, where for seventy years it remained, and remained under the influence of the French king. Clement then allowed Philip to destroy the

Order of Knights Templar—to seize the money he needed to continue financing his royal ambitions.

P. 209, L. 127. *the Cripple of Jerusalem:* Charles II of Anjou (cf. 6.106 and note). Charles succeeded his father, Charles I, against whom the Sicilians had revolted in Palermo in the Sicilian Vespers (cf. notes at 8.72 and 78). He was compelled to recognize Frederick II of Aragon as king of Sicily, while he himself ruled the kingdom of Naples. His titular designation—"of Jerusalem"—is savagely ironic, the more so when to that lackluster Crusader is applied Gregory the Great's definition of a cripple: "A man is lame who does, indeed, see the way he should go, but through infirmity of purpose is unable to follow persistently the way of life which he sees" (*Past. Care* 1.11; Gregory is glossing Lev. 21:17–20, on prohibiting a crippled man from sacrificing in the temple).

P. 209, L. 142. *Fortunate Hungary:* The Eagle predicts a reprieve for Hungary, whose king in 1308 will be Carlo Roberto (Caroberto) of Anjou, son of the Charles Martel we have met in Canto 8.

CANTO TWENTY

In him we live and move and have our being, said the apostle Paul to the Athenians, declaring that the "unknown god" they worshiped in ignorance, in dim intuition, was the true God, the one Creator of all things. God was far from their minds, he said, and yet near to them, intimately near. A strand of Christian theology thus has always held out the hypothetical possibility of the mysterious union in the Church of all who follow the light they have been granted, such as it is. To know that God exists and is good, and that man is a sinner and requires God's gift to be made just, is about as slender a strand of revelation as can be imagined for fulfilling the requirement of Christian faith. In this canto Dante will not quite assert that it is enough.

P. 211, L. 19. *the rushing of a stream:* It is the glory of God speaking in the Eagle: "And behold, the glory of the God of Israel came from the way of the east: and his voice was like a noise of many waters" (Ezek. 43:2).

P. 215, L. 37. *the pupil:* the clearest-sighted part of the eye, and the most precious. So in one of the Psalms David describes himself, not as king, but as a man graced by God: "Keep me as the apple of the eye" (Ps. 17:8). His composing of sacred music was appropriate for a ruler, says Augustine: "It was to serve him that David made use of music in order to express a tremendous truth by means of mystical symbols, for what can better suggest the unity in variety of a well-ordered city than the harmony produced by the rational and controlled concord of differing tones?" (*City of God* 17.14). Cf. note at 8.116.

P. 215, L. 40. *Now does he understand:* For a close examination of the following descriptions of the six souls that form the Eagle's eye, see introduction.

P. 215, L. 43. *The spirit:* that of Trajan; see introduction. Legend had it that so impressed was Pope Gregory the Great by Trajan's love of justice, he prayed that the emperor might be brought to life again to hear the word of God and believe. Regardless of what he believed about the fanciful story, Dante may be using Trajan here as a representative of souls whose salvation, in ways we cannot fathom, may be owing to the intercessory prayer of believers. It is interesting to note, however, that the wicked use the brevity of man's life and the impossibility of resurrection as excuses to practice injustice: "The time of our life is short and tedious, and in the end of a man there is no remedy, and no man hath been known to have returned from hell" (Wis. 2:1–2); "Come, therefore, and let us enjoy the good things that are present.... Let us oppress the poor just man, and not spare the widow, nor honor the ancient gray hairs of the aged. But let our strength be the law of justice, for that which is feeble, is found to be nothing worth" (2.6, 10–11). Trajan's life, suggests Dante, proves otherwise: "The souls of the just are in the hand of God, and the torment of death shall not touch them. In the sight of the unwise they seemed to die, and their departure was taken for misery; and their going away from us, for utter destruction; but they are in peace" (3:1–3).

P. 217, L. 82. *What things are these:* Dante echoes the incredulity and astonishment of the people when they witnessed Christ's miracles and heard his preaching (Mark 6:2).

P. 219, L. 94. *suffers violence:* "From the days of John the Baptist until now the kingdom of heaven suffereth violence, and the violent take it by force" (Matt. 11:12). The mystery of the Incarnation is akin to the mystery of the efficacy of prayer: God, as it were, becomes small in order to redeem, or submits himself to the entreaties of his own creatures. But their very prayers are the fruit of his grace working in them—and so it is that his being vanquished by prayer is the God of love's most winsome victory. Note that prayer can be offered only by one who possesses faith in *the kingdom of Heaven* and is moved by *living hope and burning charity*—the three theological virtues. Thus effective prayer cannot arise in the unbaptized (cf. *Purg.* 6.37–42; the Eagle's speech answers the question about prayer that Dante had asked in Ante-Purgatory). For the just, "their hope is full of immortality" (Wis. 3:4).

P. 221, L. 130. *predestination:* not the double predestination, to salvation or reprobation, preached by Calvin. Aquinas defines it thus: "Predestination, properly understood, is a certain divine ordering, from eternity, of those things which are to be brought about in time by the grace of God" (*Summa Theol.* 3.24.1).

P. 221, L. 138. *we too will so:* As Piccarda rejoiced in the lowest rung of beatitude (3.70–87), so the souls of the just rulers rejoice that by the will of God some matters remain hidden from them in the depths of divine providence.

P. 221, L. 140. *to clear the haze from vision all too near:* The limitation suggested at 19.79–81 is now cleared away precisely by a humble acceptance of one's limitations.

P. 221, L. 148. *eyes that blink in perfect harmony:* After the wondrous tales of salvation, Dante ends the canto with this quiet image of assent and harmony and perfect peace. Trajan and Ripheus gleam with joy, seeing now a justice whose contemplation is as natural and as effortless as the blinking of the eyes.

CANTO TWENTY-ONE

None can look upon the face of God and live. But the contemplatives long to do just that, remembering the words of the apostle Paul, that in eternity the blessed shall know even as they are known. The Incarnation removes all doubt: God is no being dwelling in splendid isolation, but the Bridegroom, glad when the bride boldly addresses him and asks for a kiss. Nor were the saints in the sphere of Saturn of the shy and retiring sort.

P. 223, L. 5. *Semele:* daughter of Cadmus and mother of Bacchus. Juno heard of her affair with Jupiter and planted the presumptuous idea in Semele's mind that Jupiter should come to her next time in the fullness of his deity. When, against his will, he granted her request, Semele was reduced to ashes (Ovid, *Met.* 3.253–315; cf. *Inf.* 30.1). This is not the only instance of Dante's using a classical myth as a warning against temerity in approaching the holy; cf. *Purg.* 1.8–12; *Par.* 1.19–21.

P. 225, L. 29. *a ladder:* Dante is clearly inspired by Jacob's dream: "And behold a ladder set up on the earth, and the top of it reached to heaven: and behold the angels of God ascending and descending on it" (Gen. 28:12). Exegetes from the earliest Christians to those of Dante's day spoke unanimously in seeing the mysterious ladder as an allegorical sign. Peter Damian, whom we will meet in this canto, held that it was a sign of the riches of the hermit's life: "You are that ladder of Jacob that lead men to Heaven and let the angels down to assist them. You are that golden path that leads men back to their true country" (*Dominus vobiscum*, in *Patrologia Latina* 145.248). In his Rule, Benedict (whom we meet in the next canto) sees it as a sign of the lowly works of devotion and charity that the monk must perform. Since Richard of Saint Victor devoted a whole work, *The Twelve Patriarchs*, to showing the manner by which one ascends, through acts of virtue and through contemplative prayer, into the presence of the Holy One, it seems clear that the ladder represents a way of life, common to monk and hermit both, that integrates labor into the life of the mystic contemplative. The contemplation, then, is intimately sprung from, and productive of, the tireless acts of charity whereby the souls descend the ladder to do the will of

God. Gregory the Great links the passage in Genesis with Paul's pastorally motivated account of his rapture in 2 Cor. 12, and his subsequent descent: "Thus Jacob, as the Lord leaned on the ladder above and the anointed stone was below, saw angels ascending and descending, which was a sign that true preachers do not only aspire by contemplation to the Holy Head of the Church above, namely, the Lord, but also descend to its members in pity of them" (*Past. Care* 2.5). From a more metaphysical angle, Bonaventure suggests that the trinitarian hierarchy of flesh, reason, and contemplation, the first two embodied in man's very being and the last infused as a gift, is itself the ladder by which man ascends to God (*Brev.* 2.12); so too, properly seen, is the universe (*Itinerarium* 1.2).

P. 225, L. 57. *why you have approached me here:* Dante is curious about two particulars: why this soul and not some other has approached him, and why the souls in this sphere do not sing. Dante is mistaken about the latter: the souls sing, but the harmonies of contemplatives cannot be heard by the ear of reason. As for the former, Dante might well be excused: in the sphere of the moon he met Piccarda, the beloved sister of his old friend Forese Donati; in Mercury he met the one soul, Justinian, most appropriate to expound his beliefs regarding the reverence men owe to the empire and to Rome; in Venus he first spoke to Charles Martel, a prince he had met and esteemed, who, had he lived, might yet have unified headstrong Italy under the imperial standard; in the sun he spoke to Thomas Aquinas, the theologian to whom his work is most indebted; in Jupiter the Roman eagle spoke to him about his deepest doubt. There must then be a reason why Peter Damian has been chosen to greet Dante here. Poetically, it works: with Peter and, in the canto following, Benedict, we revisit the discussion by Thomas and Bonaventure of true and corrupt friars (11.28–139; 12.37–145), only now we are looking at hermitages and monasteries. Yet Dante wishes to stress the point made by the Eagle in the last canto: that some things (the why of this or that particular) are hidden in the secrets of providence (20.133–38). Even *the most God-contemplating of the Seraphim,* says the contemplative, cannot answer Dante's question fully. Yet Peter Damian and Dante were kindred spirits in their zeal for reform and in their esteem for the empire; see note at line 121 below.

P. 231, L. 111. *a hermitage:* Santa Croce di Fonte Avellana, a Camaldolese monastery. *Catria* is a mountainous region near Gubbio, in Umbria.

P. 231, L. 118. *a rich yield:* The language of harvest is scriptural; cf. Matt. 13:8; Luke 10:2.

P. 231, L. 121. *Peter Damian:* Saint Peter Damian (1007–72), Camaldolese hermit and avid reformer of the Church. Peter's devotion to the ascetic life can be summed up thus: he believed that the monk should abjure all property in order to claim Christ as his only possession—and to possess Christ fully; and thus his habits of self-mortification were motivated not by hatred of food and drink but by love for Christ. In 1043 Peter became prior of the hermitage at Fonte Avellana, which he reformed according to his severe ideals of fasting, prayer, study, and self-discipline. He called himself, and signed his letters, Petrus Peccator—Peter the Sinner. He worked closely with several of the reforming monks elevated to the papacy in the eleventh century, including—despite his rather high esteem for the spiritual purpose of the empire—the great Hildebrand, Saint Gregory VII. His detestation of worldliness among men of the Church, expressed with horrific intensity in his *Book of Gomorrah,* is well captured by Dante in his image of the fat churchman needing to be boosted onto his mount. Late in his life Peter was made a cardinal, against his will, since his duties would take time from what he loved most in life, and that was contemplation: "For I recall that I have often been so kindled by the fire of divine love that I might wish at once to break through the prison of the flesh . . . and breathe in the light of eternity" (*On the abdication of the episcopacy* 5).

P. 233, L. 127. *Shoeless and gaunt:* echoing Christ's instructions as he commissioned his disciples to go forth and preach (Matt. 10:7–10).

P. 233, L. 129. *eating what they were given to eat:* as did Saint Paul, working for his bread lest he be a burden to those to whom he wished to preach (1 Cor. 4:11–12; 2 Cor. 11:9, 27; 1 Thess. 2:9; 2 Thess. 3:8–10).

P. 233, L. 134. *patience, so much do you bear:* Peter Damian has just referred to Saint Paul as the *vessel of the Holy Spirit;* the word "vessel" seems to motivate the present exclamation, alluding to Paul's justification of God's sufferance of the wicked: "What if God, willing to shew his wrath, and to make his power known, endured with much longsuffering the vessels of wrath fitted to destruction?" (Rom. 9:22).

CANTO TWENTY-TWO

In returning and rest shall ye be saved. The hard work of prayer and contemplation requires rest from the busy affairs of the world. The souls of the contemplatives here are among the most visibly active in the *Paradise,* ever ascending and descending the ladder, like the angels Jacob saw as he lay dreaming in the field of Luz. Labor on earth is usually a grindstone or treadmill; it was Saint Benedict's wisdom to sanctify earthly labor by uniting it to the restful work of Heaven.

P. 235, L. 1. *oppressed with wonder:* Dante echoes the words of Lady Philosophy to Boethius: "But I see that astonishment is weighing upon you" (*Cons. phil.* 1 pr. 2).

P. 235, L. 10. *zeal:* The shout of the souls in the sphere of Saturn was a violent burst of prayer, rising from zeal, the intense love that moves them to see the Church made holy (cf. John 2:13–17).

P. 235, L. 15. *before you die:* Beatrice may be referring to the death of one of the popes Dante has assigned to Hell, Boniface VIII or Clement V.

P. 235, L. 16. *too slow:* "The Lord is not slack concerning his promise, as some men count slackness; but is longsuffering to us-ward, not willing that any should perish, but that all should come to repentance" (2 Pet. 3:9; for the image of *the sword,* cf. Heb. 4:12).

P. 237, L. 40. *I am he:* Saint Benedict of Nursia (480–543). The debt that the West owes to Saint Benedict is as ponderous as it is unacknowledged. There had long been a tradition of monastic life in the East, marked by spiritual exercises, or ascesis, of an impressive sort—but marked by the outrageous piety of the glorious Desert Fathers or the half-mad pillar-sitting saints Simon and Daniel. But the much less Platonic West, with its ancient traditions of the practical virtues of hearth and farm, and its cultural belief in the nobility of manual labor, required a monasticism suited to the old Roman temper. That is what the Rule of Saint Benedict (who founded the monastery of Monte Cassino after having razed a temple to Apollo on that site) provided. While attempting to uproot the hardy paganism of the countryside, Benedict adopted Roman virtues for life in the monastery. Diet was sufficient yet simple; prayer was regular but not incessant; all monks were to perform manual labor; all monks were to obey the abbot (the title derives from Hebrew *abba,* "father") just as good Roman sons obeyed the paterfamilias; the abbot, like the paterfamilias, was to consult with the elders of the monastery, but as with the paterfamilias, the abbot's decisions were absolute and final. Last, the monk was not to go wandering about in search of mystical or maybe less than mystical thrills. Rather, he took a vow of stability, remaining in one monastery for the rest of his life, unless his abbot ordered him to serve elsewhere. The ancient Roman farmers worshiped the god of boundary stones, Terminus, and much of that same devotion to the particular place, to this hearth and no other, beats warmly in the Rule of Saint Benedict. The Rule not only provided spiritual stability and order during chaotic times; because of its emphasis on obedience and work, it allowed, eventually, for the birth of Europe: the clearing of forests and draining of swamps; the introduction of agriculture and viticulture to northern and central Europe; the preservation and dissemination of ancient pagan and Christian learning. The reader should consider how much work a monastery of a hundred able men living an ordered life of obedience can accomplish. The monasteries grew rich because they had the best-managed farmland in the West, perhaps in the world; and they had made it so. Dante derives his details concerning the life of Benedict from the hagiography of Pope Gregory the Great (*Dialogues* 2).

P. 237, L. 51. *where they held their feet:* Benedict refers to the monk's vow of stability; see note at line 40 above.

P. 239, L. 60. *unveil . . . sight:* As with Peter Damian (21.76–78), Dante makes a request that Benedict cannot honor. He will see Benedict and all the saints in their human forms, but only in the Empyrean, in the presence of God (32.35).

Why so? Recall what Statius said to Dante about the generation of the human soul and about its ability to feel pleasure or pain after death (*Purg.* 25.79–108); the soul's intellectual and generative powers fashion for it a shade, a ghostly body made from the circumambient atmosphere. Here in Heaven that element, air, is absent. It seems that the souls possess "bodies"—not yet their true bodies, but similitudes—in the Empyrean, for that sphere is located in the mind of God, who sees them as they are.

Critics also ask why Dante should single out Saint Benedict—after all, Dante did not ask to see the unveiled face of Thomas Aquinas. Perhaps the answer lies in the theology of the monastic life—the height of the life of the laity—as developed by the Pseudo-Areopagite. For Dionysius says that the union of the monks at the table of the Eucharist under the abbot as head makes them a Body of Christ, whose body they also receive; they in their union become a microcosm, bringing together the elements of the world. The purpose of such a life is not only to dwell together in harmony but literally to contemplate the Word through whom all things were made, and in that contemplation to become conformed to Christ: "So they tend to a unity like that of God and to the perfection of the love of God" (*Eccl. Hier.* 533A). Conversely, contemplation was in turn thought of as a mystical Eucharist, allowing the faithful "to make the pasch, the passover, resting dead in the tomb with him, but hearing the words of Christ to the thief" (Bonaventure, *Itinerarium* 7.2; cf. Luke 23:43). Dante's request to see Benedict's face, then, has the same urgency, and the same ardent contemplative aim, as does the desire of the pilgrim to see the Veronica (cf. 31.103–11), and foreshadows the contemplative Bernard's exhortation that Dante gaze "into the face" of Mary, who "most resembles Christ" (32.85–87).

P. 239, L. 71. *Jacob:* Cf. Gen. 28:12; see also note at 21.29.

P. 239, L. 77. *dens for thieves:* Cf. Matt. 21:13.

P. 239, L. 79. *usury:* As Dante saw it, usury was the unnatural—sodomitic—way of procuring one's wealth (cf. *Inf.* 11.95–96). The monks, says Benedict, are worse Sodomites, because they filch money given to them to assist the poor.

P. 239, L. 84. *not . . . repute:* bastard children, mistresses, whores, and such.

P. 239, L. 88. *without silver and gold:* "Then Peter said, Silver and gold have I none; but such as I have I give to thee: In the name of Jesus Christ of Nazareth rise up and walk" (Acts 3:6). But silver and gold are the idols of the unwise (cf. Bar. 3:16–20). Dante has accused the popes of his day of being just such idolaters (Inf. 19.112).

P. 241, L. 96. *the help:* Dante does not specify, nor can the critics specify, what divine intervention in cleaning up the monasteries Benedict predicts.

P. 241, L. 108. *beat my breast:* in token of penitence; so did the tax collector in the parable, crying out, "Lord, have mercy upon me, a sinner" (Luke 18:13).

P. 243, L. 128. *gaze down:* as did the dreaming Scipio Nasica, when in a vision he was shown the physical (and moral) cosmos by his grandfather Scipio

Africanus. To the younger Scipio the earth appears tiny, hardly more than a point, and far surpassed by the other spheres in magnitude, which his grandfather proceeds to show him, describing their motions and their harmonies. Highlighting this contrast between the tiny earth, most of which is not even habitable, and the expanses of the stars, the elder Scipio urges his grandson to scorn earthly power and glory (Cicero, *Somnium* 3–6). The reader may recall other times when Dante has looked back to see how far he has come—in particular, the time at the opening of the *Comedy* when he thought he had reached safety, and was only beginning the dread pilgrimage (*Inf.* 1.22–27).

P. 243, L. 152. *little winnowing floor:* The image may derive from Augustine; this life is a trial wherein men may, by the grace of God, be made virtuous: "Under the same flail the stalk is crushed and the grain threshed; the lees are not mistaken for oil because they have issued from the same press. So, too, the tide of trouble will test, purify, and improve the good, but beat, crush, and wash away the wicked" (*City of God* 1.8).

CANTO TWENTY-THREE
And on his vesture and his thigh a name is written: King of Kings and Lord of Lords. In this canto Dante beholds, at immeasurable distance, the whole of the Church Triumphant, that is, the Church in its glorious military parade, led by the incomprehensible light of Christ.

P. 245, L. 12. *least precipitant:* As usual Dante impresses with his visual precision. Because of the light-bending effects of our concave atmosphere, the air acts as a magnifying glass for celestial bodies appearing near the horizon. These look larger and seem to move more quickly than when they are overhead.

P. 245, L. 20. *behold the grain:* the blessed souls, fruit of the harvest (cf. Luke 10:2).

P. 247, L. 30. *are lit by ours:* It was thought (correctly, except in the case of the stars) that the sun conferred light upon the other heavenly bodies (cf. 10.28–30).

P. 247, L. 37. *the wisdom and the might:* "Christ, the wisdom of God and the power of God" (1 Cor. 1:24).

P. 247, L. 38. *the road:* Christ Himself: "I am the way, the truth, and the life" (John 14:6).

P. 247, L. 42. *opposite its nature:* Fire naturally rises (cf. 1.139–41). Dante's mind now moves like a lightning bolt in reverse, ascending and transcending its limits as far and as fast as a bolt that strikes the earth.

P. 247, L. 48. *the glory of my smile:* In the sphere of the contemplatives, Beatrice did not smile, because Dante's mind was not yet prepared to behold the surge of glory (21.4–12; cf. *Purg.* 31.133–45).

P. 247, L. 50. *a trace of a lost dream:* So Dante will describe his trying to remember and record a trace of the beatific vision (33.67–75).

P. 249, L. 71. *garden:* The word translates the Persian-derived "Paradise." So the Groom (read as an allegory of Christ) describes his Bride, the Church: "A garden inclosed is my sister, my spouse; a spring shut up, a fountain sealed" (Sg. 4:12). The scent of this garden leads the humble to salvation and the proud, who hate it, to death: "For we are unto God a sweet savour of Christ, in them that are saved, and in them that perish: to the one we are the savour of death unto death; and to the other the savour of life unto life" (2 Cor. 2:15–16).

P. 249, LL. 73–74. *the Word divine / was made incarnate:* "And the Word was made flesh, and dwelt among us" (John 1:14).

P. 251, L. 91. *that living star:* another epithet for Mary, called Morning Star in the litany of the saints.

P. 253, L. 128. *Queen of Heaven:* Lat. *Regina coeli,* an Easter hymn, the only song specified in the *Paradise:* "O Queen of Heaven, rejoice, alleluia! For He whom you merited to carry in your womb, alleluia! is risen as He said, alleluia! Rejoice and be glad, O Virgin Mary, alleluia, for the Lord is truly risen, alleluia!"

P. 253, L. 132. *such good fields to sow:* The apostles heard the word of God and kept it in their hearts; cf. Matt. 13:23. The Italian *bobolce* may mean, instead, "husbandmen," "reapers"; the Apostles thus may be seen as not only the harvest but the harvesters; cf. Gal. 6:7.

CANTO TWENTY-FOUR

We were eyewitnesses of his majesty, wrote Peter in his second epistle, confirming the faith of his flock. Yet many were eyewitnesses of the same majesty who did not believe. Beyond all the arguments from physics and metaphysics, beyond the signs and wonders, there remains the simple truth that faith is a gift. It is not by his own power but by God's grace that in this canto Dante can say, "I believe."

P. 255, L. 2. *feast of the blessed Lamb:* "Blessed are they which are called unto the marriage supper of the Lamb" (Rev. 19:9). The wedding feast is more than an image for eternal bliss: it is meant to convey the marriage, the intimacy, between Christ and his Church (cf. Luke 14:16; Matt. 22:14). At this supper the Lamb is both host and victim, giving of himself, his life: "Whoso eateth my flesh, and drinketh my blood, hath eternal life; and I will raise him up on the last day. For my flesh is meat indeed, and my blood is drink indeed. He that eateth my flesh, and drinketh my blood, dwelleth in me, and I in him" (John 6:54–56).

P. 255, L. 6. *the crumbs:* like those spiritual leavings the Canaanite woman begged from Christ (Matt. 15:27).

P. 255, L. 22. *three turns:* The motion expresses the Trinity, and Saint Peter will repeat it at the end of the canto.

P. 257, L. 35. *the keys:* those of the kingdom of Heaven, conferred particularly upon Peter and, as Catholics hold, upon Peter's successors (cf. Matt. 16:19).

P. 257, L. 39. *you walked upon the sea:* Peter was in a boat with James and John when he saw Jesus approaching them upon the water. "And Peter answered him and said, Lord, if it be thou, bid me come unto thee on the water. And he said, Come. And when Peter was come down out of the ship, he walked on the water, to go to Jesus" (Matt. 14:28–29). Peter had faith enough to make the bold request and to attempt it, but after he began to fear, and to sink, he cried for help, and Jesus lifted him up, rebuking him for his little faith. Beatrice recalls this scene, however, as one of triumph for Peter, and of course it is: since faith is not in one's own power of will, paltry as that is, but in Christ.

P. 257, LL. 43–44. *what...faith:* "The just shall live by faith" (Rom. 1:17); "They which be of faith are blessed" (Gal. 3:9). In the heavenly city dwell citizens, whose citizenship is granted not by birth, not by money, nor by political maneuvering, but by *the true faith.*

P. 257, L. 46. *bachelor:* The metaphor of the oral examination shows clearly that, for Dante and his contemporaries, Paradise was conceived as a realm of intellectual fulfillment. The form of this part of the examination (the most difficult of the three parts, since James and John, examining Dante on hope and love, will never seem, as Peter does, to contradict what Dante says) resembles, distantly, the form of disputation in the schools or in a summa. Peter poses a question, Dante responds, Peter objects, Dante responds to the objection.

P. 259, L. 62. *your beloved brother Paul:* quoting Peter himself (2 Pet. 3:15); Paul *joined* Peter in his *work* in Rome in that he, like Peter, went there to preach, and he, like Peter, was martyred there.

P. 259, L. 64. *Faith:* the great definition by Saint Paul: "Now faith is the substance of things hoped for, the evidence of things not seen" (Heb. 11:1). Aquinas discusses this precise matter of faith being both substance and argument (*Summa theol.* 2.2.4.1). What is not yet seen, but is an object of exultant faith, is the fullness of the glory of Christ (1 Pet. 1:6–12).

P. 259, L. 90. *is founded every other virtue:* "But without faith it is impossible to please him: for he that cometh to God must believe that he is, and that he is a rewarder of them that diligently seek him" (Heb. 11:6).

P. 259, L. 91. *the generous rain:* For the image, cf. 14:27.

P. 259, L. 93. *parchment:* Dante refers to the Old and New Testaments, but, since he is discussing the demonstrability of the faith, he may also have an eye to the story of Gideon, who "spread a fleece," a parchment if you will, on two successive nights, to prove to himself that it was God who was speaking to him: on one night the ground was to be dry while the fleece was soaked with dew, while on the next the fleece was to be dry while the ground was wet (Judg. 6:36–40).

PP. 259–260 LL. 93–94. *train / Of reasoning:* Ital. *silogismo.* Dante asserts that the words inspired by the Holy Spirit are more powerfully persuasive than a syllogism; in other words, more certainly true than a conclusion whose truth follows with absolute necessity from the very definitions of terms and the predicates used in the premises. Faith is not fideism but faith in what has been preached through the Holy Scriptures, though reason may show that this faith is in accord with reason (Aquinas, *Summa theol.* 2.2.6.1).

P. 261, L. 105. *You call to witness what you seek to prove:* Peter objects that Dante's reasoning is circular. How can the miracles attest to the divine provenance and truth of the Scripture, when Scripture is the only witness that the miracles actually happened? To answer the objection, Dante must move outside Scripture temporarily, and he does so, pointing to the greatest miracle of all, one that he surely believed was prophesied by Scripture: the conversion of the whole world to Christianity (Matt. 27:18–20), begun by a few poor ragtag apostles. The argument derives from Augustine (*City of God* 20.30, 22.5) and was picked up by Aquinas (*Summa con. gen.* 1.6).

P. 261, L. 111. *wine...thorn:* For the imagery, see 12.86–87 and note.

P. 263, L. 130. *And I respond: I believe in one God:* It is a stupendous and moving line. Its first half, *And I respond,* repeats the confident first words of Aquinas's explanation of his own position, in every article of the *Summa theologiae.* The second half gives the thundering first words of the *Credo: "Credo in unum Deum."* In this compact creed Dante asserts the unity of God, the providence of God, and the Trinity of God. Notice that the act of faith confidently enlists both physics and metaphysics for support: it is not a fideism, or a faith in faith, but an intellectually coherent faith in a Being about whom reason can reveal a few important truths—for example, that he exists (cf. Aquinas, *Summa theol.* 1.2.3; Hugh of Saint Victor, *On the Sacraments* 7–9; Boethius, *Cons. Phil.* 3 pr. 10)—and who has revealed other truths about himself in Scripture.

P. 263, LL. 136–138. *Moses...inspired:* That covers all of Scripture. Moses represents the Pentateuch, *the Psalms* the book of that name, and *the prophets* all the other historical, sapiential, and prophetic writings of the Old Testament; *the evangelists* wrote the four gospels, and the other writers inspired by the Holy Spirit wrote the rest of the New Testament. All of these point to Christ, the Word of God made flesh: "These are the words which I spake unto you, while I was yet with you, that all things must be fulfilled, which were written in the law of Moses, and in the prophets, and in the psalms, concerning me" (Luke 24:44).

P. 263, L. 141. *'are' and 'is':* Dante's language derives from the Athanasian Creed: "This is the catholic faith, that we worship one God in Trinity and the Trinity in Unity, neither confounding the persons, nor separating them in substance."

P. 263, L. 144. *gospel teaching:* The evangelists and apostles teach, without philosophical elucidation, the doctrine of the Trinity (cf. Matt. 28:19; John 14:16–17, 26; 2 Cor. 13:13; 1 Pet. 1:2; 1 John 5:7). From this one doctrine, Dante asserts, everything else flows, as flame from a single spark.

P. 263, L. 154. *I'd spoken... delight:* If Dante boasts now, he boasts in the Lord (1 Cor. 1:31).

CANTO TWENTY-FIVE

Give reasons for the hope that is in you. In the noblest of pagan systems, whether the brave stoicism of Rome or the glad Norse will to fight in a losing cause, there is no hope. Nor for the Christian, as Dante sees it, is hope an easy virtue. Though it is a gift of grace, it is also a habit of placing always before one's mind the promise, however distant, when all around seems to give cause to despair. Hope is the virtue that lifts the heart of the soldier.

P. 265, L. 1. *If it should happen:* Dante opens this canto on hope with a hope of his own: that someday justice may reign in his beloved Florence—his *sheepfold,* the place of his childhood and youth—and that he may return, not as a vindicated politician, but as the *poet* of the promises of Heaven. His poetic triumph here has its source in the humble waters of the baptismal font of Saint John the Baptist (cf. 15.134).

P. 265 L. 5. *lamb:* Dante's words might imply that he is both a lamb in the flock and a guardian of that flock, unlike some: "But he that is an hireling and not the shepherd, whose own the sheep are not, seeth the wolf coming, and leaveth the sheep, and fleeth" (John 10:12). More directly, Dante is himself the lamb attacked by *wolves:* "But I was like a lamb... that is brought to the slaughter; and I knew not that they had devised devices against me" (Jer. 11:19).

P. 265, L. 7. *other vellum:* The word denotes parchment made from sheepskin; thus it can refer both to the poetry of the *lamb* Dante or to the grizzled skin and white hair of Dante's old age.

P. 265, L. 8. *my crown:* "Blessed is the man that endureth temptation: for when he is tried, he shall receive the crown of life, which the Lord hath promised to them that love him" (Jas. 1:12). The verse from the epistle of James signals a return to the invocation of Apollo at the beginning of the poem (1.13–36); again a crown is hoped for, but there is no mention of Apollo, and Dante will find that crown at his life's *baptismal* source.

P. 265, LL. 10–11. *the faith... His:* "Abraham believed God, and it was imputed unto him for righteousness: and he was called the Friend of God" (Jas. 2:23).

P. 267, L. 29. *renowned spirit:* Beatrice refers to James's writing of the epistle that bears his name. Other than to establish a poetic symmetry between the three chief apostles and the three theological virtues, critics are not sure how justified it is to see James as an emblem of hope. In fact, however, a great deal of James's epistle has to do with hope, and particularly with the sort of hope that the exiled Dante had to pursue. James recommends the patient endurance of the just, those who suffer not only persecution with "the patience of Job" (5:11), but the strife within their own members: "My brethren, count it all joy when ye fall into divers temptations; knowing this, that the trying of your faith worketh patience. But let patience have her perfect work, that we may be perfect and entire, wanting nothing" (1:2–4); he reproves the false hopes of the worldly, predicting that they will come to an unexpected and bad end: "For what is your life? It is even a vapor, that appeareth for a little time, and then vanisheth away" (4:14). Rather, says James, we are to hope that the prayers of a just man will be efficacious (5:16); that prayer for the sick may work healing of body and soul (5:13–14); and that the Lord will give what we ask in faith (1:5–6), even "the crown of life" (1:12). James also serves as the link between faith and love, for it is in the hope of Christ's promises that we perfect faith by means of love (2:18–22).

P. 267, L. 39. *those mountains:* "I will lift up mine eyes unto the hills, from whence cometh my help" (Ps. 121:1; the verse seems to have inspired the image of the sun-clad mountain at the beginning of the *Comedy, Inf.* 1.13–18).

P. 267, L. 42. *nobles:* Ital. *conti,* "counts," like the twelve counts or paladins, the peers of Charlemagne. The image of the warfaring Christian underlies Dante's conversation with Saint James.

P. 267, L. 44. *comfort:* Ital. *conforte,* "strengthen." Dante uses forms of this word to describe the strengthening comfort given him by Virgil and Beatrice. Here, Saint James makes Dante himself the strengthener; he, like Saint Paul (*Inf.* 2.28–30), is to tell what he has seen in Paradise, to confirm the faithful in their faith. Before Dante entered Hell he doubted his worthiness to go to the other world: "I'm not Aeneas, I'm not Saint Paul" (*Inf.* 2.32). In his conversation with Cacciaguida he was assigned, implicitly, the role of Aeneas, founder of the Roman people (15.25–27; 17.13–99), and here he is assigned the role of the Chosen Vessel, Paul, returning from Paradise (cf. 2 Cor. 12:2–4) to bring hope to his fellow Christians.

P. 267, L. 51. *answering:* It might seem boastful if Dante himself told James of his great hope (cf. James's warning against boastfulness, 4:16). The interruption marks the first time in the *Comedy*—and perhaps the only time—Dante is praised by Beatrice for his virtue. Why here, and why this virtue? Perhaps Dante is supreme in hope because of how much tribulation he has endured—the calumny and exile (*Par.* 5.6–8); perhaps too his hope is manifest in his daring prayer to be inspired by God to write a poem about all times and all creation. Whatever the reason, Beatrice, once distressed by the possibility that Dante would lose all hope (cf. *Inf.* 1.49–54; 2.58–66), now pronounces him a *son* of the *Church Militant,* a warrior with hope in his every stride.

P. 269, L. 57. *from Egypt to behold Jerusalem:* "When Israel went out of Egypt, the house of Jacob from a people of strange language; Judah was his sanctuary, and Israel his dominion" (Ps. 114:1; this is the psalm sung by the souls on the boat to Purgatory, *Purg.* 2.46). Dante is being freed from bondage to sin—the fleshpots of Egypt—to behold Jerusalem, the City of Peace, the City of God (Rev. 21:2).

P. 269, L. 69. *merits we have won:* Dante gives the school-text answer: "Hope is the certain expectation of future beatitude, rising from the grace of God and from our past merits" (Lombard, *Sentences* 3.26; also Aquinas, *Summa theol.* 2.2.17.1–2).

P. 269, L. 76. *shed your rain upon me too:* See note at line 29 above. For the image of rain, note James 5:7: "Be patient therefore, brethren, unto the coming of the Lord. Behold, the husbandman waiteth for the precious fruit of the earth, and hath long patience for it, until he receive the early and latter rain."

P. 269, L. 81. *lightning bolt:* echoing the name that Jesus gave to James and John, the Sons of Thunder (Mark 3:17).

P. 269, L. 83. *held me near:* "Draw nigh to God, and he will draw nigh to you" (Jas. 4:8).

P. 269, L. 84. *the palm:* James was put to death by Herod Agrippa (Acts 12:2). He is the only apostle whose death is recorded in the Bible.

P. 269, L. 90. *His friend:* Cf. Jas. 2:23.

P. 271, L. 92. *robed with a double robe:* "Therefore in their land they shall possess the double: everlasting joy shall be unto them" (Is. 61:7). Dante interprets the verse from Isaiah as implying that the highest hope involves the full beatitude of body and soul in union.

P. 271, L. 98. *Let them hope in you:* Lat. *Sperent in te,* repeating Ps. 9:11, quoted by Dante in Italian in lines 73–74.

P. 271, L. 101. *Cancer:* The constellation Cancer is high in the midnight sky during the dead of winter. If one of its stars were as bright as the soul approaching, winter would be as bright as day for a whole month.

P. 271, L. 110. *like a still and silent spouse:* In their dance the three great apostles do honor to Beatrice, and she responds by introducing them to Dante (24.34–36; 25.17–18), naming them by describing an honor granted to them: Peter was given the keys, and James's tomb in Spain is the destination for pilgrims from all over Christendom. But now, in her silent wonder, she suggests that the honors granted to John—that he reclined upon Christ's breast at table (John 13:23), and that from the Cross Christ gave to him the care of his mother, Mary, who lived with John from that day forth (John 19:26–27)—were the greatest, if not in authority, then in love. The association of the apostle John with love and light is a natural one to draw: the gospel and the three letters that bear his name present a veritable theology of love, whereof these verses are perhaps the most famous: "Beloved, let us love one another: for love is of God; and every one that loveth is born of God, and knoweth God. He that loveth not knoweth not God; for God is love. In this was manifested the love of God toward us, because that God sent his only begotten Son into the world, that we might live through him. Herein is love, not that we loved God, but that he loved us" (1 John 4:7–10).

P. 271, L. 113. *Christ our Pelican:* Christ, the Suffering Servant: "I am like a pelican of the wilderness: I am like an owl of the desert" (Ps. 102:6). Due to a confusion regarding a bird the people of the Middle Ages had heard of but rarely seen, it was thought that the pelican fed its young from its own substance. Artistic representations show the bird pricking its breast with its own beak, and the young feeding upon the blood. Naturally, the pelican was therefore considered a sign of Christ, whose body and blood nourish the faithful in the sacrifice of the Eucharist. The motif inspires one of the stanzas of Aquinas's hymn *Adoro te devote:* "O pelican of mercy, Jesus Lord and God, / Cleanse me of my uncleanness by your saving blood, / Whereof a single drop would evermore suffice / To heal the world and save it from all its wickedness." (see Appendix C).

P. 271, L. 119. *an eclipse of the sun:* Dante's metaphor is dramatically and theologically perfect. He is straining his eyes, trying to see whether John is in Heaven with his body, as Jesus hinted might be possible, without however asserting that it should be so, as the gospel writer is himself quick to note (John 21:21–23). Ironically, that body would not eclipse the soul but would, as Solomon has said (14.52–57), outshine it with its glorious incandescence. The result of the staring is that Dante goes temporarily blind—and that loss of vision, while he is being examined on love, is like a passage to a more perfect sight. Indeed, blindness is a central theme in the gospel of John; see, for instance, the curing of the blind man in chapter 9.

CANTO TWENTY-SIX

Not that we loved God, but that he loved us. It may be a surprise that in this canto on love, neither affections nor specific acts of love, such as almsgiving, are focused upon. That is because Dante's view of love is as far from the narcissistic as is imaginable. His love can, fundamentally, be no other than anyone else's love, since he, Dante, is a creature whose desired goal has already been set for him in his own creation, as it has in the creation of every other human being. The only reason why we love at all, Dante would say, is that God has made us for love—for his love.

P. 275, L. 8. *its single end:* Aquinas thus defines charity: "The love of God whereby he is loved as the object of our blessedness, whereto we are ordered by faith and hope" (*Summa theol.* 2.1.65.5). So too Augustine, linking love of God and love of one another: "It is this Good which we are commanded to love with our whole heart, with our whole mind, and with all our strength. It is toward this Good that we should be led by those who love us, and toward this Good we should lead those whom we love" (*City of God* 10.3).

P. 275, LL. 14–15. *the gate / she entered:* Dante's blindness will be cured by a loving glance from Beatrice's eyes, and justly so, since it was through his eyes that her beauty once wounded him with love (cf. *Purg.* 30.40–42).

P. 275, L. 17. *Alpha and Omega:* God is the beginning and end of all love: "I am Alpha and Omega, the beginning and the end, the first and the last" (Rev. 22:13).

P. 275, L. 19. *my instructor, Love:* Compare this theological statement with Dante's description of his poetic inspiration: "I'm one who takes the pen / when Love breathes wisdom into me, and go / finding the signs for what he speaks within" (*Purg.* 24.52–54). There, Dante was the poet, the crafter; here, the attentive hearer of words granted to him by the grace of Love.

P. 279, L. 25. *Arguments of philosophy:* As in his justification of the faith (24.133–34), Dante begins by asserting the capacity of natural human reason to see that only the Supreme Being is worthy to be the ultimate object of our love. Revelation sharpens and deepens what reason sees, and reveals what reason does not see.

P. 279, L. 37. *He lays this bare before my intellect:* The structure of Dante's statement implies that "he" must refer to a philosopher; if not, we might conclude that Dante has in mind Dionysius the Areopagite, who wrote a treatise on the nine celestial hierarchies. It should also be a pagan philosopher, to set up a progression and climax: philosopher to whom only the light of natural reason is granted; Old Testament prophet, granted also the light of revelation; New Testament evangelist, granted the fullest light of revelation. My guess is that the philosopher referred to is Plato, whose *Timaeus*—thought by the early Christians to have been influenced by the book of Genesis—describes God's creation of a beautiful and orderly cosmos, reflecting the eternal pattern of that cosmos existing in his mind.

P. 279, L. 42. *I shall reveal all worth to you:* When Moses asked the Lord to reveal to him the fullness of his glory, the Lord replied thus: *Ego ostendam omne bonum tibi* (Ex. 33:19, Vulgate), "I shall reveal all good to you." What does that have to do with love? The glory and the beauty of the Lord instill love and are the objects of love. We must consider that the revelation of this glory results, as it was thought, in Moses' writing of the Pentateuch, and in particular his writing of the first chapters of Genesis, describing the great act of love whereby God created the universe. The reader might also note that Dante uses this very verse in *La vita nuova* 3 to describe his first sight of the lovely Beatrice and the dream of Love that followed. When asked to interpret the dream, his friend Guido Cavalcanti replied, writing, "I believe you have beheld all worth."

P. 279, L. 43. *your proemion:* The gospel of John also begins with a cosmology of love, only here the emphasis is upon the inner love of the Trinity and upon the love of God for sinful man, redeeming him by the Incarnation of Christ, the Light of the World. Thus in the three examples we see a natural view of the Love that binds the world, the supernatural revelation of the Love that made the world, and the supernatural revelation of the Love that precedes the world and redeems the world.

P. 281, L. 58. *this world's very being:* The world is beautiful and worthy of love: "The heavens declare the glory of God; and the firmament sheweth his handiwork" (Ps. 19:1). Dante's reply to Saint John shows the ramification of love: because he loves the Creator, he loves all things according to the gifts the Creator has bestowed upon them.

P. 281, L. 62. *the ocean that deceives:* It is love that has saved Dante from "the dangerous sea" of sin (cf. *Inf.* 1.24; 2.106–8).

P. 281, L. 65. *Master of the vine:* Cf. John 15:1.

P. 281, L. 68. *Holy, holy, holy:* The beginning of the liturgical prayer *Sanctus:* "Holy, holy, holy, Lord God of hosts, heaven and earth are full of your glory. Hosanna in the highest. Blessed is he who comes in the name of the Lord. Hosanna in the highest" (for the triple repetition of the word "holy," see Is. 6:3; Rev. 4:8). Dante having passed his examination on the three theological virtues, the heavens resound with a doxology celebrating the Trinity and the One, Christ, who comes in the name of the Lord (John 12:12–13). At this point Dante's sight returns, and he sees the first embodied being created in the image and likeness of the Trinity, the being who was, in his disobedience, the type or shadow of the obedient Redeemer to come. We are joining the Alpha with the Omega: nearing the fulfillment of human desire, we meet the first man, progenitor of our race, Adam.

P. 283, L. 95. *my will:* It is not a burning doubt, as when Dante pleaded that the Eagle of justice teach him about the fate of virtuous pagans (19.22–33), but a set of intellectual questions that some readers might (wrongly) think idle or curious. These have to do with time (how long Adam dwelled in Paradise, and how long it has been since he was driven out of it), language (which one he used), and sin (exactly why Adam was condemned). We see that in one manner or another the questions deal with the limitations of a corporeal being. All bodies dwell in time and are subject to change; the language we use, a human construct, is also subject to change. Had Adam not sinned in Paradise, there still would have been time, and Adam's response to Dante suggests that there would have been linguistic change, too. That marks a sharp departure from the traditional view, expounded by Dante himself (*De vera eloquentia* 1.6.4–7), that Hebrew was instilled into Adam by God and was allowed to remain unchanged indefinitely. Adam's sin, then, is a violation of the truth that linguistic change teaches: that we are beings bounded in space and time, and thus must submit to the boundaries set for us by our Creator. To wish to speak a never-changing language is to wish not to be an embodied being but a god. The reader should note too that the punishment for such presumption, in the account of the Tower of Babel, is linguistic confusion (Gen. 11:1–9).

P. 283, L. 115. *My son:* No mere affectionate epithet: Dante in fact is Adam's son.

P. 283, LL. 119–120. *four thousand and / three hundred and two turnings of the sun:* from his death to the death of Christ that freed him from Limbo. Adding to that the number of years Adam lived on earth and the number of years since the death

of Christ, by 1300, the year of this vision, it will have been 6,498 years since
Adam's creation.

P. 285, L. 134. I *was the name:* perhaps the *Yah* of the Hebrew name for God, the
never-pronounced tetragrammaton YHWH. Adam says that it was followed by
El, a Hebrew word meaning "Lord" (as in Bethel, "House of the Lord").

P. 285, L. 137. *a branch's leaves:* The image comes from Horace (*Ars poetica* 60–62).

P. 285, L. 142. *Six hours:* Such was the opinion of Peter Comestor (the Book De-
vourer of 12.134), in his *Scholastic History* 24. That shockingly short time is at
least longer than the less than twenty seconds Dante says Satan existed before
he fell (29.48–51).

You are the Christ, the Son of the living God. So said Simon, inspired by the
Holy Spirit, when Jesus asked his disciples who they—as opposed to the wonder-
ing people in the towns and villages—thought he was. At which profession of
faith Jesus pronounced him Peter, the rock upon which he would build his
Church. Thus when Peter grows angry at the misuse of his chair, the papacy, he
is expressing once again his faith and his zeal—he shed his own blood in Rome to
spread the gospel of Christ.

P. 287, L. 1. *To Father and to Son and Holy Ghost:* The souls sing the doxology "Glory
be to the Father, and to the Son, and to the Holy Ghost: as it was in the begin-
ning, is now, and ever shall be, world without end. Amen." Having listened to
talk of human mutability and the changes wrought by sin, the souls give glory
to the changeless Trinity. This song—and its joy—will burst into the indigna-
tion of the zealous Saint Peter, who beholds with shame the changes wrought
upon the Holy See by those who care for power and money more than they
care for God, and who will not respect the limits of the power granted to them.

P. 287, L. 5. *inebriating:* "They shall be inebriated with the richness of your house"
(Ps. 36:9, Vulgate).

P. 287, L. 8. *riches . . . desire:* "Lay up for yourselves treasures in heaven, where nei-
ther moth nor rust doth corrupt, and where thieves do not break in and steal"
(Matt. 6:20).

P. 287, L. 15. *their plumage:* Peter's anger shows that individuality is not effaced in
Heaven; he is still that impetuous apostle who cut off the ear of the high priest's
servant (John 18:10), and who burst out, when the others were silent, with the
first confession that Jesus was the Son of God (Matt. 16:16).

P. 287, L. 22. *my Holy See:* Ital. *il luogo mio,* "my place," that is, the Chair of Peter.
After the singing of the thrice-blessing *Sanctus* and the Trinitarian *Gloria Patri,*
the repetition of Peter's words strikes like the thunder of a liturgical curse. The
pope may think himself secure because of the high dignity he is afforded, but

he should heed the warning of the prophet Jeremiah: "Thus saith the Lord of hosts, the God of Israel, Amend your ways and your doings, and I will cause you to dwell in this place. Trust ye not in lying words, saying, The temple of the Lord, The temple of the Lord, The temple of the Lord, are these" (7:3–4); "Is this house, which is called by my name, become a den of robbers in your eyes? Behold, even I have seen it, saith the Lord" (7:11).

The movement of this canto replicates that of the end of the preceding canto and applies the wisdom to be learned there: we turn from the changeless Trinity to a world of change that is now, since Adam's fall, also a world of sin. There we find the Church of Christ, the Ark wherein we are to sail over the tempestuous sea to our salvation, in the clutches of sin. For the head (Boniface VIII) has turned Rome—the sacred ground whereon Peter and Paul and so many of the early martyrs died—into a sewer, for the delight of Satan. Even though Boniface is by Church law the true vicar of Christ (cf. *Purg.* 20.86–90), morally—in the presence of God's Son—that chair is now vacant. That leaves a pretty state of affairs on earth: an emperor who is no emperor, and a pope who is no pope.

P. 289, L. 35. *an eclipse:* Cf. Luke 23:45.

P. 289, L. 40. *the Bride of Christ:* the Church (cf. 11.32–33; Eph. 5:25–32).

P. 289, L. 41. *by my blood:* Dante echoes the saying of Tertullian "The blood of the martyrs is the seed of the Church." The first popes are all saints and martyrs: Peter (d. 66, under Nero), *Linus* (78, under Vespasian), *Cletus* (91, under Domitian); skipping some, these are followed by *Sixtus* (127, under Hadrian), *Pius* (149, under Antoninus Pius), *Calixtus* (222, under Alexander Severus), and *Urban* (230, under Alexander Severus).

P. 289, L. 42. *gold:* Peter once adjured his disciples to take care of his flock, "not for filthy lucre" (1 Pet. 5:2), and indeed asserted that Christ's blood and not "silver or gold" had redeemed them (1 Pet. 1:18–19).

P. 289, L. 47. *to left, to right:* Peter accuses the pope of playing God, arrogating to himself and perverting the judgment of Christ, who when he returns will separate the good from the wicked, the sheep from the goats (Matt. 25:31–33). The pope instead separates Christians into partisan camps for the power he can gain thereby.

P. 289, L. 50. *blazon the banners of some new Crusade:* Ital. *divenisser signaculo in vessillo,* "become the insignia upon the banner." The words echo the opening of the crusading hymn *Vexilla Regis prodeunt* (cf. *Inf.* 34.1). The pope uses his sign not to win back the Holy Land but to battle his Christian rivals (cf. *Inf.* 27.86–88).

P. 289, L. 55. *wolves in every fold:* Cf. Matt. 7:15; Jer. 23:1.

P. 289, L. 57. *why do you sleep:* "Awake, why sleepest thou, O Lord? Arise, cast us not off forever. Wherefore hidest thou thy face, and forgettest our affliction and our oppression?" (Ps. 44:23–24); see also *Purg.* 6.118–20.

P. 291, L. 63. *the world's glory:* The Lord once defended the Roman state by raising up Scipio Africanus; now the Lord will defend the Roman papacy by avenging himself upon the churchmen who illegitimately fight the just claims of the empire.

P. 291, L. 66. *Do not conceal:* Dante's commission, to write what he has seen (cf. *Purg.* 32.103–105; 33.52–57; *Par.* 17.127–42). Compare with Cacciaguida's command that Dante speak fearlessly about Florence and political corruption (17.124–32).

P. 293, L. 85. *this little threshing floor:* a reprise of the phrase Dante used to describe the earth the last time he glanced down at it (22.152). This marks our final vision of earth in the *Comedy*—now, as we are about to ascend to the Primum Mobile.

P. 295, L. 119. *time:* Time begins in the mysterious providence that impels the Primum Mobile, but comes to fruition in the corporeal spheres below. The previous canto ended with an account of the misuse of Adam's brief time in Paradise; this canto ends with the consequent falling away of human beings from childhood and innocence into wickedness. But since the Redeemer is the Lord of time, time will also bring the restoration of justice and of beauty in the Church on earth.

P. 295, L. 126. *swell the true plums and turn them soft and sour:* making them unnatural, unjust, as if one's wicked deeds were not one's true children but bastards: "But the multiplied brood of the wicked shall not thrive, and bastard slips shall not take deep root, nor any fast foundation.... For the branches not being perfect, shall be broken, and their fruits shall be unprofitable, and sour to eat, and fit for nothing" (Wis. 4:3, 5).

P. 295, L. 128. *among the children:* an indictment of the decadence of Dante's day; Dante is probably also thinking of Christ's warning "Except ye be converted, and become as little children, ye shall not enter into the kingdom of Heaven" (Matt. 18:3).

P. 295, L. 137. *the lovely daughter:* Interpretations of the tercet cover quite a range: "the sunlight, daughter of the sun, *him who brings the dawn,* can turn a fair complexion dark"; or "the Church, daughter of God, in its corruption can [do the same]"; or "the lure of the sorceress Circe [representing worldly goods], daughter of the sun god Hyperion, can corrupt, transforming white to black."

P. 295, L. 148. *good fruit:* not the sour plums of line 126.

CANTO TWENTY-EIGHT

And the sons of morning sang for joy—not those effeminate, wispy-winged things with rosy faces, but sons of morning, of unimaginable power, incorporeal beings, immortal because incorporeal. The existence of angels, of course, is attested by Scripture; nor is it unreasonable that an incorporeal God could or would create rational beings not limited by body. The reader will note that just as the angels fill a reasonable place in the scale of being extending from God to dust, so they themselves are hierarchically ordered, divided into ranks. Indeed, Dante would argue that there could be no harmonious choir otherwise.

P. 297, L. 2. *miserable and mortal humankind:* Dante echoes Virgil's *Georgics* 3.66; the Roman's point is that the wise husbandman must seize the best age for the breeding of cattle, since old age follows too soon. Here the direction is the reverse: after the suffering come restoration and glory.

P. 297, L. 3. *she... Paradise:* Beatrice raises Dante's mind to the contemplation of Heaven not only by her speaking of theological truth but by her womanly beauty.

P. 297, L. 11. *her lovely eyes:* By looking into Beatrice's eyes Dante glimpses a vision of what he turns around to see: the cosmos as concentric spheres revolving around God.

P. 297, L. 16. *a point:* With audacity Dante represents the infinite God by an image of the infinitesimally small—a point that, like God, is indivisible and has no extension in space and time. Dante is thinking of the traditional formulation of the Deity as both center and circumference of all things; we have heard him call God the "uncircumscribed" (14.30), but He is that uncircumscribed One about whom all things turn, since their turning is the created, embodied reflection of His unchanging stillness, as He is ever in act and ever at rest (Augustine, *Conf.* 13.37).

P. 299, L. 42. *whence... depend:* Dante echoes Aristotle: "On such a principle, then, depend the heavens and the world of nature" (*Metaphysics* 30.7). Yet the visible image—the whole cosmos, literally hanging from a single dimensionless point—is far more powerful than the bare philosophical statement.

P. 299, L. 53. *angelic temple:* Heaven, as God's temple (cf. 2 Sam. 22:7; Ps. 10:5; Rev. 7:15).

P. 301, L. 93. *a chessboard's squares:* more than two to the sixty-third power. Legend had it that the inventor of chess was offered a reward by the king of Persia. The inventor asked for a grain of wheat on the first square, two on the second, and so on for all sixty-four squares. The king soon saw that not all the grain in his kingdom would suffice to honor the request. The number of angels is finite but is greater than any practical human numeration (cf. Aquinas, *Summa con. gen.* 2.92).

P. 305, L. 95. *where:* Lat. *ubi,* used as a noun to describe "place" in an ontological more than in a spatial sense. The power and grace of God hold the angels in being and preserve them in beatitude.

P. 305, L. 99. *the Seraphim and Cherubim:* highest of the angels. Dante follows the angelic hierarchy described by Pseudo-Dionysius the Areopagite (see lines 103, 122–126): *Seraphim, Cherubim, Thrones, Dominations, Virtues, Powers, Princes, Archangels, Angels.* Of course, there are ranks within the ranks; and each rank has its proper virtue, the power of God it is most meant to manifest. The angels are close to God according to the degree to which God has granted them vision of

Himself; such vision stirs and fulfills love (14.46–51; cf. *Summa theol.* 2.1.3.8). This love makes the soul like unto God: "Beloved, now are we the sons of God, and it doth not yet appear what we shall be: but we know that, when we shall appear, we shall be like him, for we shall see him as he is" (1 John 3:2).

P. 305, L. 111. *love…afterward:* Dante follows the opinion of Aquinas, who argues that beatitude consists in the vision of God, and that the joy of fulfilled love is concomitant with it, as a necessary consequence (*Summa theol.* 2.1.4.1).

P. 305, LL. 112–113. *grace…along with virtuous will:* The free will cooperates with grace by sacrificing itself to it (*Purg.* 11.10–12), not by adding anything of its own.

P. 305, L. 119. *Hosanna:* Cf. John 12:13.

P. 305, L. 129. *toward God:* So Beatrice has already said of the heavenly spheres whereof the angels are the intelligences (2.118–23).

CANTO TWENTY-NINE

God saw that it was good. Dante answers the question "Why did God create?" by referring us back to the first chapter of Genesis. In polytheistic systems the world is always created to fulfill the motive of some god or other, or as an aftereffect of some conflict in the immortal regions. Genesis gives no motive, implying that there was none, none that we would call a motive anyway, since God is not moved, not troubled, as there is nothing prior to God. If we wished, we could say, instead of "God created," "God loved," and leave it at that—for perfect love is its own motive.

P. 309, L. 12. *terminus of* where *and* when: Latin *ubi* and *quando*. After giving us a vision of God as a dimensionless point of light, Dante says that Beatrice pauses for what is a "dimensionless" *instant* of time. We move, then, from discussing "space" that is no space to "time" that is no time, for there is no passage of time in eternity. Dante has seen the plan of the cosmos in the moment; now he wonders about that cosmos from the perspective of eternity and time. Specifically, for what end did God set these rings in motion?

P. 309, L. 18. *into new loves burst the Eternal Love:* God created out of the superabundance of His love (cf. 7.64–66 and note at 7.65). The tenet resembles the Neoplatonic theory of emanations: that the cosmos, corporeal and incorporeal, flows in a succession of emanations from the fountain of the One. But the difference is decisive: in Plotinian thinking as in all pantheistic and quasi-pantheistic systems, such procession from God is necessary. The universe is, as it were, God's body, and God is a necessary feature of the universe. But Jewish and Christian thought asserts the contrary: there is nothing at all necessary about the existence of the universe. God created it out of love, for His purposes, for Himself, that He might communicate with it His goodness (cf. Augustine, *Conf.* 13.4; Aquinas, *Summa con. gen.* 2.46).

P. 309, L. 19. *he did not lie adrowse and still:* "Lo, are not those men full of their old carnal nature who say to us, 'What was God doing before he made heaven and earth?' " (Augustine, *Conf.* 11.10; cf. also *City of God* 11.5). Augustine replies that there is no "before" and "after" in God.

P. 309, L. 21. *the hovering... waters:* "And the Spirit of God moved upon the face of the waters" (Gen. 1:2). According to the schoolmen, the waters above which God hovered were the already created celestial spheres. Augustine suggests that the verse "Let there be light" (Gen. 1:2) describes the creation of the angels, who participate from the beginning in the light of Christ: "Thus, the angels, illuminated by that Light which created them, became light and were called 'day' because they participated in that unchangeable Light and Day which is the Word of God, by whom they and all things were made" (*City of God* 11.9).

P. 311, L. 24. *three-cord bow:* The language suggests that the universe, comprising pure form (the incorporeal beings), pure matter (unformed matter), and matter and form combined (all objects in the physical world), bears the stamp of the Trinity, its Creator. The image derives from Scripture: "A triple cord is difficult to break" (Eccl. 4:12), and is cited by Richard of Saint Victor in his argument for a plurality of persons in the Deity (*The Trinity* 3.5). Aquinas uses the metaphor of the archer to show that God acts freely, by intellect and will, and not by necessity (*Summa con. gen.* 2.23).

P. 311, L. 32. *their order and their essence, concreate:* When God created the angels—literally, his "messengers," the manifesters of his power, wisdom, and love—he created at that same moment their separate beings (for each angel, being an incorporeal essence, belongs to its own single species, as Aquinas argues, *Summa theol.* 1.50.4), the rank to which each would belong (not, therefore, by common features, but by the grace of vision granted to them by God), and the harmonious order of the ranks. At the same time, God created the physical cosmos wherein the angels would be his messengers. If the discussion sounds hopelessly abstruse, the reader should bear in mind that what Dante is touching on here is the unity and harmony of all created things as manifesting God and as bringing into being his eternal providence. The whole—the incorporeal angels, the rational beings united to bodies, the nonrational animals, the nonsentient plants, and mere body—expresses the unity and trinity of God more fully and beautifully and fittingly, says Aquinas (*Summa con. gen.* 2.46) than would a universe lacking any of these things. The angels, then, *belong* to this cosmos, just as do the grains of sand on the shore.

P. 311, L. 37. *Jerome:* In his letter to Titus (1.2), Saint Jerome wrote that the angels existed long before the creation of the physical world, but his opinion is not the common one, and he is specifically refuted by Aquinas, whose reasoning Dante follows: "No part is perfect if it is separated from the whole. Therefore it is not probable that God, 'whose works are perfect' (Dt. 32:4), would create the angels alone before the other creatures" (*Summa theol.* 1.61.3).

P. 311, LL. 48–49. *in less time . . . twenty:* Aquinas says that the angels were not created in a state of beatitude, since beatitude follows merit; nor can beatitude be lost. But a single act of grateful love was sufficient in the angels to merit beatitude, and those who were so blessed were blessed immediately—although "time," for angels, pertains not to a succession of moments, but to a succession of movements of the will (*Summa theol.* 1.62.5). It follows, then, that the angels who fell with Satan fell, as it were, directly upon their creation, since it is impossible to imagine a suspension of the will in an intellectual creature, and since one movement of love toward their Creator would have confirmed them in sinlessness and would have showered upon them eternal blessedness, for "a blessed angel can in no way sin" (*Summa theol.* 1.62.8). The surprising instantaneousness of the sin of Satan is reflected, in his temporally sequential acts, by the original sin of Adam, who Dante says spent only six hours in Paradise (26.139–42). That should illustrate how fundamental the sins were: the turning away from one's own source, one's principle of being.

P. 313, LL. 56–57. *the angel . . . pressed:* Satan, locked in ice at the center of the earth (*Inf.* 34.111).

P. 313, L. 62. *merit and illuminating grace:* The angels who did not fall are rewarded by such grace that their perseverance in beatitude is assured, as they are granted the fullness of their desires in the vision of God (cf. Aquinas, *Summa theol.* 1.62.8).

P. 313, L. 72. *remembers, understands, and wills:* The rather corporeal angels of *Paradise Lost* experience time-dependent activities of the mind; Dante's angels do not. Just as the angels possess no physical extension in space, so, since they behold the face of God wherein all things are present, they transcend the mental faculties corresponding to past, present, and future. They will, but do not wish (since they see the future); and they know the past, but they do not, in our sense of the word, "remember." This assertion—which is not required by Catholic doctrine—seems to spring from Aquinas's argument that angels do not know by the slow intellectual motions of discursive reasoning: "At once in those things which they know first by nature, they see all that in them can be known" (*Summa theol.* 1.58.3). Their mode of knowledge is to be opposed to the vain ramblings of the speculators whom Dante is about to reprove. It should be noted, however, that Aquinas himself, and Bonaventure (*Brev.* 2.6) argued that the angels do possess memory.

P. 313, L. 75. *that must speak equivocally:* without, that is, acknowledging the equivocation.

P. 315, L. 94. *For show:* Beatrice's condemnation of egotism among philosophers appears to echo Richard of Saint Victor: "In our time there have arisen certain pseudo-philosophers, fabricators of untruth. Wanting to make a name for themselves, they are eager to discover new things. Nor was it a concern of theirs so much that they might affirm truth, as that they might think that they had discovered a new thing" (*Ark* 2.2).

P. 315, L. 97. *This one:* Two explanations were offered for the darkness in the afternoon of Christ's death: one, that the moon retreated and caused an eclipse; the other, that the sun withheld its rays. Dante accepts the second as truer to Scripture (Matt. 27:45) and as more fitting, since it would mean that darkness covered the whole earth (an eclipse of the sun would have been seen by *the Jews* in Jerusalem but not by people in India and Spain).

P. 315, L. 103. *Jacks and Jips:* Ital. *Lapi* (from *Jacopo*, "James," "Jacob") *e Bindi* (from *Ildebrando*, "Hildebrand"). I have translated nicknames with nicknames.

P. 315, L. 110. *Go… earth:* a bitter parody of the words of Christ: "Go ye into all the world, and preach the gospel to every creature" (Mark 16:15).

P. 315, L. 114. *the shield and lance:* "Stand therefore, having your loins girt about with truth, and having on the breastplate of righteousness; and your feet shod with the preparation of the gospel of peace; above all, taking the shield of faith, wherewith ye shall be able to quench all the fiery darts of the wicked. And take the helmet of salvation, and the sword of the Spirit, which is the word of God" (Eph. 6:14–17).

P. 317, L. 139. *love… perceives:* Cf. 28.110–11.

P. 317, L. 145. *One:* If God is One, and if God creates, how can He reflect his oneness in His creatures? Aquinas's answer is that He can most fittingly do that by means of a harmonious ordering of an extravagant multiplicity and diversity of creatures (*Summa con. gen.* 2.45). Dante's words also echo Solomon's description of the Wisdom of God, making and ordering all things, while remaining one (Wis. 7.27, 8:1).

CANTO THIRTY

Who is she that looketh forth as the morning, sings the Groom, fair as the moon, clear as the sun, and terrible as an army with banners? Such is Beatrice, when she falls silent at the end of this canto. In Beatrice we have seen beauty and, at times, womanly tenderness; we have also seen the clarity of justice and the terribleness of total love. It does not mar her portrait that the last words we hear her utter are the last words of the *Comedy* that refer to the pains of Hell—for Hell too has been part of this vision of love and beauty. Yet it will not be our last *sight* of Beatrice—that is reserved for a moment of deep affection, thankfulness, and hope.

P. 321, L. 35. *more brilliant than my trumpet:* Cf. 1.34–36.

P. 321, L. 39. *the highest body:* The Empyrean is the so-called heaven of heavens, its name deriving from Greek *pyros,* "fire." It was, however, thought to be motionless and incorporeal fire, imparting its influence upon all the moving spheres below it (cf. Aquinas, *Summa theol.* 1.66.3).

P. 321, LL. 49–50. *enveloped in a live / gleaming of light:* Dante's experience resembles that of Paul in his own account of what happened on the way to Damascus (Acts 22:6–11).

P. 323, L. 60. *a stream:* It almost violates the poetry to comment upon an image so beautiful. The river is reminiscent of the garden of Eden and brings to its magnificent climax the series of rivers we have seen in the hereafter. More, the river, in its *flowing round,* suggests the flowing of humanly experienced life (if not time) in a changeless eternity. For the image, cf. Rev. 22:1–2.

P. 323, L. 66. *rubies…gold:* Cf. Ecclus. 32:7; also Virgil, *Aen.* 10.134.

P. 323, L. 67. *inebriated with perfumes:* The joy of Heaven is wild and exuberant in its order, expressing the love of the Church for her Groom: "His cheeks are as a bed of spices, as sweet flowers: his lips like lilies, dropping sweet smelling myrrh" (Sg. 5:13). The fragrance, if we follow Pseudo-Dionysus, is the "infinitely divine Sweetness" which is "content to impress its authentic stamp on the souls that are true likenesses of itself" (*Eccl. Hier.* 476A); the invisible fragrance is also the Light.

P. 325, L. 99. *I saw:* Dante uses the word *vidi* as a so-called improper rhyme, as elsewhere he uses the name of Christ (for no word is worthy of rhyming with that name). He now stresses how incomparable is the vision he is being granted.

P. 325, L. 102. *his only peace:* "You have made us for yourself, and our hearts will never rest until they rest in you" (Augustine, *Conf.* 1.1).

P. 325, L. 117. *the heavenly rose:* The second great image Dante uses to describe the *courts* of the blessed, the rose of human beatitude may be thought of as growing from God's river of light. Its manifold petals figure forth both equality (all within the rose are within the rose) and hierarchy (the souls dwell upon different petals, different tiers). The reader should also recall that complexly numbered and organized roses of stained glass, to express the life of blessedness, had been adorning the facades of Gothic cathedrals for 150 years.

P. 327, L. 129. *robes of white:* Cf. 25.96; also Rev. 7:9–14.

P. 327, L. 130. *our city:* the New Jerusalem (Rev. 21:2).

P. 327, L. 145. *Not long:* Clement V died a few months after Henry of Luxembourg; justly, Dante thought.

P. 327, L. 148. *Him of Anagni deeper down his hole:* Beatrice will not deign to name Boniface VIII; we are to contrast the emperor Henry, not yet in Paradise but destined to be there, with Boniface, not yet in Hell but equally so destined. In his last words, Virgil gave over his charge of Dante and triumphantly pronounced him free, needing the discipline neither of Church nor of empire: "Lord of yourself I crown and miter you" (*Purg.* 27.142). The last words of Beatrice—all the more shocking coming from the mild and lovely woman—reaffirm the divine provenance of the empire in her praise of Henry VII, and deliver a bitter judgment against the pope who would oppose it.

CANTO THIRTY-ONE

We are compassed about with so great a cloud of witnesses. It is odd that many modern men should find little enough trouble believing in some transcendent Being or force that made the world—but should then scruple about trusting that this same Being could be personal, could or would care about any particular man or woman on earth, before or after death. Perhaps it is because we, if we were gods, would not so care. But the wonder and beauty of the doctrine of the saints touches this canto with joy, as Dante sees the face of his first saint other than Beatrice. He does not speak to the soul of, but really *meets*, Bernard of Clairvaux.

P. 329, L. 13. *living flame:* So Ezekiel describes the angels: "Their appearance was like burning coals of fire, and like the appearance of lamps" (1:13).

P. 329, L. 23. *according to their dignity:* The lines return us, fittingly, to the beginning of the poem. We are about to transcend even those things that theology can show; all the rest of *Paradise* was, as it were, a preparation for this. Just as the last four cantos of *Inferno* are devoted to the traitors, those most satanic of sinners, and as the last four cantos of *Purgatory* find us in Earthly Paradise and in the company of Beatrice, so these last cantos of *Paradise*—three, not four—show us the beatitude whereof the scheme of the spheres, the Eagle, the ladder, and so forth, were but allegories adapted to our human understanding.

P. 333, L. 30. *look on our battering tempest here below:* Beatrice's prophecy against Boniface is repeated here in Dante's plea—the last such plea he will make—that divine justice look with mercy upon the people of Italy and return to the empire its rightful authority.

P. 333, L. 39. *Florence:* the last time Dante will mention the city. The parallelism with the saints—the citizens who are *just and sane*—casts Florence as an epitome of the broken and unredeemed. But more: Dante is about to enter his true land, leaving behind an exile more sorrowful than was his banishment from the city of his birth: "We must cross over from land to land, from an alien land to our own land, from exile to the fatherland, from people to people, and from a kingdom to another people, from the land of the dying to the land of the living, if we wish by this experience to know true and inner joy" (Richard of Saint Victor, *Twelve Pat.* 38).

P. 333, L. 40. *speechless awe:* The silence signals that we are moving into a fuller experience of Paradise, one more befitting contemplative rapture than theological elucidation.

P. 335, L. 58. *another answers me:* When Dante turned to Virgil to exclaim his renewed love for Beatrice, he found to his shock that Virgil had returned to Hell (*Purg.* 30.40–54). So here, when Dante turns to Beatrice to ask her about the nature of the celestial rose, he finds, with some dismay, that Beatrice is no longer there. But there is not a hint of tragedy in this moment. The man he does see is Saint Bernard of Clairvaux (1090–1153), one of the greatest men, and greatest personalities, of the Middle Ages. Though frail and sickly, the young Bernard chose to enter the new Cistercian Order—an order of Benedictine monks who believed that the famously successful monastery at Cluny and all her daughter houses had become too wealthy, indeed so wealthy that very few of the monks had to perform any manual labor. Bernard was a powerful persuader, and from his own determination other men caught the desire to go to the swamplands of Champagne, to drain the marshes, clear the forest, and till the land. He founded the monastery of Clairvaux and served as its abbot.

Bernard's formidable preaching against laxity in the monastic life made him the most renowned reformer of his day; he was an adviser to several popes, including his own onetime student the reformist Eugenius III. When Pope Eugenius III wished to rouse the Christian princes to go crusading in the Holy Land, it was to the great abbot of Clairvaux he turned. Bernard was also at the center of the scandal involving the theologian Peter Abelard, whose adulterous relationship with his pupil Héloïse resulted in Abelard's castration and Héloïse's banishment to a convent. Though Bernard had nothing to do with the crime committed against Abelard, he was a bitter opponent of the latter's methods of disputation, believing that Abelard's *Sic et non* attributed altogether too much capacity to reason to decide where truth lay. Indeed, when Abelard stated that one cannot believe what one does not understand, he might well have appeared (and wished to appear, since he was a self-promoter) to have reversed the formula we find in Augustine and Anselm, that we will not understand unless we first believe.

It was a struggle between a brilliant but high-living and somewhat effeminate rationalist and a brilliant, austere, masculine mystic. And Bernard was both theologian and mystic, particularly stirred by the bridal imagery of the Song of Songs and by the humble sinlessness of the Virgin Mary (see Appendix E). Legend had it that, because of his devotion to Mary, Bernard was granted a glimpse of Paradise while he was yet on earth. His appearance here as the reverend old man should recall that of Cato at the base of Purgatory (*Purg.* 1.31–33), although Bernard's "age" is a measure of his wisdom and the reverence it is due, and not to any bodily decay.

Beatrice "disappears" here because we have reached the limit of theological speculation; what follows is the direct vision of the invisible things of God. Thus, says Richard of Saint Victor, Rachel (symbolizing the rational-contemplative mind) must die that Benjamin may be born, "because when the human mind is carried above itself it passes beyond all narrowness of human reasoning" (*Twelve Pat.* 73).

P. 335, L. 79. *Lady:* Dante's last words to Beatrice, and her last response—a lovely look of peaceful approval. Here and only here does Dante pray for her intercession, and only here does he address Beatrice with the familiar pronoun *tu* (our early modern English familiar "thou"). His prayer calmly and confidently acknowledges the grace he has been given, and the freedom he enjoys. All that is left to ask is that he be given the grace to persevere unto the end. That is what Dante the character asks from her; all Dante the poet has done is pay Beatrice a tribute such as no man had ever paid any woman, or perhaps ever will.

P. 335, L. 84. *to you I owe the grace:* as intercessor and instrument of God's grace, exactly as someone might attribute his conversion to a certain good friend, while knowing, of course, that the gift was God's.

P. 335, L. 93. *the eternal Spring:* God is "the fountain of living waters" (Jer. 2:13).

P. 337, L. 103. *A pilgrim from Croatia:* from somewhere, that is, very far away. The powerful simile, with its stupendous exclamation of awe and joy, applies immediately to Dante's beholding of the great Bernard; but this moment and similar moments in the *Comedy*—Dante's astonishment when he learns that he is looking upon Virgil (*Inf.* 1.79); his wonder at the yet veiled face of Beatrice (*Purg.* 30.31–39), then at her eyes (31.115–20), and finally at the revealing of her smile (31.136–45); his repeated gazing, throughout the *Paradise,* into the ever-increasing beauty of her face; his request to see the face of Saint Benedict (*Par.* 22.58–60) and his striving to see beneath the blinding light the form of Christ's beloved apostle John (25.118–23)—are meant to lead us to the final vision, not of a man in the image of Christ, nor of the image of Christ preserved on a linen cloth, but of Christ himself, face-to-face (1 Cor. 13:12).

P. 337, L. 111. *by contemplating:* Again, we must keep in mind that to contemplate God is not merely to behold God as from without, but to become conformed to God from within.

CANTO THIRTY-TWO

Blessed art thou among women. We are apt to consider Dante's devotion to Mary a fossil of his medieval Catholic culture. A lazy error that is. Certainly medieval Christians in the West (and even more so in the East) gave honor to Mary, but this honor derives its meaning from the Incarnation of Christ. It is Christian doctrine that man's redemption and union with God is effected only by the incarnate Word: the very flesh of man is redeemed. Through proud Eve came the generations of sin into the world; and through humble Mary, in the flesh, came the Redeemer. As there is no closer intimacy on earth than that between the mother and the child in the womb, so in Heaven no human being enjoys greater intimacy with Christ than does his mother, Mary.

P. 341, L. 8. *Rachel:* the beloved wife of Jacob, and traditionally considered a personification of the contemplative life, while her sister, Leah, personified the active life (cf. *Purg.* 27.101–108). *The Twelve Patriarchs* by Richard of Saint Victor is a mystical meditation upon the sons of Leah and Rachel as steps in the intertwining orders of a life of active and contemplative virtue, leading to the youngest son, Benjamin (in giving birth to whom Rachel died), symbolizing the acceptance of grace in the beholding of things that *appear* to violate reason: "And so the hearer falls down at the thunder of the divine voice because the capacity of human sense succumbs to that which is divinely inspired, and unless it abandons the limitations of human reasoning it does not expand the bosom of the understanding in order to hold the secret of divine inspiration. And so there the hearer falls, where human reason fails. There Rachel dies, that Benjamin may be born" (82). Just such a "death" of Rachel must now occur in Dante, that he may be granted the fullness of the beatific vision. It is also important to note that, as we saw at the very beginning of the *Comedy* (*Inf.* 2.102), Beatrice sits beside Rachel: theology descends and ascends, descends to do the work that Leah personifies, and ascends to lead to the threshold of a vision that passes understanding. See the diagram below for the seating arrangement Dante describes.

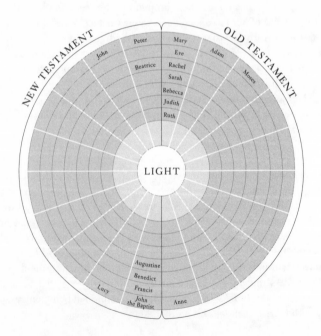

P. 341, L. 10. *Sarah ... Rebecca ... Judith:* Sarah was the wife of Abraham and mother of Isaac; Rebecca was the wife of Isaac and mother of Jacob; Judith was the heroine whose brave slaying of the Assyrian captain Holofernes saved the Hebrew people (cf. *Purg.* 12.58–60), and whose tale is told in the (for Catholic and Orthodox) Old Testament book of Judith.

P. 343, L. 31. *the great John:* The Baptist, herald and cousin of Christ, corresponds with Mary, mother of Christ: "Verily I say unto you, Among them that are born of women there hath not risen a greater than John the Baptist" (Matt. 11:11).

P. 343, L. 35. *Francis, Benedict, and Augustine:* For Saint Francis see note at 11.40; for Saint Benedict see note at 22.40. Saint Augustine (354–426), bishop of Hippo, was simply one of the most powerful intellects the world has known, building his Christian theology in part upon the foundational truths of Greek philosophy, particularly Neoplatonism, and, in *The City of God,* implicitly devising the world's first theory of history. His *Confessions* is the world's first (and in my opinion greatest) autobiography, a work that established the theme of pilgrimage as central to the medieval understanding of life. These three saints mark a progression and correspond to the women Eve, Rachel, and Beatrice already named: Eve is consort of Adam, the type of Christ to whom Francis was assimilated in the stigmata; Rachel is an allegory of mystic contemplation, that for which Dante praises Benedict; and Beatrice symbolizes theology, to which Augustine devoted his intellectual life.

P. 343, L. 46. *childlike piping of the voice:* Dante imagines the baptized infants retaining their infant bodies in Paradise—as Fra Angelico would portray children dancing in the garden in his *Final Judgment.* Aquinas, however, had opined that the glorified bodies of the blessed would be at the prime of youth, "the state of ultimate perfection ... just at the point when growth ends and decay begins" (*Summa theol.* suppl. 81.1). But the children here again convey the inequality—the freedom—of the gifts of grace: as not all are granted the same light, so not all are of the same age, and there is even a hierarchy among the children, according to a hierarchy of grace that only God can know (*Summa theol.* 2.1.112).

P. 343, L. 54. *hunger, thirst, or grief:* "They shall hunger no more, neither thirst anymore ... and God shall wipe away all tears from their eyes" (Rev 7:16–17).

P. 345, L. 81. *circumcision:* Before Abraham, all a child needed was his parents' belief in the Redeemer to come (Aquinas, *Summa theol.* 3.70.4); with Abraham, the rite of circumcision was established, males dedicating themselves to God in the very members of generation that transmitted original sin but that were also the means whereby the parents of the Redeemer would be born (3.70.3). Circumcision was an act of faith, foreshadowing the death and regeneration enacted in baptism: "In [Christ] also ye are circumcised with the circumcision made without hands, in putting off the body of the sins of the flesh by the circumcision of Christ: buried with him in baptism, wherein also ye are risen with him through the faith of the operation of God, who hath raised him from the dead" (Col. 2:11–12).

P. 345, L. 85. *the face that most resembles Christ:* Mary was Jesus' mother; quite literally, no face of a human being more closely resembles his. But also in her sinless submission to the will of God, she is closer to Christ than any human being ever was or will be. This marks the final time Dante will rhyme on the name of Christ.

P. 347, L. 107. *adorned by Mary's ray:* Ital. *abbelliva.* The word derives from the love poetry of the Provençal troubadours, as does much of the language used to describe Bernard and the angel Gabriel, faithful champions of the beautiful Mary.

P. 347, L. 112. *the palm:* of victory. In her submission to God's will, Mary would be exalted beyond all other women, so that all generations would call her blessed (Luke 1:48).

P. 347, L. 116. *patricians:* The word moves us from the world of courtesy to that of glorious rule; it is followed by a daring Roman epithet for Mary: *Augusta.*

P. 347, L. 117. *clement and most just:* Ital. *giustissimo e pio.* As always in the poem (cf. *Inf.* 2.5), *pio* has a range of meanings: "pious," "devoted," "reverent," "merciful." All are in force here, but I have chosen "clement," considering that in this empire the problem of the reconciliation of justice and mercy has been resolved: "Mercy and truth are met together; righteousness and peace have kissed each other" (Ps. 85:10).

P. 349, L. 137. *Lucy:* legendary saint and martyr of Syracuse, whose intercession has assisted Dante; cf. *Inf.* 2.97; *Purg.* 9.52–63.

P. 349, L. 139. *hour of sleep:* Ital. *il tempo che t'assonna.* The language suggests—yet only suggests—that the whole *Comedy* or at least *Paradise* has been a vision in a dream. I remain skeptical of that interpretation, but will note the association of sleep and dreams with prophetic visions, an association to be found in Scripture from Genesis to the Revelation of Saint John (cf. *Purg.* 29.143–44), and particularly with regard to the last things: "And it shall come to pass afterward, that I will pour out my spirit upon all flesh; and your sons and your daughters shall prophesy, your old men shall dream dreams, your young men shall see visions" (Joel 2:28). In any case, since Dante is still alive and since his commission is to speak the truth to those below, his vision in Paradise must needs be temporary.

P. 349, L. 151. *And he began to speak this holy prayer:* Master dramatist that he is, Dante closes his cantos with a rhetorical climax or a moment of solemn stillness; this is the only canto he leaves open, as we rush with longing into the next and final song.

CANTO THIRTY-THREE

I am the Bread of Life. God creates what is not God. That is a mystery of love. This creator God is Himself a Trinity of Persons. That is a mystery of love. The

Second Person united Himself with human flesh to redeem mankind. That is a mystery of love. He rose from the dead and sits at the right hand of the Father, both God and man. That is a mystery of love. The final Christian mystery, implicit in the whole of *Paradise*, is that this Christ is with us still, abiding within the faithful, making them like unto Himself, giving them His very flesh in the Eucharist, as once he gave it on the Cross. This is the love that moves the sun and the other stars.

P. 351, L. 1. *Virgin Mother:* Saint Bernard's prayer is rich in biblical allusions and in the paradoxes of the Incarnation, paradoxes captured by the Marian devotions. The *Magnificat* celebrates Mary's humility and exaltation: "He hath regarded the low estate of his handmaiden: for, behold, from henceforth all generations shall call me blessed" (Luke 1:48). Saint Ambrose first described the womb of Mary as bringing forth flowers: "The grace of the lily flower came to bloom in the womb of the Virgin"; the *Ave Maria* cites Elizabeth's cry to Mary (Luke 1:42) to the same effect: "Blessed is the fruit of thy womb."

P. 351, L. 3. *the fulcrum of the everlasting plan:* God had determined from eternity that the Son would be born to Mary. In this sense the words of Wisdom can be applied to the mother of Christ: "The Lord possessed me in the beginning of his way, before his works of old" (Prov. 8:22).

P. 351, L. 12. *ever-living hope:* There is no hope in Hell (*Inf.* 3.9); there is no need for hope in Paradise. Hope is the characteristic virtue of Purgatory, and the virtue in which mortal men must dwell, since they have been offered what they do not yet possess.

P. 351, LL. 17–18. *often . . . race:* That is because her help is an effect of divine grace. Mary came to Dante's assistance before he prayed (*Inf.* 2.94–99).

P. 351, L. 21. *all things that come to be:* literally, all creatures, including the angels themselves. In the order of being, all human beings are inferior to all angels, but in the order of grace and redemption it need not be so.

P. 353, L. 29. *I pray:* Bernard prays that Dante may be granted the vision of God, and that he may persevere in grace so as to be numbered among the blessed (cf. 31.88–90).

P. 353, LL. 46–47. *the end of all desires:* not only to love God or to be loved by God, but to know the love that is God: "By knowing and loving Christ, by being confirmed in faith and rooted in love, we can know the breadth, length, height, and depth of Scripture, and, through such knowledge, attain unto the all-surpassing Knowledge and measureless Love which is the Blessed Trinity. To this the saints' desires tend; this is the final state, replete with all that is true and good" (Bonaventure, *Brev.* prol. 1.5).

P. 355, L. 65. *the Sibyl's prophecy:* This is the last tribute to the poetry of Virgil, a tribute and at the same time a poignant acknowledgment of the distance that separates the pagan from the Christian poet. Any knowledge of the Deity, even that which is enabled by the exercise of reason, is owing to the grace of God; without the gift of revelation, without the Word made flesh and dwelling among men, any vision of God must be as fleeting and as insubstantial as the scattered messages of the Sibyl's *leaves*.

P. 355, L. 67. *Summit of light:* Dante invokes God directly, without a shade of classical mythology or allegory. His mission is both humble and grand: it is to show forth even the *palest flicker* of the *glory* of God, to give praise to God, and to help turn the reader's heart and mind to God. The character Dante has gone on the arduous pilgrimage for his own salvation; now we see that Dante considers it his glorious labor to have led the reader on that same pilgrimage.

P. 355, L. 77. *I'd have gone blind:* This last image of blindness (cf. 25.118–39) reverses the reader's expectations. It is the blinding light of God that restores vision, filling it with light. To turn one's eyes away from God is to turn from the source of light and vision, and therefore to go blind. Thus as Dante gazes upon that light, it descends to him, folding the poet's small power of vision into its own omnipotence.

P. 355, L. 85. *I saw the scattered elements unite:* The first of the three mysteries beheld by the poet is that of the unity of all things and their harmonious dependence upon and permeation by the providence of God. The image of the book derives from Bonaventure: "From this we may gather that the universe is like a book reflecting, representing, and describing its Maker, the Trinity" (*Brev.* 2.12).

P. 357, L. 96. *sea god gape at Argo's shade:* This final glance toward the classical past—itself like the most fleeting shadow across the light—casts *the sea god* as small and astonished before a bravery that, after two thousand years, is hardly a memory; and that *bravery* is as nothing compared with what Dante is trying to recall; yet more of what Dante is trying to recall will *fade* in an instant than has faded, over those *two millennia*, of the memory of the Argonauts. This tercet brings to its climax the sea metaphor woven throughout the poem (e.g., *Purg.* 1.1–3; *Par.* 2.1–18). Dante is now near the port—or rather, near the deepest profundities of the sea. His wood is of God's making, whose ship does not founder (cf. Wis. 14:1–7).

P. 357, L. 102. *one would not consent:* Once one sees the divine, the fulfillment of all desires, one cannot turn away (Aquinas, *Summa theol.* 2.1.5.4).

P. 357, L. 107. *what a baby says:* The power of language to describe God is less than the babbling of an unweaned infant. Dante casts himself as helpless before God—but it is a God who, like the mother in the image, will feed him and will enable him to speak what he can. With these words Dante sums up the many images of domestic life, especially of motherhood and childhood, delightfully to be found throughout the *Comedy* and particularly in the *Paradise*. For the saint is not a generality but a particular man or woman, who lived in a certain place, a certain house, before a certain hearth, and took nourishment from his or her mother there (cf. note at 14.64). Moreover, we are instructed to become as children: "Crave, as newborn babes, pure spiritual milk" (1 Pet. 2:2).

P. 357, L. 113. *I changed by seeing:* "Enlightened by the knowledge of the things we contemplate—we shall take on the form of Light" (Pseudo-Dionysius, *Eccl. Hier.* 372B).

P. 357, L. 116. *three rings:* The second mystery is that of the Trinity, one in substance (*one measure*), with a plurality of Persons (*three colors*). There were many attempts to grasp the truth of the paradoxical doctrine of the Trinity. Dante follows one of the most traditional: the Father knows (if He did not know, He would fail in omniscience), the Son is known, and the Spirit is the Love that breathes forth in this knowledge. Richard of Saint Victor puts matters in terms of love: if God is perfect, then God must love; then there must be a plurality of persons, one who loves and one who is loved; but love is not fulfilled unless there is a third with whom one can communicate, can share, one's love for the beloved. The Son shares the Father's riches; the Spirit shares the love between the Father and the Son (*The Trinity* 7). Cf. also Bonaventure, *Brev.* 1.2. These, the highest mysteries, are those which appear to contradict human reason, says Richard (*Twelve Pat.* 86).

P. 359, L. 127. *circle:* The final mystery is that of the Incarnation. This mystery, if you will, folds up within itself the other two. A God who is Himself a relationship of Persons, equal yet distinct, equal yet dwelling within an order of authority, creates a universe out of the bounty of His love, and the creatures in this universe range from angels to dust. Some are free to love or to sin; those who sin lose their divine gifts, but perhaps do not lose them either, because the same God who made man can, in love, remake man; and the same Wisdom that steers all things in the universe can Himself become one of the creatures in that universe, allowing mere man, mortal man, to imitate Him and do what no angel can do, giving of himself utterly, even unto death. The paradox is one of those things that Richard of Saint Victor says not only is beyond reason, but appears (the operative word is "appears") to violate reason. Hence Dante returns here to yet another image he has used, in *Paradise* especially: that of the *geometer.* The geometer exercises all his reason to try to understand an incorporeal reality— indeed, to try to solve what was then suspected and what is now known to be an insoluble problem: how to construct a square with the same area as a given circle, using nothing but a straightedge and a compass (tools that are, essentially, nothing other than arithmetic and algebraic logic made material). Theologically, the problem is how to reduce the infinite-sidedness and no-sidedness of the divine with the world of our foursquare elements. It cannot be done by man; but it can be done for man by God; most fittingly it can be done for man by God made man. Beatrice gave the theological reasons why it was fitting that man be redeemed by the incarnate Word (7.55–120); now we glimpse that the universe and man himself, man foreknown to sin and foreknown to be redeemed, are made by the power of the Father, in the love of the Spirit, through the wisdom of the redeeming Son.

P. 359, L. 142. *Here ceased:* No more can be said. So the last words of the *Celestial Hierarchy* of Pseudo-Dionysius, reminding us that there are "mysteries beyond us" to be "honored by silence."

P. 359, L. 144. *a wheel in equal balance:* See 15.73–87 and note at 15.73. Mortal, sinful man is beset with decay—with inequality and disharmony between his faculties. Now Dante himself is set to rights, no longer suffering the war within his members (Rom. 8:23–25); he no less than the great heavenly spheres is taken up into eternity, turning as they turn. It is God—Christ—dwelling within him (Gal. 2:20).

P. 359, L. 145. *the other stars: Paradise* ends as did the other canticles of the *Comedy,* with "stars," man's origin and his home.

ABOUT THE TRANSLATOR

ANTHONY ESOLEN is a professor of English at Providence College. He is a published poet who has written numerous scholarly articles on Renaissance and medieval literature. He is the author of *Peppers,* a book of poetry, and his translations include Lucretius's *De rerum natura* and Torquato Tasso's *Gerusalemme liberata,* along with Dante's *Inferno* and *Purgatory,* published by the Modern Library.

A Note on the Type

The principal text of this Modern Library edition
was set in a digitized version of Janson, a typeface that
dates from about 1690 and was cut by Nicholas Kis,
a Hungarian working in Amsterdam. The original matrices have
survived and are held by the Stempel foundry in Germany.
Hermann Zapf redesigned some of the weights and sizes for
Stempel, basing his revisions on the original design.